Story by
Norie Yamada

Art by
Kumichi Yoshizuki

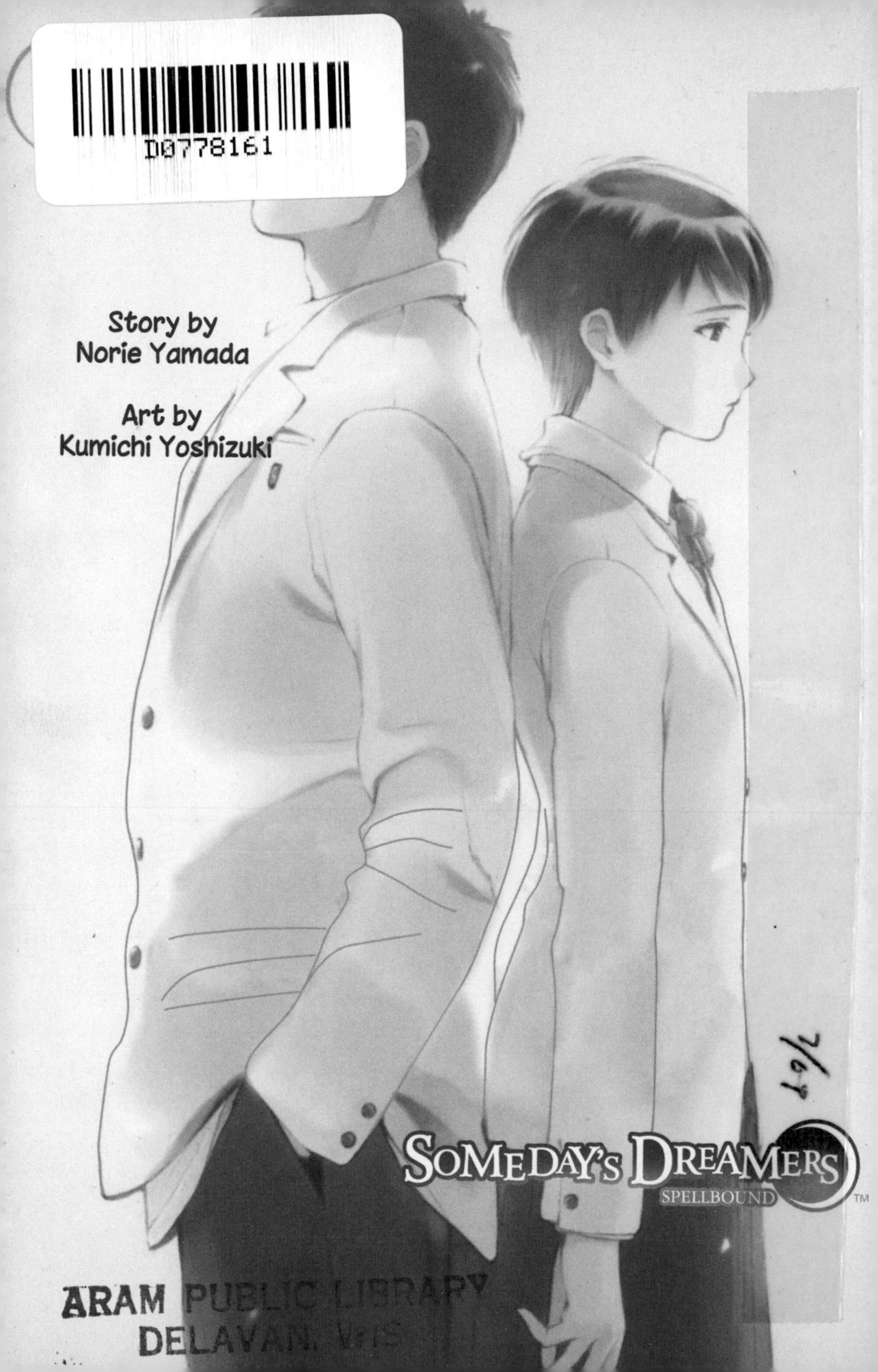

SOMEDAY'S DREAMERS
SPELLBOUND™

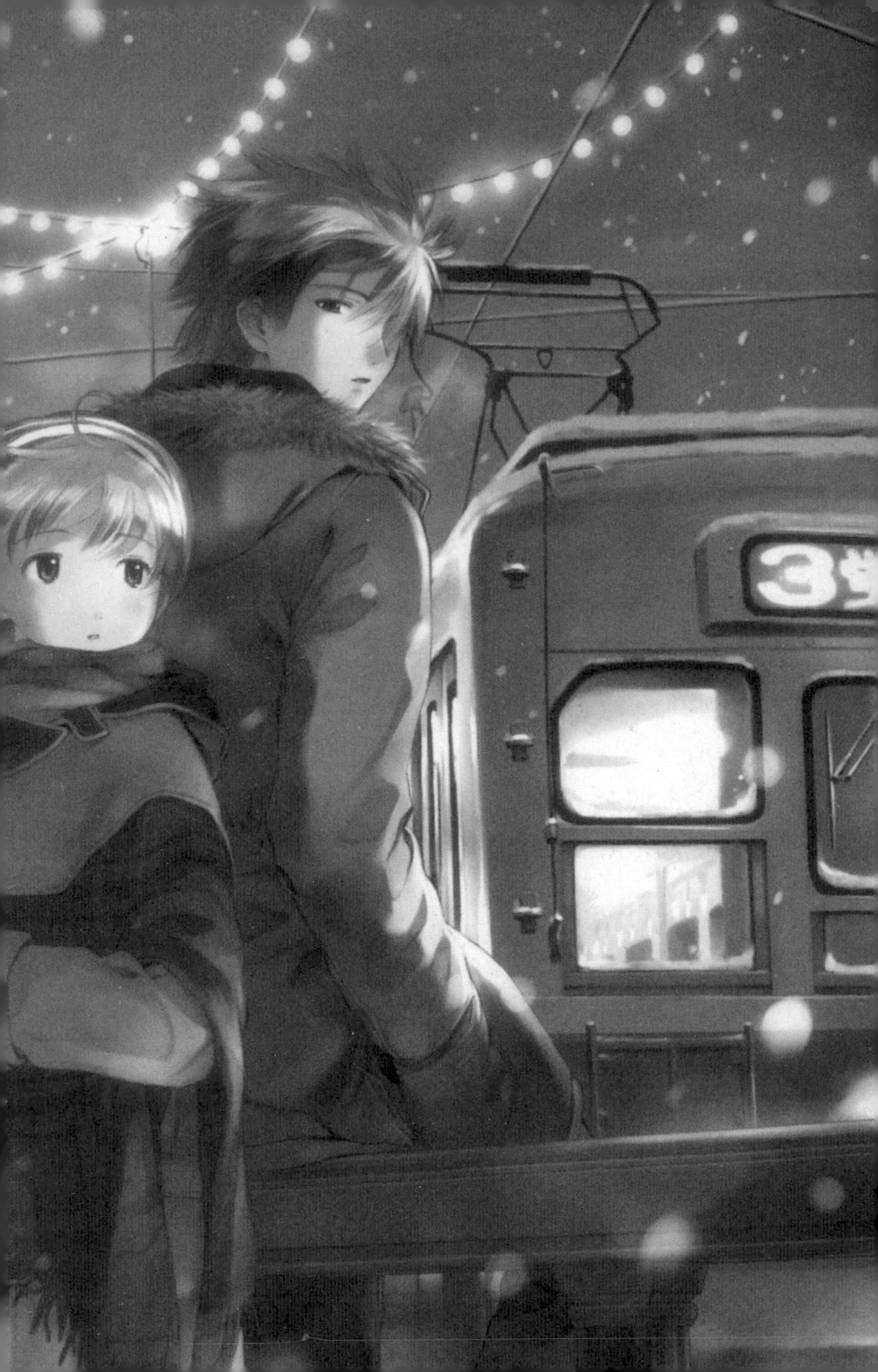
3

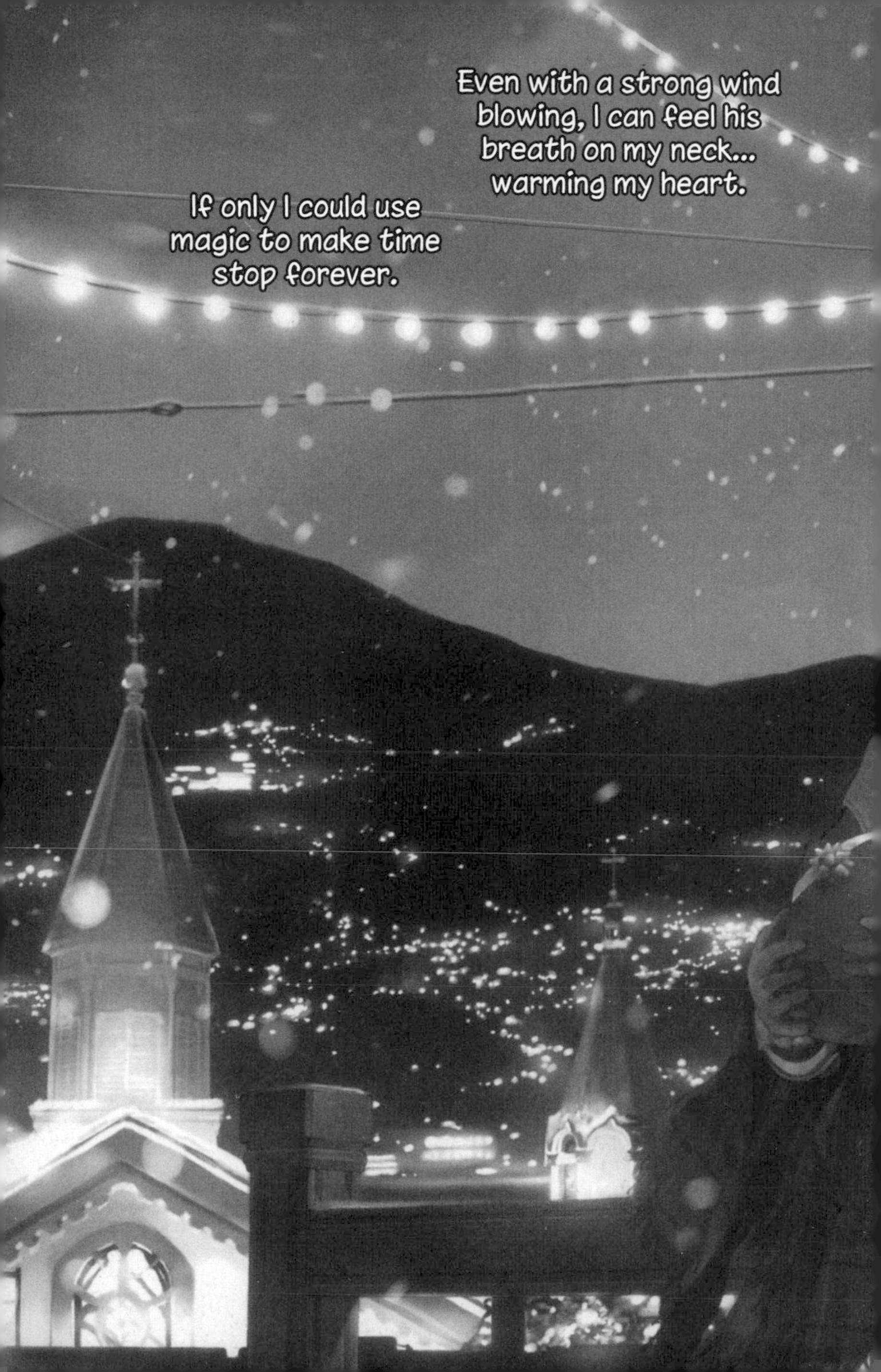
Even with a strong wind blowing, I can feel his breath on my neck... warming my heart.
If only I could use magic to make time stop forever.

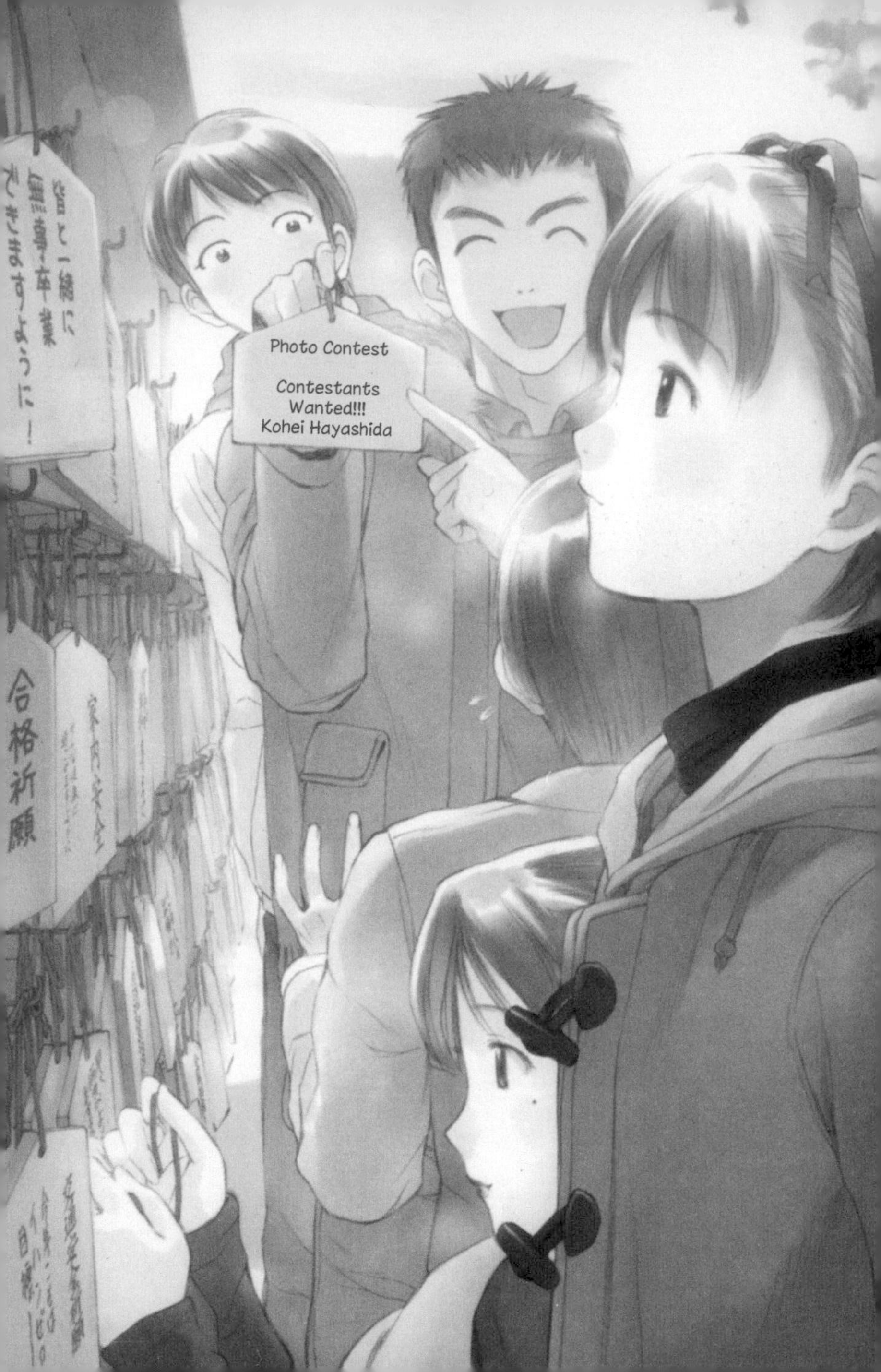
Photo Contest
Contestants Wanted!!!
Kohei Hayashida
皆と一緒に無事卒業できますように！
合格祈願

SOMEDAY's DREAMERS
SPELLBOUND
Volume 4

Story by Norie Yamada
Art by Kumichi Yoshizuki

TOKYOPOP

HAMBURG // LONDON // LOS ANGELES // TOKYO

Someday's Dreamers: Spellbound Volume 4
Story By Norie Yamada
Art By Kumichi Yoshizuki

Translation - Jeremiah Bourque
English Adaptation - Marc Goldsmith
Copy Editor - Nikhil Burman
Retouch and Lettering - Star Print Brokers
Production Artist - Courtney Geter
Graphic Designer - Jose Macasocol, Jr.

Editor - Paul Morrisey
Digital Imaging Manager - Chris Buford
Pre-Production Supervisor - Erika Terriquez
Production Manager - Elisabeth Brizzi
Managing Editor - Vy Nguyen
Creative Director - Anne Marie Horne
Editor-in-Chief - Rob Tokar
Publisher - Mike Kiley
President and C.O.O. - John Parker
C.E.O. and Chief Creative Officer - Stuart Levy

A  Manga

TOKYOPOP and ⟡ are trademarks or registered trademarks of TOKYOPOP Inc.

TOKYOPOP Inc.
5900 Wilshire Blvd. Suite 2000
Los Angeles, CA 90036

E-mail: info@TOKYOPOP.com
Come visit us online at www.TOKYOPOP.com

MAHOUTSUKAI NI TAISETSUNA KOTO TAIYOU TO KAZE
NO SAKAMICHI Volume 4 © 2005 NORIE YAMADA/
KUMICHI YOSHIZUKI First published in Japan in 2005 by
FUJIMISHOBO CO., LTD., Tokyo. English translation rights
arranged with KADOKAWA SHOTEN PUBLISHING CO., LTD.,
Tokyo through TUTTLE–MORI AGENCY, INC., Tokyo.
English text copyright © 2007 TOKYOPOP Inc.

ISBN: 978-1-59816-645-3
First TOKYOPOP printing: December 2007
10 9 8 7 6 5 4 3 2 1
Printed in the USA

CONTENTS:

SOMEDAY's DREAMERS
SPELLBOUND ™

My name is Nami Matsuo. I'm a senior at Nagasaki Ryokunan High.

I'm a magic user who's never succeeded at casting a spell in her life.

I'd been doing my best forgetting about magic...

..and focusing on studies my last year of school...

..when a mysterious transfer student, Ryutaro Tominaga, appeared.

He slugged one of my classmates his first day--
just because someone took his picture.

He brushes me off by calling me "magic user" instead of "Nami."

Still...

..I want to know more about him.

Why he is as kind as he is cruel.

He has me spellbound.

But then, the day before summer break...

..he told me to never come near him again.

It was that day...

..I realized I was in love with him.

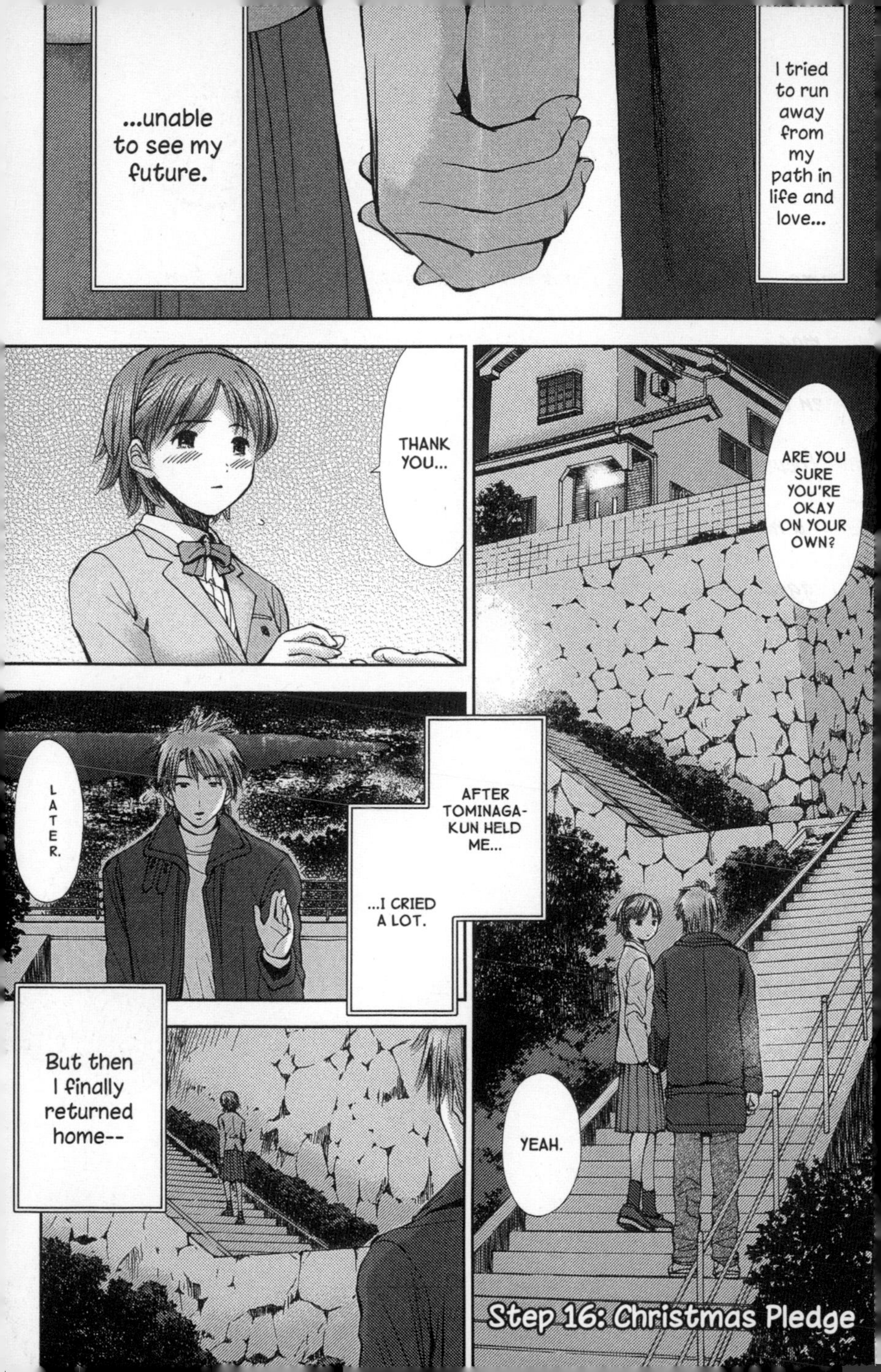
I tried to run away from my path in life and love...
...unable to see my future.
ARE YOU SURE YOU'RE OKAY ON YOUR OWN?
YEAH.
Step 16: Christmas Pledge
THANK YOU...
AFTER TOMINAGA-KUN HELD ME...
...I CRIED A LOT.
LATER.
But then I finally returned home--

Step 16: Christmas Pledge

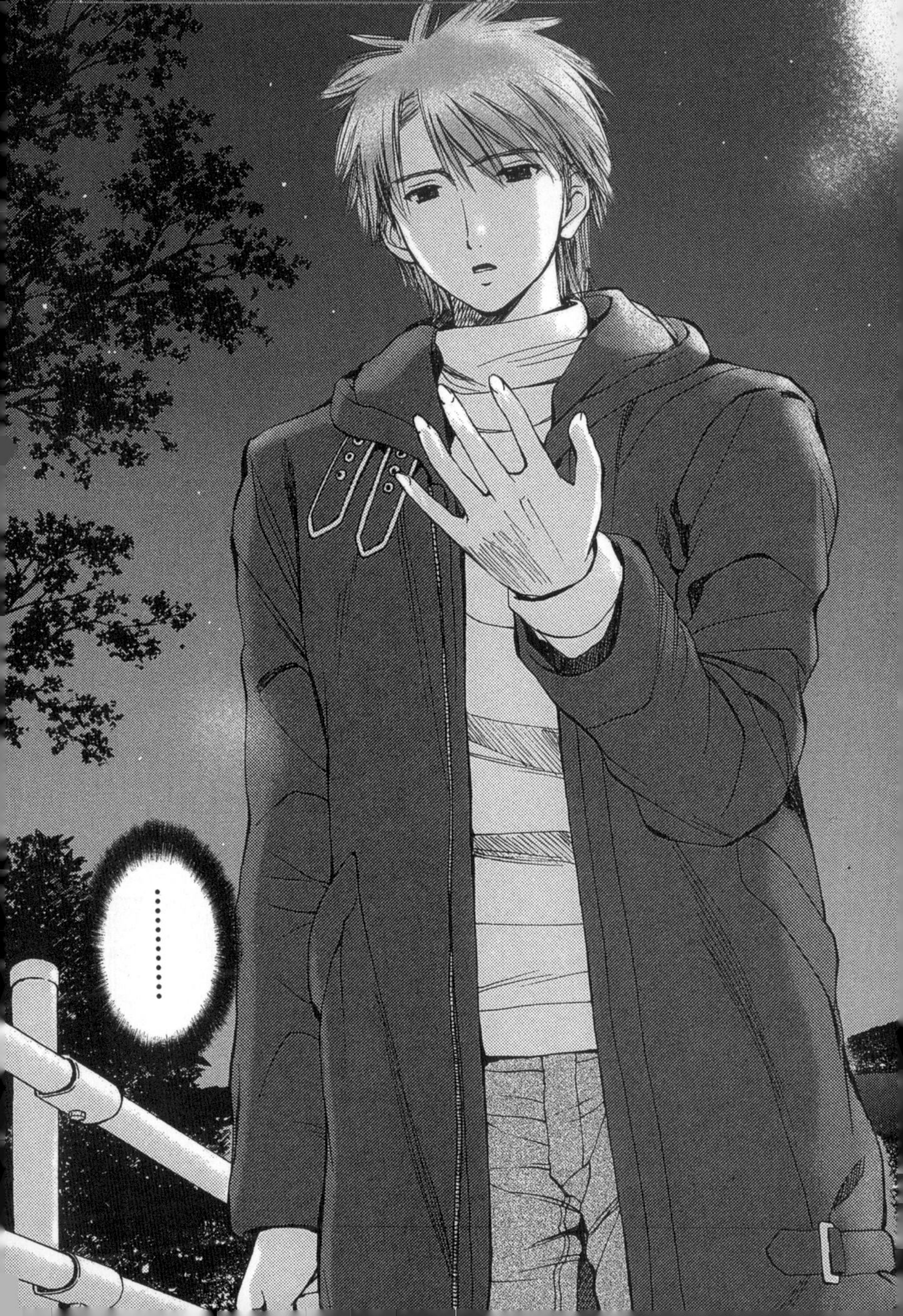
....

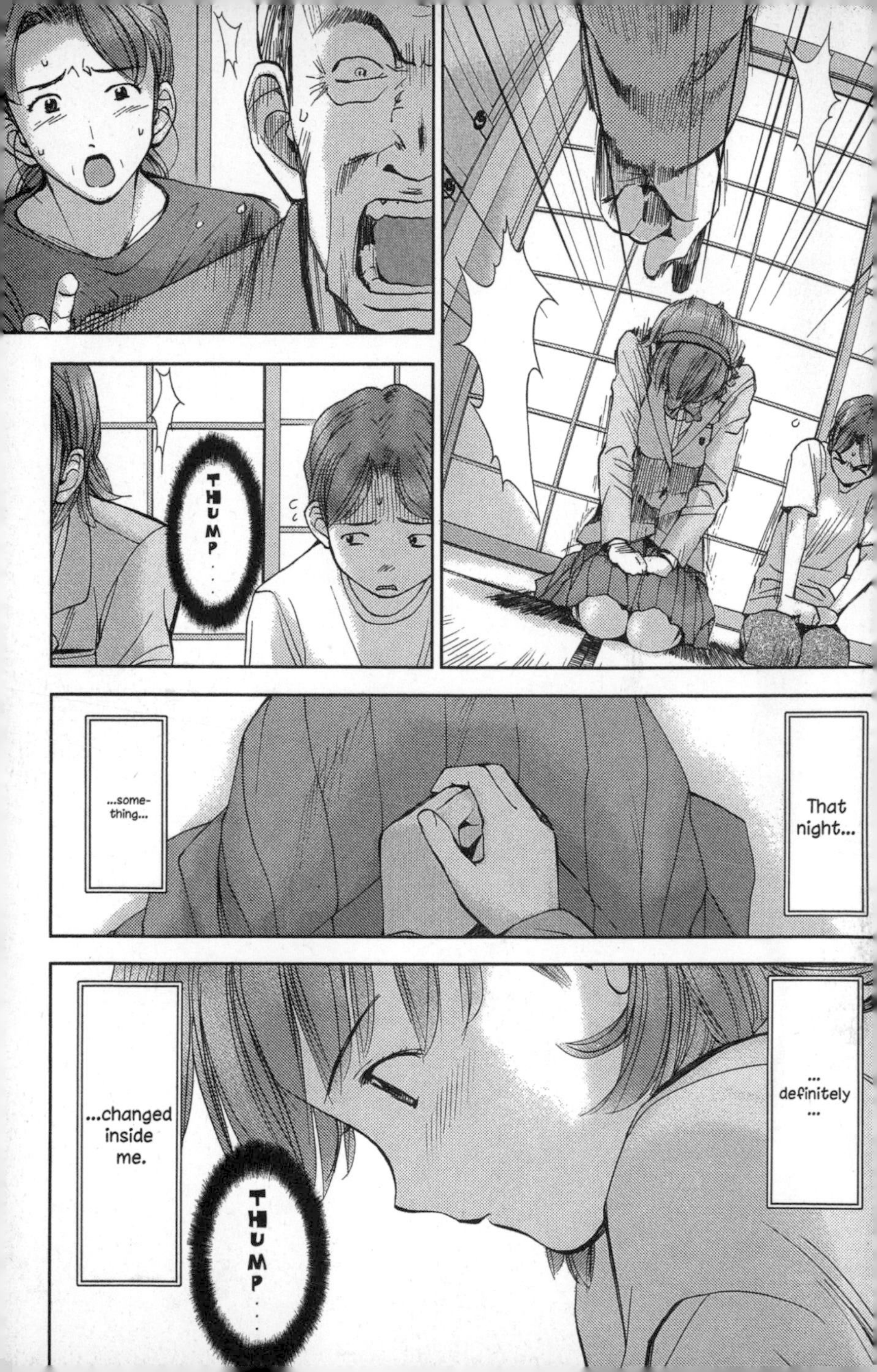
THUMP...
That night...
...something...
...definitely...
...changed inside me.
THUMP...

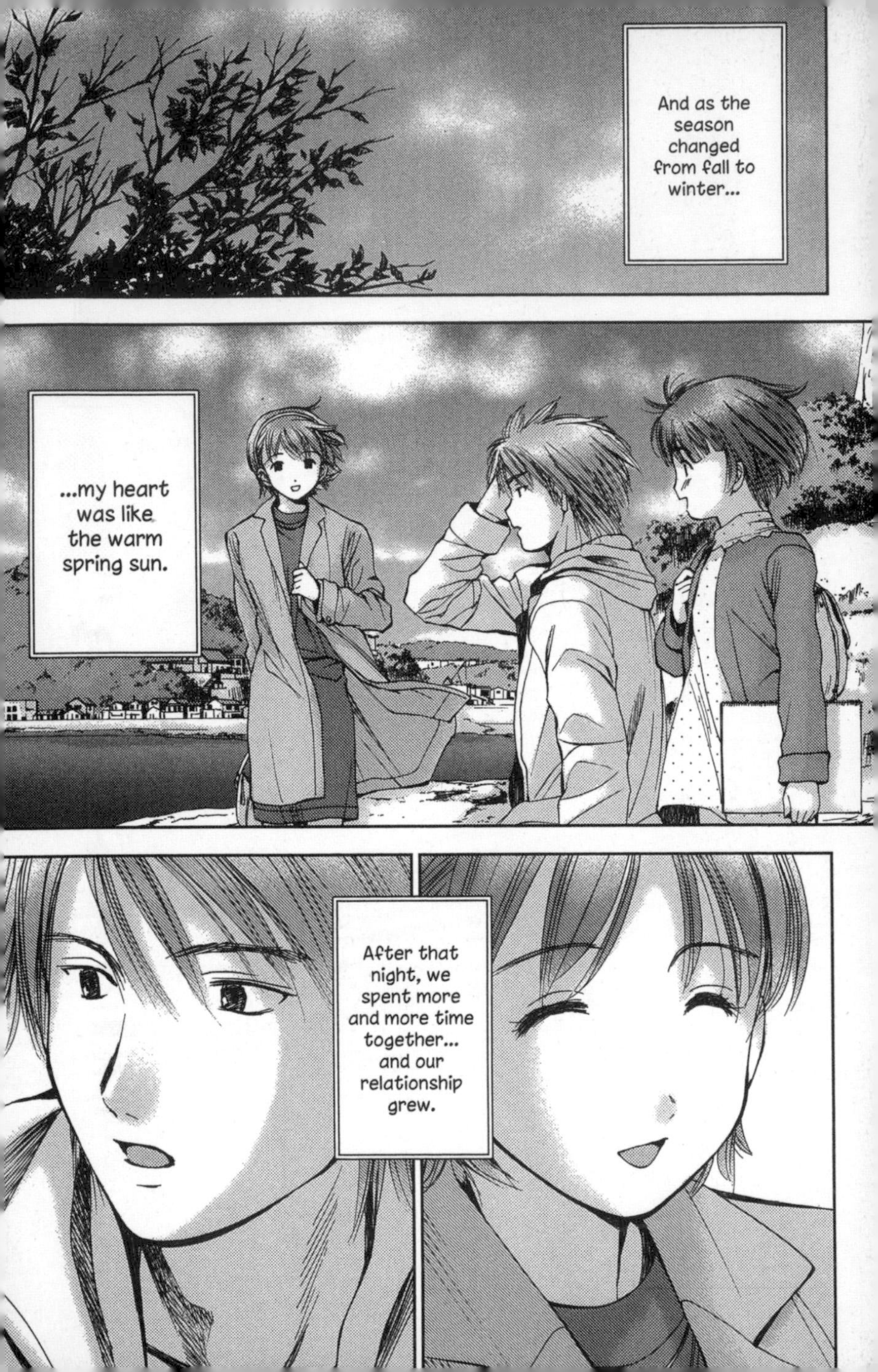
And as the season changed from fall to winter...
...my heart was like the warm spring sun.
After that night, we spent more and more time together... and our relationship grew.

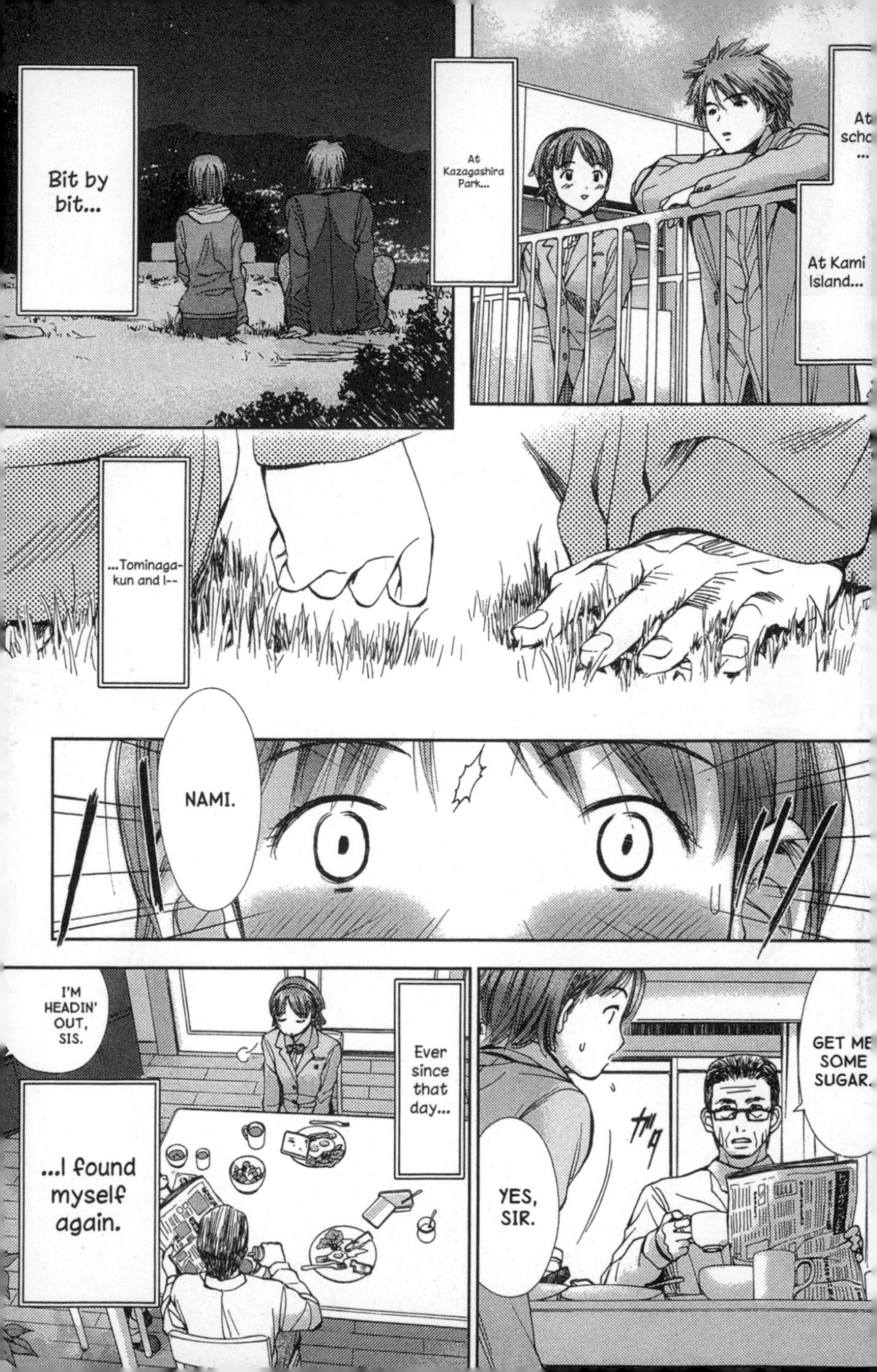

At scho ...
At Kami Island...
At Kazagashira Park...
Bit by bit...
...Tominaga-kun and I--
NAMI.
GET ME SOME SUGAR.
ガタ
YES, SIR.
Ever since that day...
I'M HEADIN' OUT, SIS.
...I found myself again.

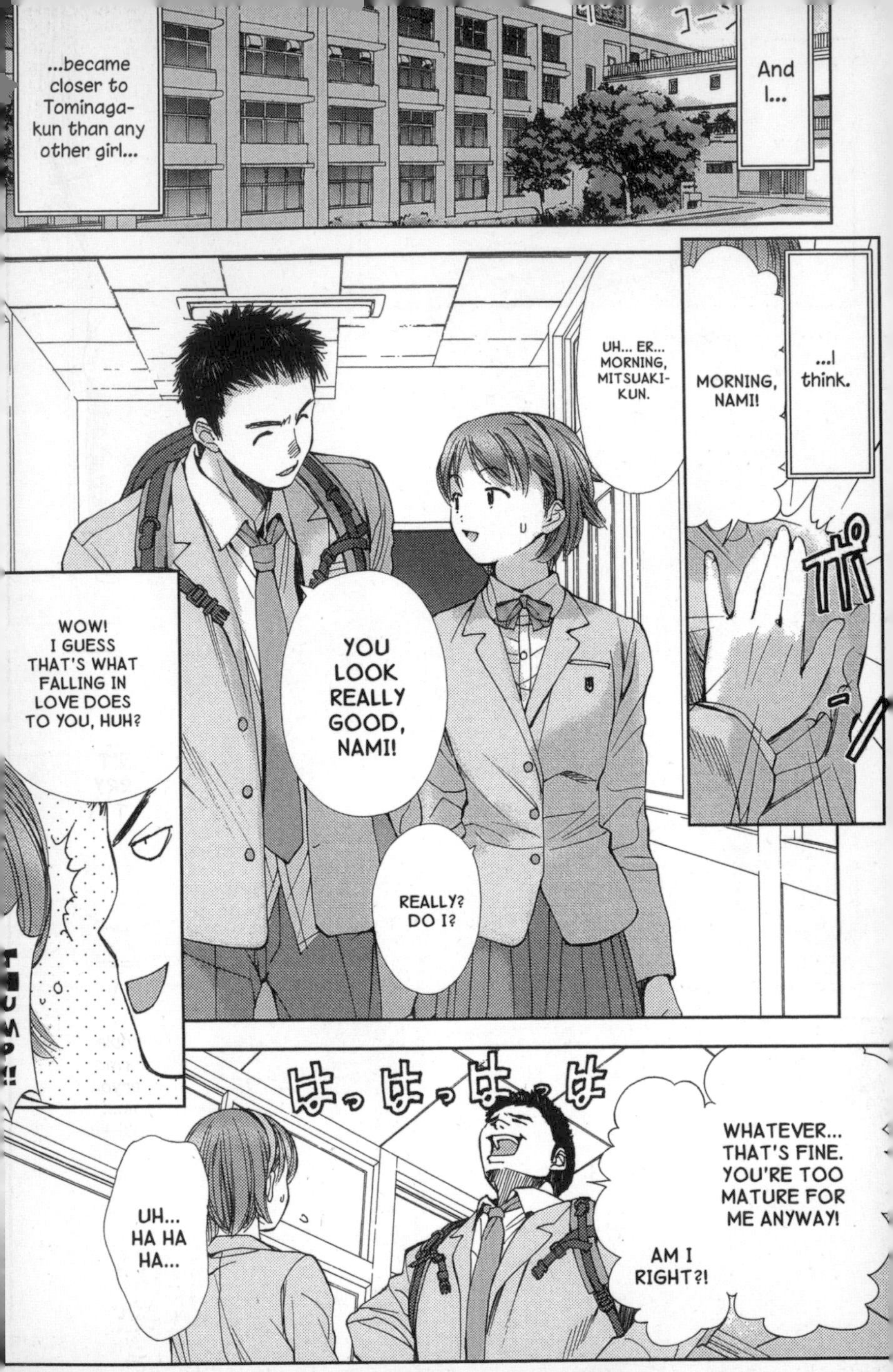
And I...
...became closer to Tominaga-kun than any other girl...
...I think.
MORNING, NAMI!
UH... ER... MORNING, MITSUAKI-KUN.
YOU LOOK REALLY GOOD, NAMI!
REALLY? DO I?
WOW! I GUESS THAT'S WHAT FALLING IN LOVE DOES TO YOU, HUH?
はっはっはっは
WHATEVER... THAT'S FINE. YOU'RE TOO MATURE FOR ME ANYWAY!
AM I RIGHT?!
UH... HA HA HA...

HEY, COME ON! CHEER UP!

WHY DO I DO THAT TO MYSELF? I AM SO DEPRESSED.

RIEKO.

SORRY. I ALWAYS SEEM TO DUMP MY STUFF ON YOU.

There was a real turning point for me, and then...

C'MON, CLASS IS STARTING!

DON'T WORRY ABOUT IT!

...I was able to talk normally to everyone again... Mitsuaki-kun, Rieko and Chika...

YEAH, I--

Although, Chika still got weird sometimes--

MATSUO.

HEY.

??

ARE YOU COMING TO KAMI ISLAND TODAY?

CHIKA!

I'M SORRY FOR ALL THE--

IT'S OKAY!

I CAN'T. I'M DOING SOMETHING WITH SUMOMO-CHAN.

HEY, TOMINAGA!

SURE. OF COURSE!

What am I to Tominaga-kun... How does he see me?

WELL, FOR THE RECORD, I HAVE TO WORK TODAY...

I'M SORRY. BUT THANKS FOR TAKING CARE OF SUMOMO FOR ME.

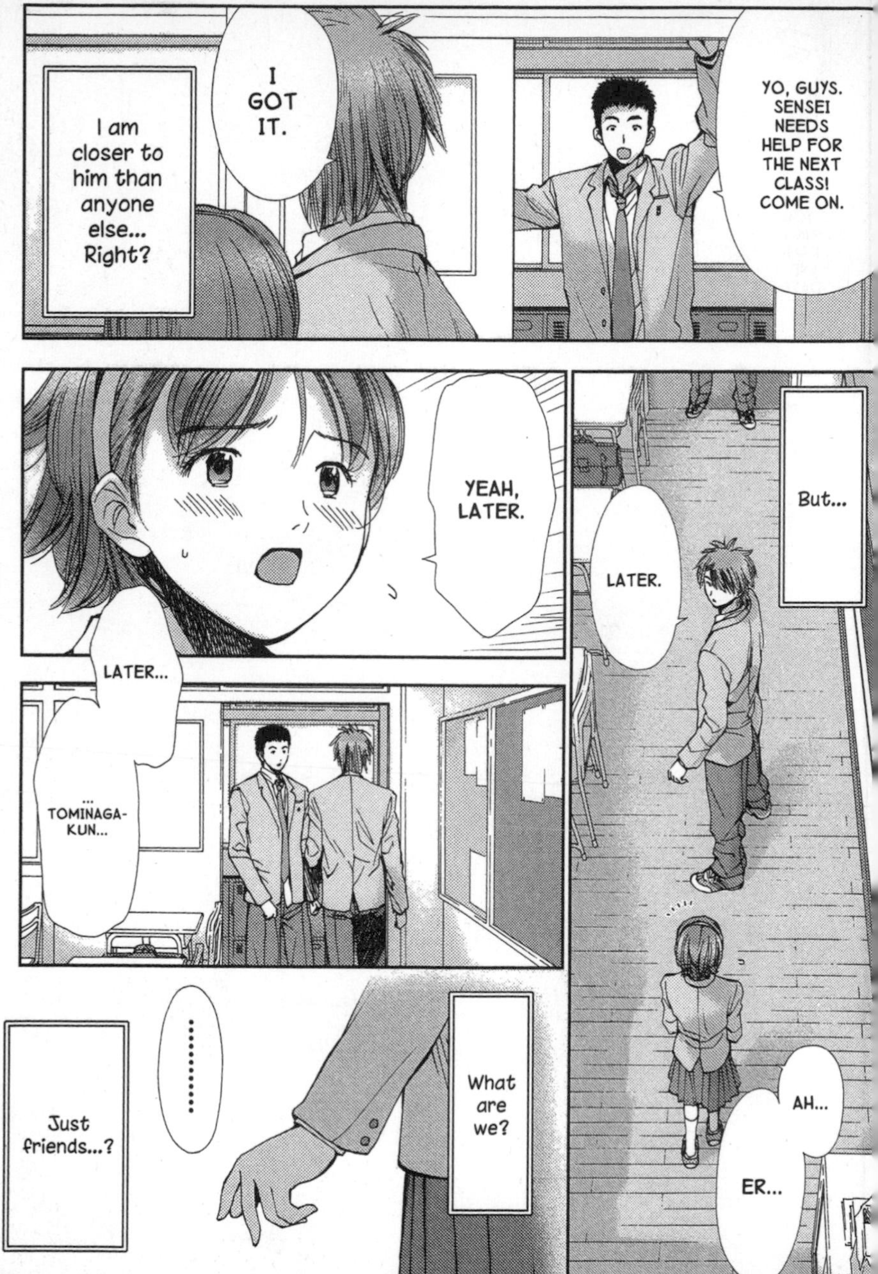
YO, GUYS. SENSEI NEEDS HELP FOR THE NEXT CLASS! COME ON.
I GOT IT.
I am closer to him than anyone else... Right?
But...
LATER.
AH...
ER...
YEAH, LATER.
LATER...
... TOMINAGA-KUN...
What are we?
....
Just friends...?

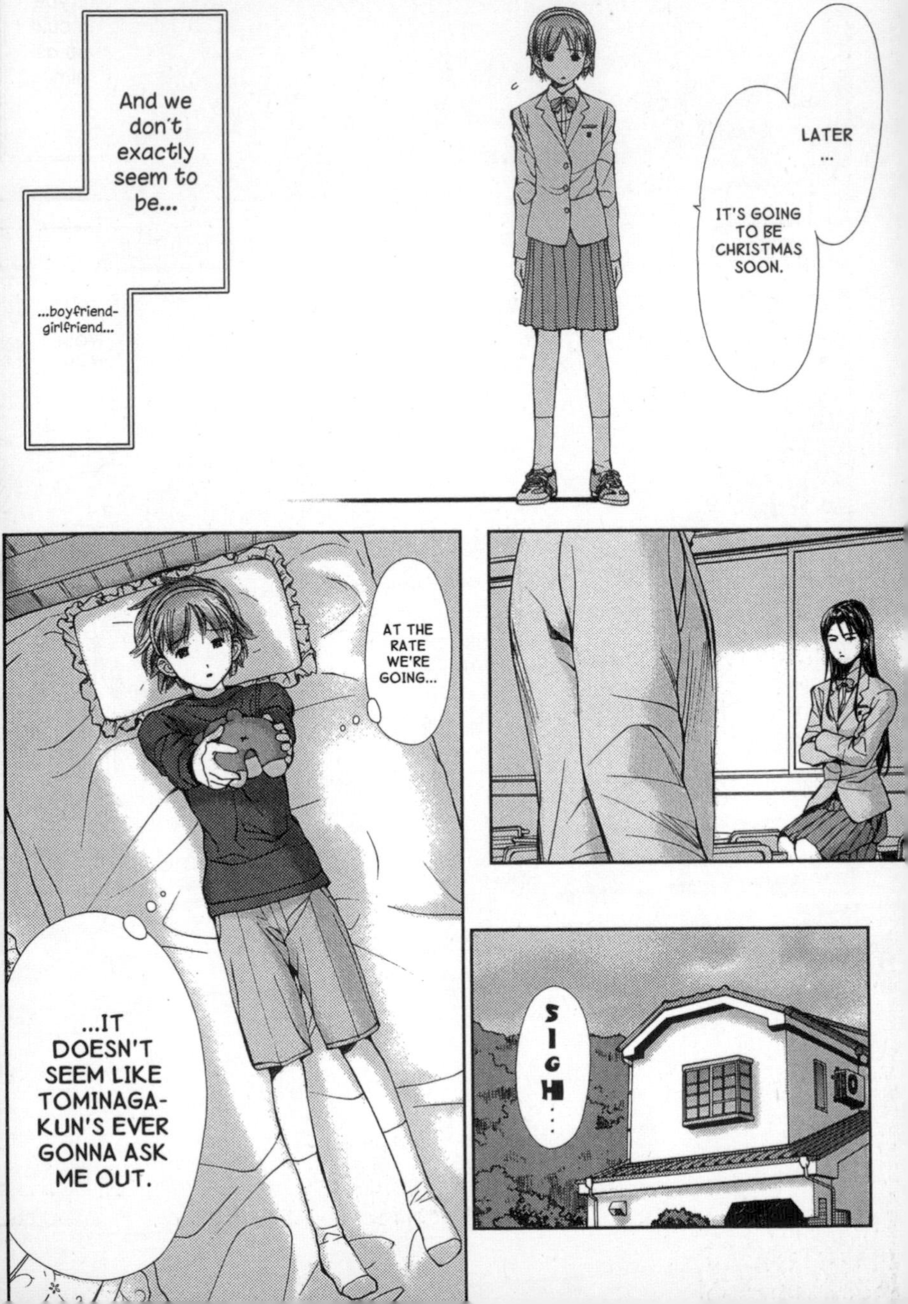
LATER ...
IT'S GOING TO BE CHRISTMAS SOON.
And we don't exactly seem to be...
...boyfriend-girlfriend...
SIGH...
AT THE RATE WE'RE GOING...
...IT DOESN'T SEEM LIKE TOMINAGA-KUN'S EVER GONNA ASK ME OUT.

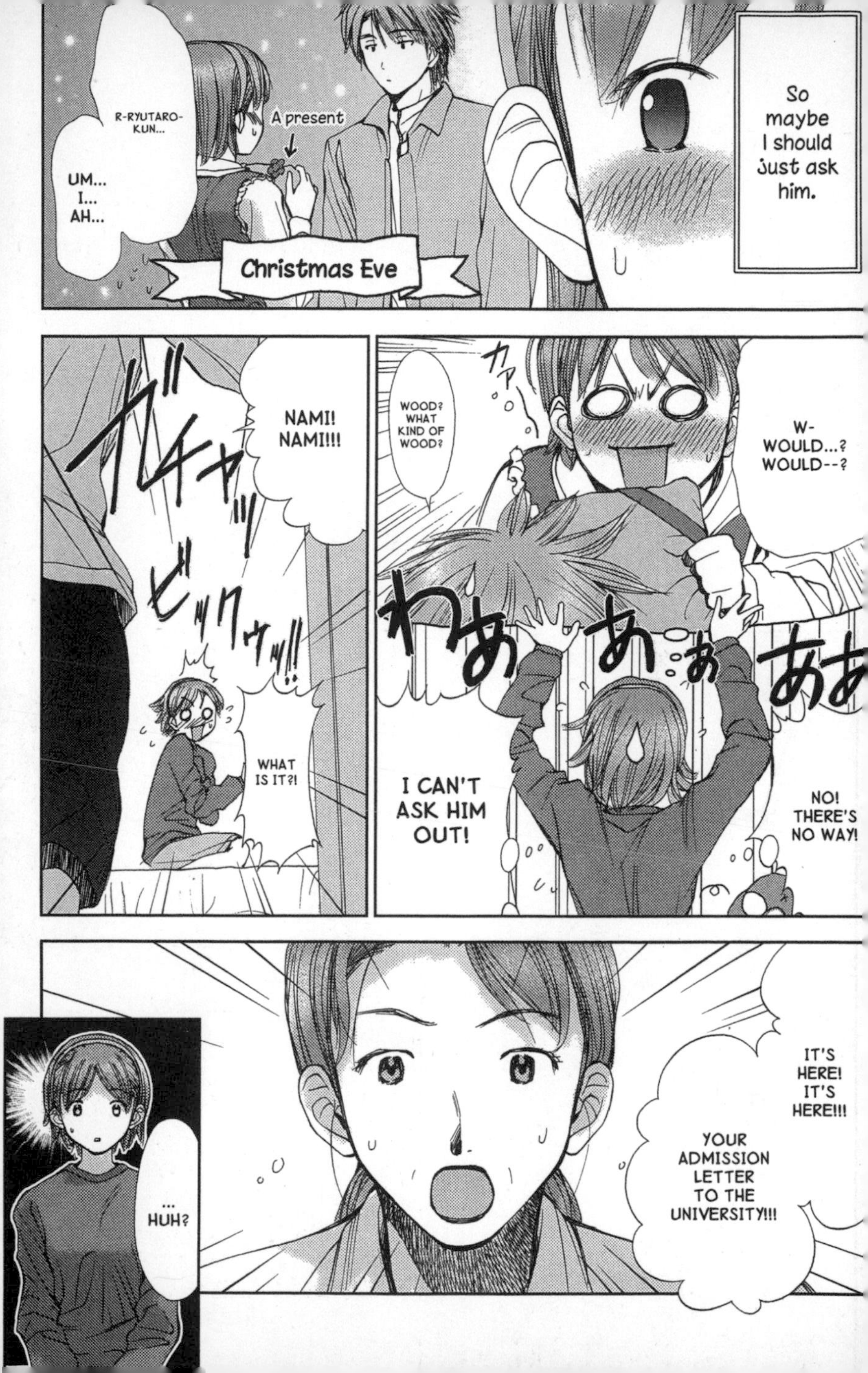
So maybe I should just ask him.
Christmas Eve
A present
R-RYUTARO-KUN...
UM... I... AH...
W- WOULD...? WOULD--?
WOOD? WHAT KIND OF WOOD?
カァ
わああぁああ
NO! THERE'S NO WAY!
I CAN'T ASK HIM OUT!
NAMI! NAMI!!!
ガチャッ
ビックゥッ!!
WHAT IS IT?!
IT'S HERE! IT'S HERE!!!
YOUR ADMISSION LETTER TO THE UNIVERSITY!!!
... HUH?

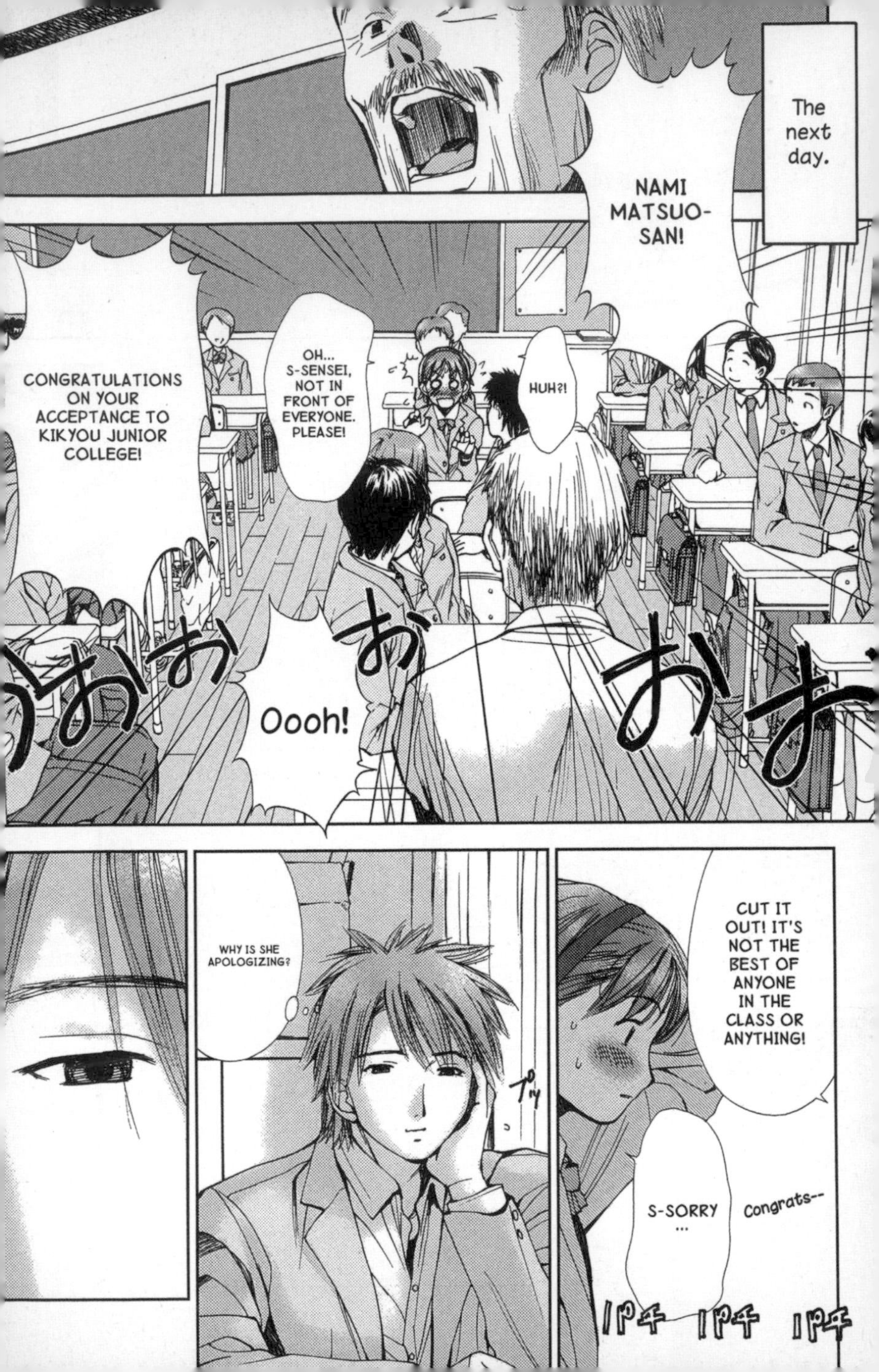
The next day.
NAMI MATSUO-SAN!
CONGRATULATIONS ON YOUR ACCEPTANCE TO KIKYOU JUNIOR COLLEGE!
Oooh!
HUH?!
OH... S-SENSEI, NOT IN FRONT OF EVERYONE. PLEASE!
CUT IT OUT! IT'S NOT THE BEST OF ANYONE IN THE CLASS OR ANYTHING!
Congrats--
S-SORRY ...
WHY IS SHE APOLOGIZING?

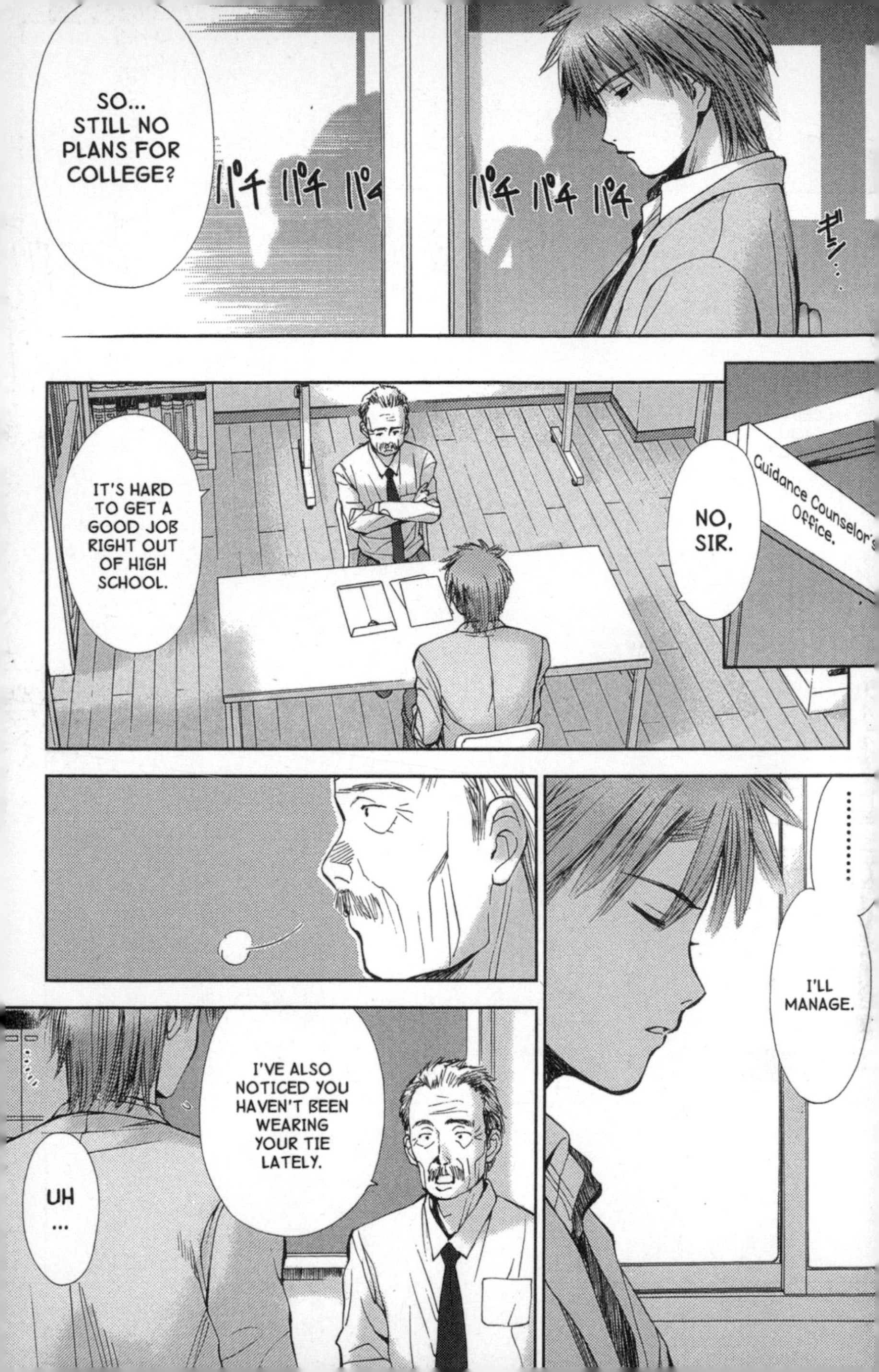
SO... STILL NO PLANS FOR COLLEGE?
パチ パチ パチ
パチ パチ パチ
Guidance Counselor's Office.
NO, SIR.
IT'S HARD TO GET A GOOD JOB RIGHT OUT OF HIGH SCHOOL.
....
I'LL MANAGE.
I'VE ALSO NOTICED YOU HAVEN'T BEEN WEARING YOUR TIE LATELY.
UH ...

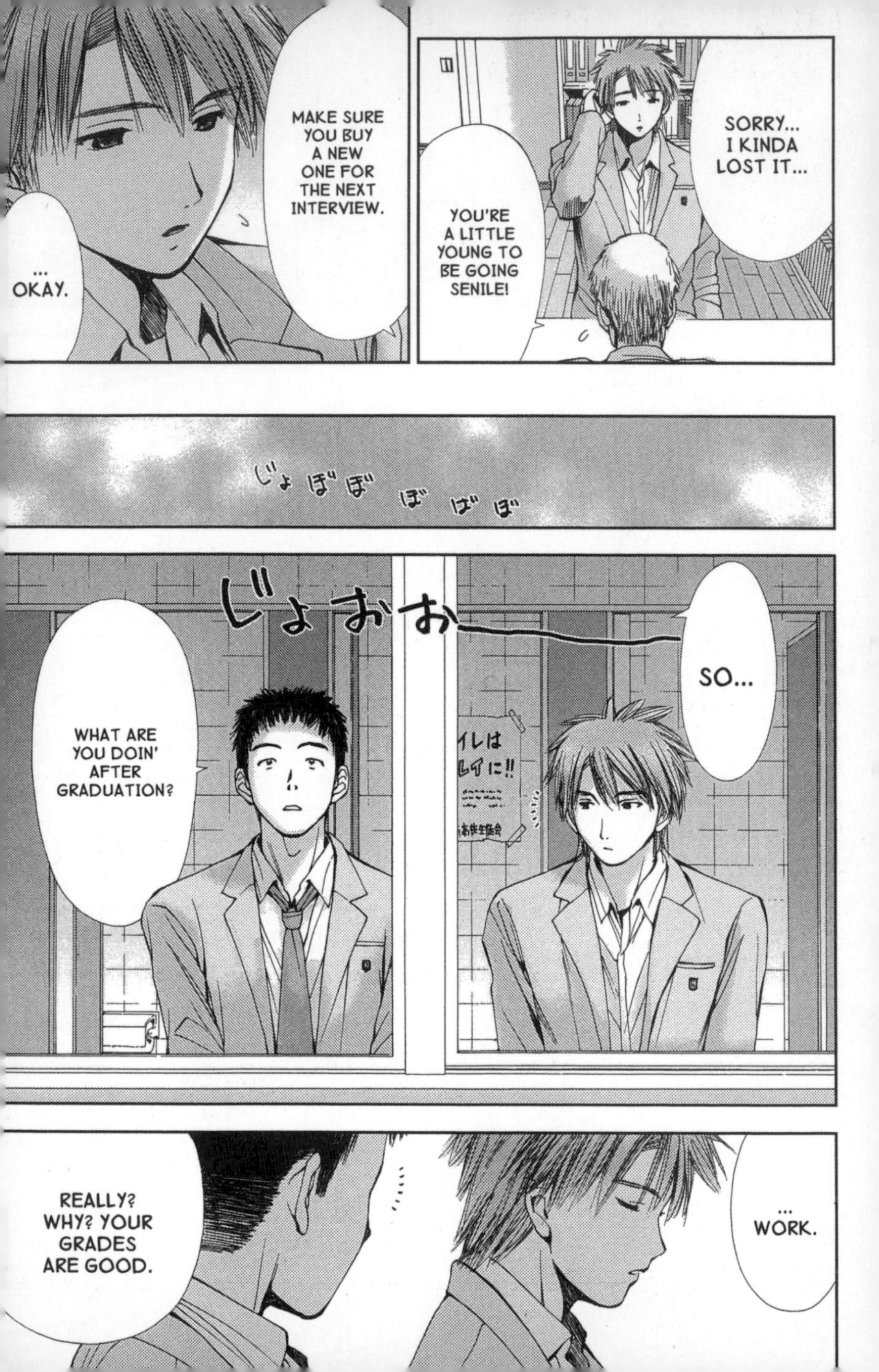
SORRY... I KINDA LOST IT...
YOU'RE A LITTLE YOUNG TO BE GOING SENILE!
MAKE SURE YOU BUY A NEW ONE FOR THE NEXT INTERVIEW.
... OKAY.
じょぼぼ ぼ ばぼ
じょおお
SO...
WHAT ARE YOU DOIN' AFTER GRADUATION?
... WORK.
REALLY? WHY? YOUR GRADES ARE GOOD.

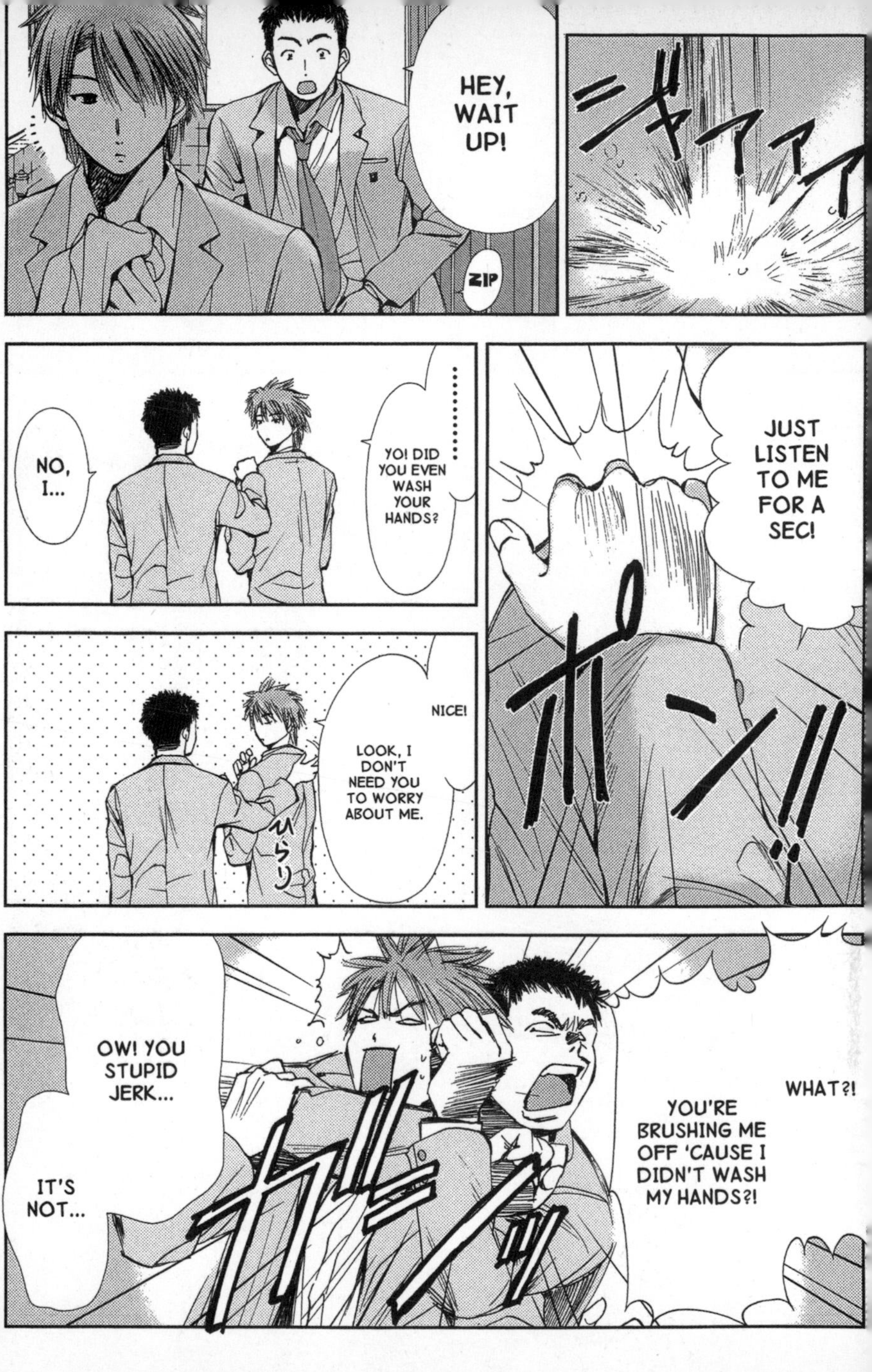
HEY, WAIT UP!
ZIP
JUST LISTEN TO ME FOR A SEC!
ポン!!
YO! DID YOU EVEN WASH YOUR HANDS?
NO, I...
NICE!
LOOK, I DON'T NEED YOU TO WORRY ABOUT ME.
ひらり
WHAT?!
YOU'RE BRUSHING ME OFF 'CAUSE I DIDN'T WASH MY HANDS?!
OW! YOU STUPID JERK...
IT'S NOT...

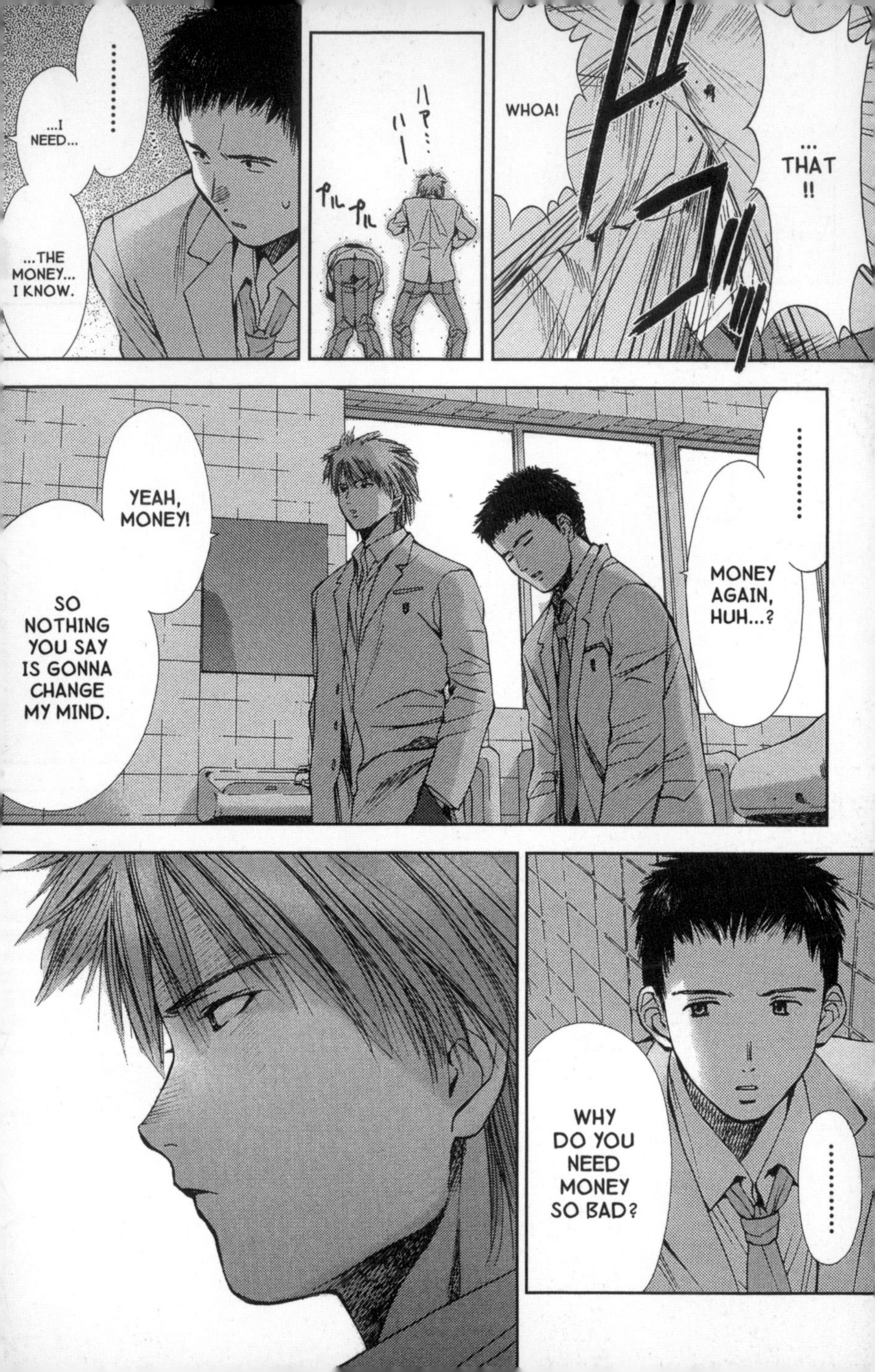
WHOA!
... THAT !!
ドゴッ
ハァ… ハー
プルプル
....
...I NEED...
...THE MONEY... I KNOW.
....
MONEY AGAIN, HUH...?
YEAH, MONEY!
SO NOTHING YOU SAY IS GONNA CHANGE MY MIND.
....
WHY DO YOU NEED MONEY SO BAD?

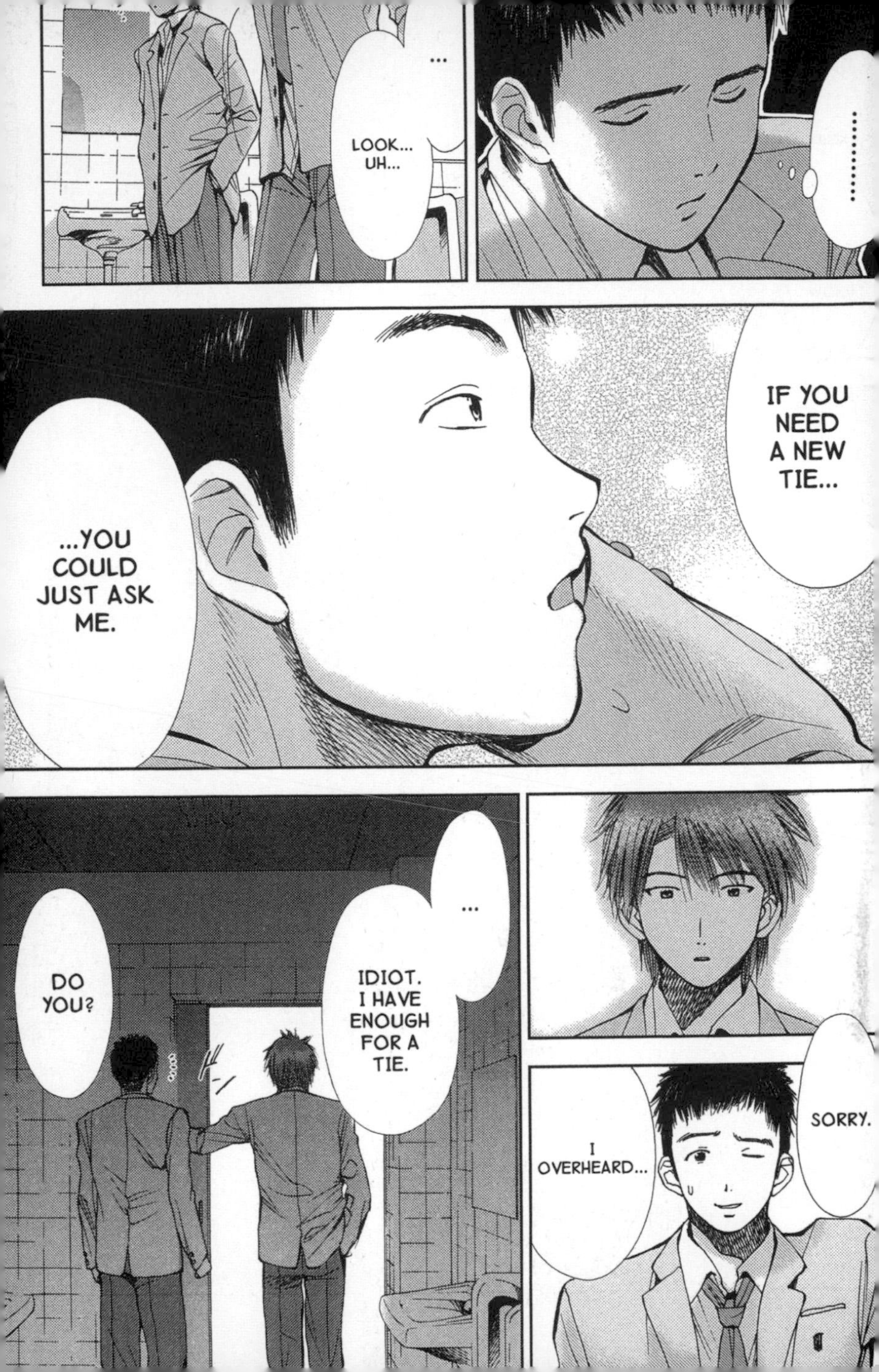
......
...
LOOK... UH...
IF YOU NEED A NEW TIE...
...YOU COULD JUST ASK ME.
SORRY.
I OVERHEARD...
...
IDIOT. I HAVE ENOUGH FOR A TIE.
DO YOU?

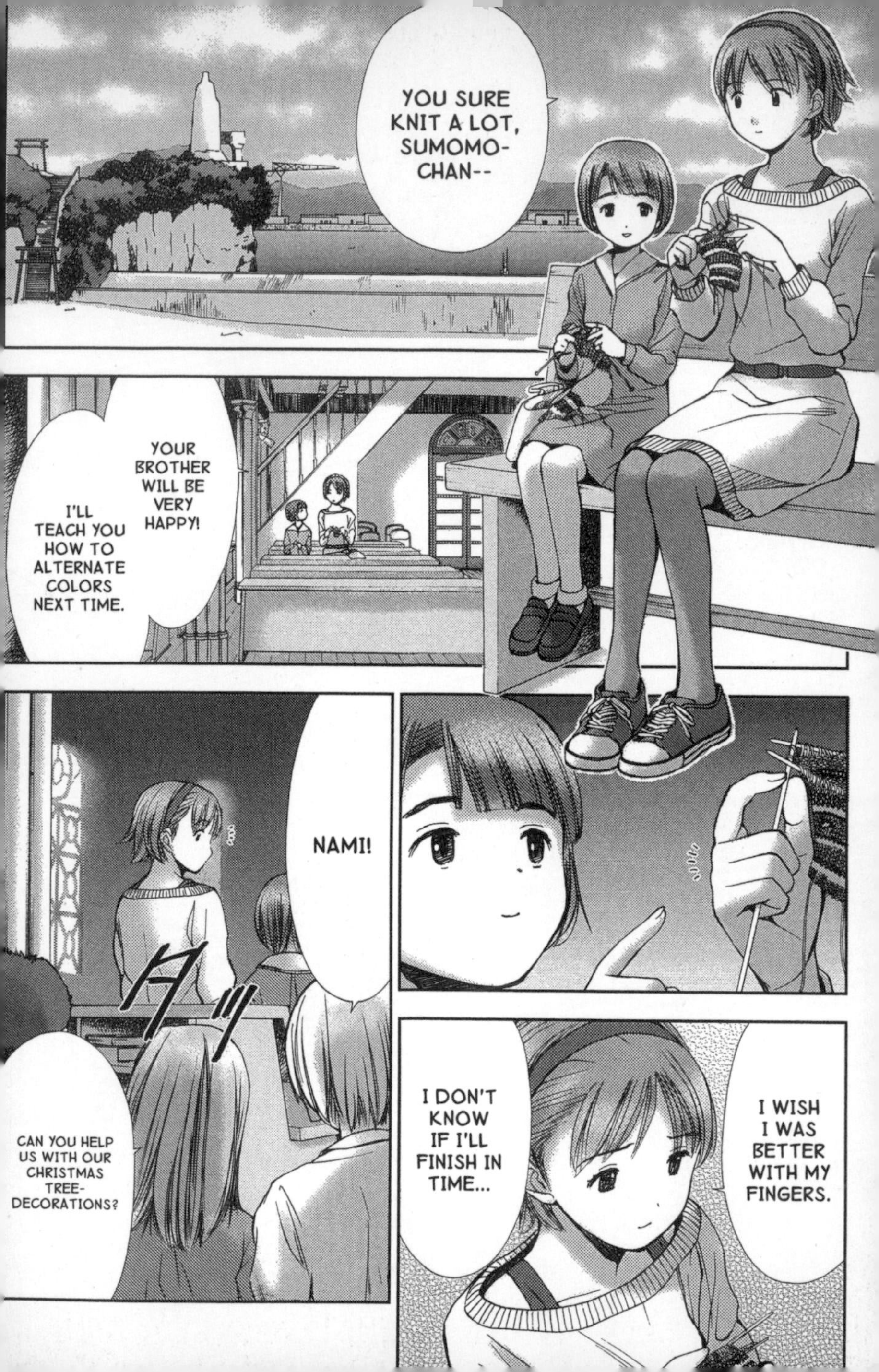
YOU SURE KNIT A LOT, SUMOMO-CHAN--
YOUR BROTHER WILL BE VERY HAPPY!
I'LL TEACH YOU HOW TO ALTERNATE COLORS NEXT TIME.
I WISH I WAS BETTER WITH MY FINGERS.
I DON'T KNOW IF I'LL FINISH IN TIME...
NAMI!
CAN YOU HELP US WITH OUR CHRISTMAS TREE-DECORATIONS?

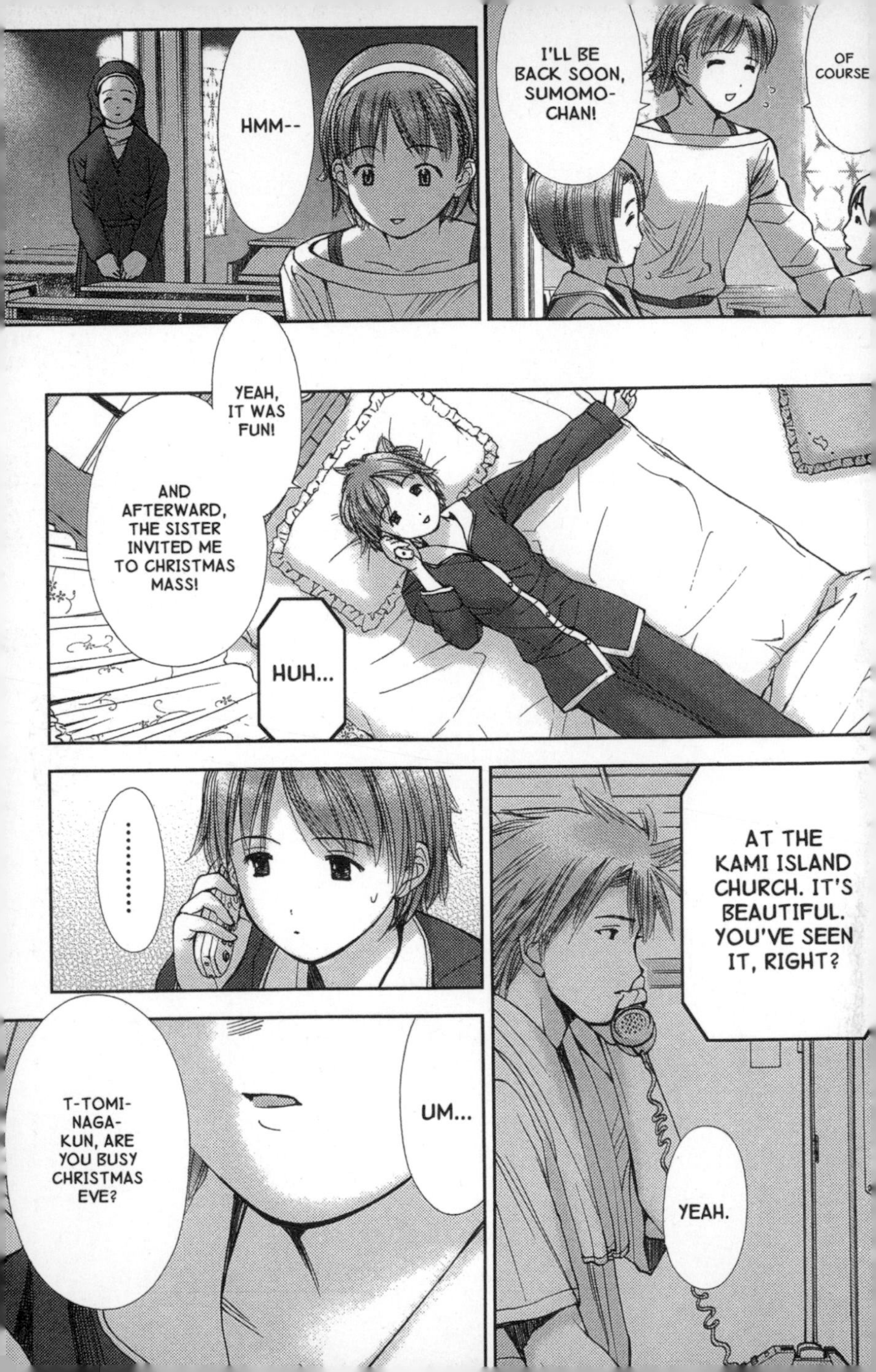
OF COURSE
I'LL BE BACK SOON, SUMOMO-CHAN!
HMM--
YEAH, IT WAS FUN!
AND AFTERWARD, THE SISTER INVITED ME TO CHRISTMAS MASS!
HUH...
AT THE KAMI ISLAND CHURCH. IT'S BEAUTIFUL. YOU'VE SEEN IT, RIGHT?
YEAH.
....
UM...
T-TOMI-NAGA-KUN, ARE YOU BUSY CHRISTMAS EVE?

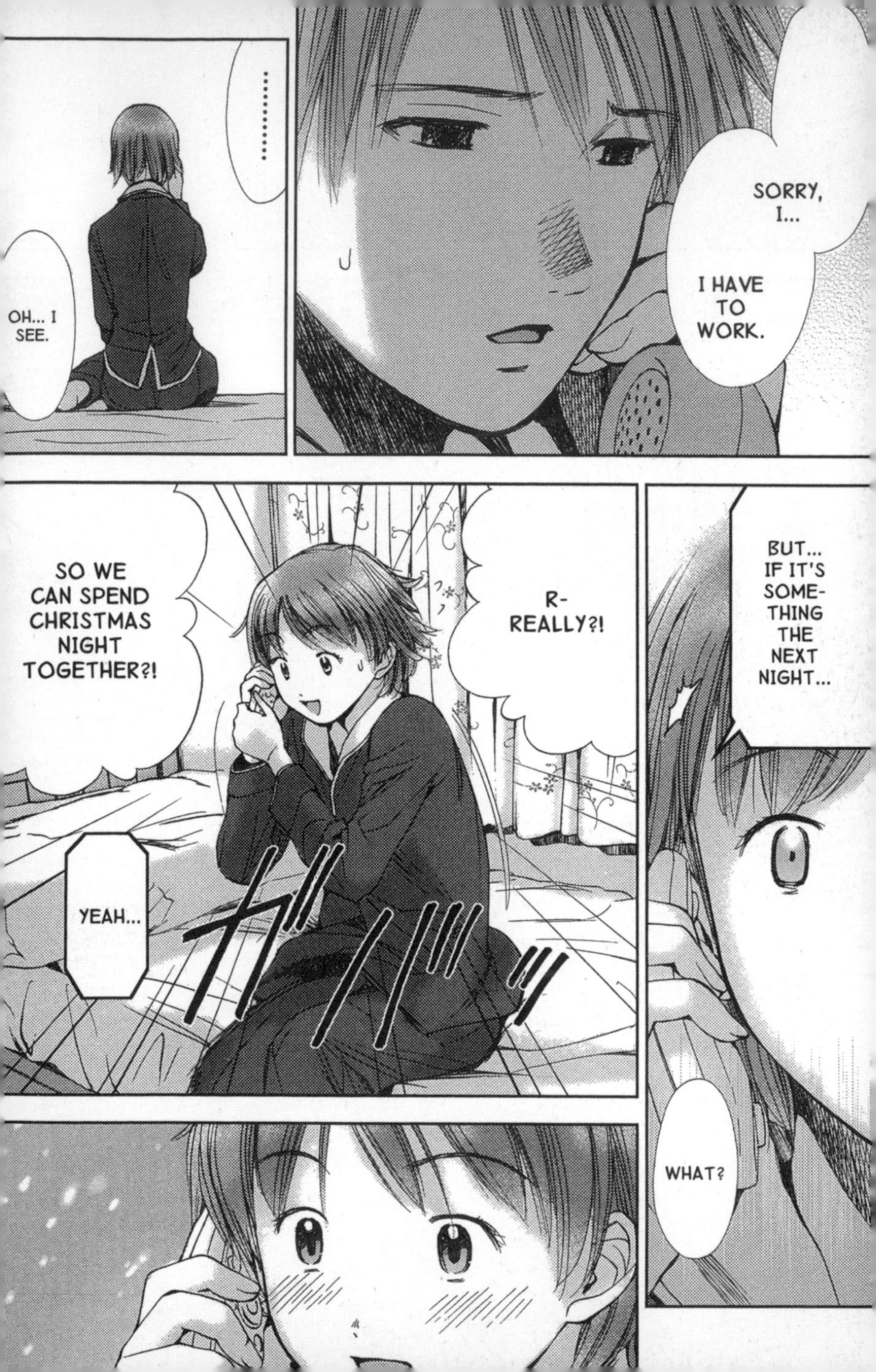
SORRY, I... I HAVE TO WORK.
......
OH... I SEE.
BUT... IF IT'S SOME-THING THE NEXT NIGHT...
WHAT?
R-REALLY?!
SO WE CAN SPEND CHRISTMAS NIGHT TOGETHER?!
YEAH...

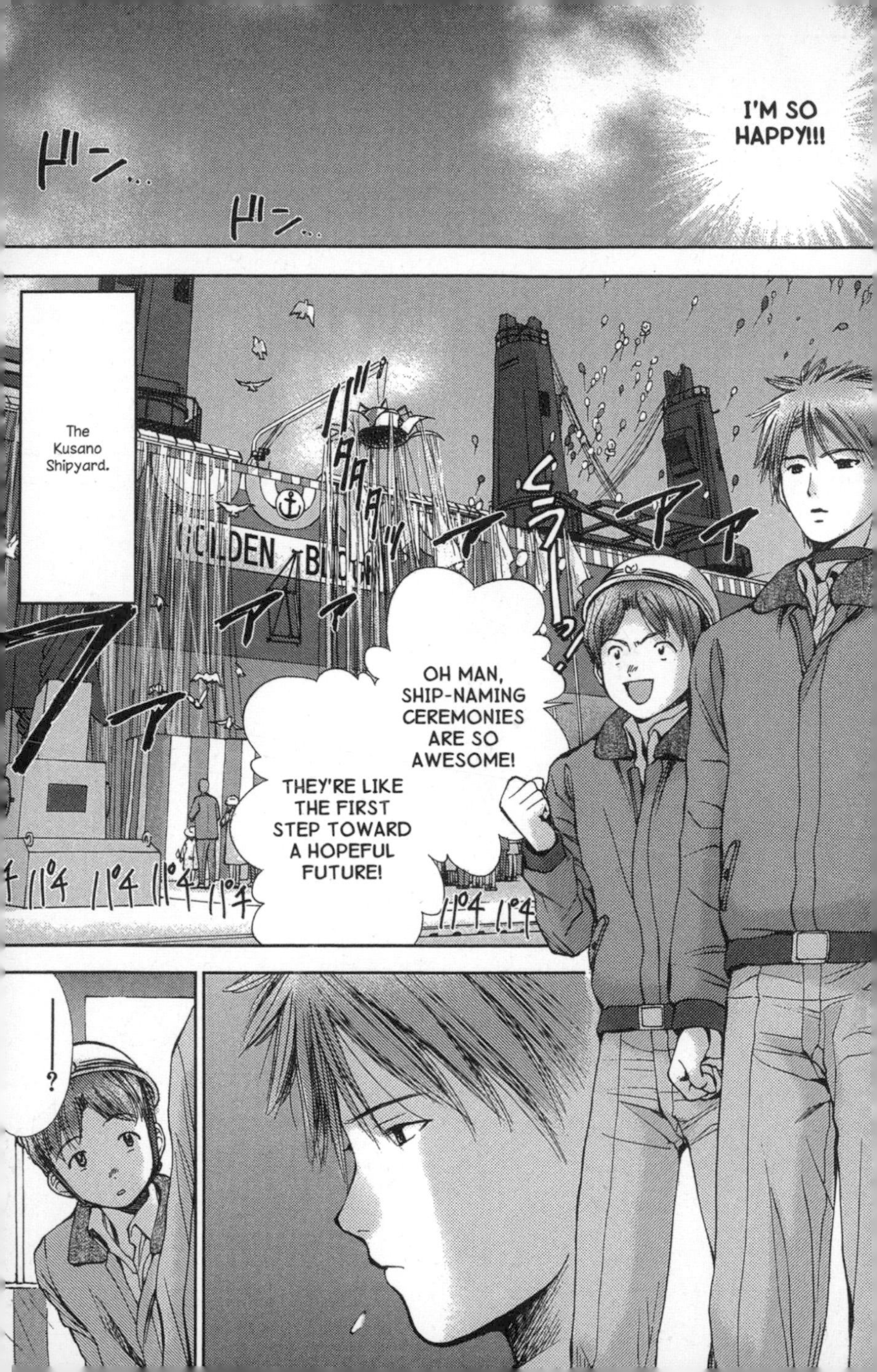
I'M SO HAPPY!!!
The Kusano Shipyard.
OH MAN, SHIP-NAMING CEREMONIES ARE SO AWESOME!
THEY'RE LIKE THE FIRST STEP TOWARD A HOPEFUL FUTURE!
—?

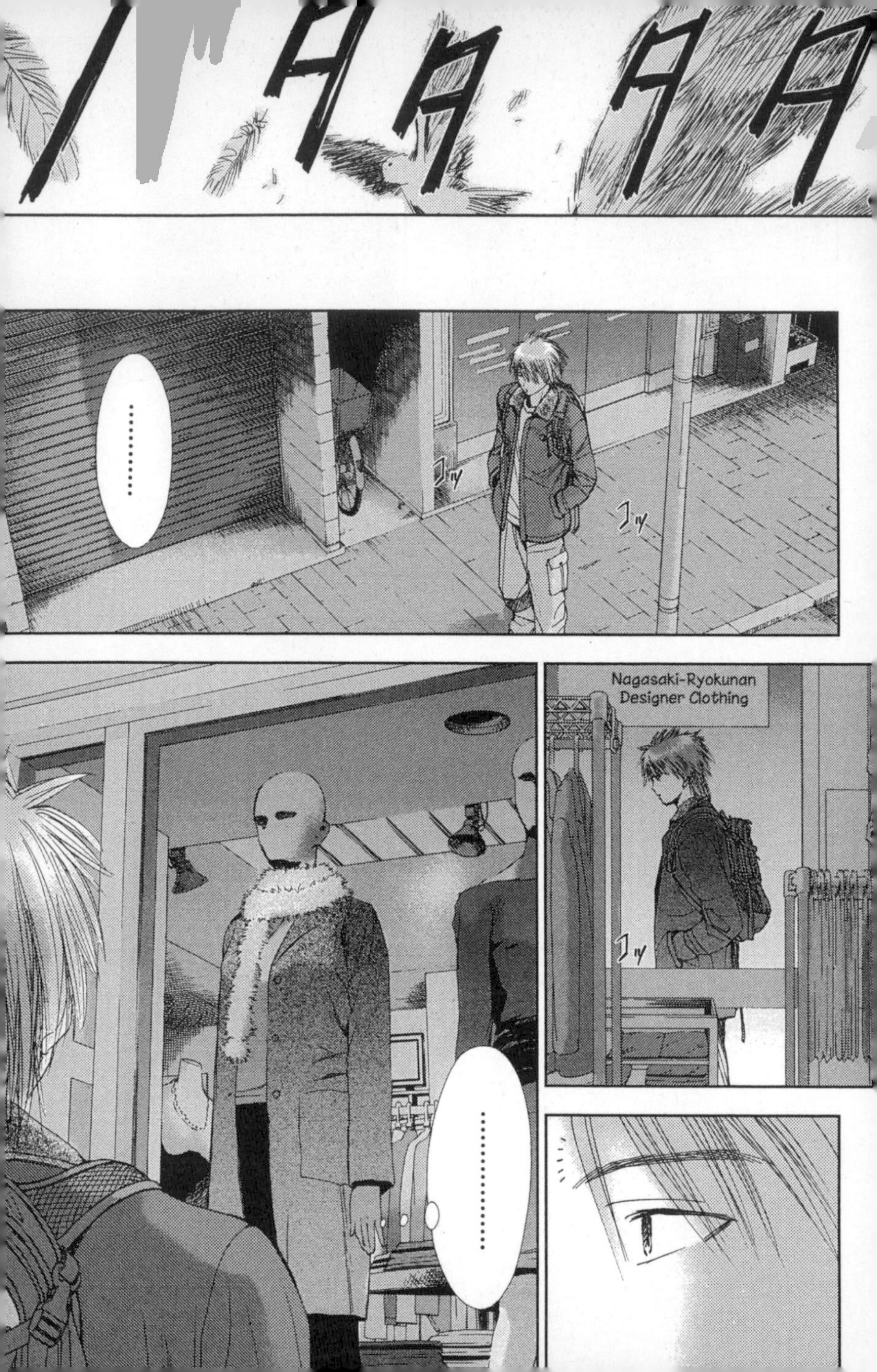
…………
コツ
コツ
Nagasaki-Ryokunan
Designer Clothing
コツ
…………

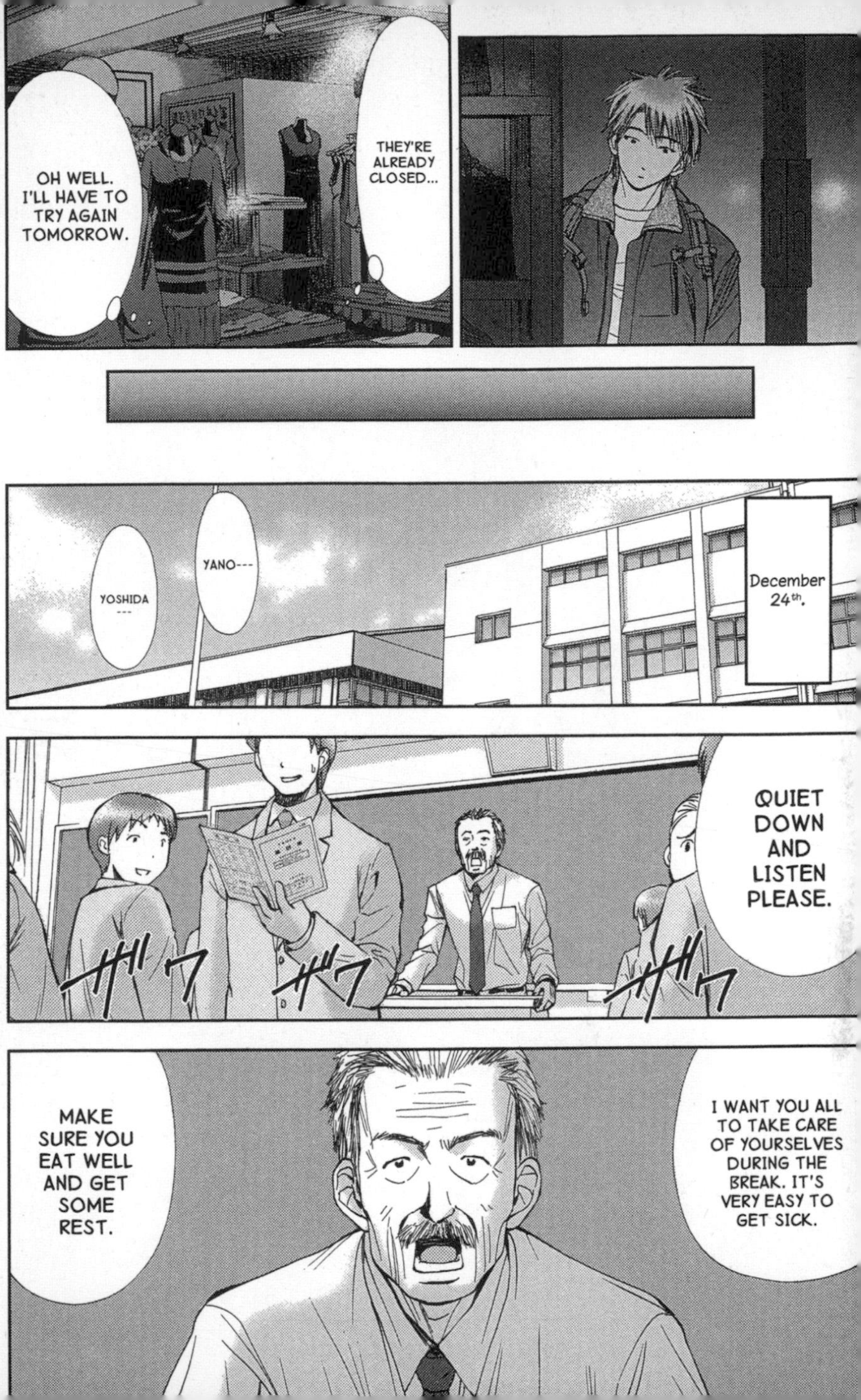
THEY'RE ALREADY CLOSED...
OH WELL. I'LL HAVE TO TRY AGAIN TOMORROW.
December 24th.
YANO---
YOSHIDA ---
QUIET DOWN AND LISTEN PLEASE.
ザワ
ザワ
ザワ
I WANT YOU ALL TO TAKE CARE OF YOURSELVES DURING THE BREAK. IT'S VERY EASY TO GET SICK.
MAKE SURE YOU EAT WELL AND GET SOME REST.

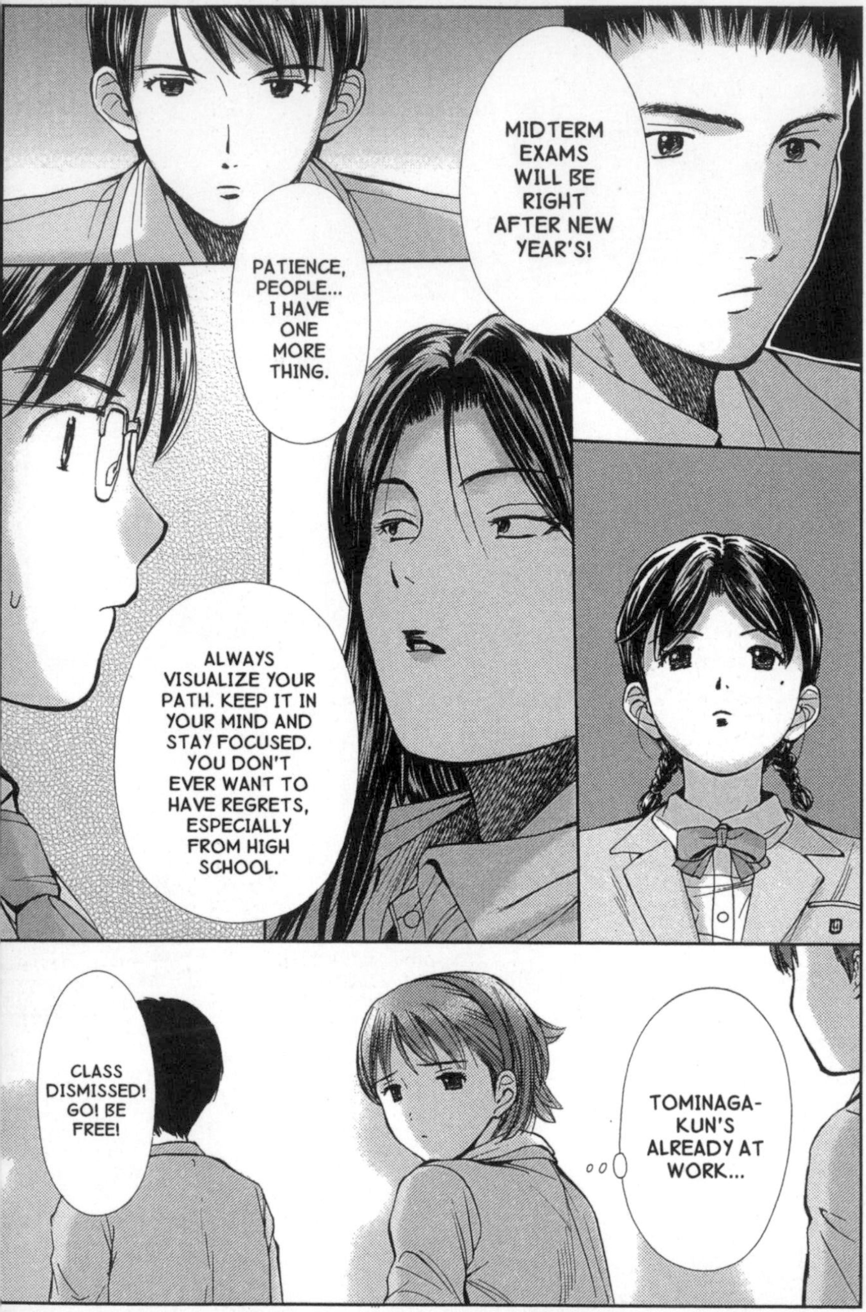
MIDTERM EXAMS WILL BE RIGHT AFTER NEW YEAR'S!
PATIENCE, PEOPLE... I HAVE ONE MORE THING.
ALWAYS VISUALIZE YOUR PATH. KEEP IT IN YOUR MIND AND STAY FOCUSED. YOU DON'T EVER WANT TO HAVE REGRETS, ESPECIALLY FROM HIGH SCHOOL.
TOMINAGA-KUN'S ALREADY AT WORK...
CLASS DISMISSED! GO! BE FREE!

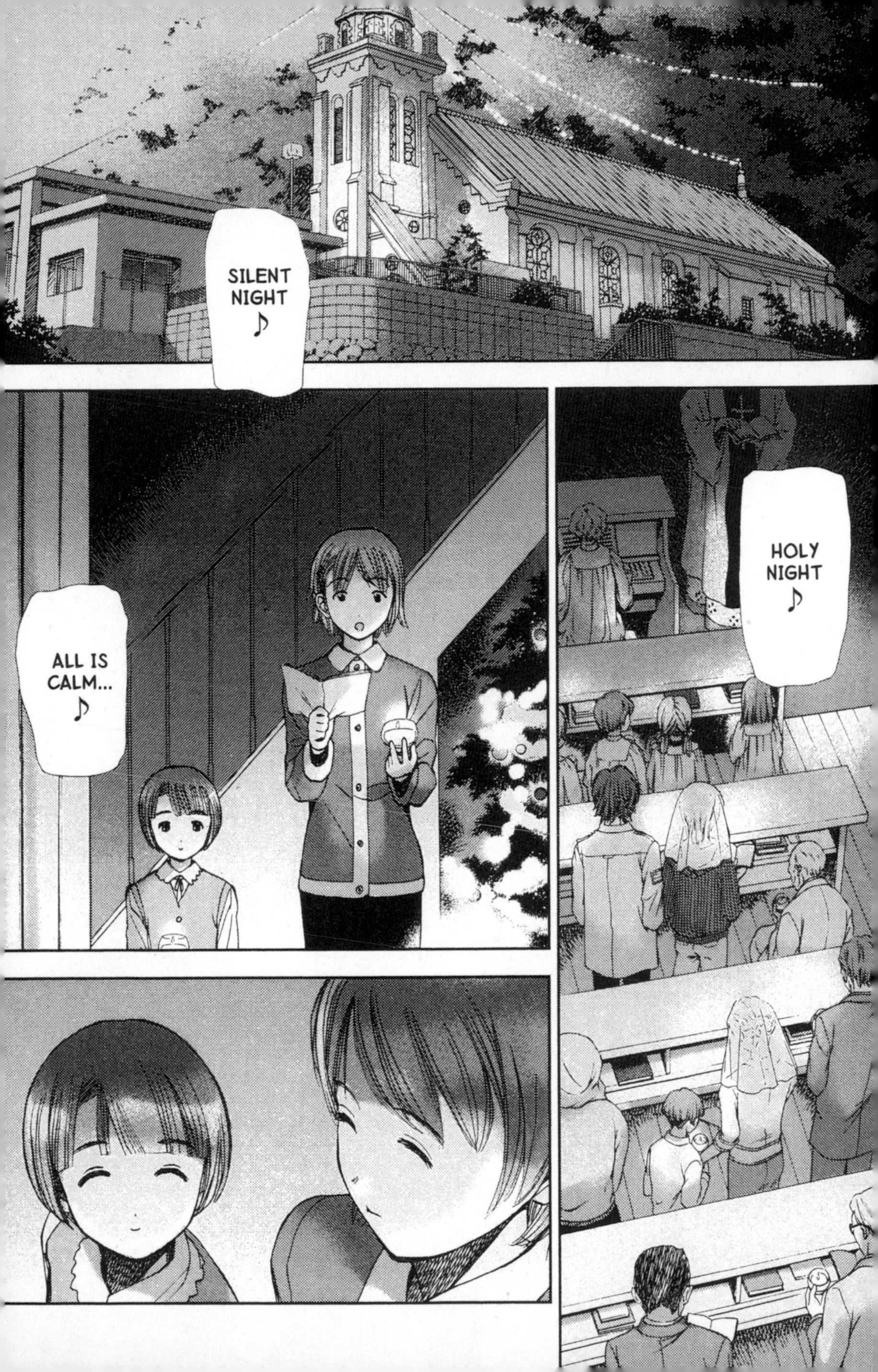
SILENT NIGHT ♪
HOLY NIGHT ♪
ALL IS CALM... ♪

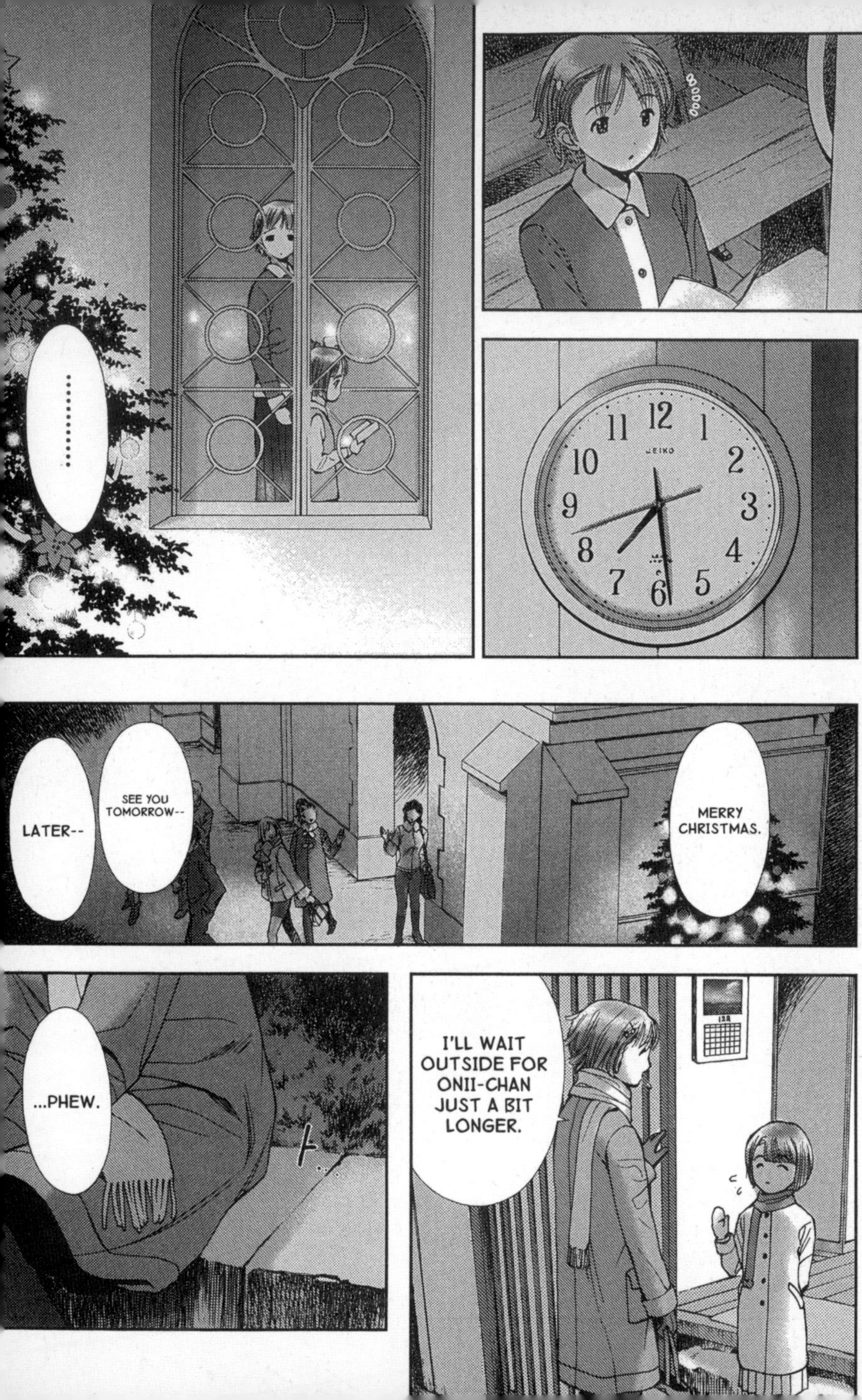

....
MERRY CHRISTMAS.
SEE YOU TOMORROW--
LATER--
I'LL WAIT OUTSIDE FOR ONII-CHAN JUST A BIT LONGER.
...PHEW.

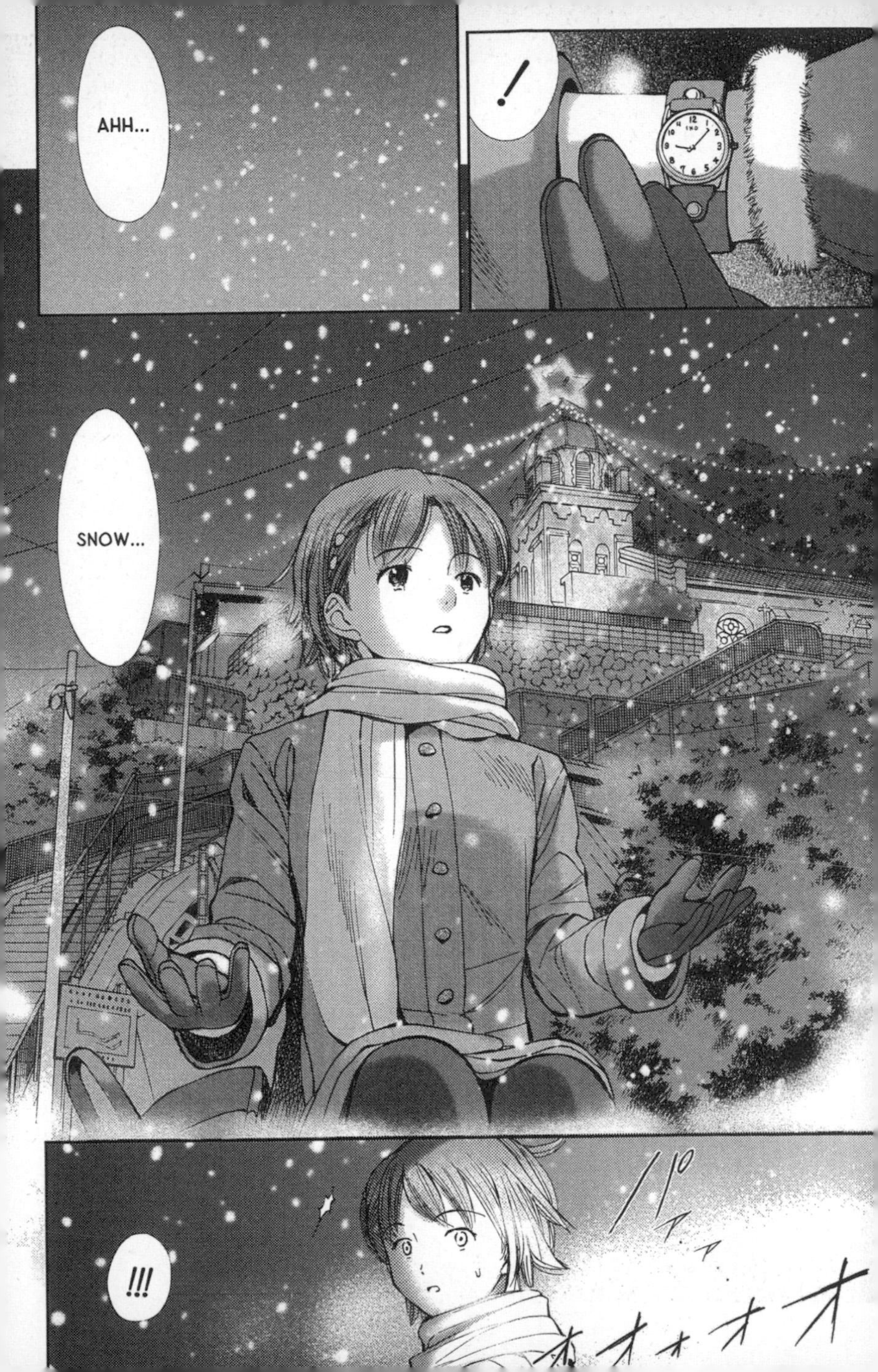
!
AHH...
SNOW...
!!!
パァァ
オオォオオ

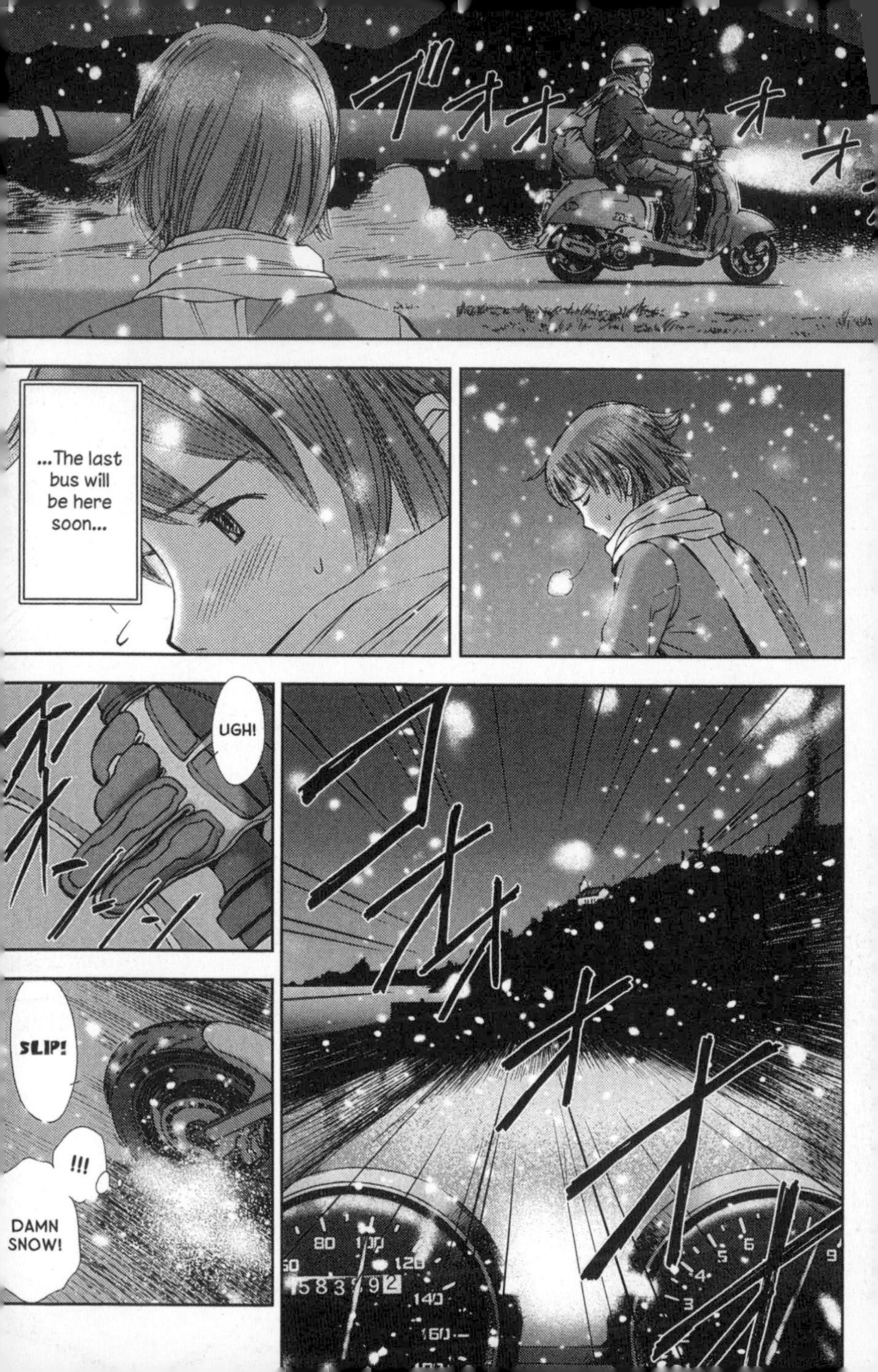
...The last bus will be here soon...
UGH!
SLIP!
!!!
DAMN SNOW!

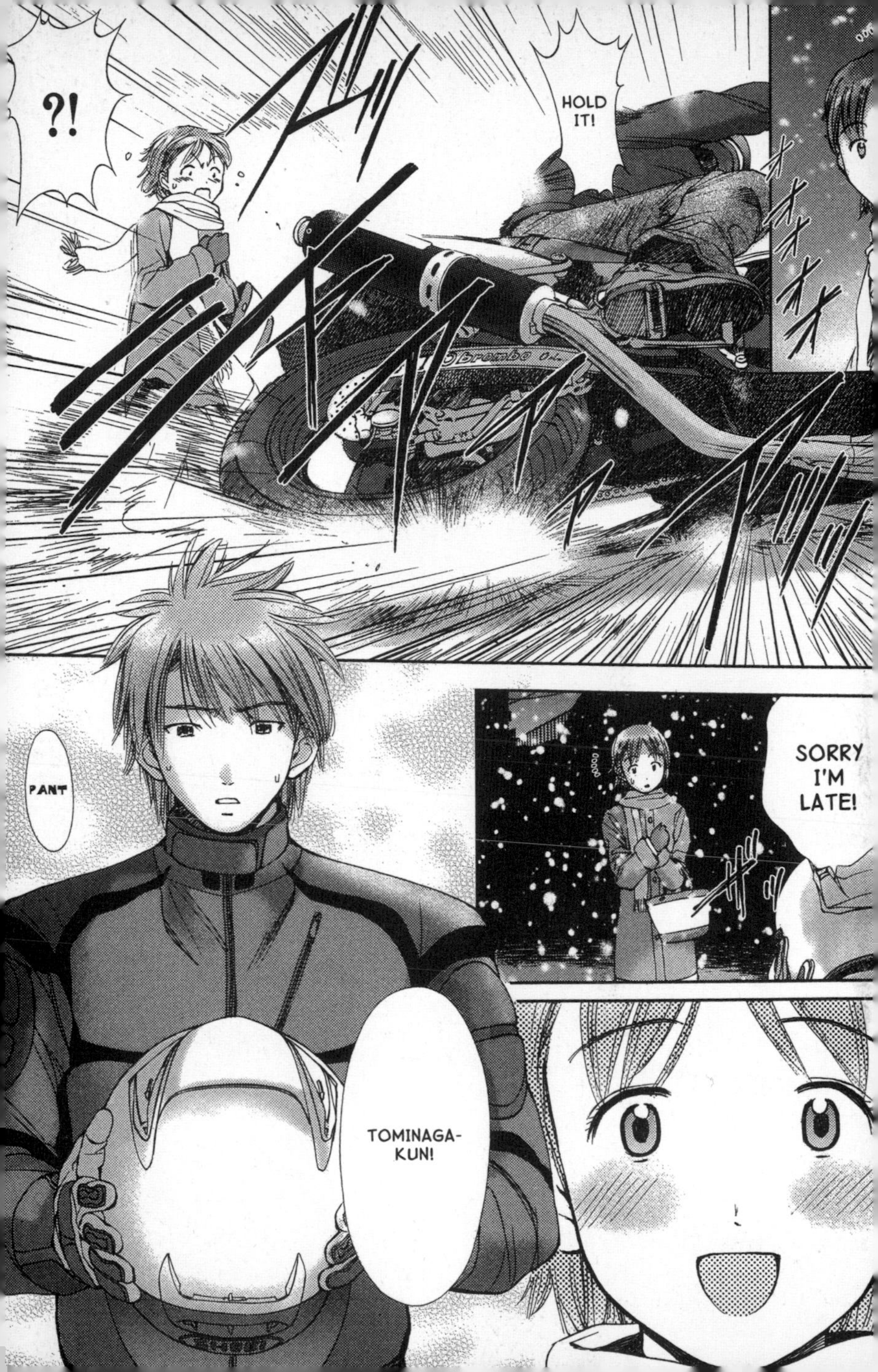
HOLD IT!
?!
SORRY I'M LATE!
PANT
TOMINAGA-KUN!

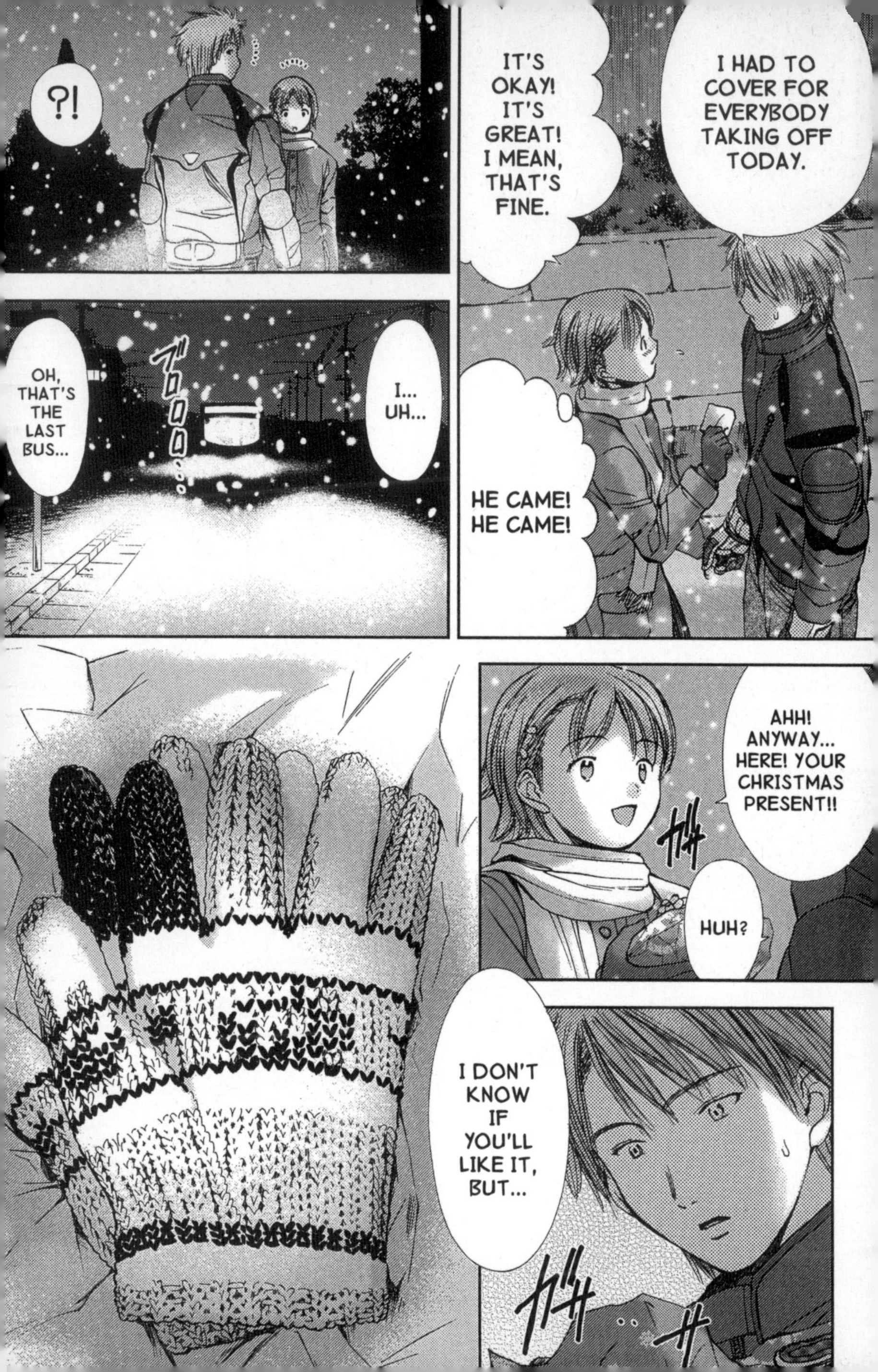
I HAD TO COVER FOR EVERYBODY TAKING OFF TODAY.
IT'S OKAY! IT'S GREAT! I MEAN, THAT'S FINE.
HE CAME! HE CAME!
?!
I... UH...
ブロロロ...
OH, THAT'S THE LAST BUS...
AHH! ANYWAY... HERE! YOUR CHRISTMAS PRESENT!!
ガサ
HUH?
I DON'T KNOW IF YOU'LL LIKE IT, BUT...
ガサ
ガサ

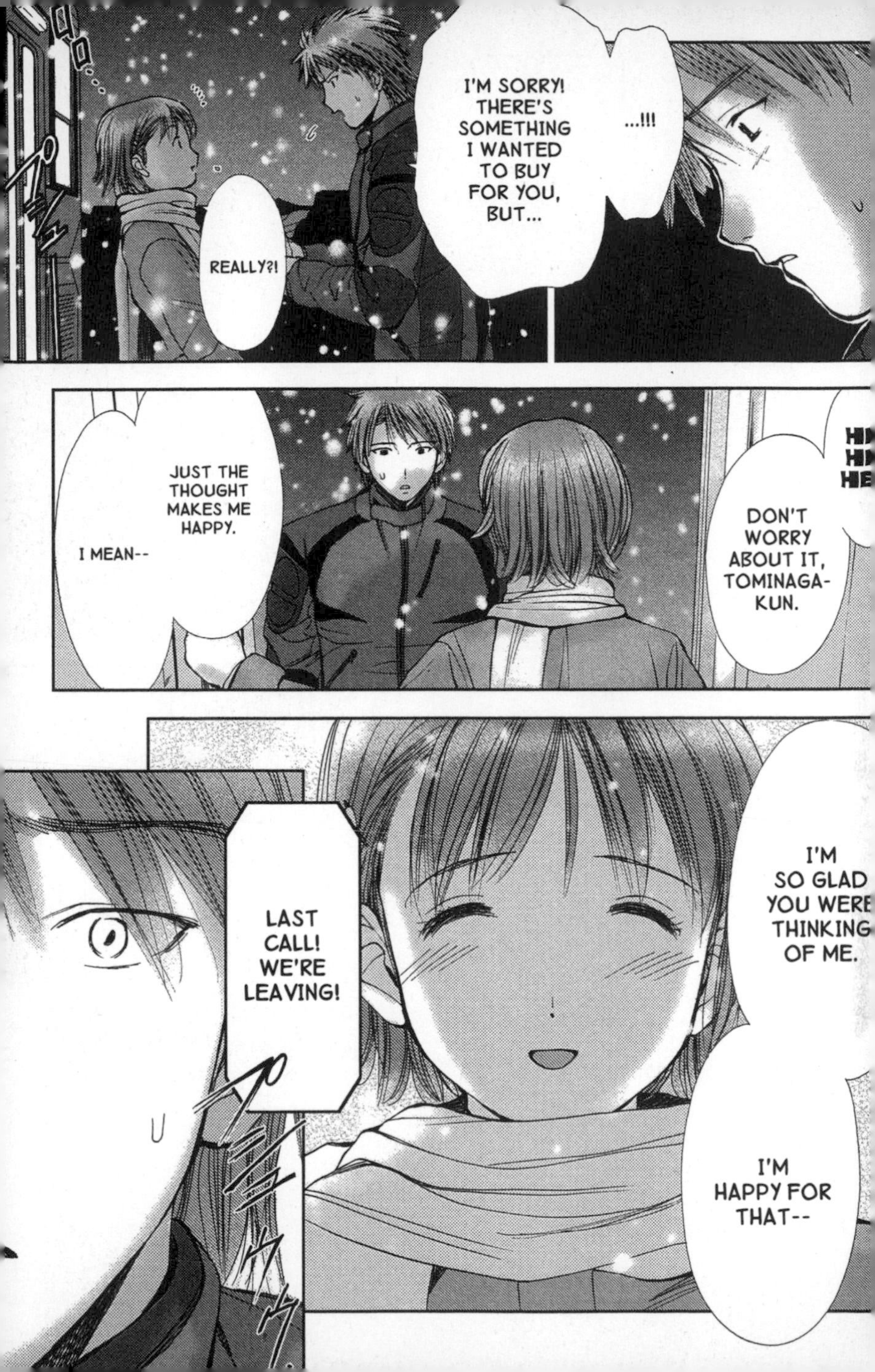
I'M SORRY! THERE'S SOMETHING I WANTED TO BUY FOR YOU, BUT...
...!!!
REALLY?!
DON'T WORRY ABOUT IT, TOMINAGA-KUN.
JUST THE THOUGHT MAKES ME HAPPY.
I MEAN--
I'M SO GLAD YOU WERE THINKING OF ME.
I'M HAPPY FOR THAT--
LAST CALL! WE'RE LEAVING!

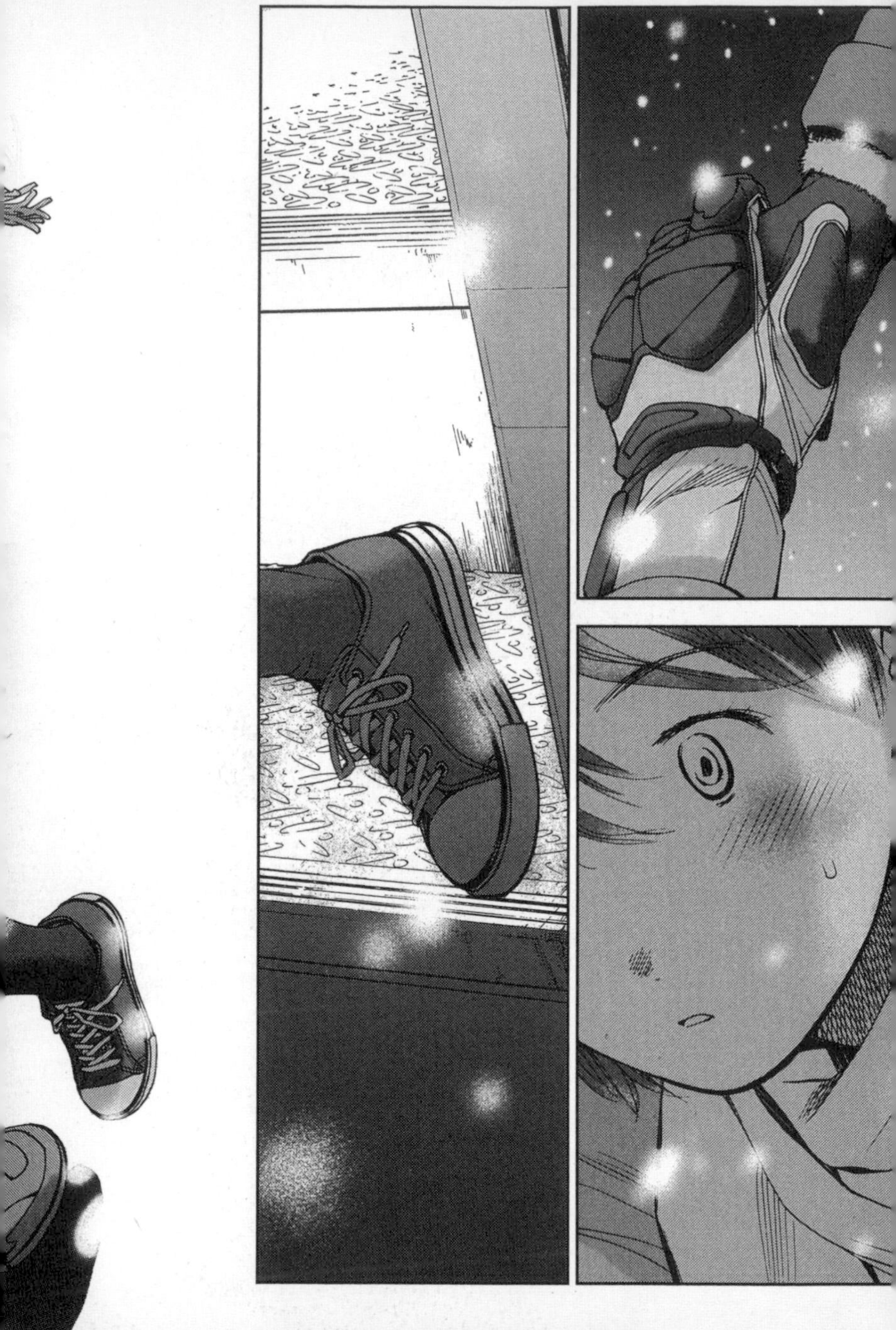

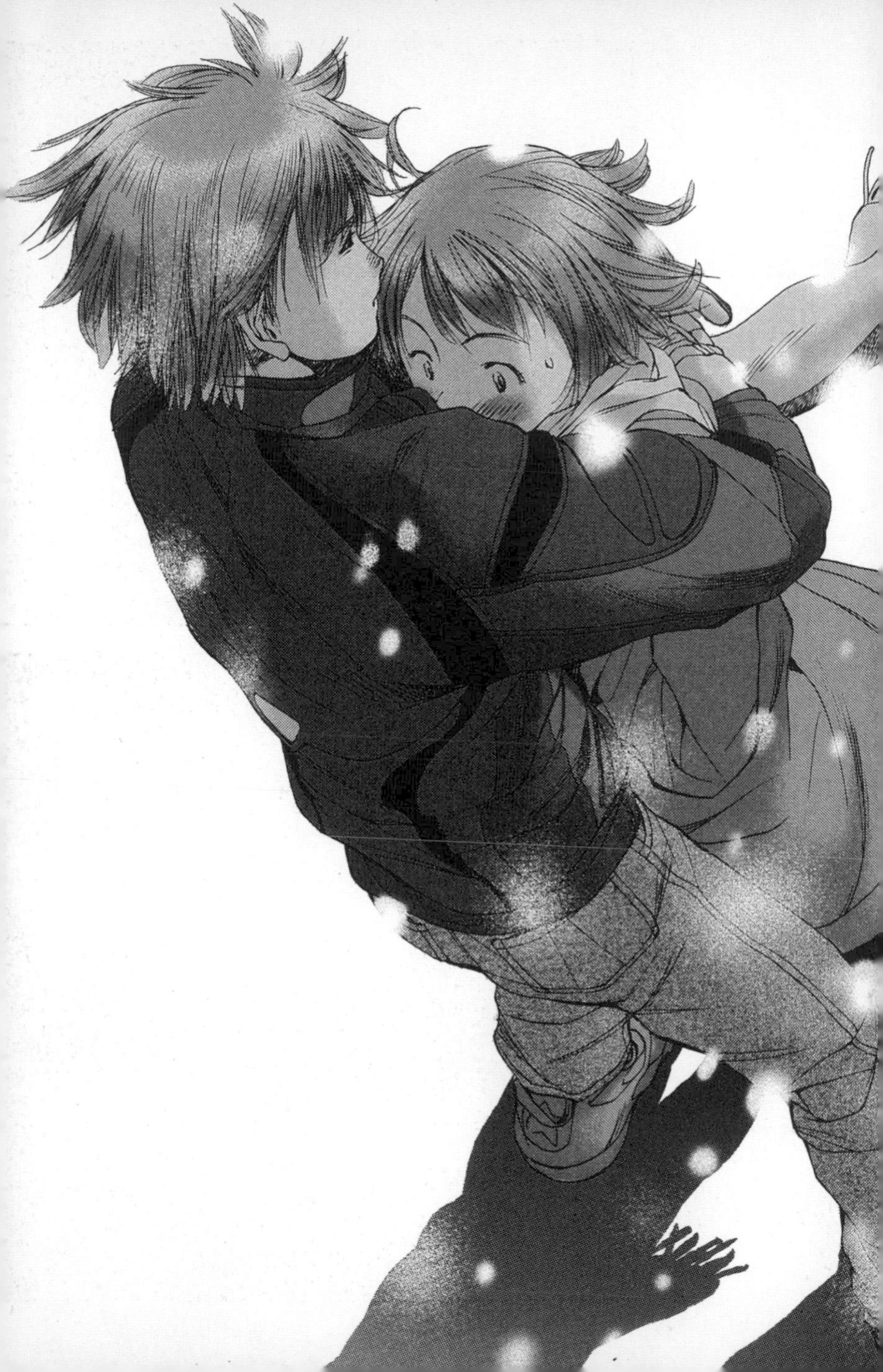

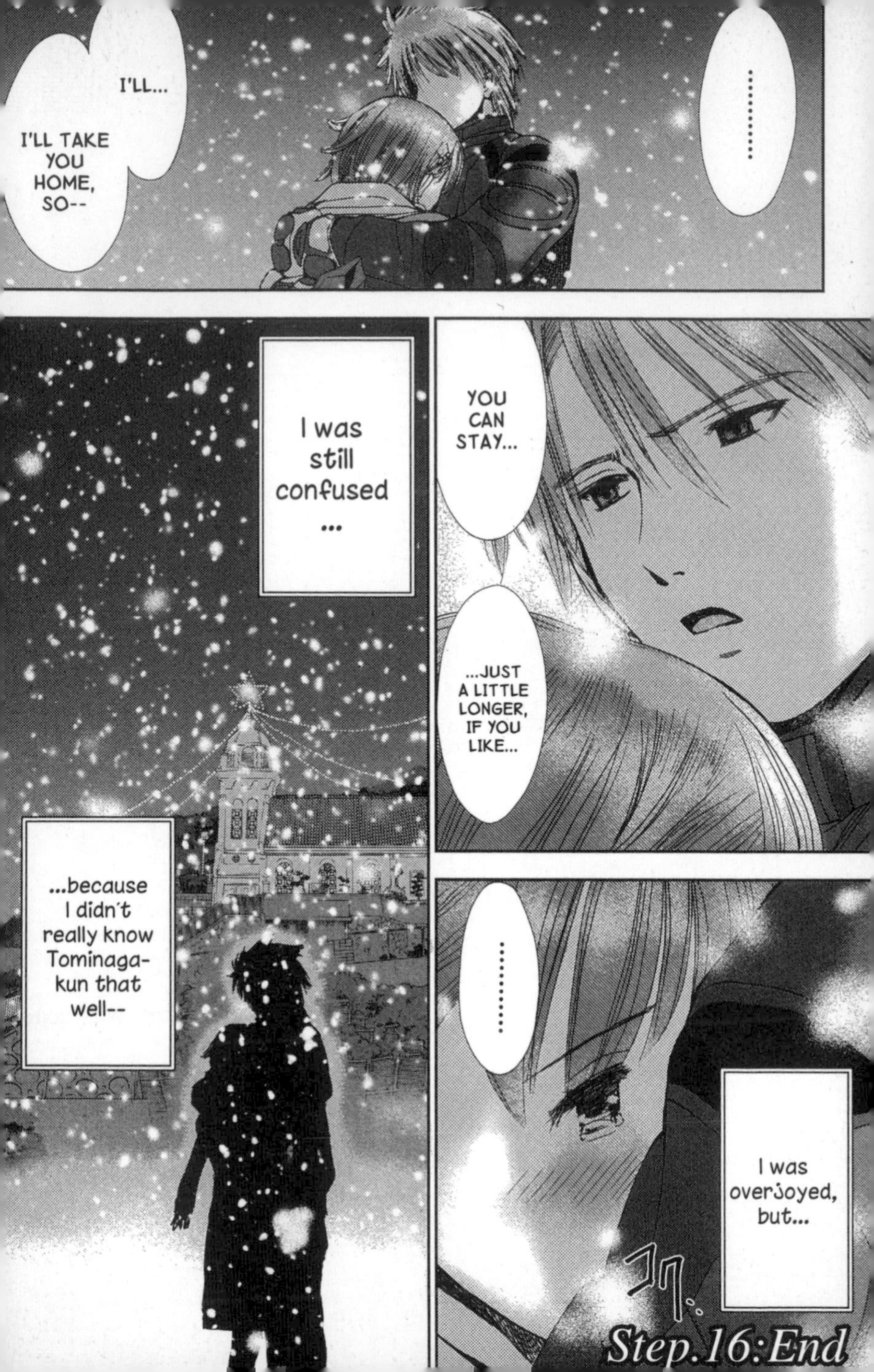

....
I'LL...
I'LL TAKE YOU HOME, SO--
YOU CAN STAY...
...JUST A LITTLE LONGER, IF YOU LIKE...
....
I was overjoyed, but...
コク
Step.16:End
I was still confused...
...because I didn't really know Tominaga-kun that well--

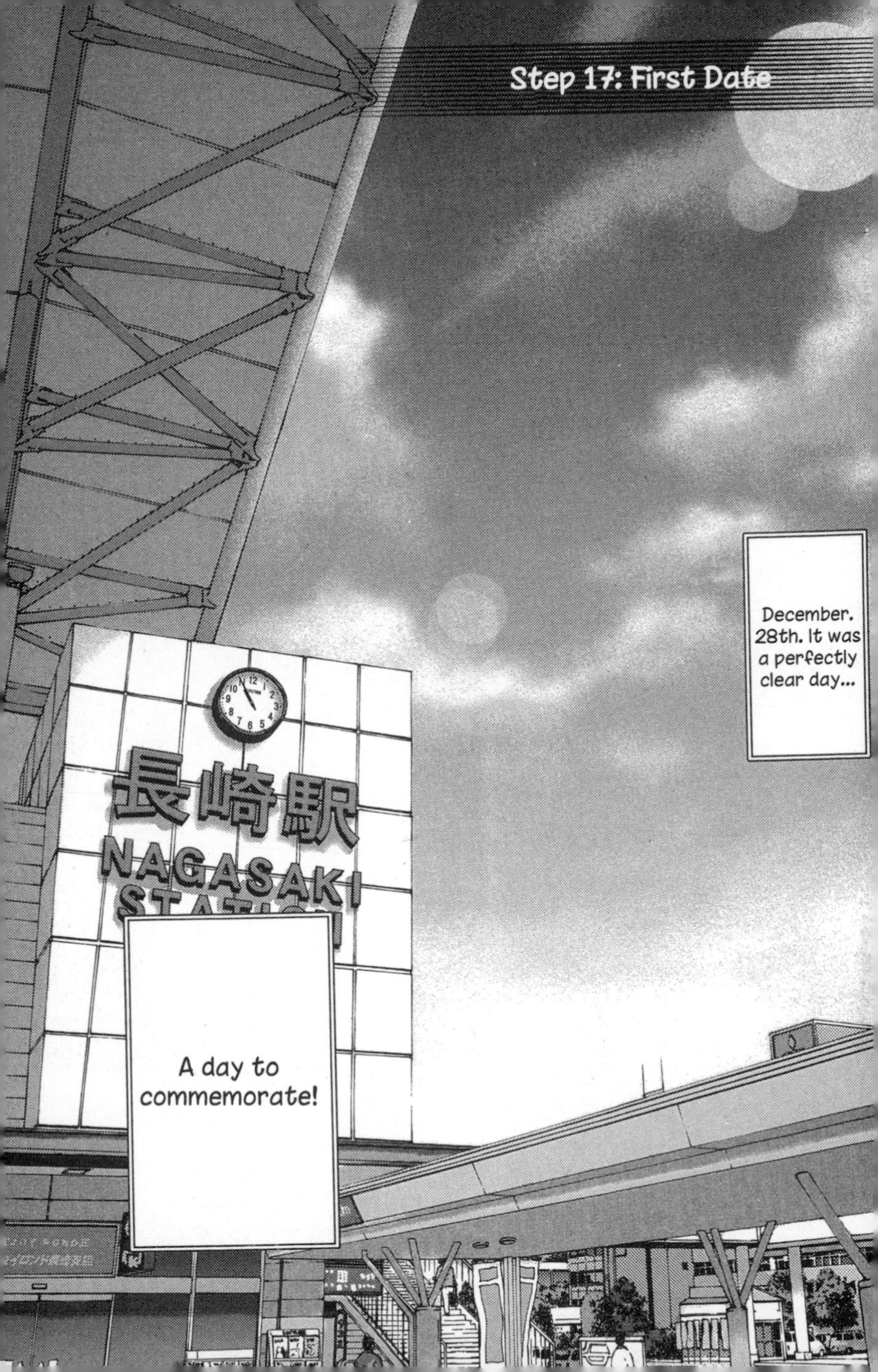
Step 17: First Date
December. 28th. It was a perfectly clear day...
長崎駅
NAGASAKI
A day to commemorate!

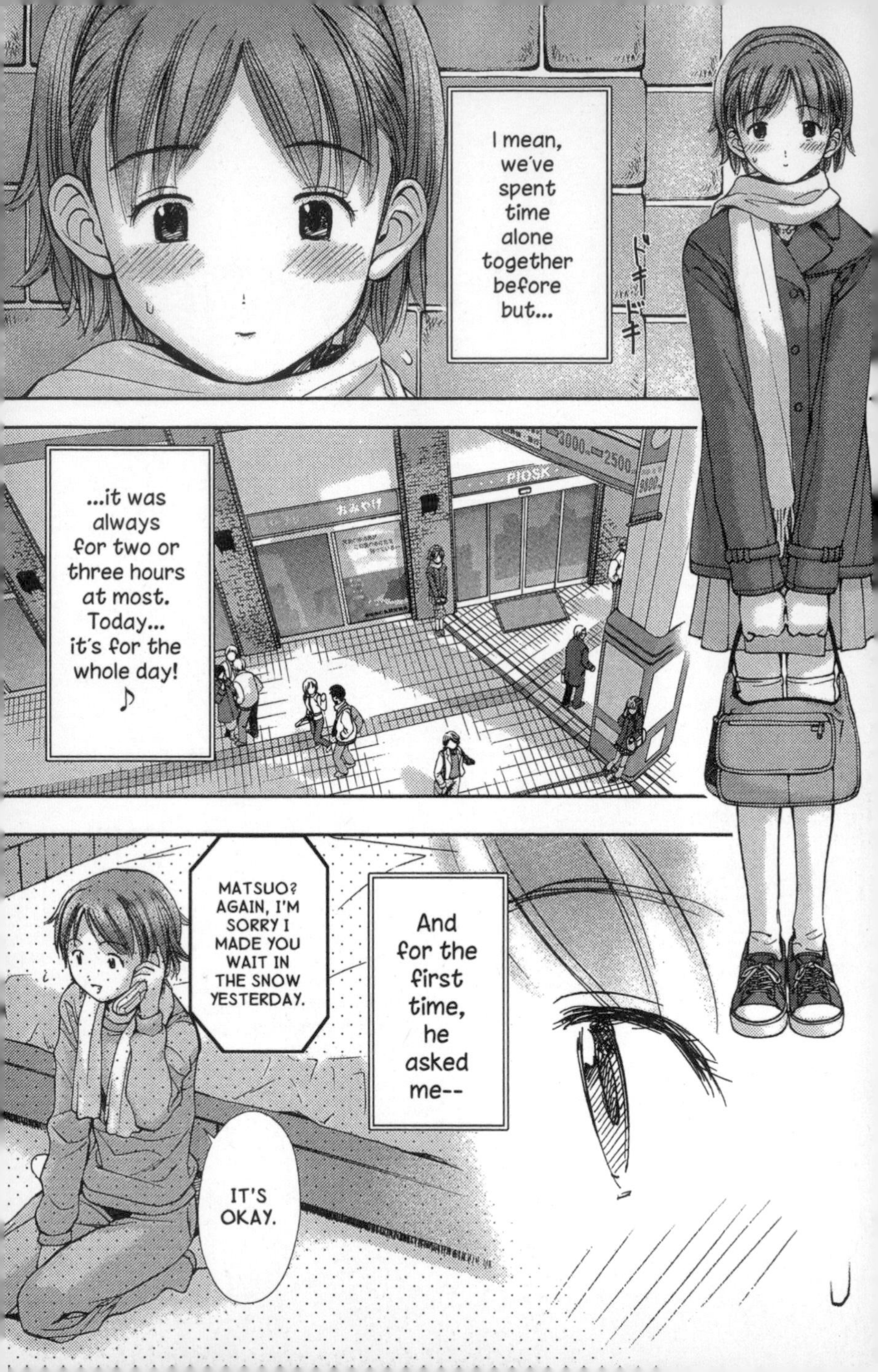
ドキドキ
I mean, we've spent time alone together before but...
...it was always for two or three hours at most. Today... it's for the whole day! ♪
And for the first time, he asked me--
MATSUO? AGAIN, I'M SORRY I MADE YOU WAIT IN THE SNOW YESTERDAY.
IT'S OKAY.

AND, WELL.

...I'D LIKE TO MAKE IT UP TO YOU...

mon	tue	wed	thu	fri	sat
		1	2	3	4
6	7	8	9	10	
13	14	15	16	17	
20	21	22	23	24	
(27) Vacation!	28	29 →	30	31	

12月

Work the A.M. shift.

I ACTUALLY HAVE THREE DAYS OFF, STARTING ON THE 28TH.

SO IF YOU'RE FREE, WOULD YOU LIKE TO GO OUT SOMEWHERE?

YES! ABSOLUTELY!!! YES, YES, YES!!!

UH...

WHA...?!

And so today is the day...

MATSUO? HELLO? HELLO?!

ぷる ぷる ぷる

|?

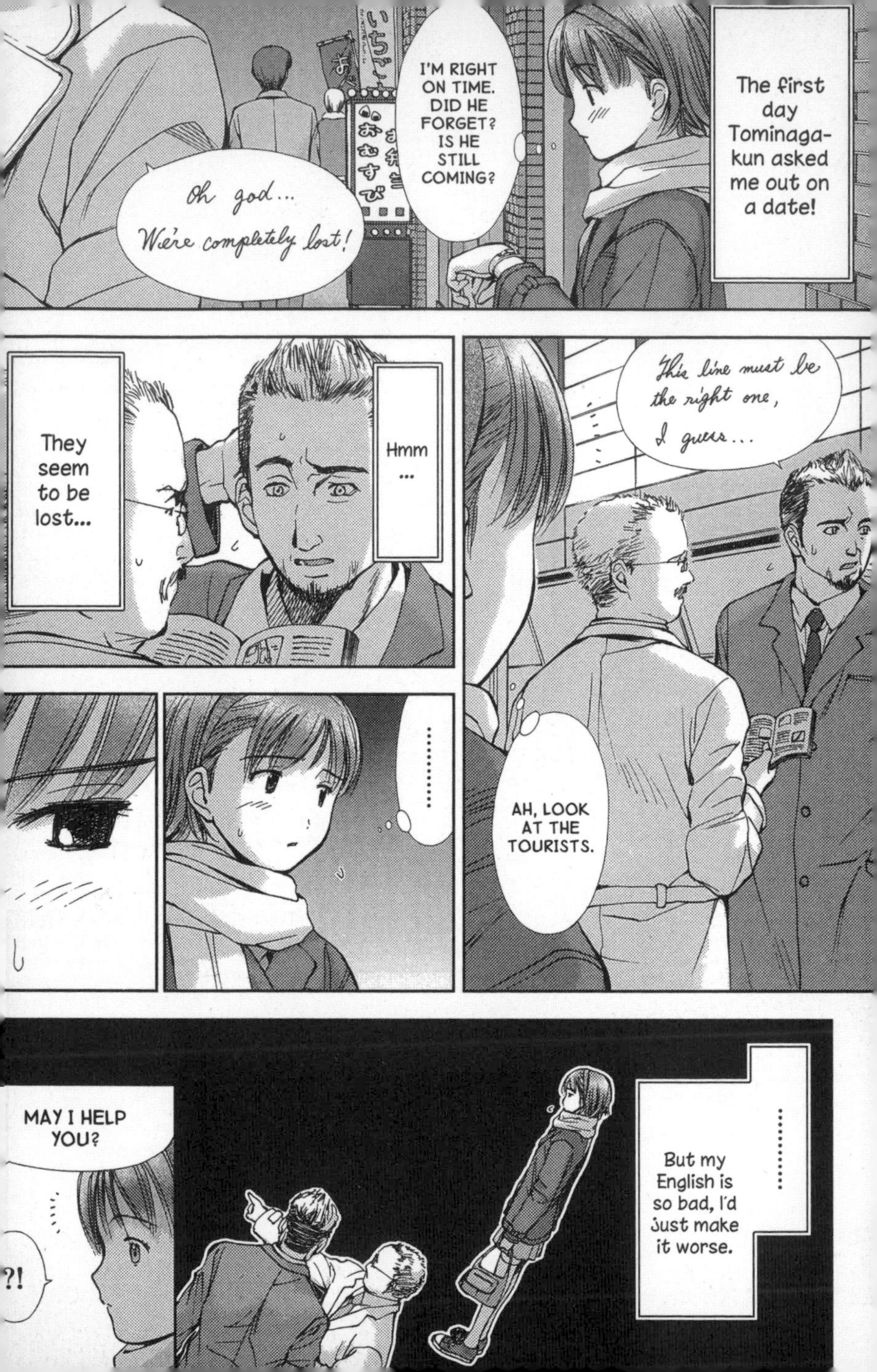
The first day Tominaga-kun asked me out on a date!
I'M RIGHT ON TIME. DID HE FORGET? IS HE STILL COMING?
Oh god... We're completely lost!
This line must be the right one, I guess...
AH, LOOK AT THE TOURISTS.
Hmm ...
They seem to be lost...
....
......
But my English is so bad, I'd just make it worse.
MAY I HELP YOU?
...
?!

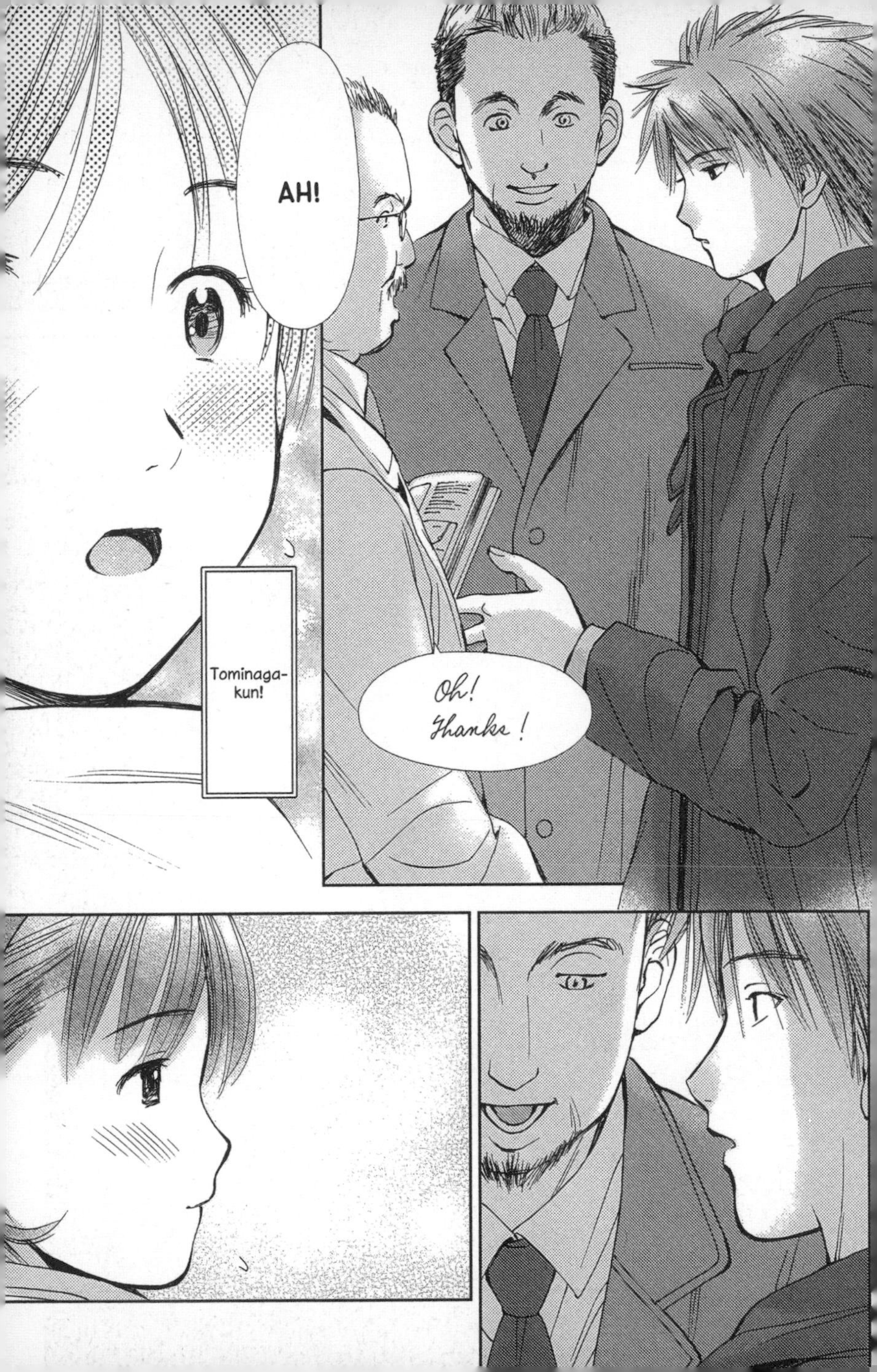
Oh! Thanks!
AH!
Tominaga-kun!

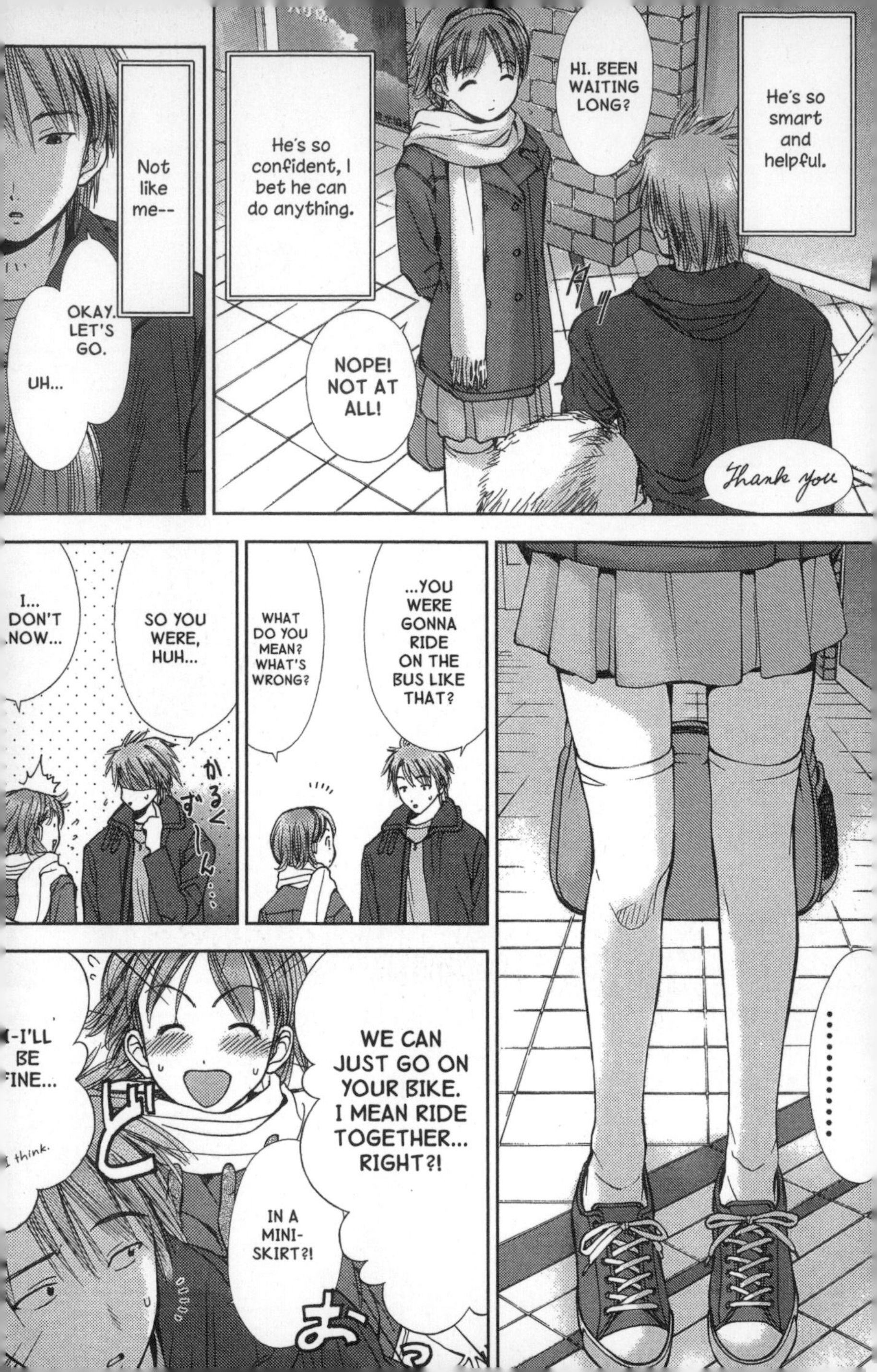
He's so smart and helpful.
HI. BEEN WAITING LONG?
He's so confident, I bet he can do anything.
NOPE! NOT AT ALL!
Thank you
Not like me--
OKAY. LET'S GO.
UH...
......
...YOU WERE GONNA RIDE ON THE BUS LIKE THAT?
WHAT DO YOU MEAN? WHAT'S WRONG?
SO YOU WERE, HUH...
かるく ずーん...
I... DON'T NOW...
WE CAN JUST GO ON YOUR BIKE. I MEAN RIDE TOGETHER... RIGHT?!
-I'LL BE FINE...
think.
IN A MINI-SKIRT?!

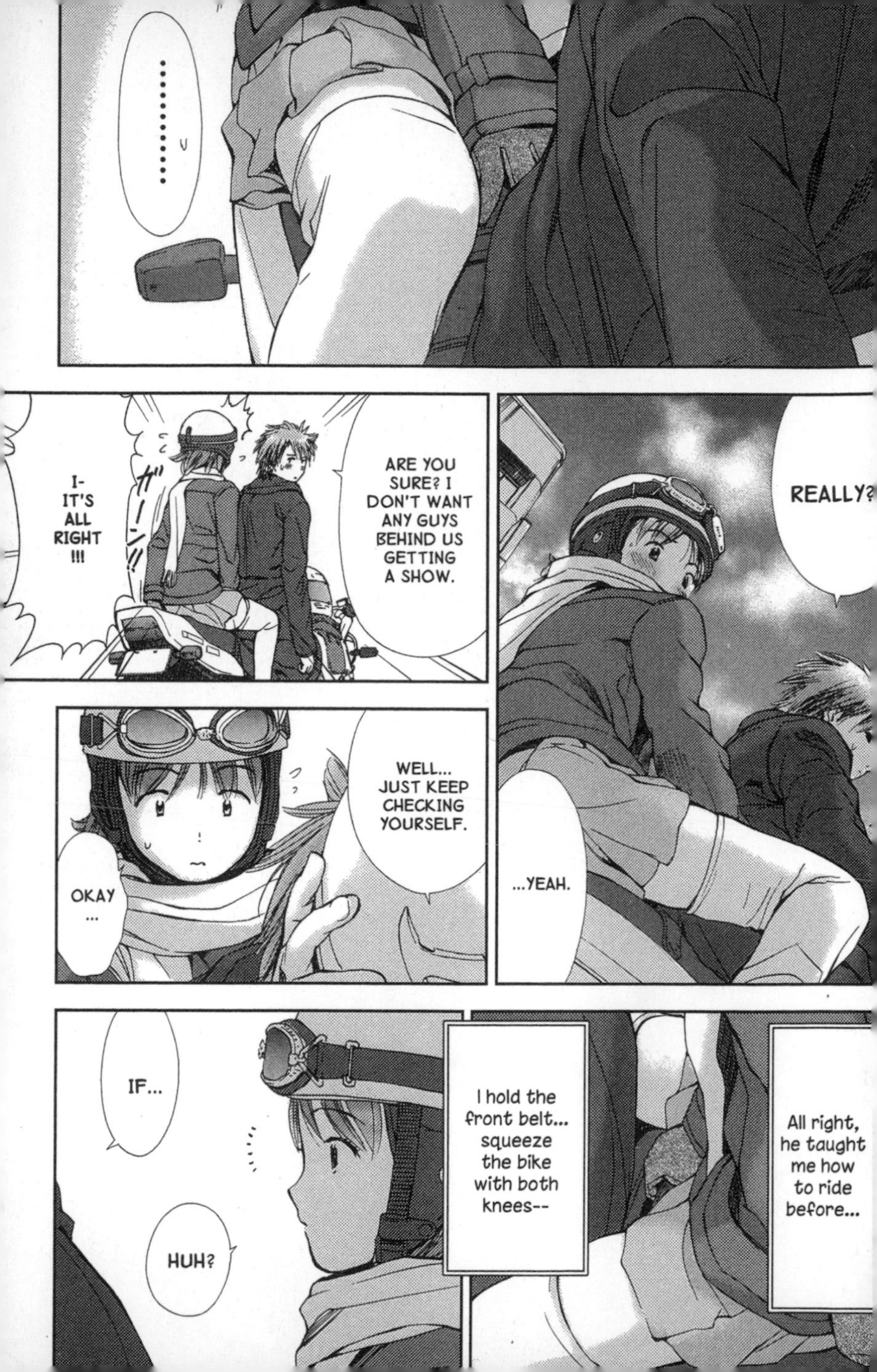
......
REALLY?
...YEAH.
ARE YOU SURE? I DON'T WANT ANY GUYS BEHIND US GETTING A SHOW.
I- IT'S ALL RIGHT !!!
WELL... JUST KEEP CHECKING YOURSELF.
OKAY ...
All right, he taught me how to ride before...
I hold the front belt... squeeze the bike with both knees--
IF...
HUH?

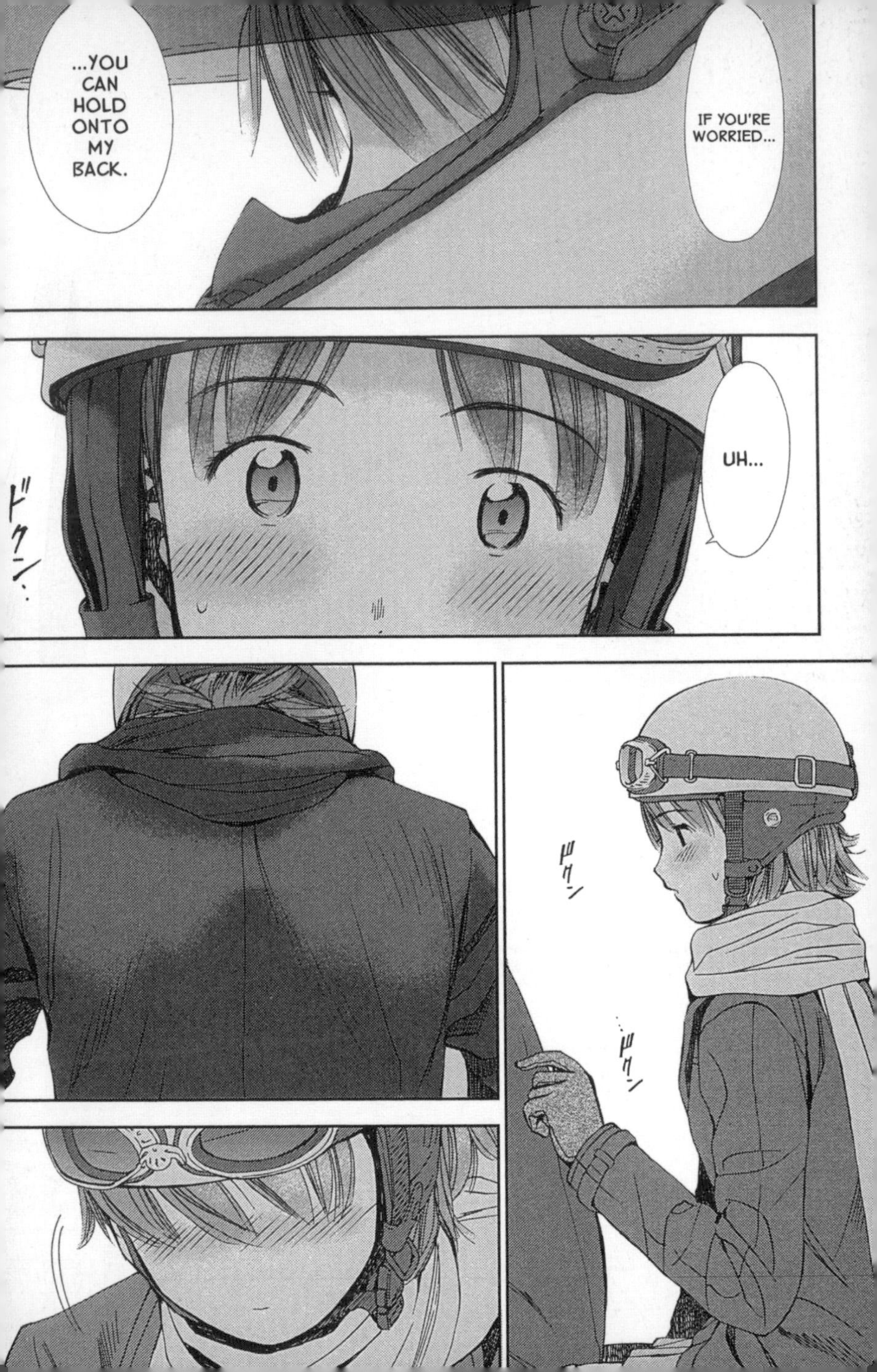
IF YOU'RE WORRIED...
...YOU CAN HOLD ONTO MY BACK.
UH...
ドクン
ドクン
...ドクン

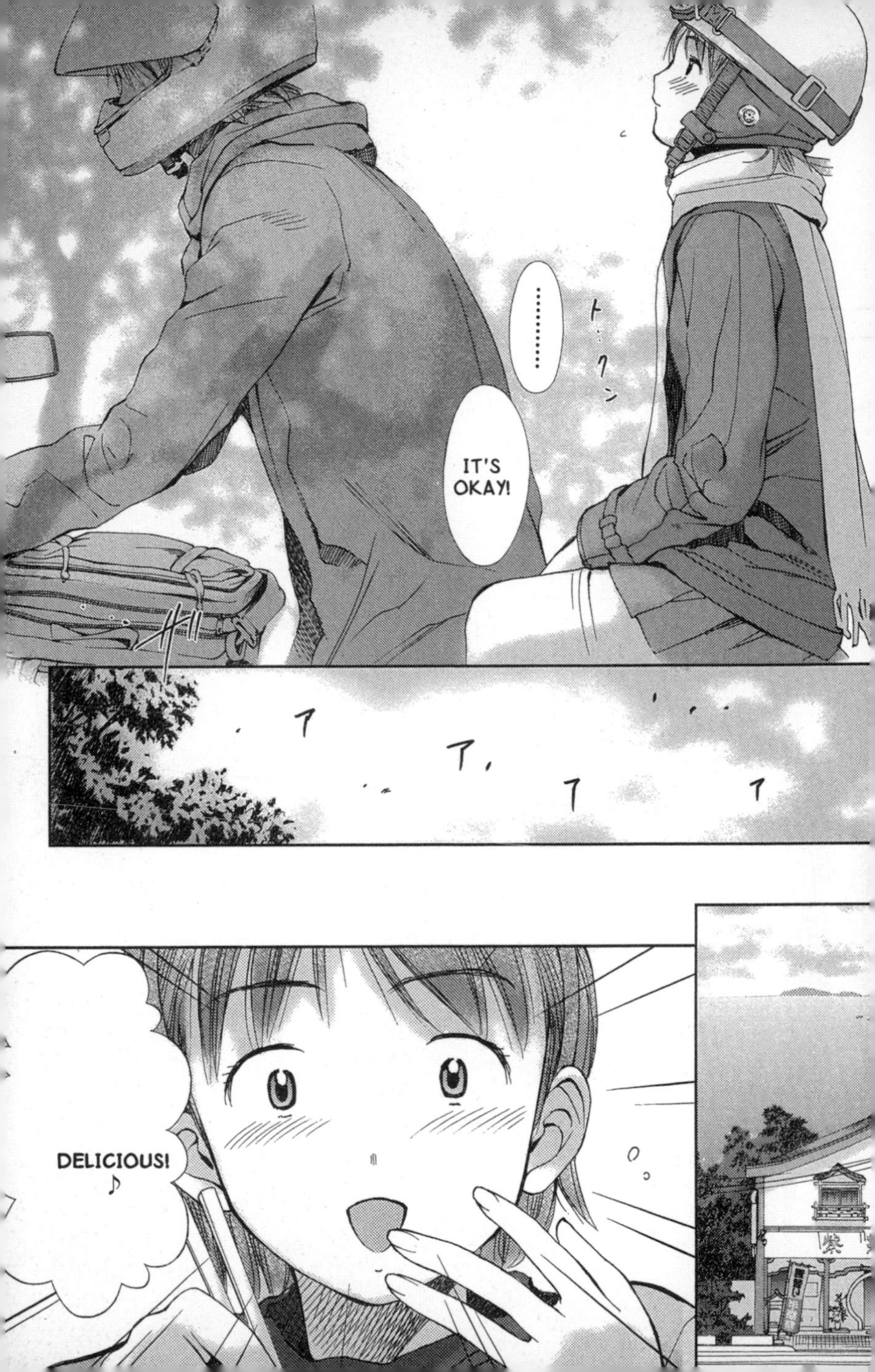
トクン
......
IT'S OKAY!
ア ア ア ア
DELICIOUS! ♪

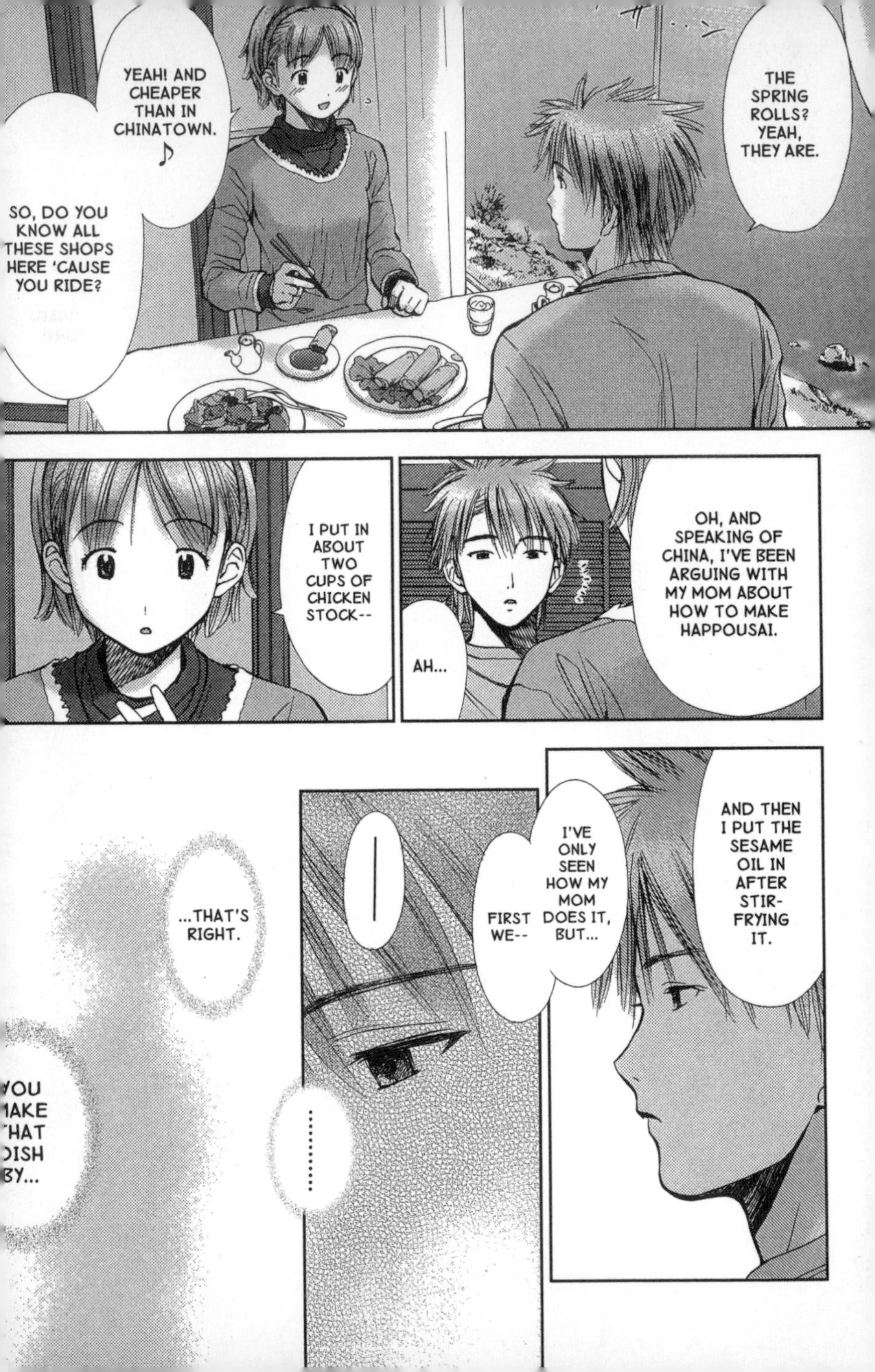
THE SPRING ROLLS? YEAH, THEY ARE.
YEAH! AND CHEAPER THAN IN CHINATOWN. ♪
SO, DO YOU KNOW ALL THESE SHOPS HERE 'CAUSE YOU RIDE?
OH, AND SPEAKING OF CHINA, I'VE BEEN ARGUING WITH MY MOM ABOUT HOW TO MAKE HAPPOUSAI.
AH...
I PUT IN ABOUT TWO CUPS OF CHICKEN STOCK--
AND THEN I PUT THE SESAME OIL IN AFTER STIR-FRYING IT.
I'VE ONLY SEEN HOW MY MOM DOES IT, BUT...
FIRST WE--
......
...THAT'S RIGHT.
YOU MAKE THAT DISH BY...

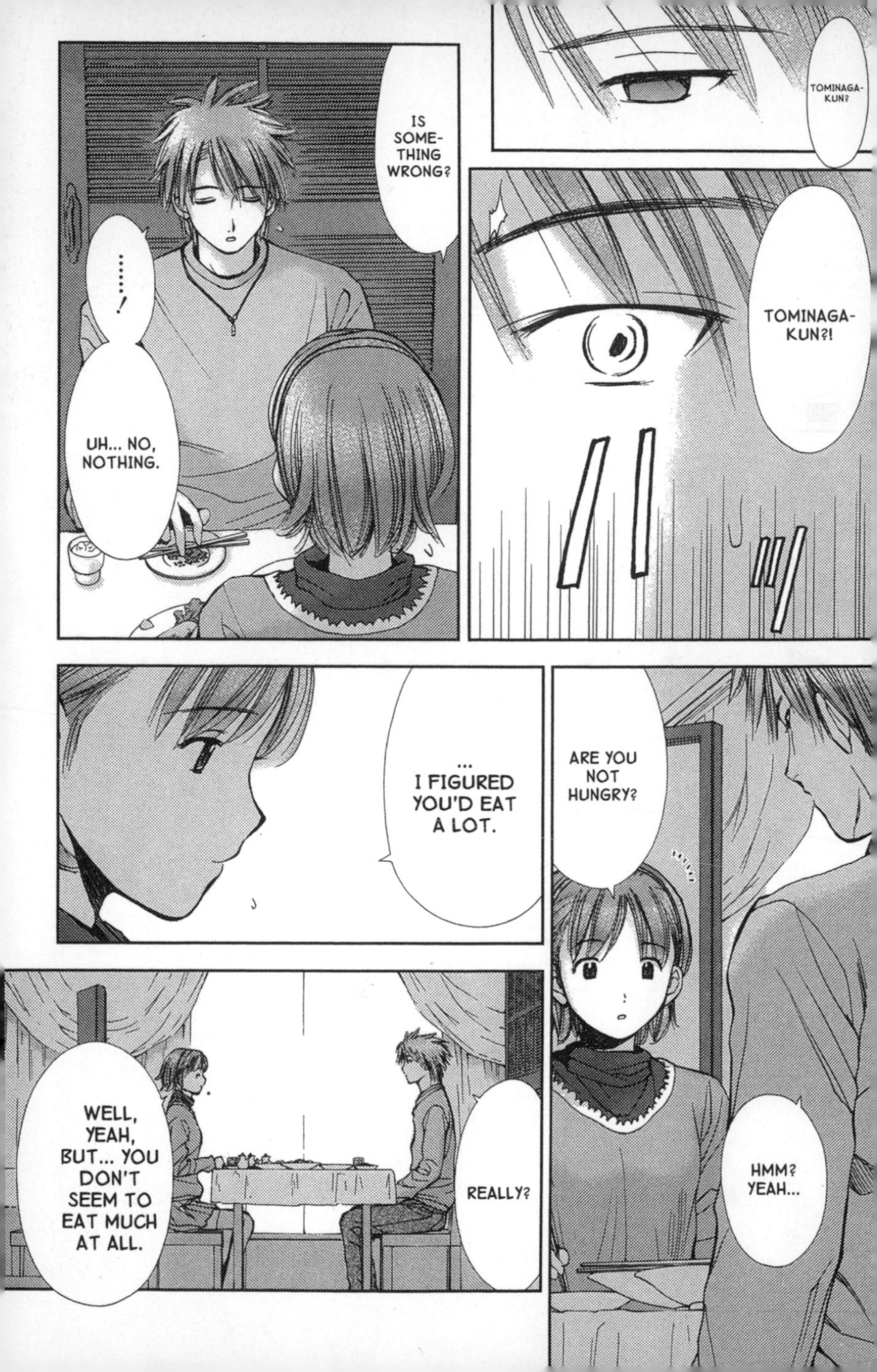
TOMINAGA-KUN?
TOMINAGA-KUN?!
IS SOMETHING WRONG?
......!
UH... NO, NOTHING.
ARE YOU NOT HUNGRY?
HMM? YEAH...
... I FIGURED YOU'D EAT A LOT.
REALLY?
WELL, YEAH, BUT... YOU DON'T SEEM TO EAT MUCH AT ALL.

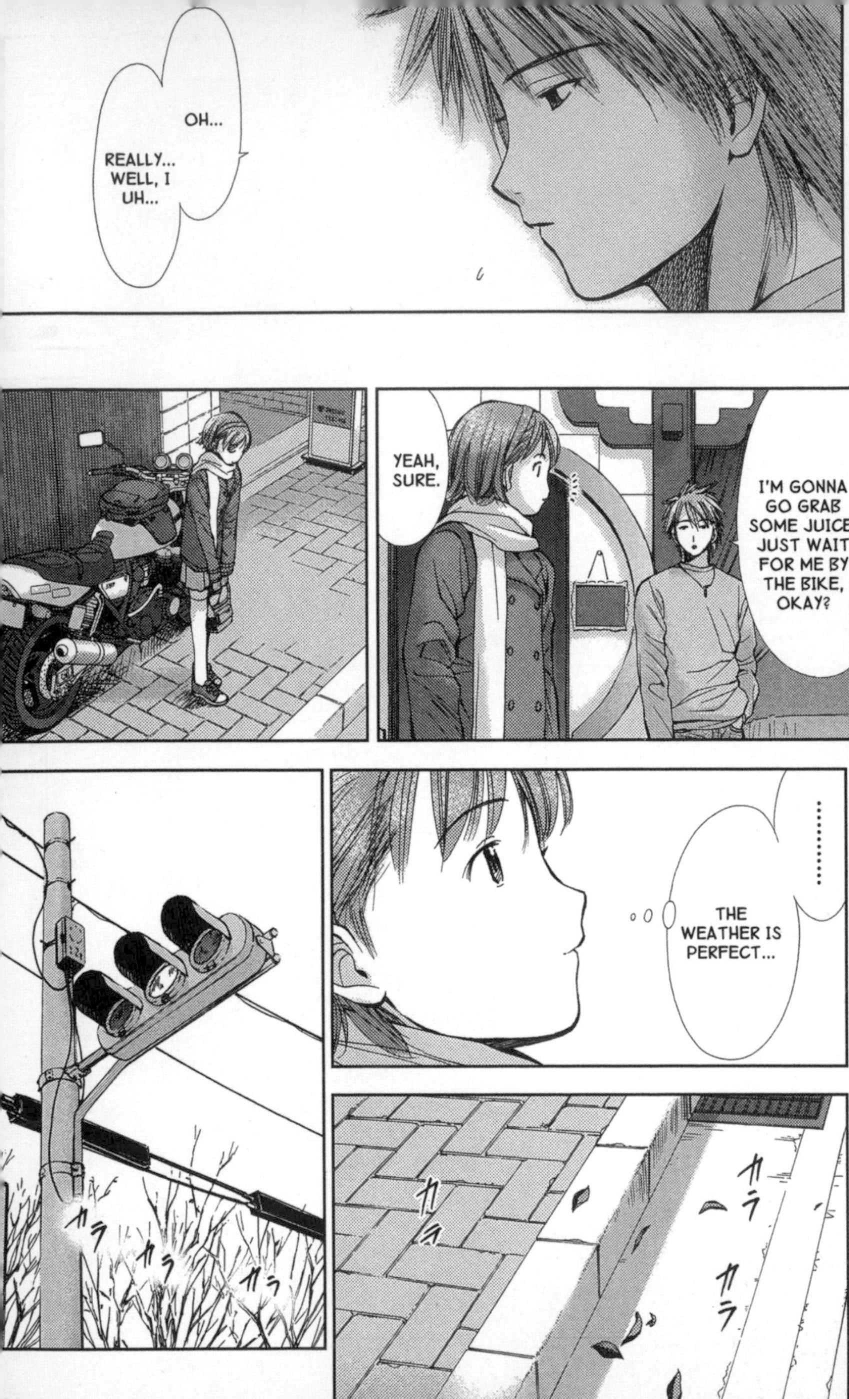
OH...
REALLY... WELL, I UH...
I'M GONNA GO GRAB SOME JUICE. JUST WAIT FOR ME BY THE BIKE, OKAY?
YEAH, SURE.
....
THE WEATHER IS PERFECT...
カラ
カラ
カラ
カラ
カラ
カラ
カラ

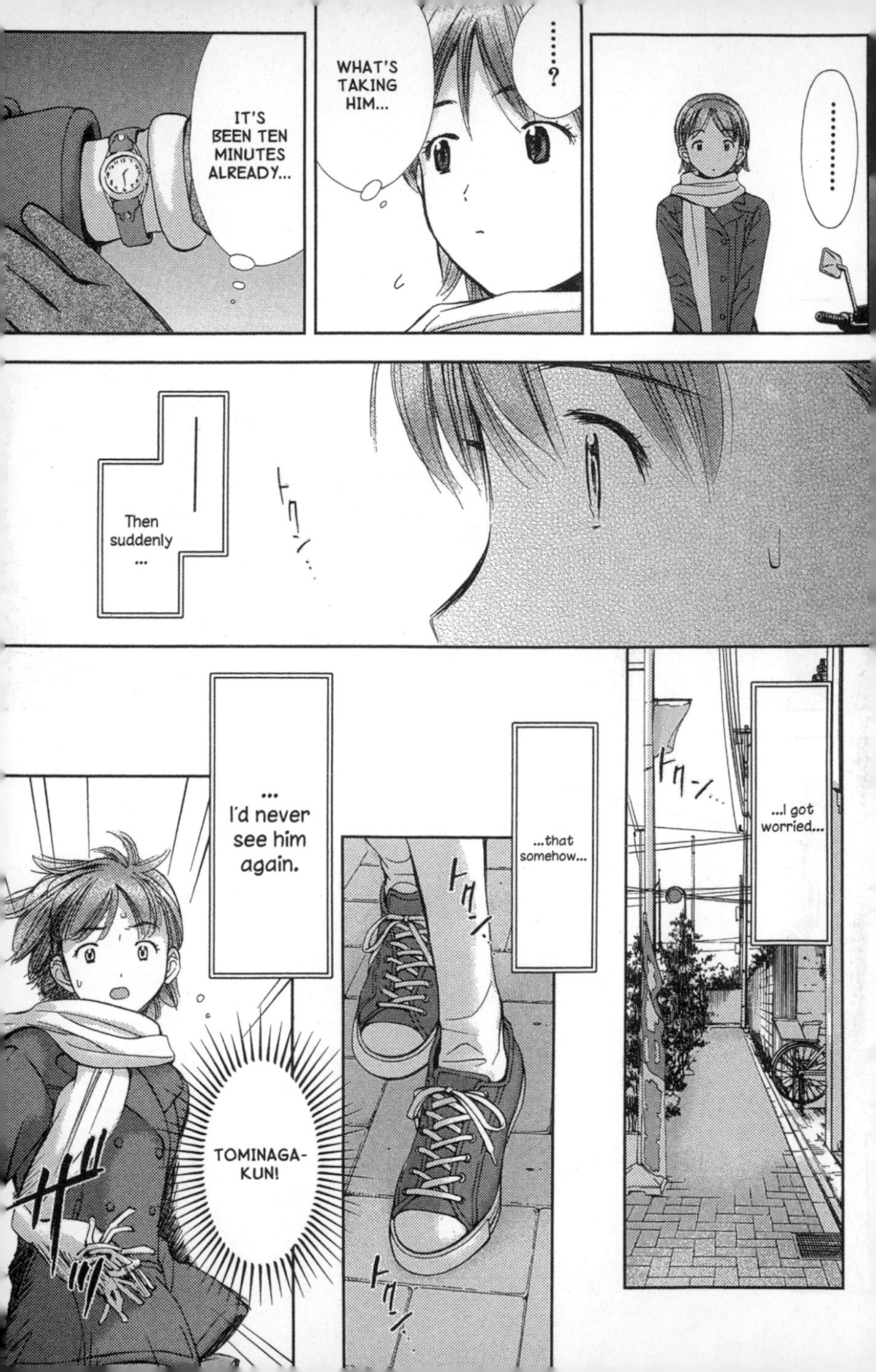
……
……?
WHAT'S TAKING HIM...
IT'S BEEN TEN MINUTES ALREADY...
Then suddenly ...
...I got worried...
...that somehow...
... I'd never see him again.
TOMINAGA-KUN!

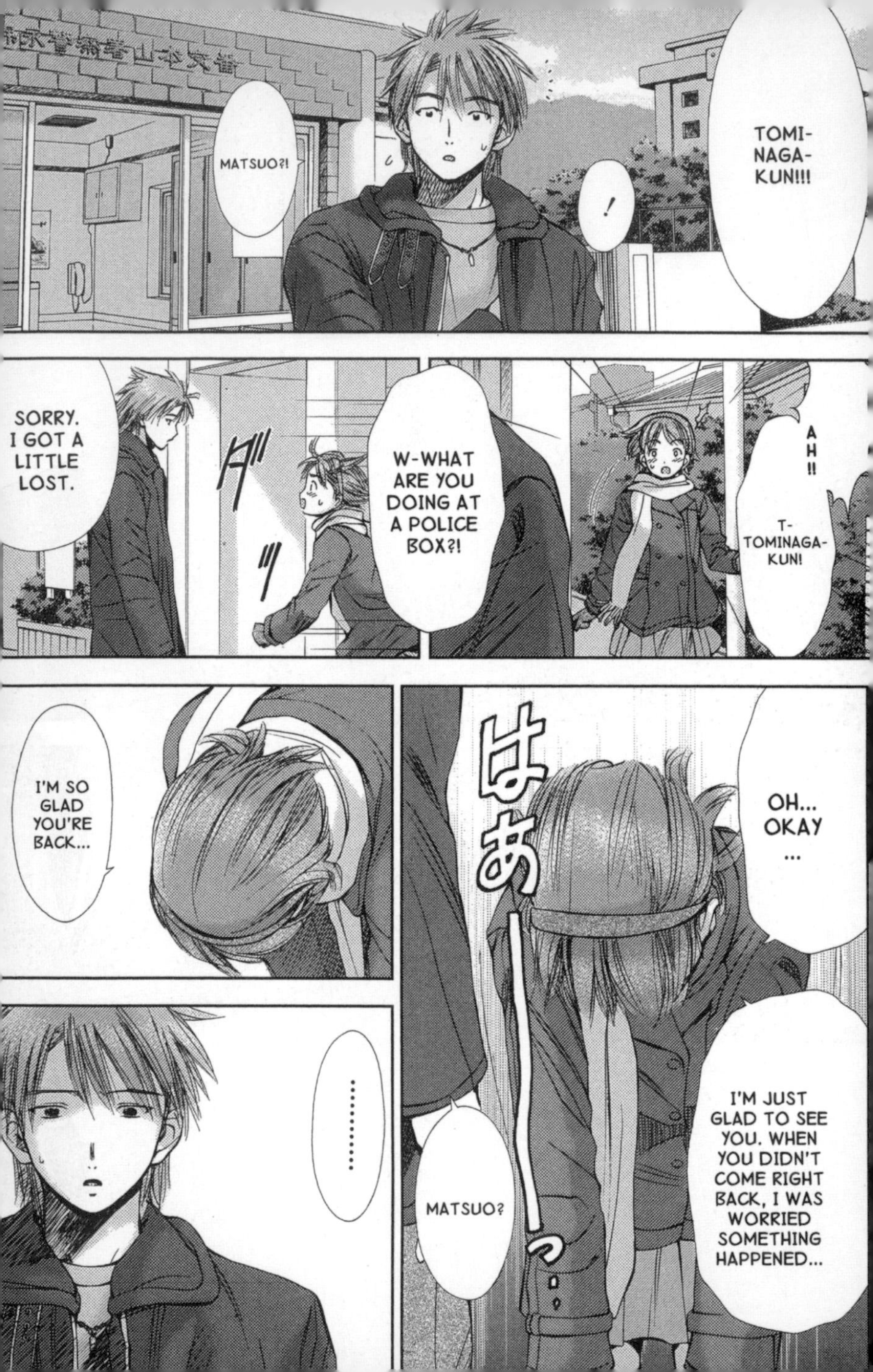
TOMI-NAGA-KUN!!!
!
MATSUO?!
AH!!
T-TOMINAGA-KUN!
ダッ
W-WHAT ARE YOU DOING AT A POLICE BOX?!
SORRY. I GOT A LITTLE LOST.
OH... OKAY ...
はあーっ
I'M SO GLAD YOU'RE BACK...
......
MATSUO?
I'M JUST GLAD TO SEE YOU. WHEN YOU DIDN'T COME RIGHT BACK, I WAS WORRIED SOMETHING HAPPENED...

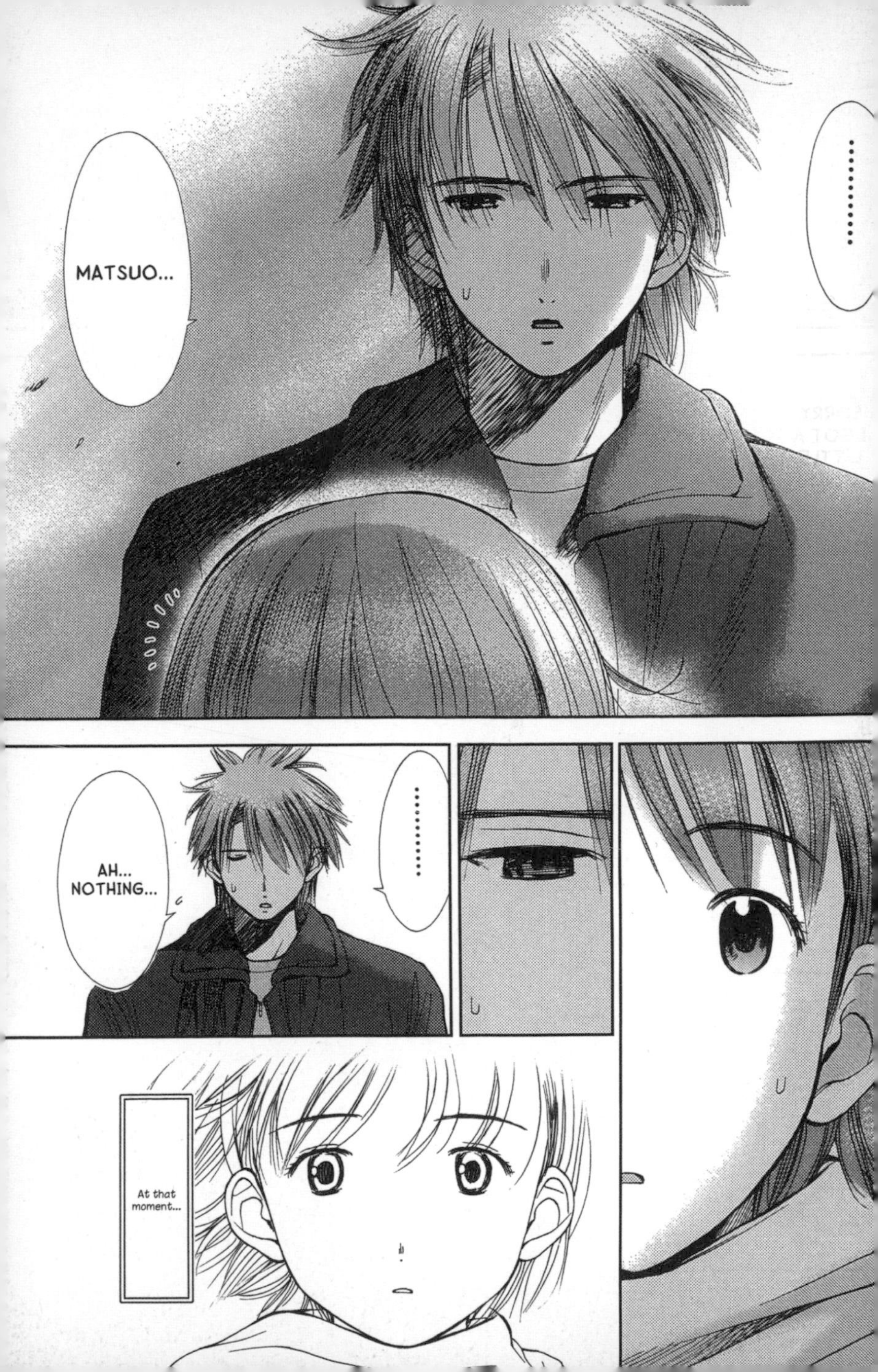

......
MATSUO...
....
AH... NOTHING...
At that moment...

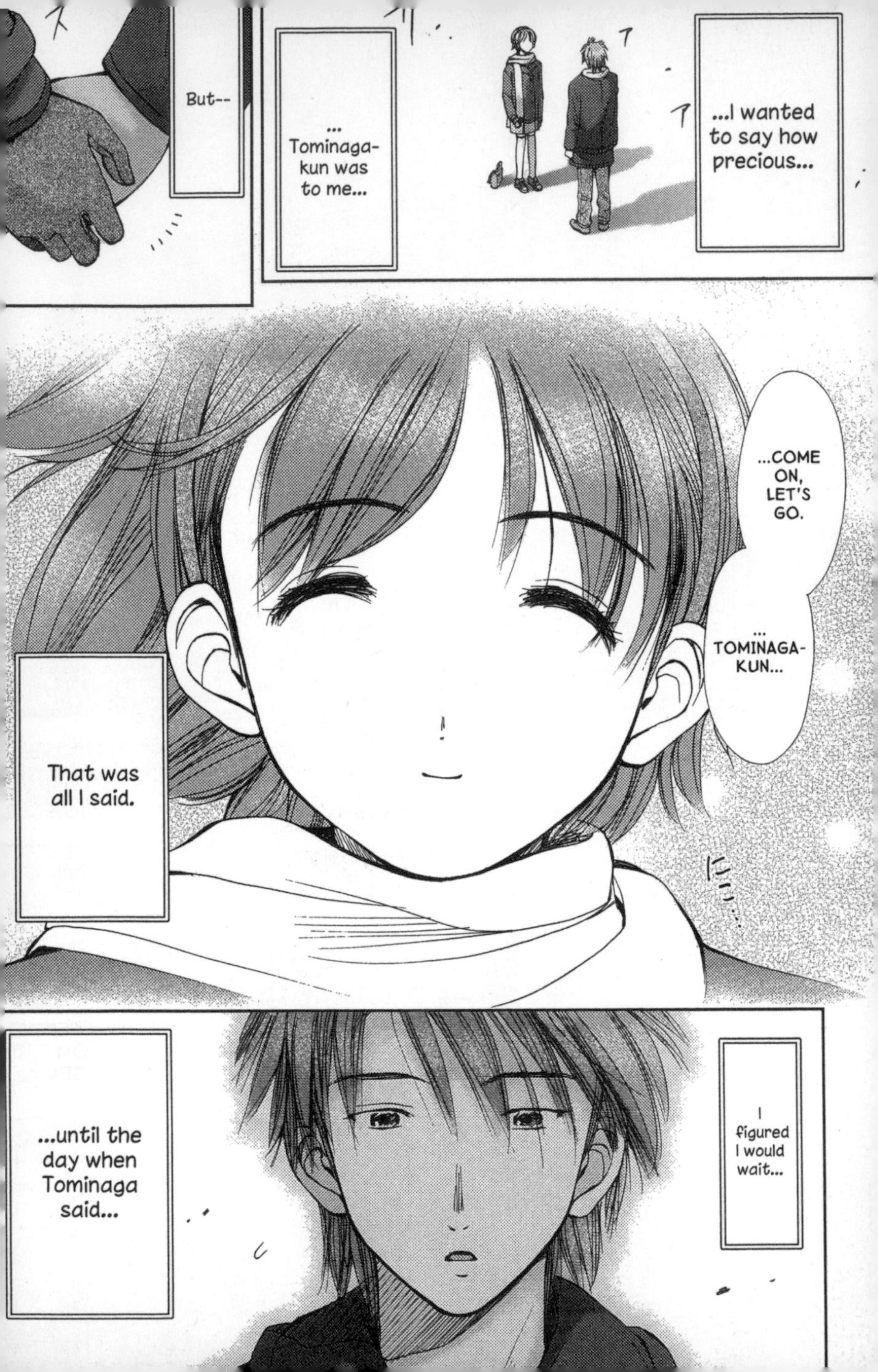
...I wanted to say how precious...
...Tominaga-kun was to me...
But--
...COME ON, LET'S GO.
...TOMINAGA-KUN...
That was all I said.
I figured I would wait...
...until the day when Tominaga said...

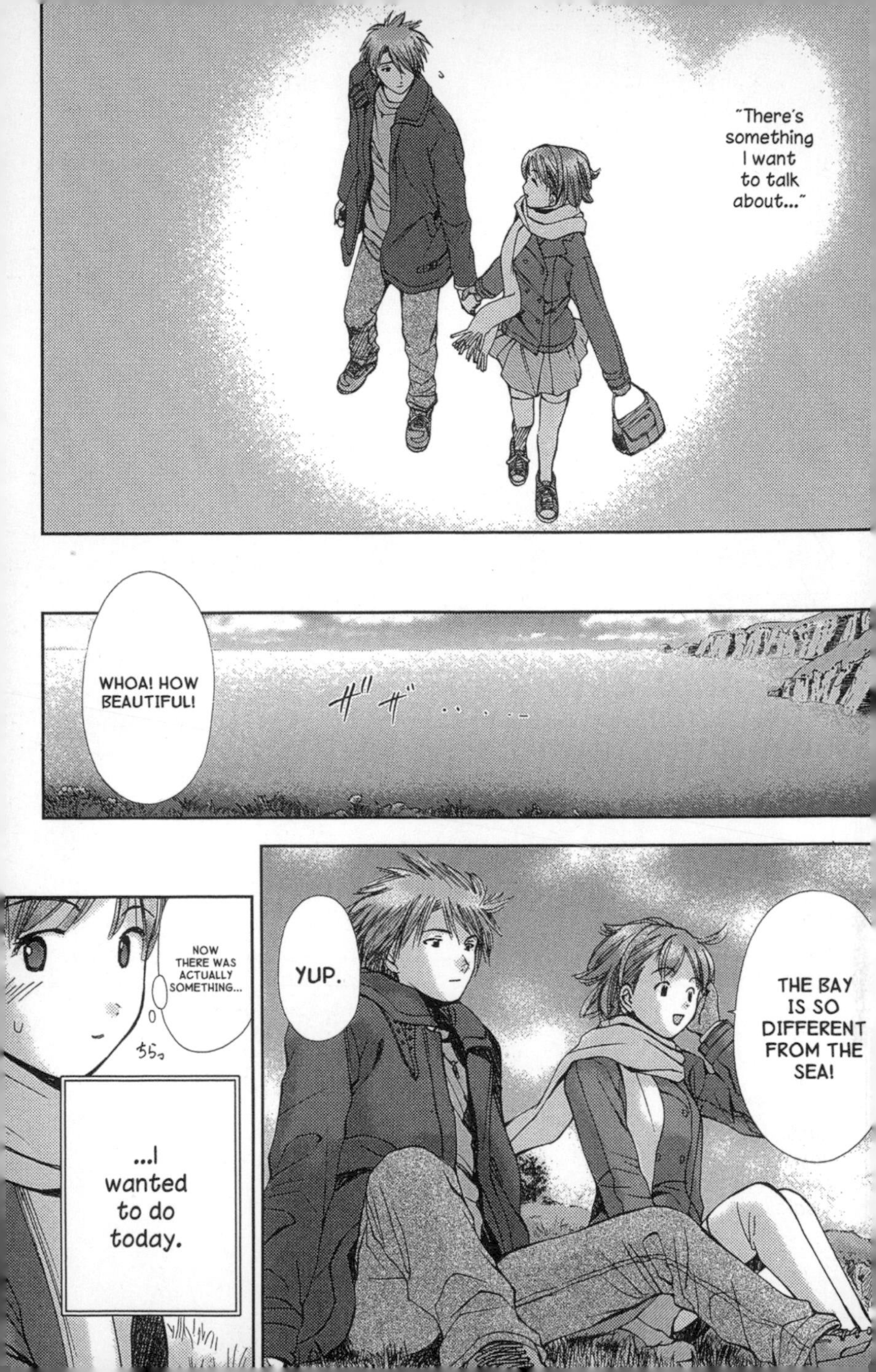
"There's something I want to talk about..."
WHOA! HOW BEAUTIFUL!
ザザ
THE BAY IS SO DIFFERENT FROM THE SEA!
YUP.
NOW THERE WAS ACTUALLY SOMETHING...
ちらっ
...I wanted to do today.

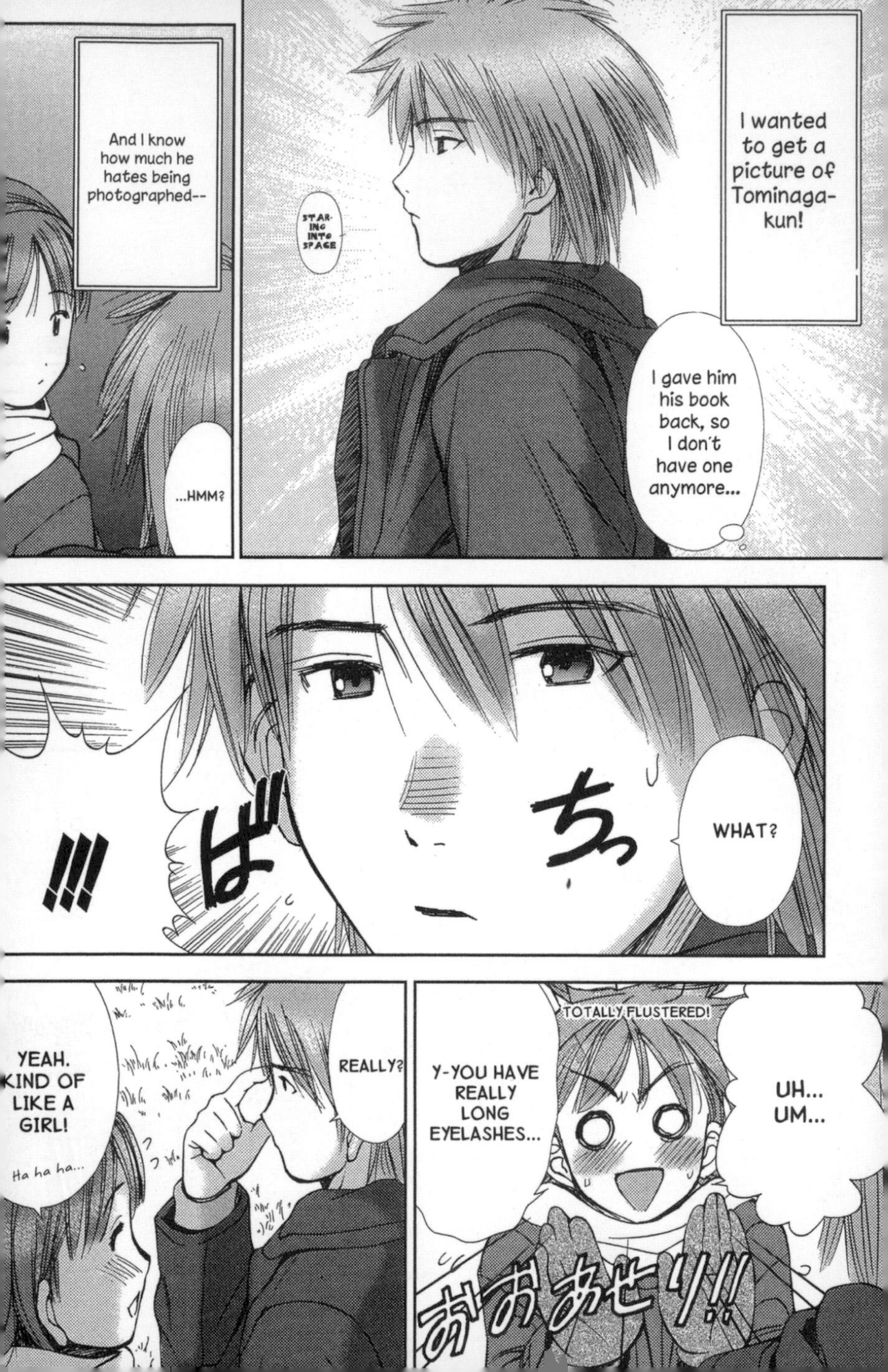
I wanted to get a picture of Tominaga-kun!
STAR-ING INTO SPACE
I gave him his book back, so I don't have one anymore...
And I know how much he hates being photographed--
...HMM?
WHAT?
ばちっ
!!!
UH... UM...
TOTALLY FLUSTERED!
Y-YOU HAVE REALLY LONG EYELASHES...
おおあせり!!
REALLY?
YEAH. KIND OF LIKE A GIRL!
Ha ha ha...

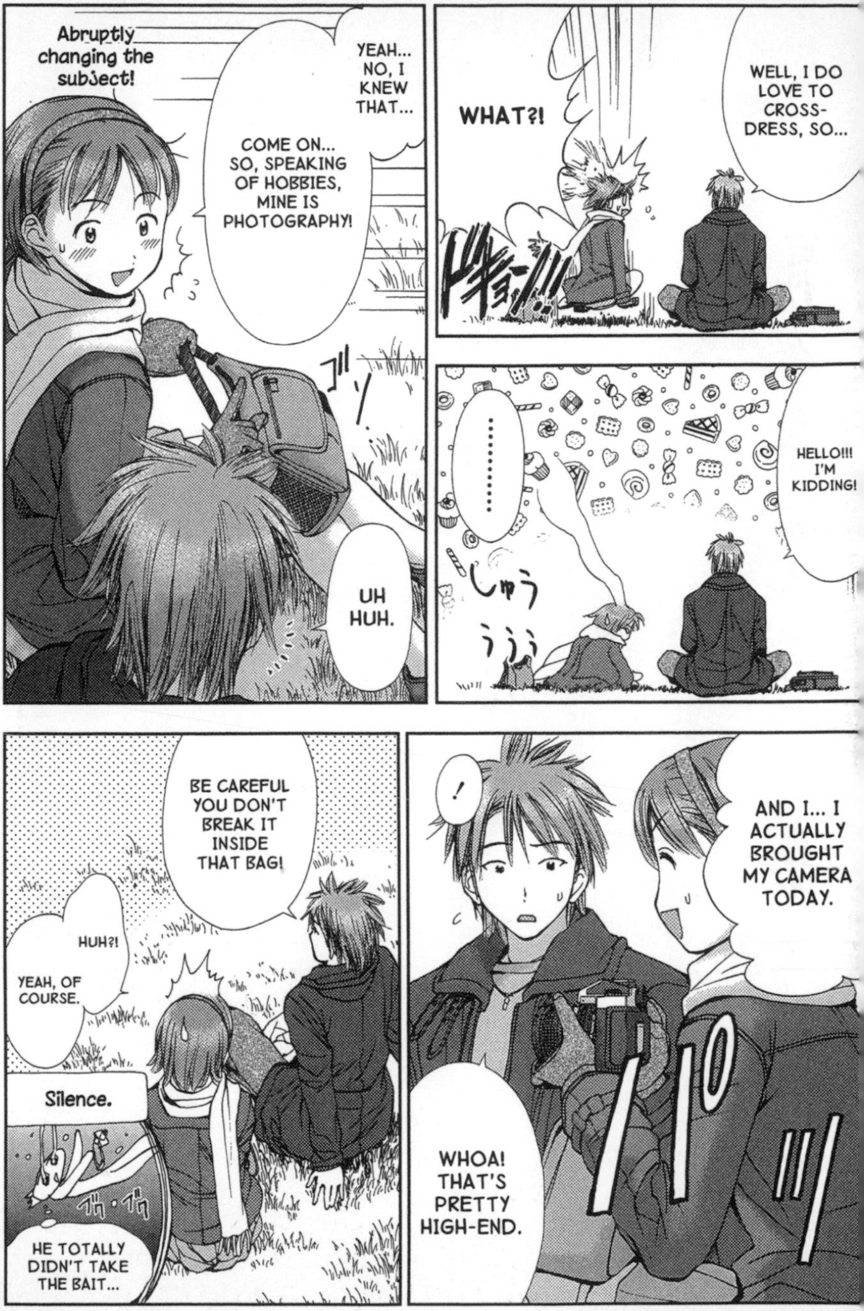
WELL, I DO LOVE TO CROSS-DRESS, SO...
WHAT?!
HELLO!!! I'M KIDDING!
....
しゅう
ううう
Abruptly changing the subject!
YEAH... NO, I KNEW THAT...
COME ON... SO, SPEAKING OF HOBBIES, MINE IS PHOTOGRAPHY!
UH HUH.
AND I... I ACTUALLY BROUGHT MY CAMERA TODAY.
!
WHOA! THAT'S PRETTY HIGH-END.
BE CAREFUL YOU DON'T BREAK IT INSIDE THAT BAG!
HUH?!
YEAH, OF COURSE.
Silence.
HE TOTALLY DIDN'T TAKE THE BAIT...

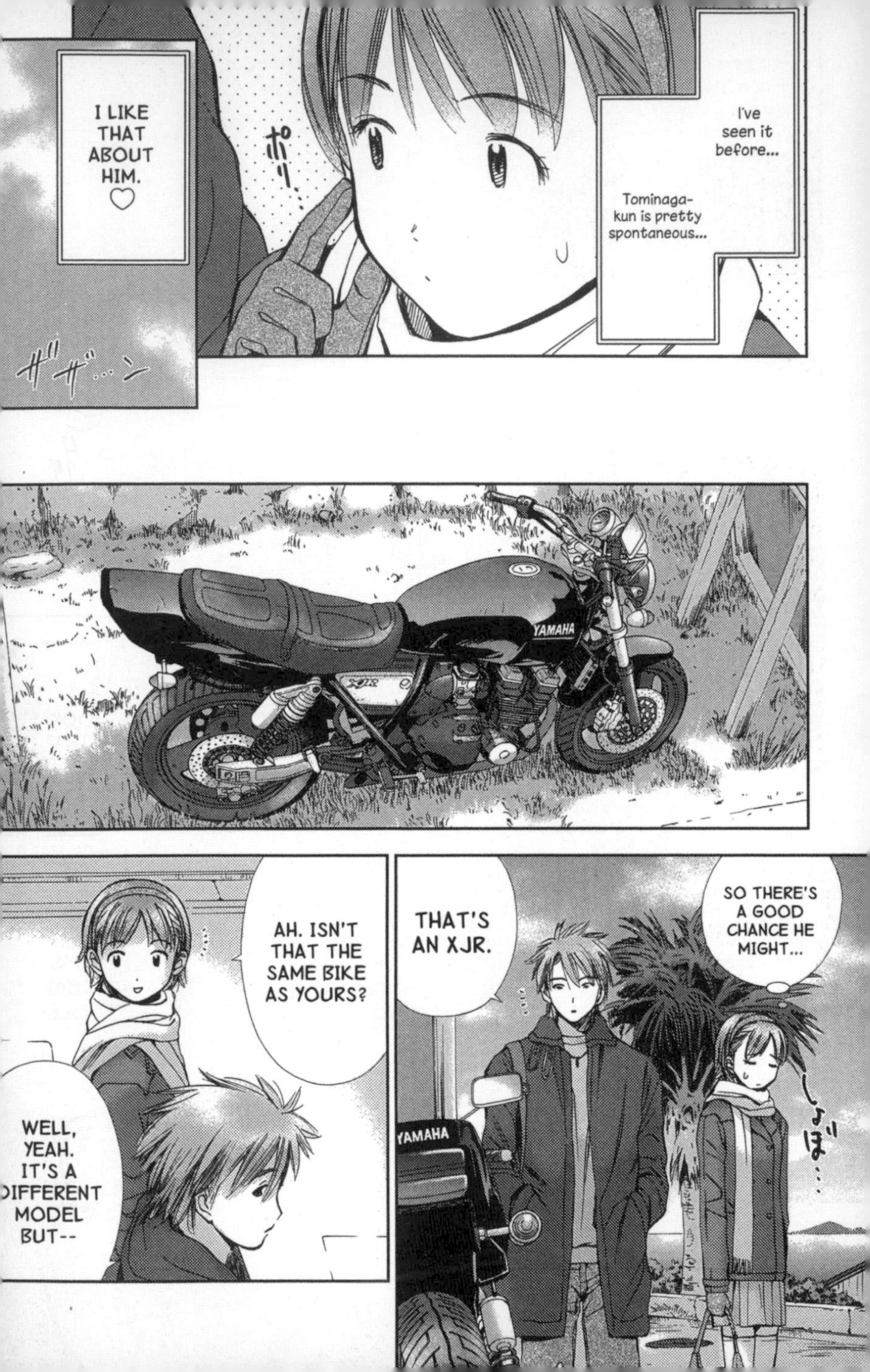
I've seen it before...
Tominaga-kun is pretty spontaneous...
ポリ...
I LIKE THAT ABOUT HIM. ♡
ザザ…ン
YAMAHA
XJR
SO THERE'S A GOOD CHANCE HE MIGHT...
しょぼ…
THAT'S AN XJR.
YAMAHA
AH. ISN'T THAT THE SAME BIKE AS YOURS?
WELL, YEAH. IT'S A DIFFERENT MODEL BUT--

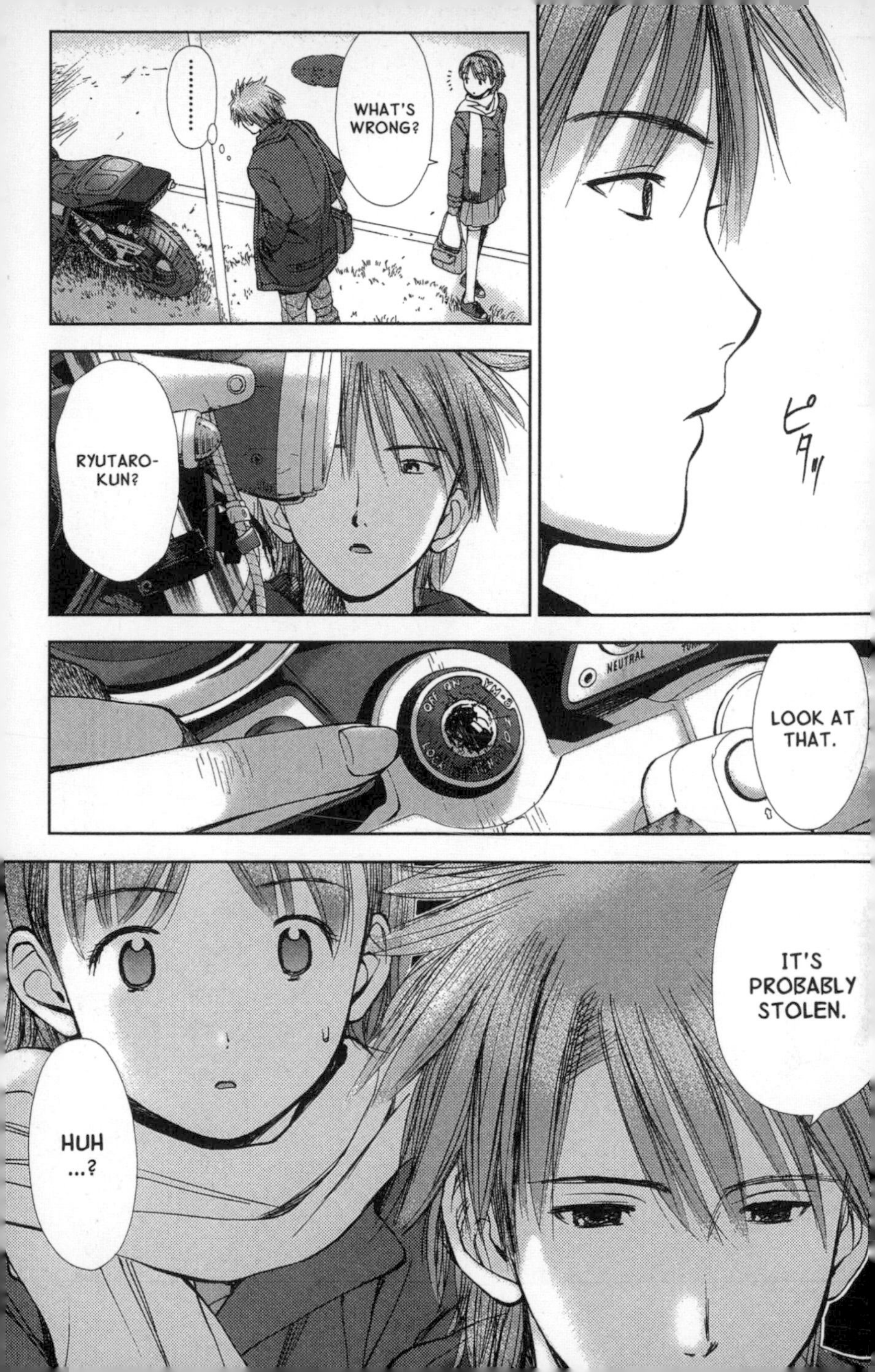
ピタッ
WHAT'S WRONG?
......
RYUTARO-KUN?
LOOK AT THAT.
IT'S PROBABLY STOLEN.
HUH ...?

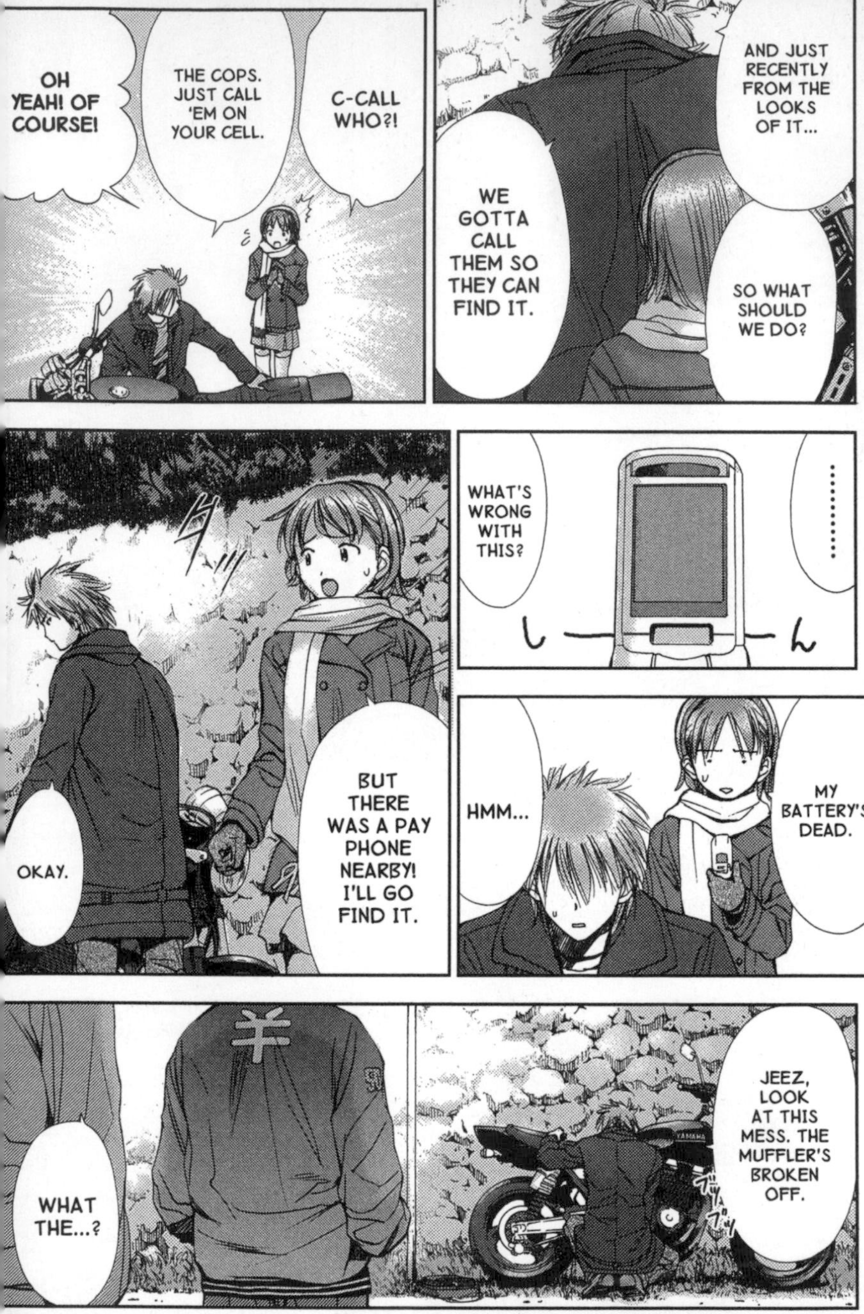
AND JUST RECENTLY FROM THE LOOKS OF IT...
SO WHAT SHOULD WE DO?
WE GOTTA CALL THEM SO THEY CAN FIND IT.
C-CALL WHO?!
THE COPS. JUST CALL 'EM ON YOUR CELL.
OH YEAH! OF COURSE!
....
WHAT'S WRONG WITH THIS?
し——ん
MY BATTERY'S DEAD.
HMM...
ザッ
BUT THERE WAS A PAY PHONE NEARBY! I'LL GO FIND IT.
OKAY.
JEEZ, LOOK AT THIS MESS. THE MUFFLER'S BROKEN OFF.
ブッ ブッ
WHAT THE...?

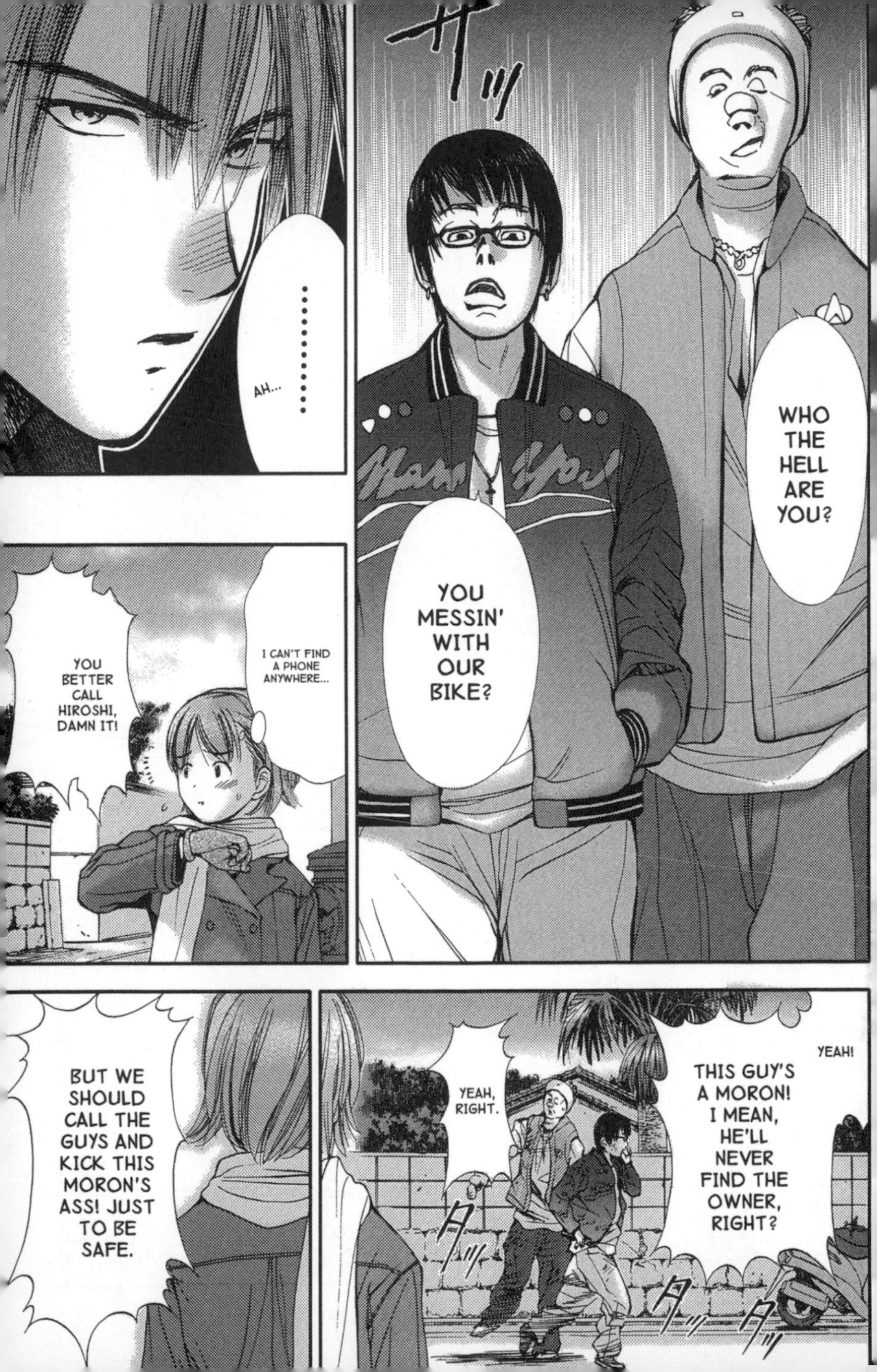
ザッ
WHO THE HELL ARE YOU?
YOU MESSIN' WITH OUR BIKE?
......
AH...
I CAN'T FIND A PHONE ANYWHERE...
YOU BETTER CALL HIROSHI, DAMN IT!
YEAH!
THIS GUY'S A MORON! I MEAN, HE'LL NEVER FIND THE OWNER, RIGHT?
YEAH, RIGHT.
BUT WE SHOULD CALL THE GUYS AND KICK THIS MORON'S ASS! JUST TO BE SAFE.

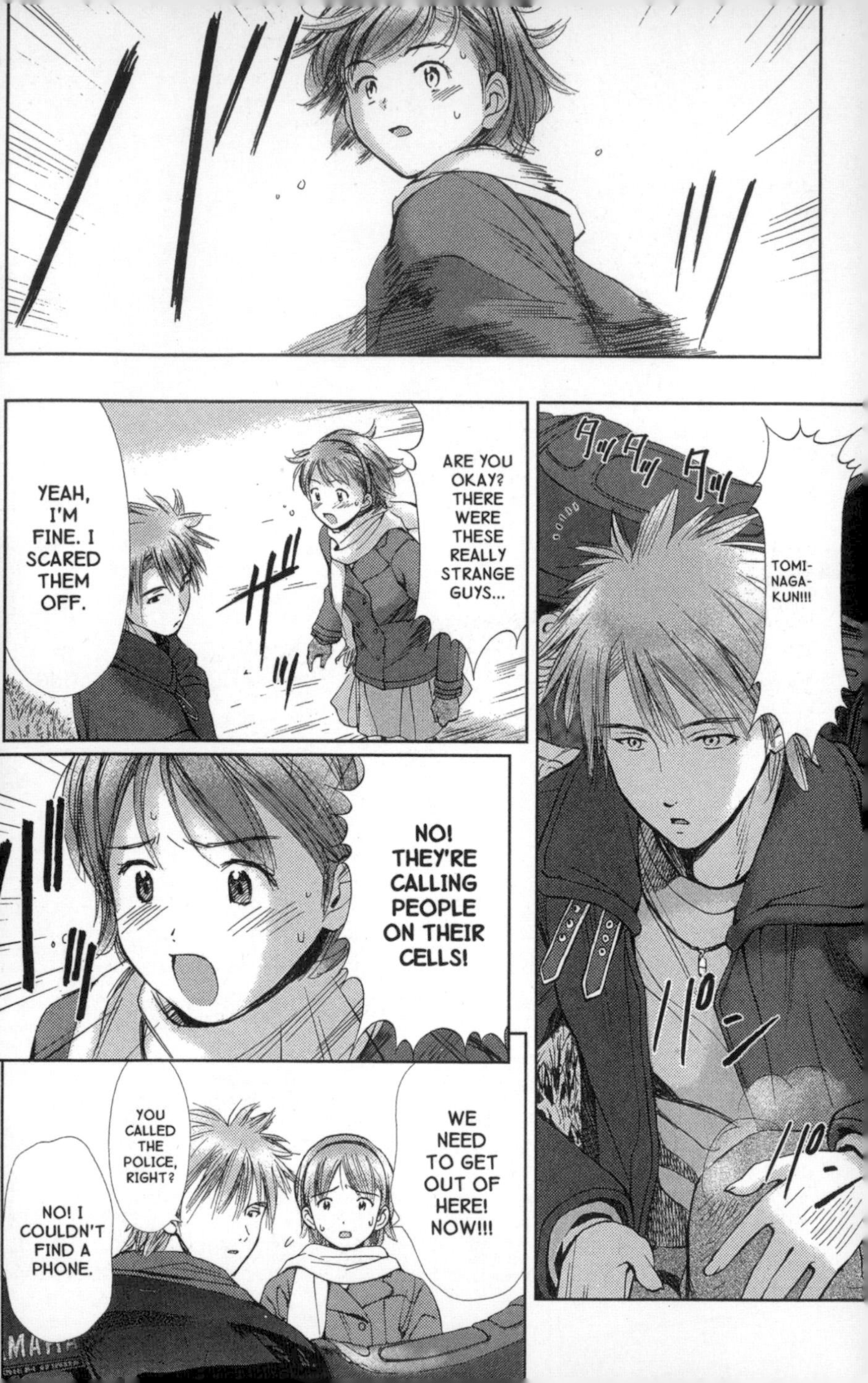
タッタッ タッ
TOMI-NAGA-KUN!!!
ARE YOU OKAY? THERE WERE THESE REALLY STRANGE GUYS...
YEAH, I'M FINE. I SCARED THEM OFF.
NO! THEY'RE CALLING PEOPLE ON THEIR CELLS!
WE NEED TO GET OUT OF HERE! NOW!!!
YOU CALLED THE POLICE, RIGHT?
NO! I COULDN'T FIND A PHONE.

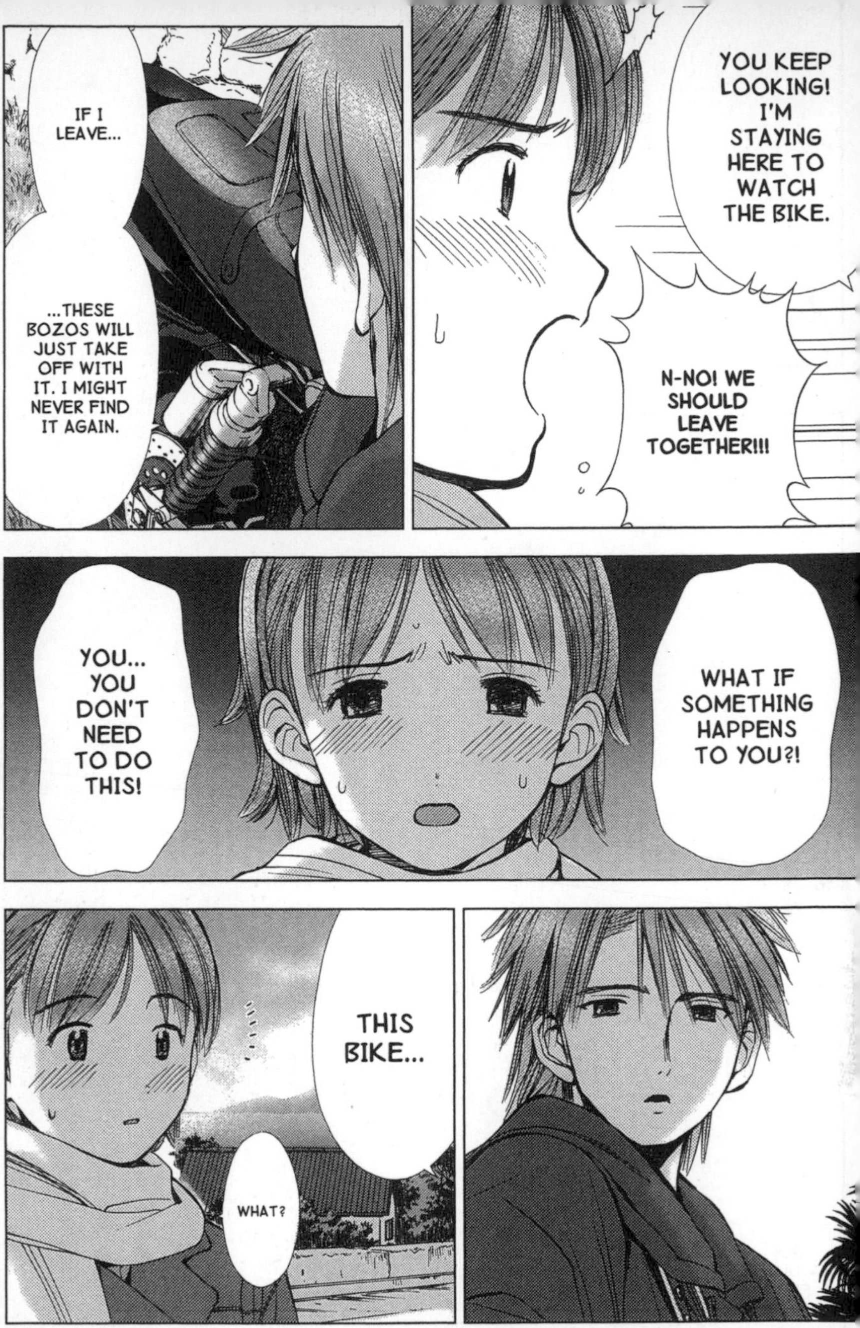
YOU KEEP LOOKING! I'M STAYING HERE TO WATCH THE BIKE.
N-NO! WE SHOULD LEAVE TOGETHER!!!
IF I LEAVE...
...THESE BOZOS WILL JUST TAKE OFF WITH IT. I MIGHT NEVER FIND IT AGAIN.
WHAT IF SOMETHING HAPPENS TO YOU?!
YOU... YOU DON'T NEED TO DO THIS!
THIS BIKE...
WHAT?

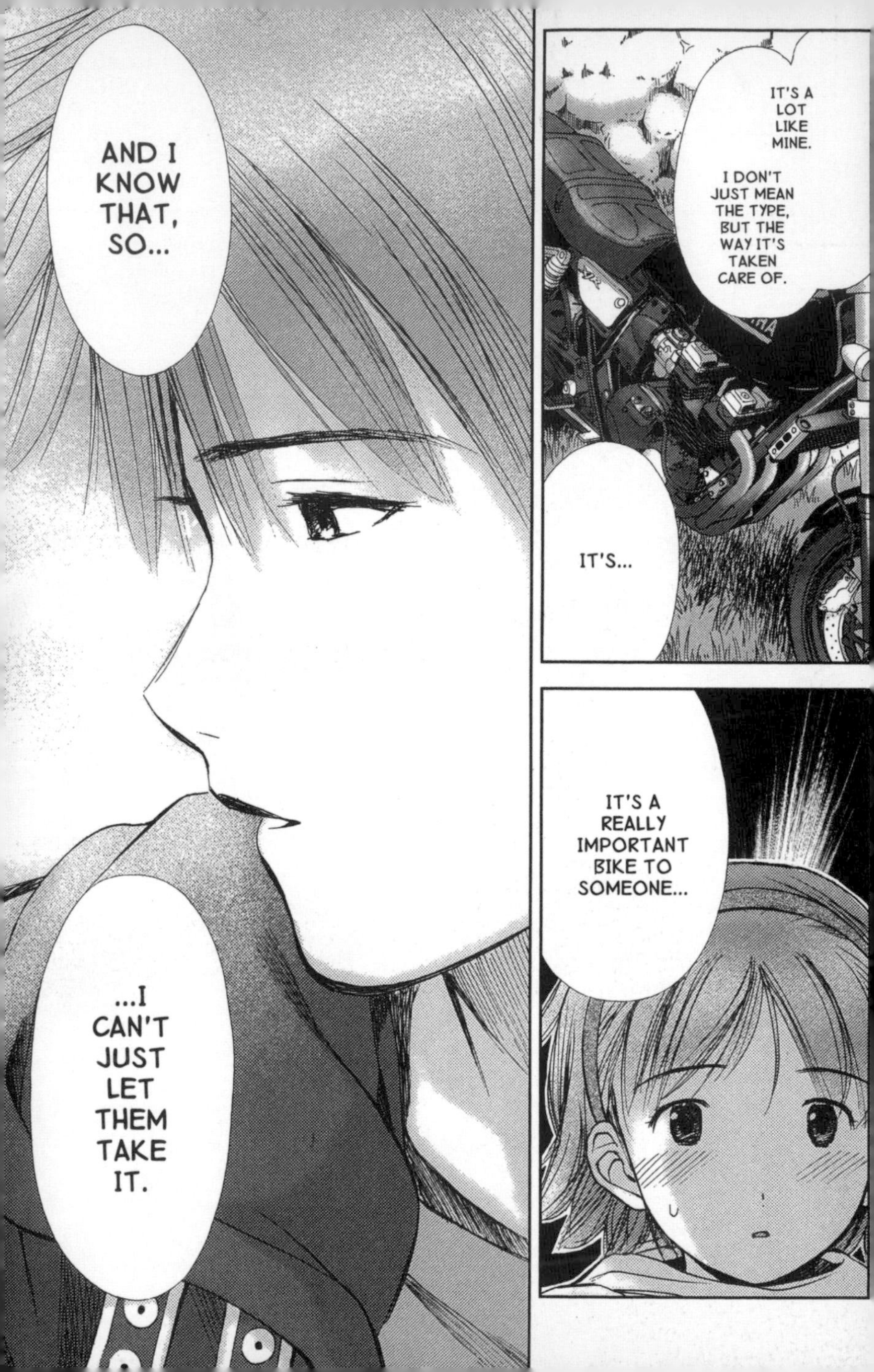
IT'S A LOT LIKE MINE.
I DON'T JUST MEAN THE TYPE, BUT THE WAY IT'S TAKEN CARE OF.
IT'S...
IT'S A REALLY IMPORTANT BIKE TO SOMEONE...
AND I KNOW THAT, SO...
...I CAN'T JUST LET THEM TAKE IT.

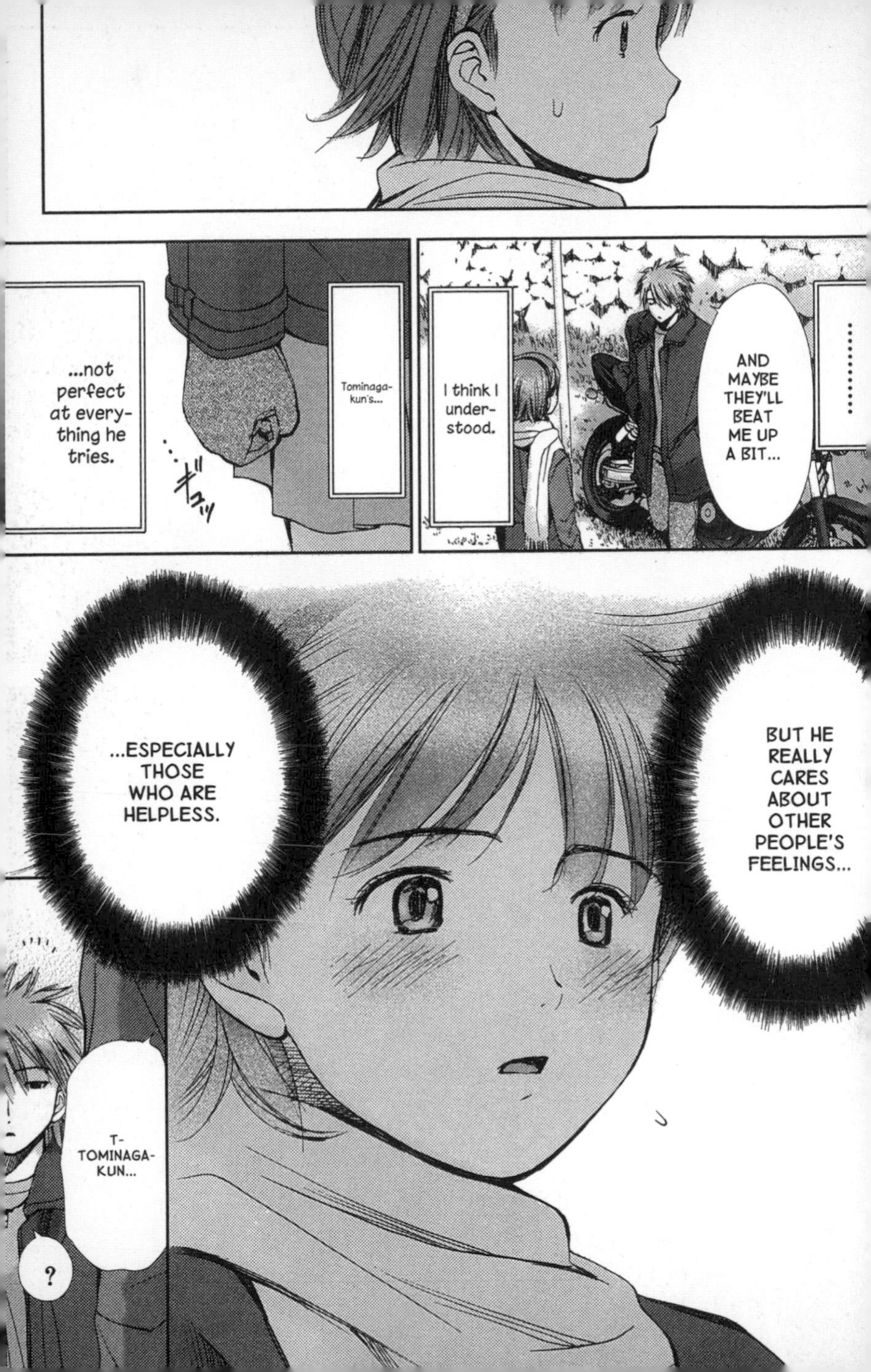
......
AND MAYBE THEY'LL BEAT ME UP A BIT...
I think I understood.
Tominaga-kun's...
...not perfect at every-thing he tries.
ギュッ
BUT HE REALLY CARES ABOUT OTHER PEOPLE'S FEELINGS...
...ESPECIALLY THOSE WHO ARE HELPLESS.
T-TOMINAGA-KUN...
?

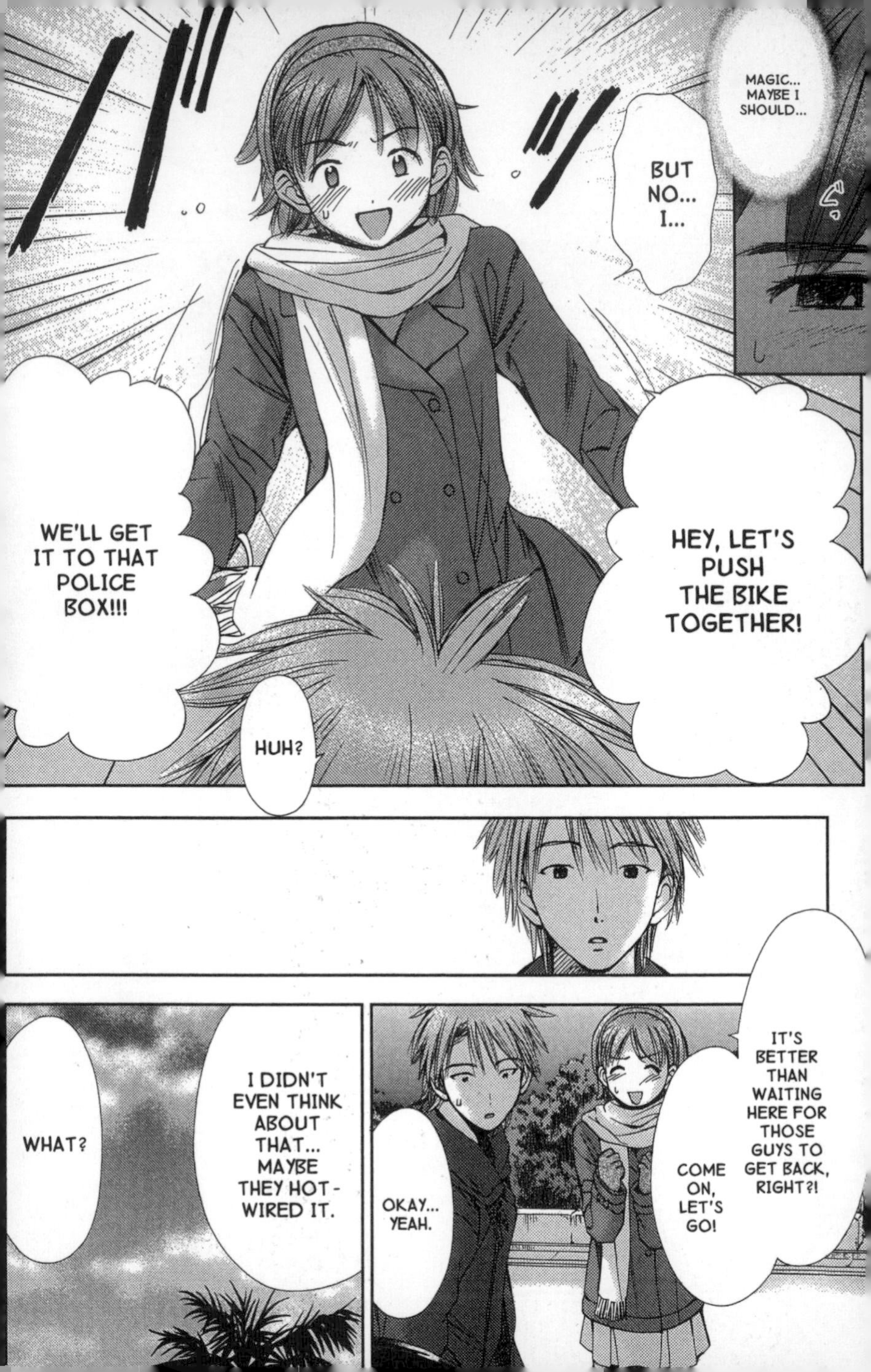
MAGIC... MAYBE I SHOULD...
BUT NO... I...
HEY, LET'S PUSH THE BIKE TOGETHER!
WE'LL GET IT TO THAT POLICE BOX!!!
HUH?
IT'S BETTER THAN WAITING HERE FOR THOSE GUYS TO GET BACK, RIGHT?!
COME ON, LET'S GO!
OKAY... YEAH.
I DIDN'T EVEN THINK ABOUT THAT... MAYBE THEY HOT-WIRED IT.
WHAT?

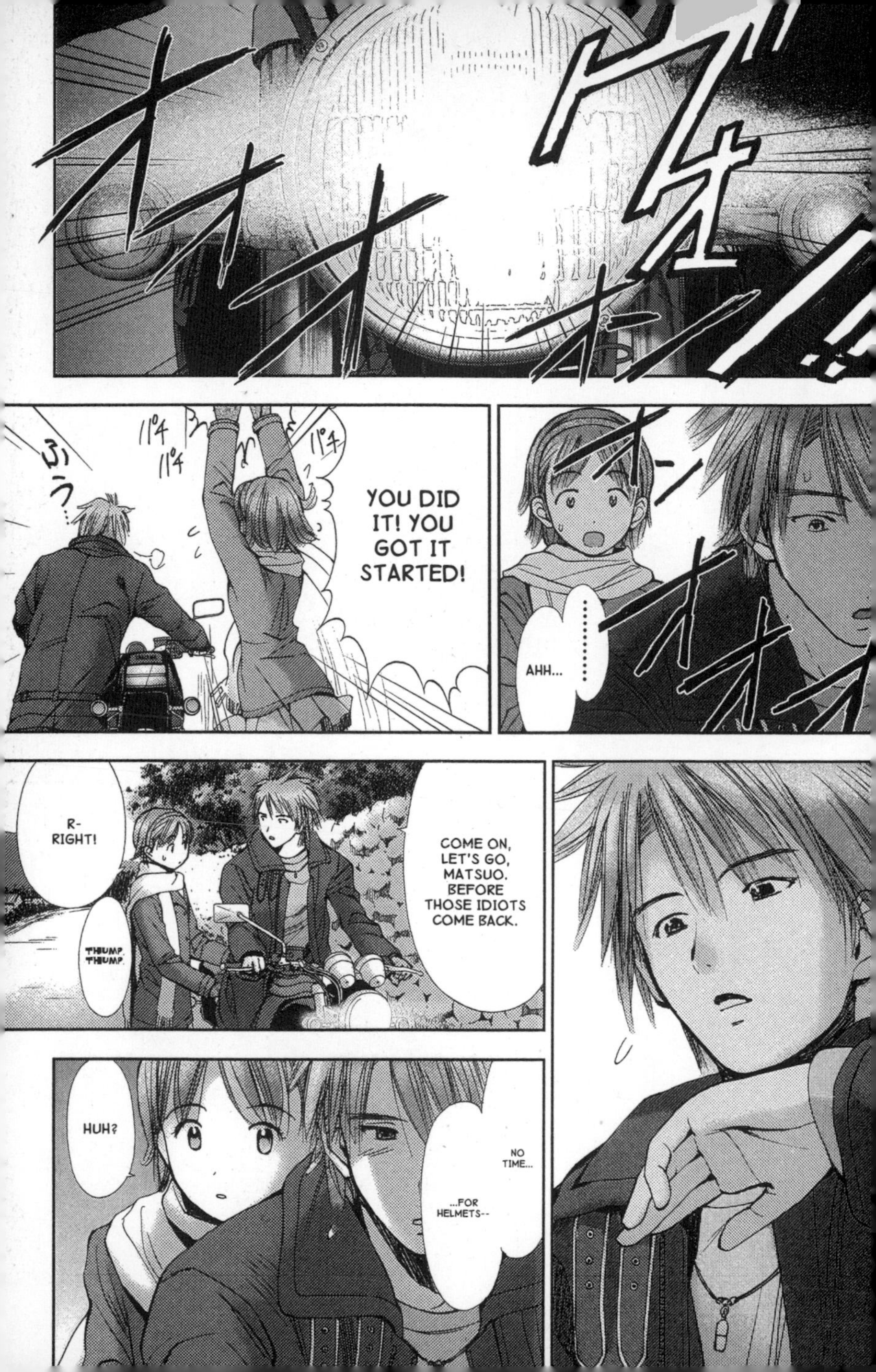
AHH...
......
YOU DID IT! YOU GOT IT STARTED!
ふう
パチ パチ
パチ
COME ON, LET'S GO, MATSUO. BEFORE THOSE IDIOTS COME BACK.
R-RIGHT!
THUMP. THUMP.
NO TIME...
...FOR HELMETS--
HUH?

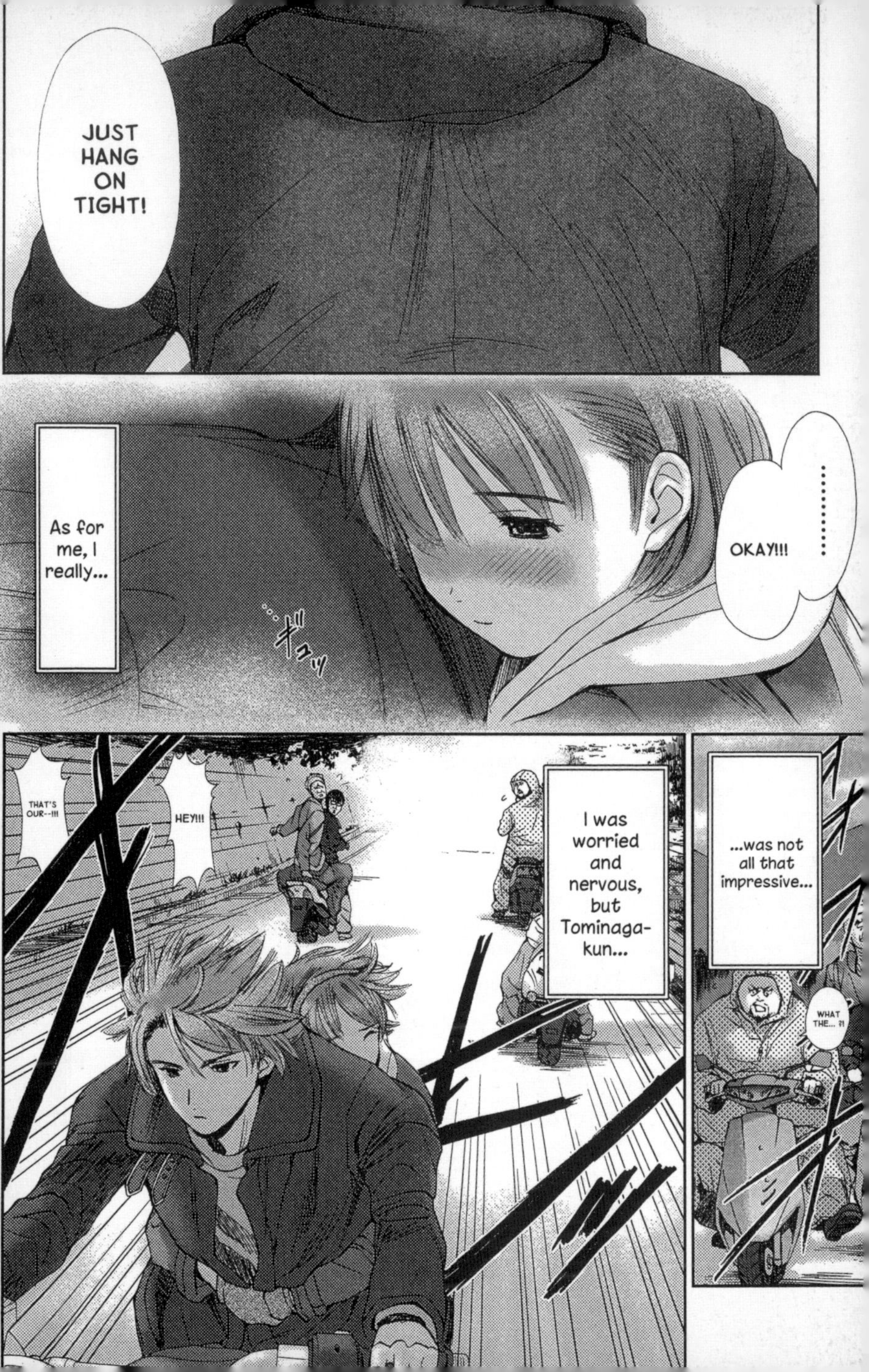
JUST HANG ON TIGHT!
......OKAY!!!
As for me, I really...
...ギュッ
...was not all that impressive...
WHAT THE... ?!
I was worried and nervous, but Tominaga-kun...
HEY!!!
THAT'S OUR--!!!

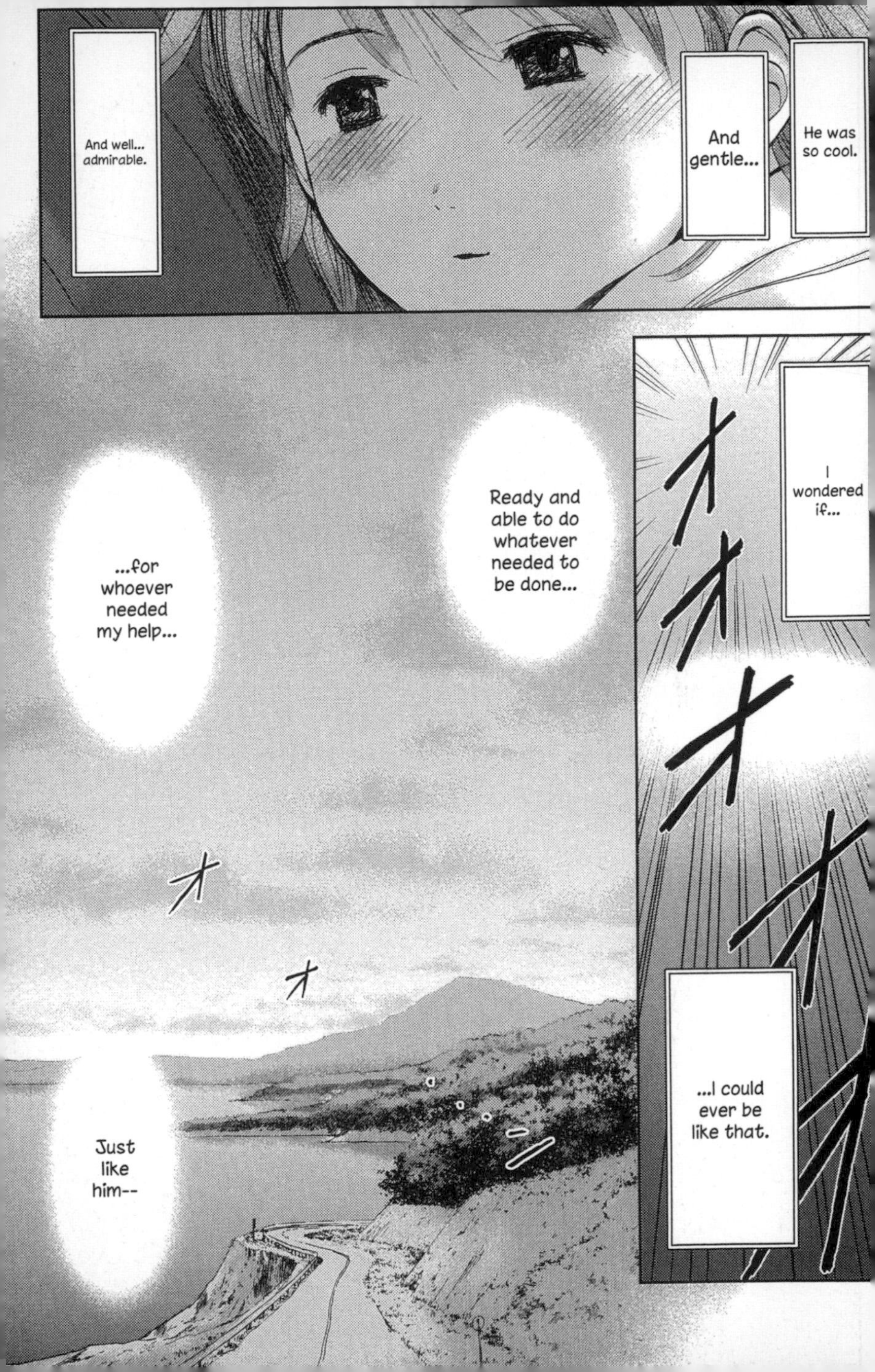
He was so cool.
And gentle...
And well... admirable.
I wondered if...
オオオオ
...I could ever be like that.
Ready and able to do whatever needed to be done...
...for whoever needed my help...
オ
オ
Just like him--

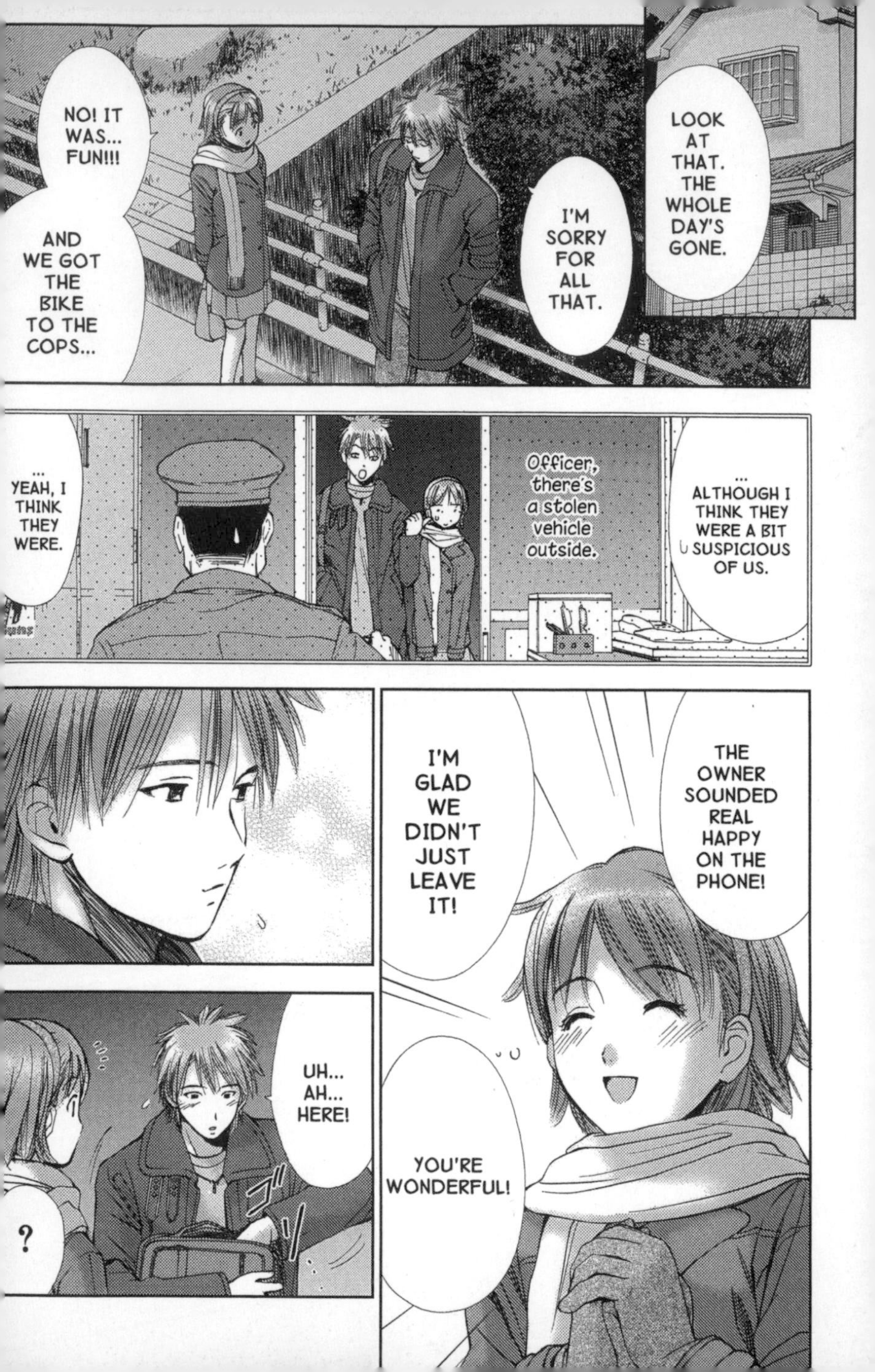
LOOK AT THAT. THE WHOLE DAY'S GONE.
I'M SORRY FOR ALL THAT.
NO! IT WAS... FUN!!!
AND WE GOT THE BIKE TO THE COPS...
... ALTHOUGH I THINK THEY WERE A BIT SUSPICIOUS OF US.
Officer, there's a stolen vehicle outside.
... YEAH, I THINK THEY WERE.
THE OWNER SOUNDED REAL HAPPY ON THE PHONE!
I'M GLAD WE DIDN'T JUST LEAVE IT!
YOU'RE WONDERFUL!
UH... AH... HERE!
?

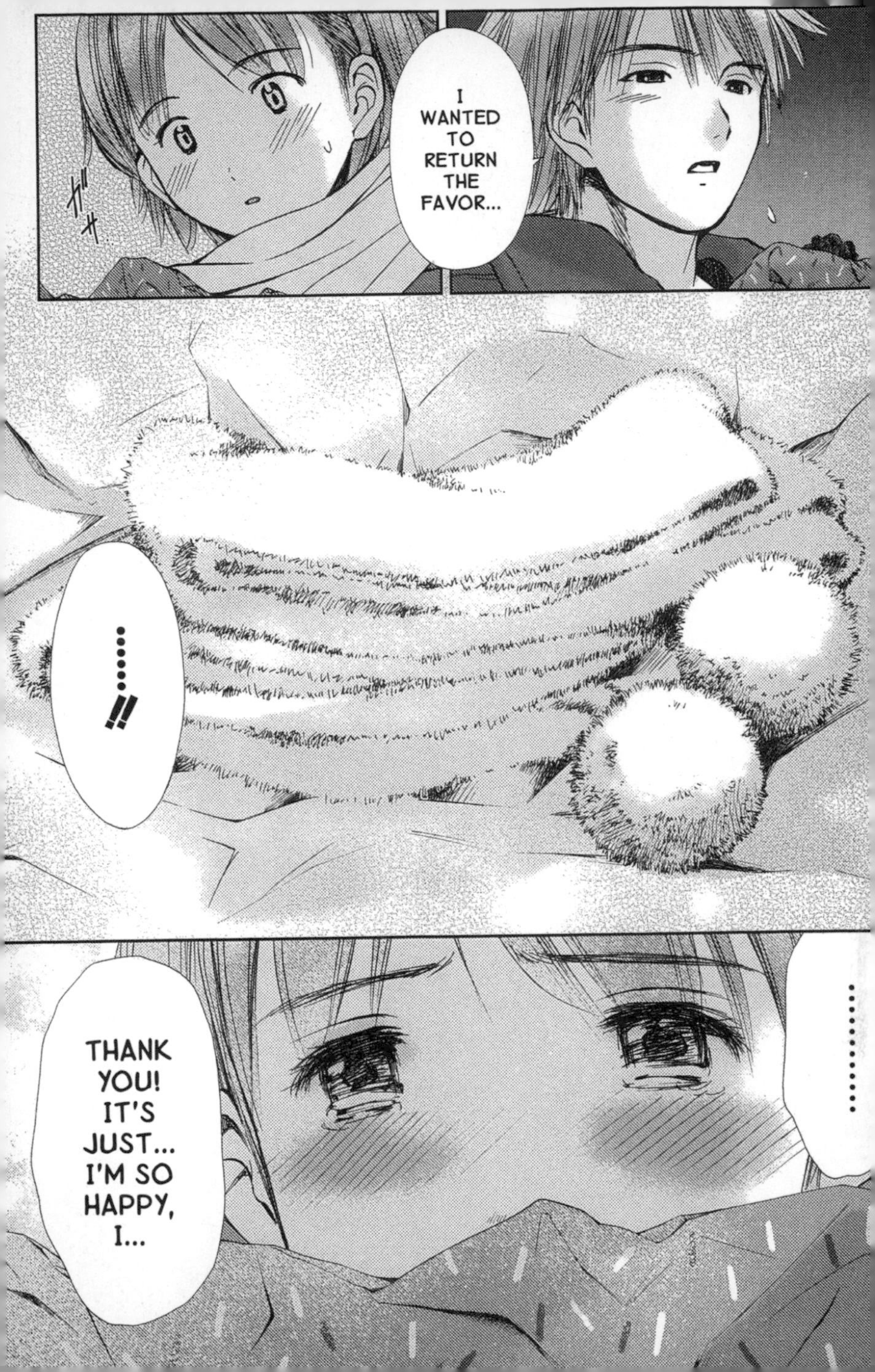
I WANTED TO RETURN THE FAVOR...
......!!
....
THANK YOU! IT'S JUST... I'M SO HAPPY, I...

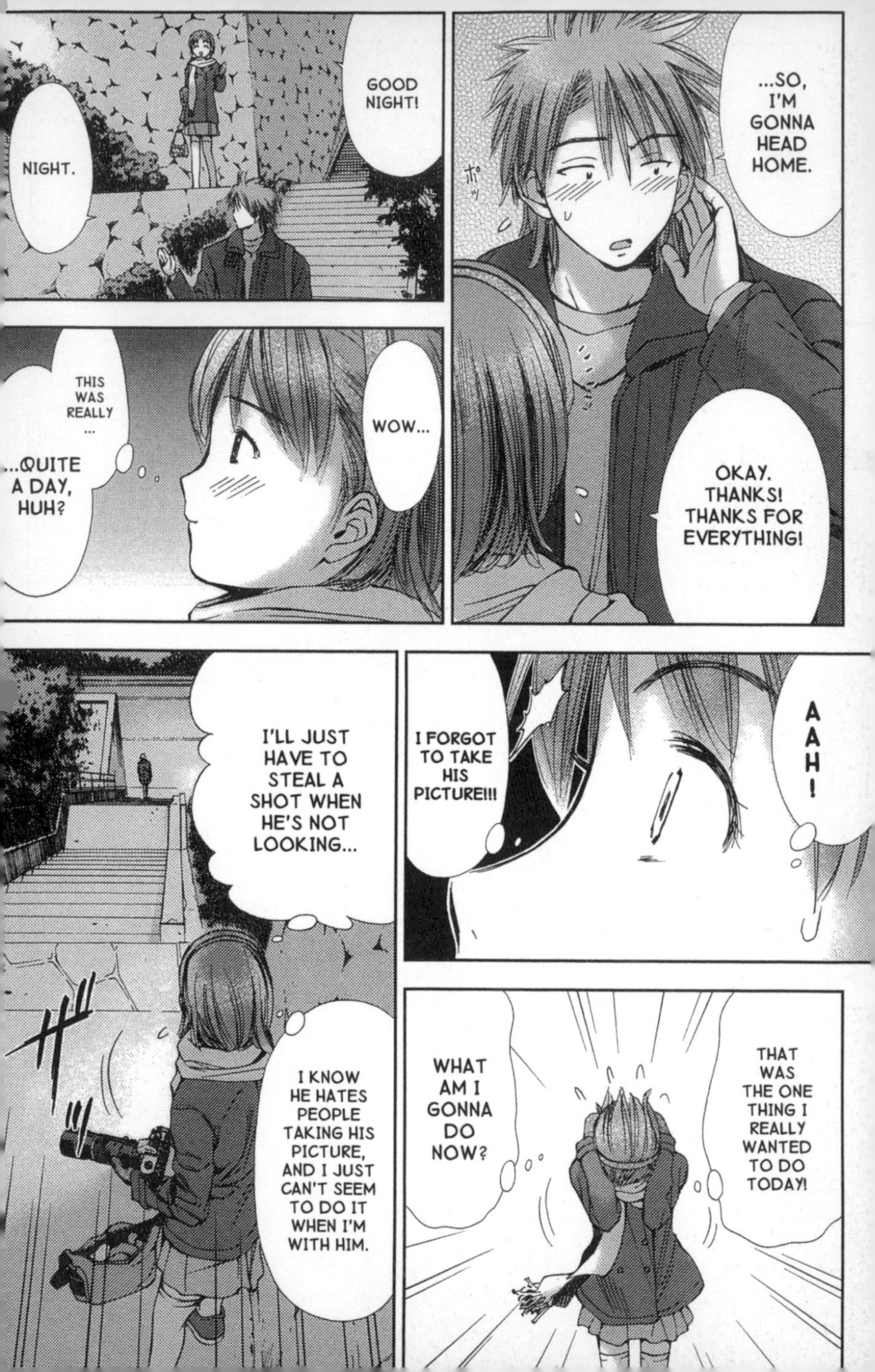
...SO, I'M GONNA HEAD HOME.
OKAY. THANKS! THANKS FOR EVERYTHING!
GOOD NIGHT!
NIGHT.
WOW...
THIS WAS REALLY ...
...QUITE A DAY, HUH?
AAH!
I FORGOT TO TAKE HIS PICTURE!!!
THAT WAS THE ONE THING I REALLY WANTED TO DO TODAY!
WHAT AM I GONNA DO NOW?
I'LL JUST HAVE TO STEAL A SHOT WHEN HE'S NOT LOOKING...
I KNOW HE HATES PEOPLE TAKING HIS PICTURE, AND I JUST CAN'T SEEM TO DO IT WHEN I'M WITH HIM.

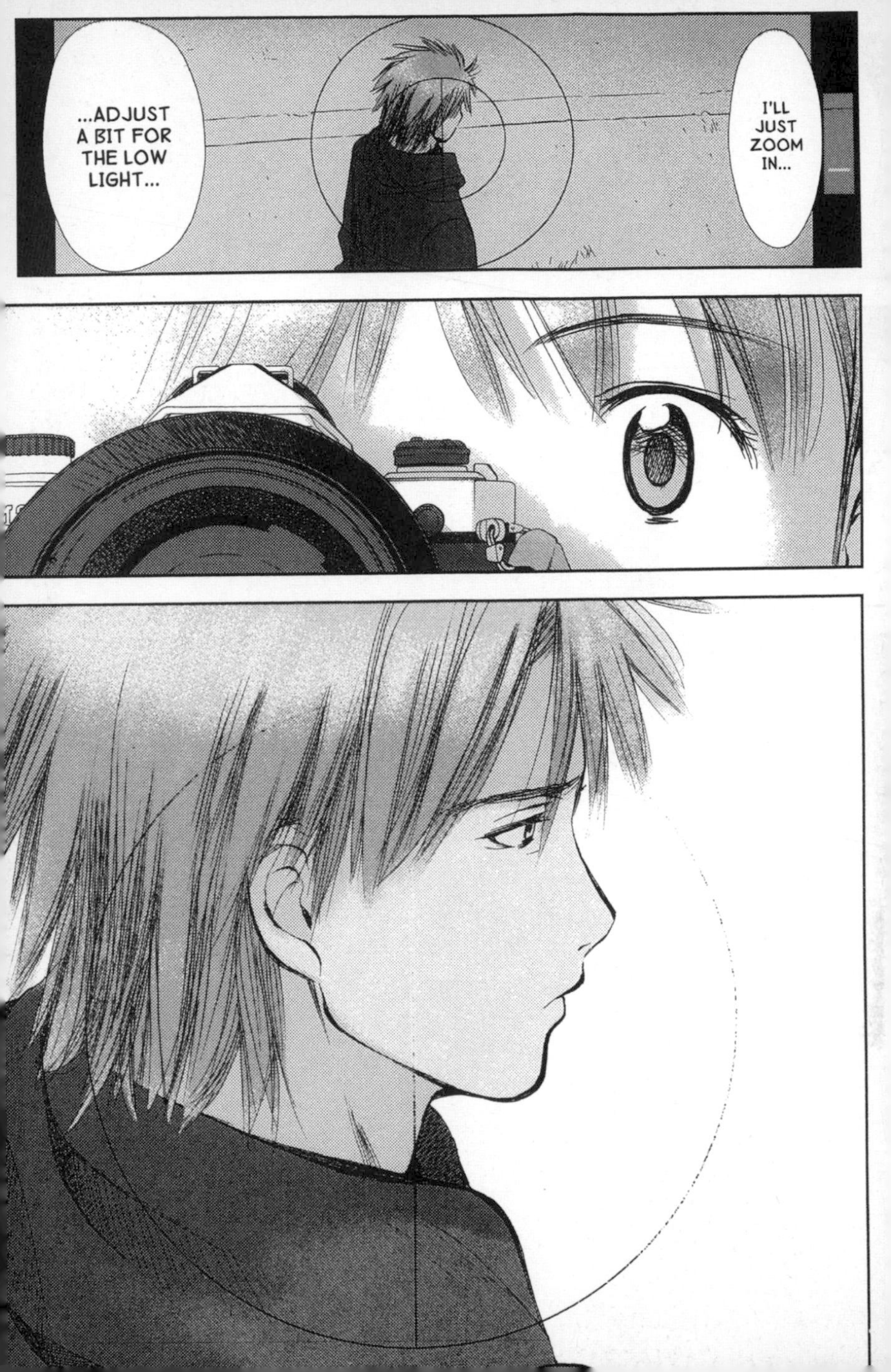
I'LL JUST ZOOM IN...
...ADJUST A BIT FOR THE LOW LIGHT...

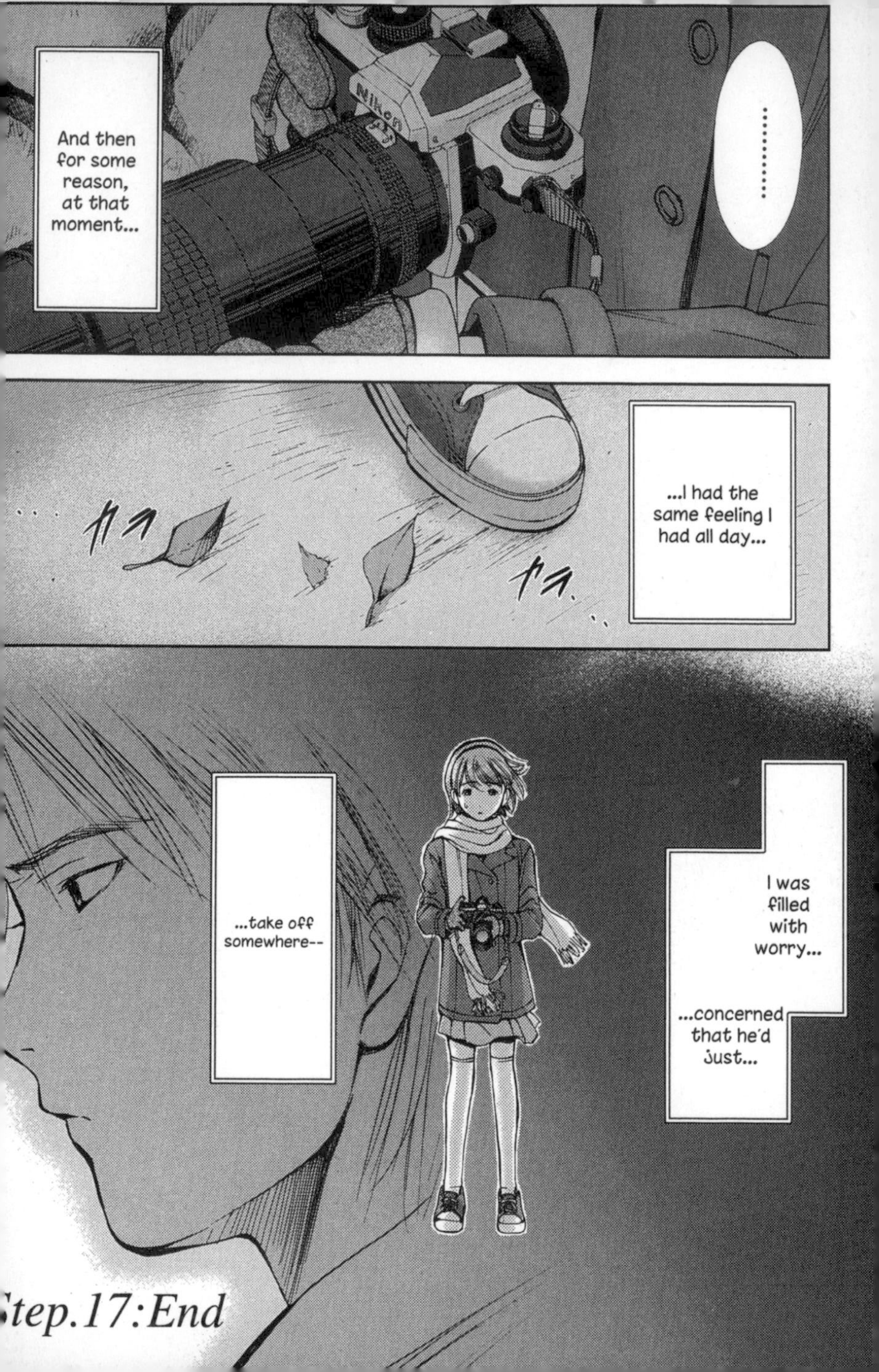

......
And then for some reason, at that moment...
...I had the same feeling I had all day...
I was filled with worry...
...concerned that he'd just...
...take off somewhere--
Step.17:End

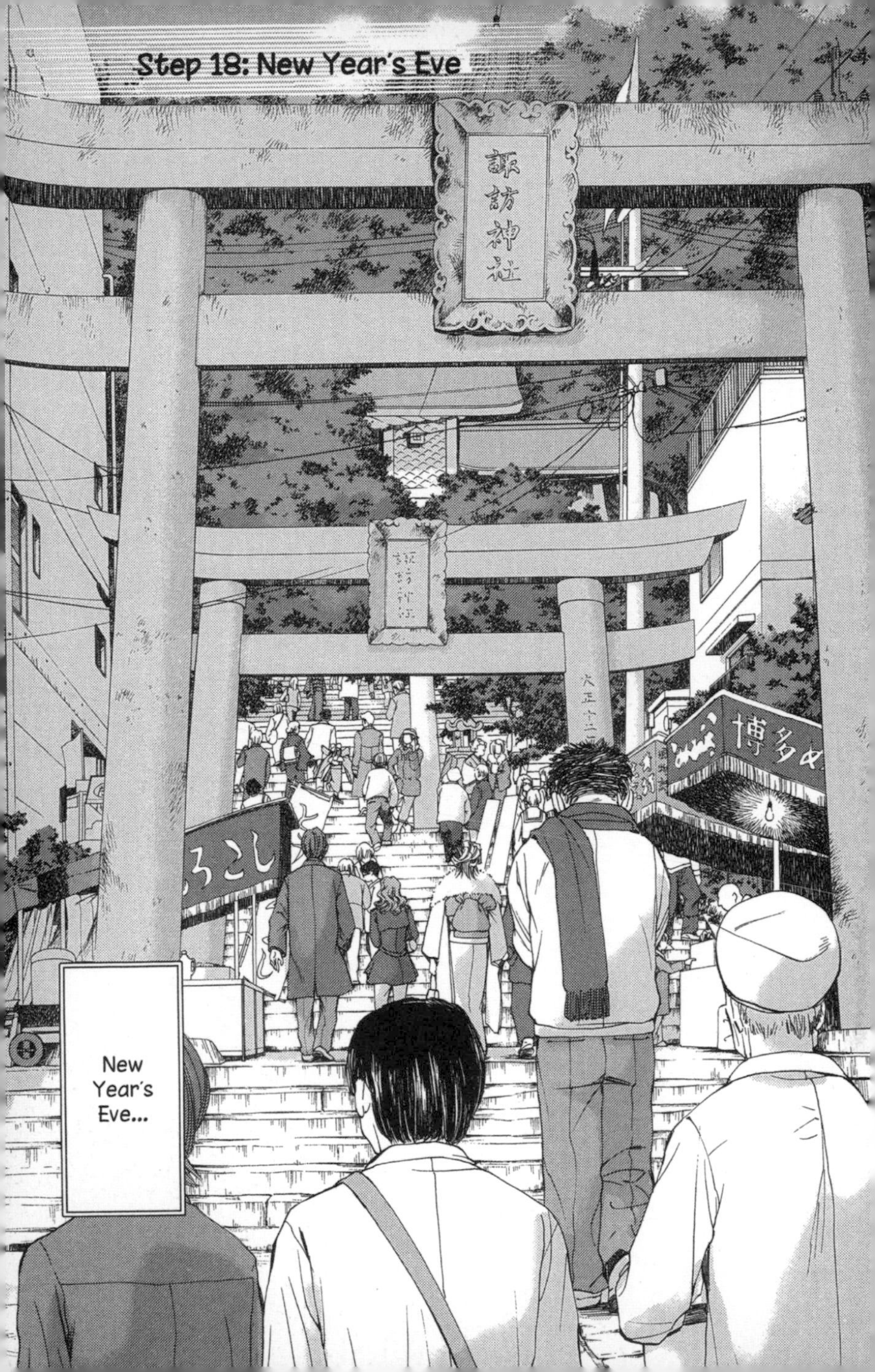
Step 18: New Year's Eve
諏訪神社
博多
New Year's Eve...

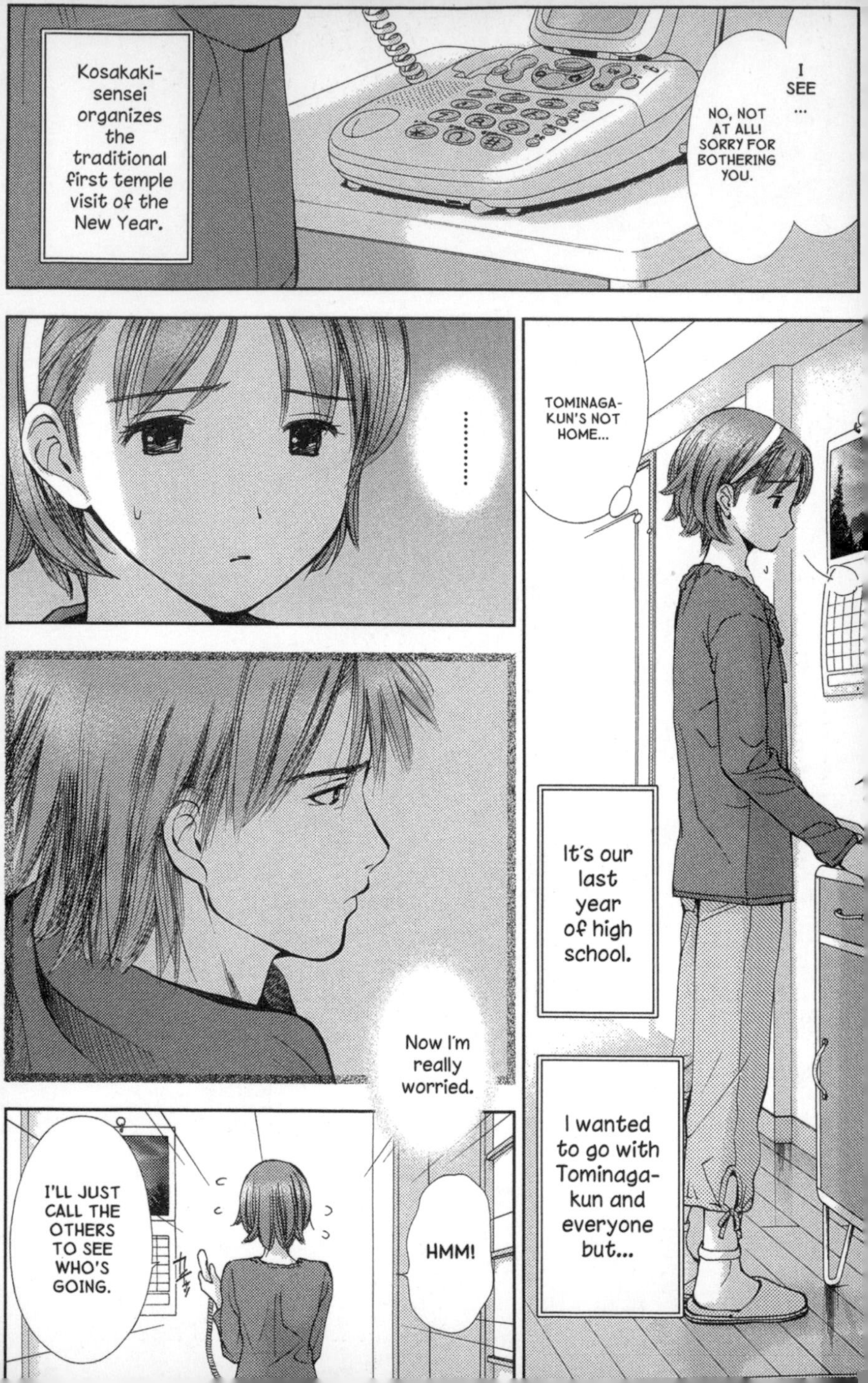
I SEE ...
NO, NOT AT ALL! SORRY FOR BOTHERING YOU.
Kosakaki-sensei organizes the traditional first temple visit of the New Year.
TOMINAGA-KUN'S NOT HOME...
It's our last year of high school.
I wanted to go with Tominaga-kun and everyone but...
....
Now I'm really worried.
HMM!
I'LL JUST CALL THE OTHERS TO SEE WHO'S GOING.

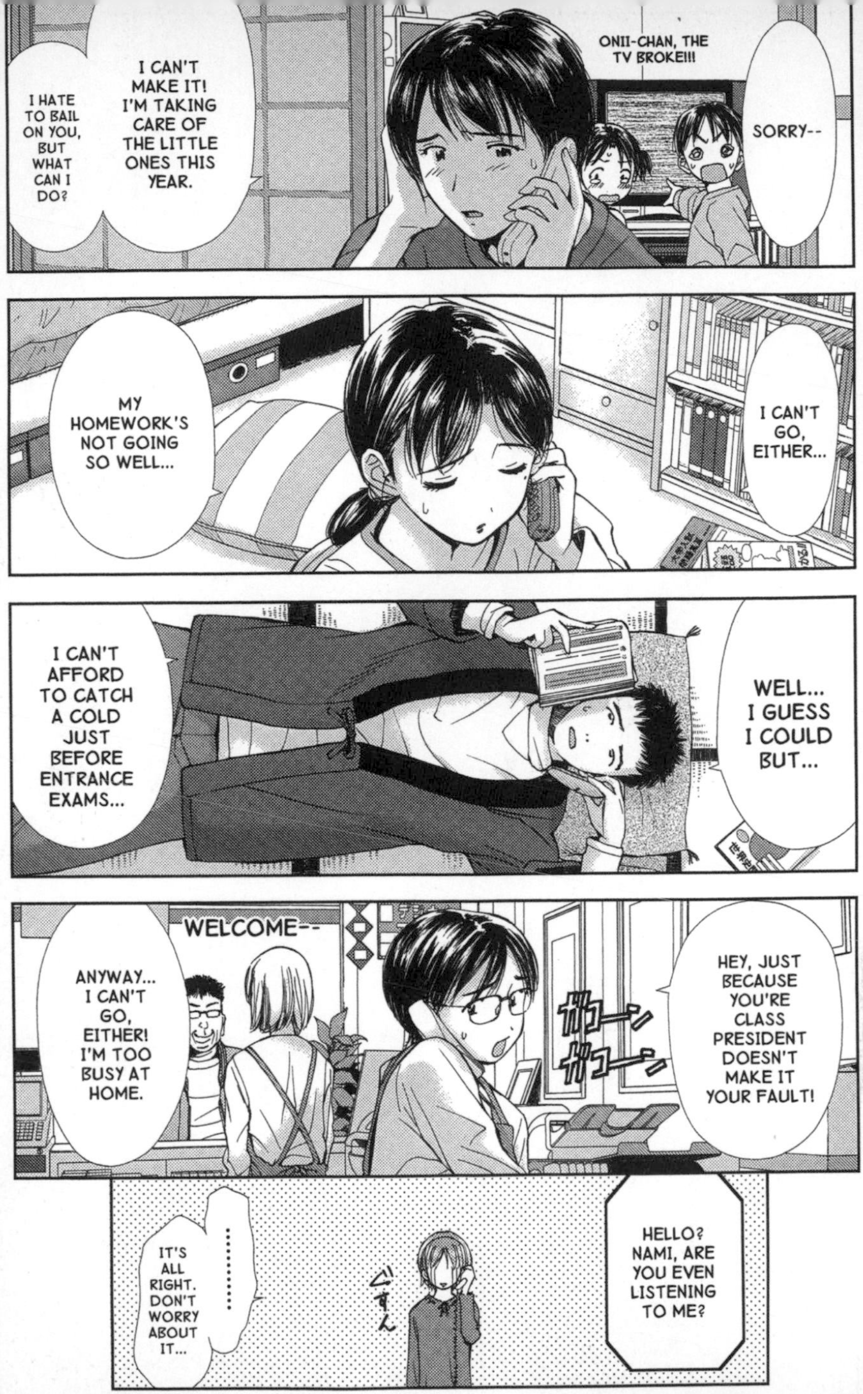
SORRY--
ONII-CHAN, THE TV BROKE!!!
I CAN'T MAKE IT! I'M TAKING CARE OF THE LITTLE ONES THIS YEAR.
I HATE TO BAIL ON YOU, BUT WHAT CAN I DO?
I CAN'T GO, EITHER...
MY HOMEWORK'S NOT GOING SO WELL...
WELL... I GUESS I COULD BUT...
I CAN'T AFFORD TO CATCH A COLD JUST BEFORE ENTRANCE EXAMS...
HEY, JUST BECAUSE YOU'RE CLASS PRESIDENT DOESN'T MAKE IT YOUR FAULT!
ガコーン
ガコーン
WELCOME--
ANYWAY... I CAN'T GO, EITHER! I'M TOO BUSY AT HOME.
HELLO? NAMI, ARE YOU EVEN LISTENING TO ME?
ぐすん
....
IT'S ALL RIGHT. DON'T WORRY ABOUT IT...

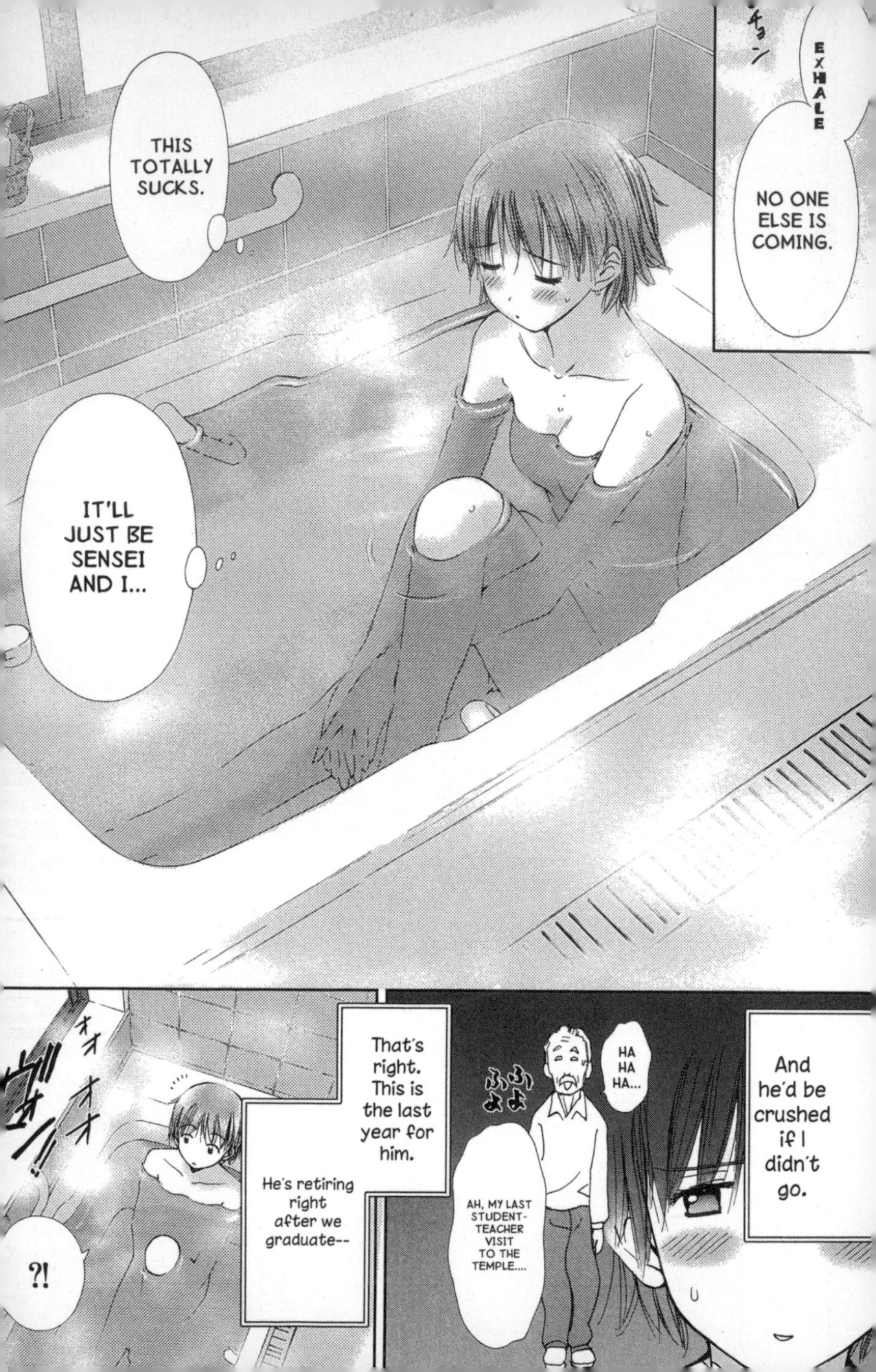

チョン
EXHALE
NO ONE ELSE IS COMING.
THIS TOTALLY SUCKS.
IT'LL JUST BE SENSEI AND I...
And he'd be crushed if I didn't go.
HA HA HA...
ふよふよ
AH, MY LAST STUDENT-TEACHER VISIT TO THE TEMPLE....
That's right. This is the last year for him.
He's retiring right after we graduate--
ヴォオオオ
?!

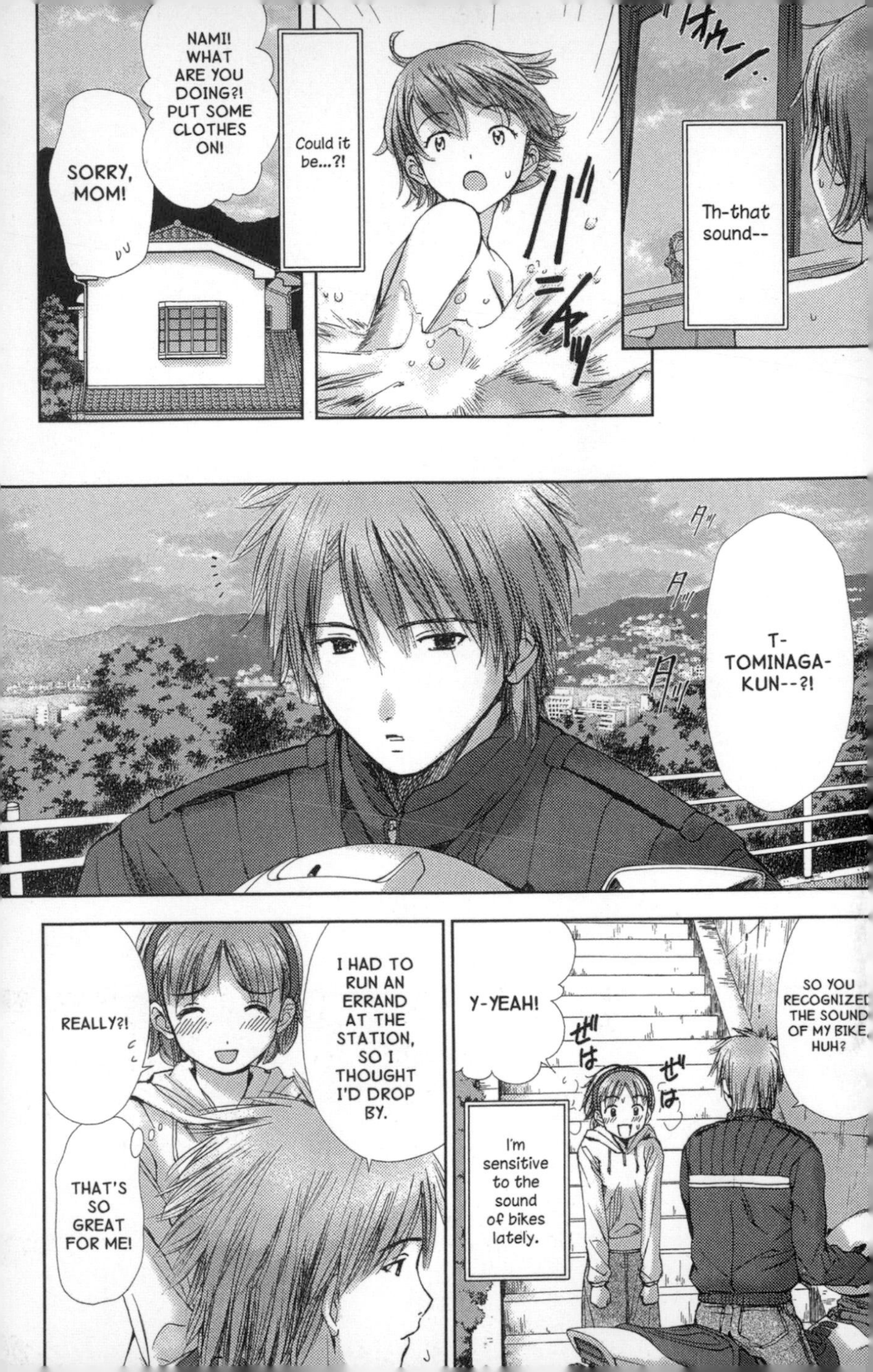
Th-that sound--
Could it be...?!
NAMI! WHAT ARE YOU DOING?! PUT SOME CLOTHES ON!
SORRY, MOM!
T-TOMINAGA-KUN--?!
SO YOU RECOGNIZED THE SOUND OF MY BIKE, HUH?
Y-YEAH!
ぜは
ぜは
I'm sensitive to the sound of bikes lately.
I HAD TO RUN AN ERRAND AT THE STATION, SO I THOUGHT I'D DROP BY.
REALLY?!
THAT'S SO GREAT FOR ME!

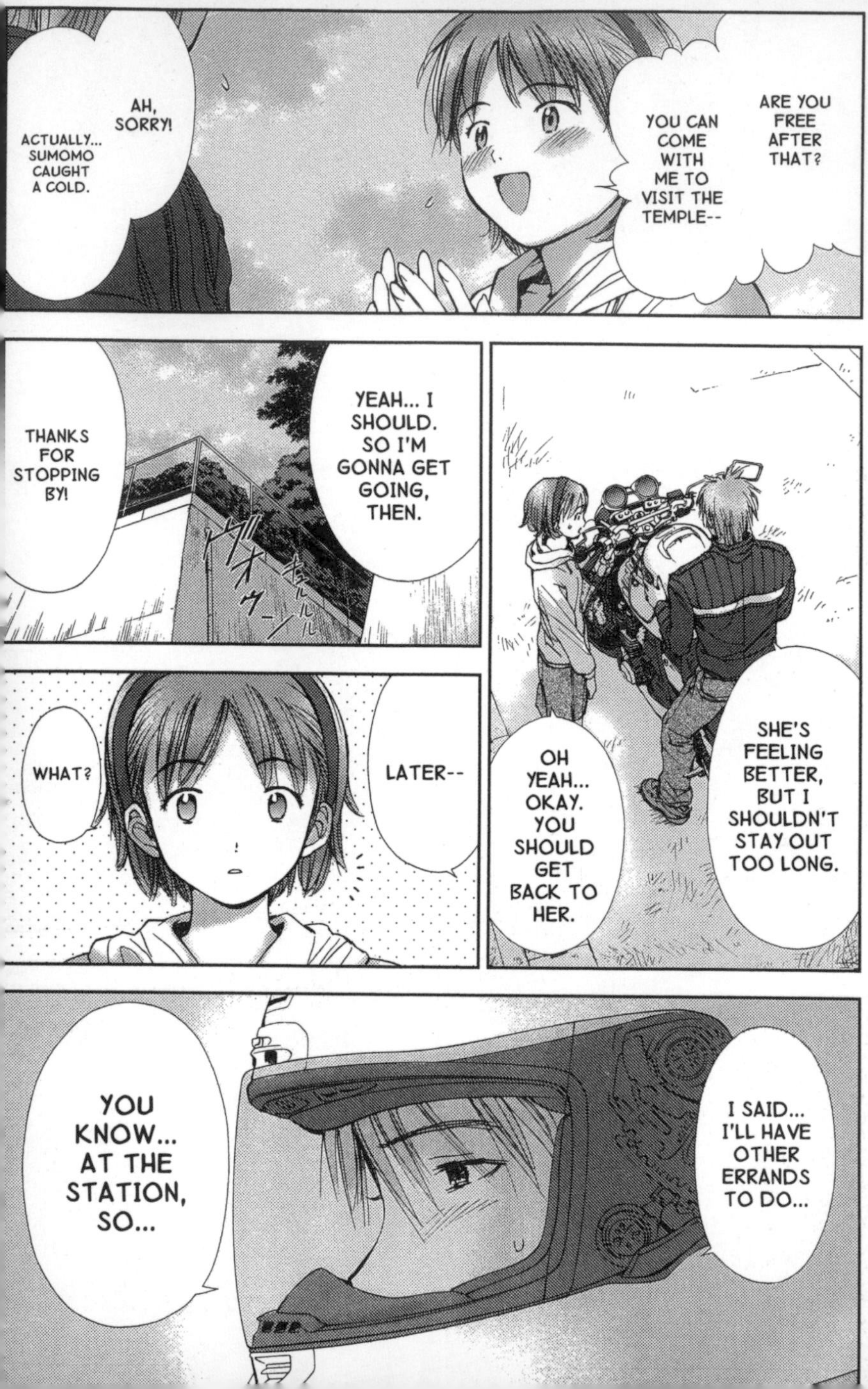
ARE YOU FREE AFTER THAT?
YOU CAN COME WITH ME TO VISIT THE TEMPLE--
AH, SORRY!
ACTUALLY... SUMOMO CAUGHT A COLD.
SHE'S FEELING BETTER, BUT I SHOULDN'T STAY OUT TOO LONG.
OH YEAH... OKAY. YOU SHOULD GET BACK TO HER.
YEAH... I SHOULD. SO I'M GONNA GET GOING, THEN.
THANKS FOR STOPPING BY!
LATER--
WHAT?
I SAID... I'LL HAVE OTHER ERRANDS TO DO...
YOU KNOW... AT THE STATION, SO...

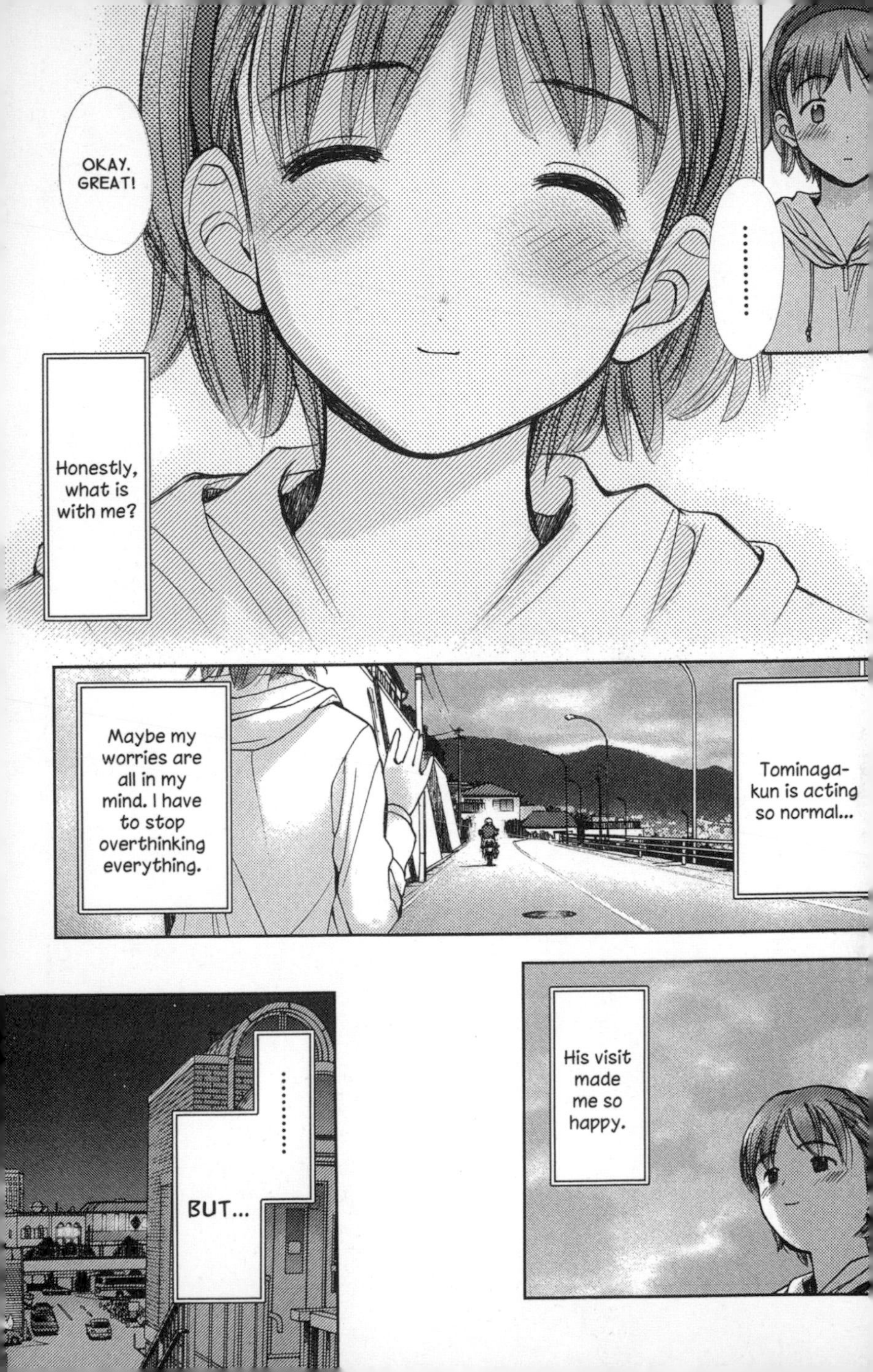
......
OKAY. GREAT!
Honestly, what is with me?
Tominaga-kun is acting so normal...
Maybe my worries are all in my mind. I have to stop overthinking everything.
His visit made me so happy.
......
BUT...

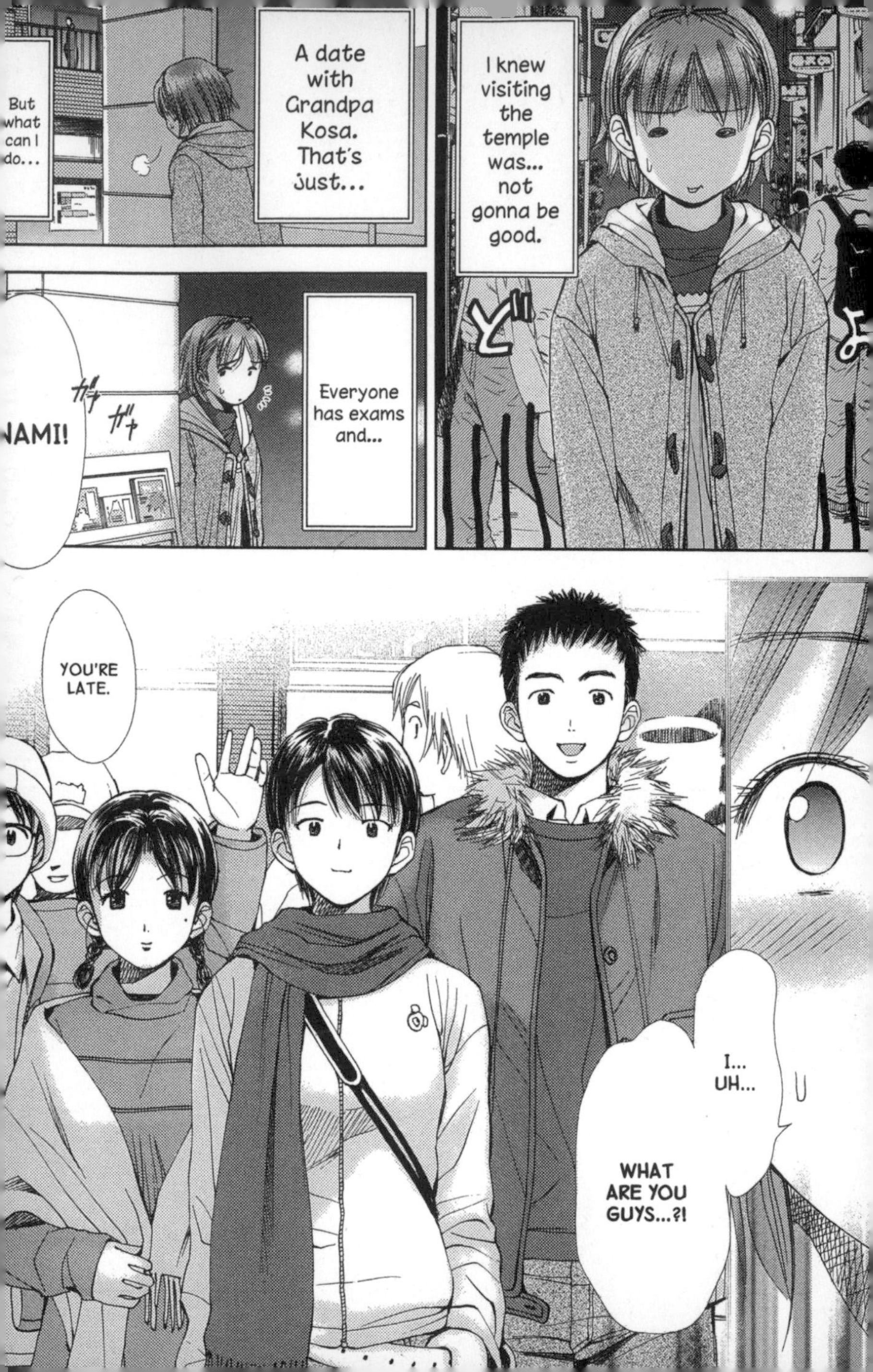
I knew visiting the temple was... not gonna be good.
A date with Grandpa Kosa. That's just...
But what can I do...
Everyone has exams and...
NAMI!
YOU'RE LATE.
I... UH...
WHAT ARE YOU GUYS...?!

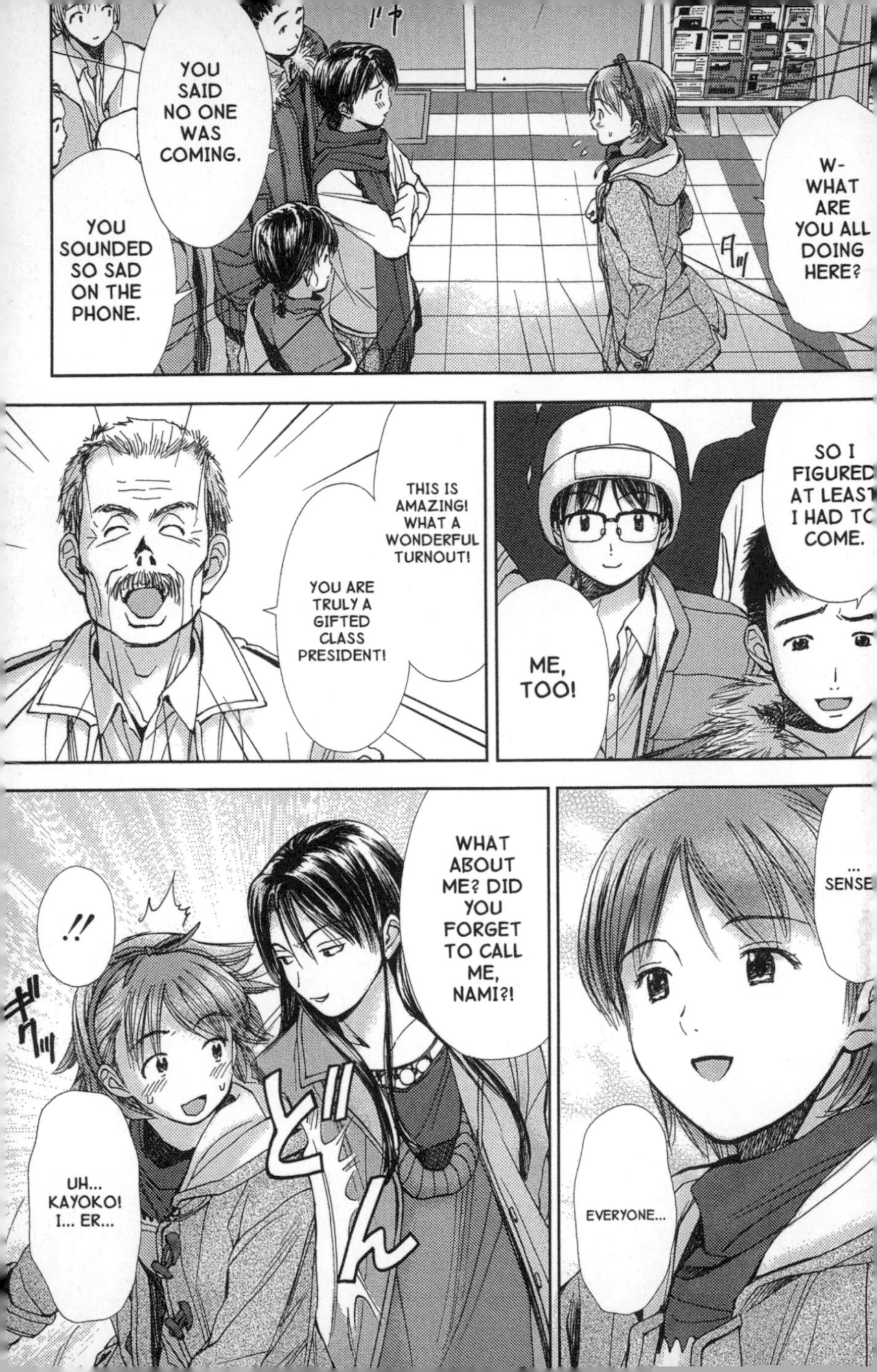
W- WHAT ARE YOU ALL DOING HERE?
YOU SAID NO ONE WAS COMING.
YOU SOUNDED SO SAD ON THE PHONE.
SO I FIGURED AT LEAST I HAD TO COME.
ME, TOO!
THIS IS AMAZING! WHAT A WONDERFUL TURNOUT!
YOU ARE TRULY A GIFTED CLASS PRESIDENT!
... SENSE
EVERYONE...
WHAT ABOUT ME? DID YOU FORGET TO CALL ME, NAMI?!
!!
UH... KAYOKO! I... ER...

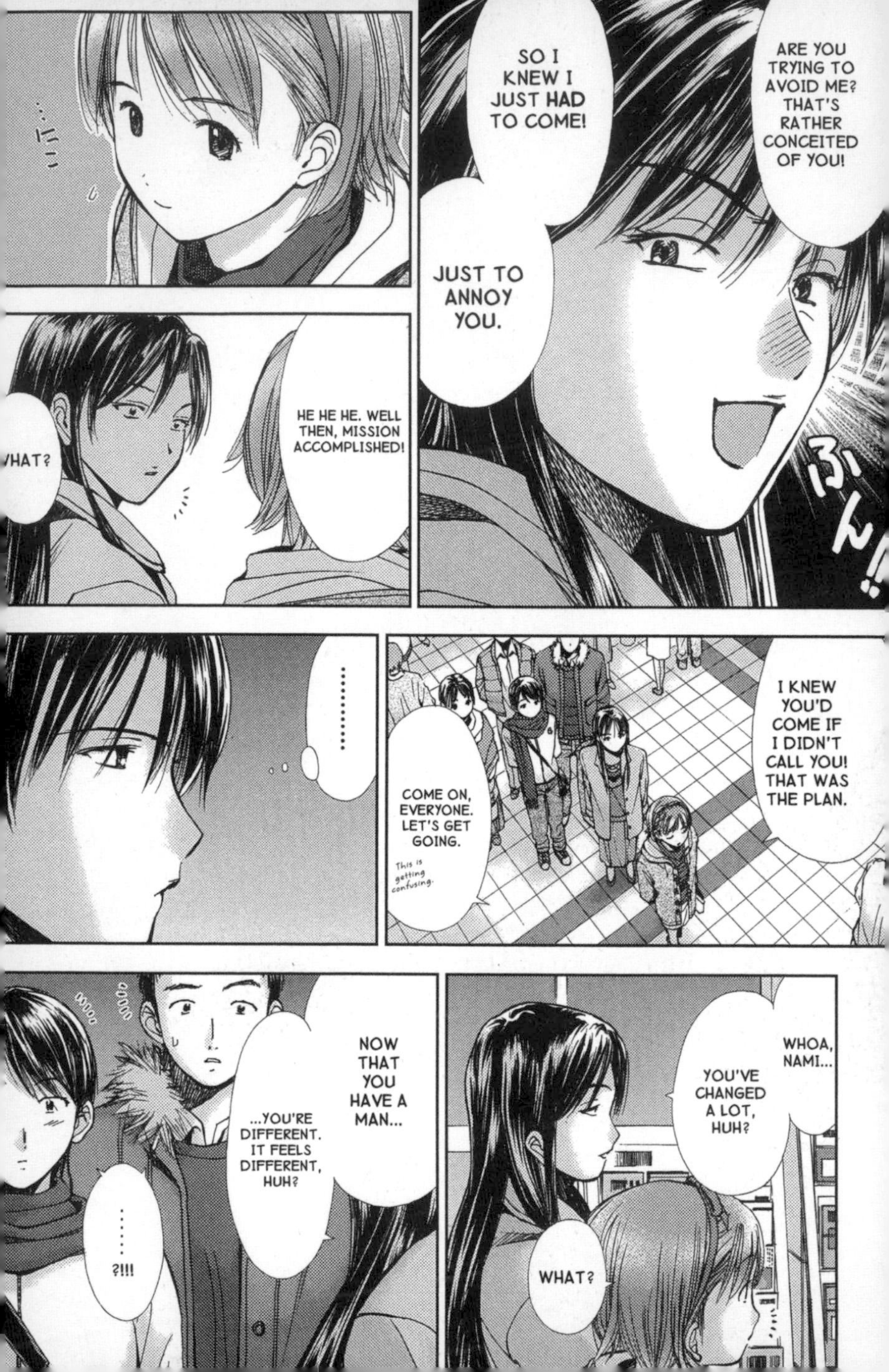
ARE YOU TRYING TO AVOID ME? THAT'S RATHER CONCEITED OF YOU!
SO I KNEW I JUST HAD TO COME!
JUST TO ANNOY YOU.
ふん!!
…にこ
HE HE HE. WELL THEN, MISSION ACCOMPLISHED!
WHAT?
I KNEW YOU'D COME IF I DIDN'T CALL YOU! THAT WAS THE PLAN.
COME ON, EVERYONE. LET'S GET GOING.
This is getting confusing.
....
WHOA, NAMI...
YOU'VE CHANGED A LOT, HUH?
WHAT?
NOW THAT YOU HAVE A MAN...
...YOU'RE DIFFERENT. IT FEELS DIFFERENT, HUH?
......
?!!!

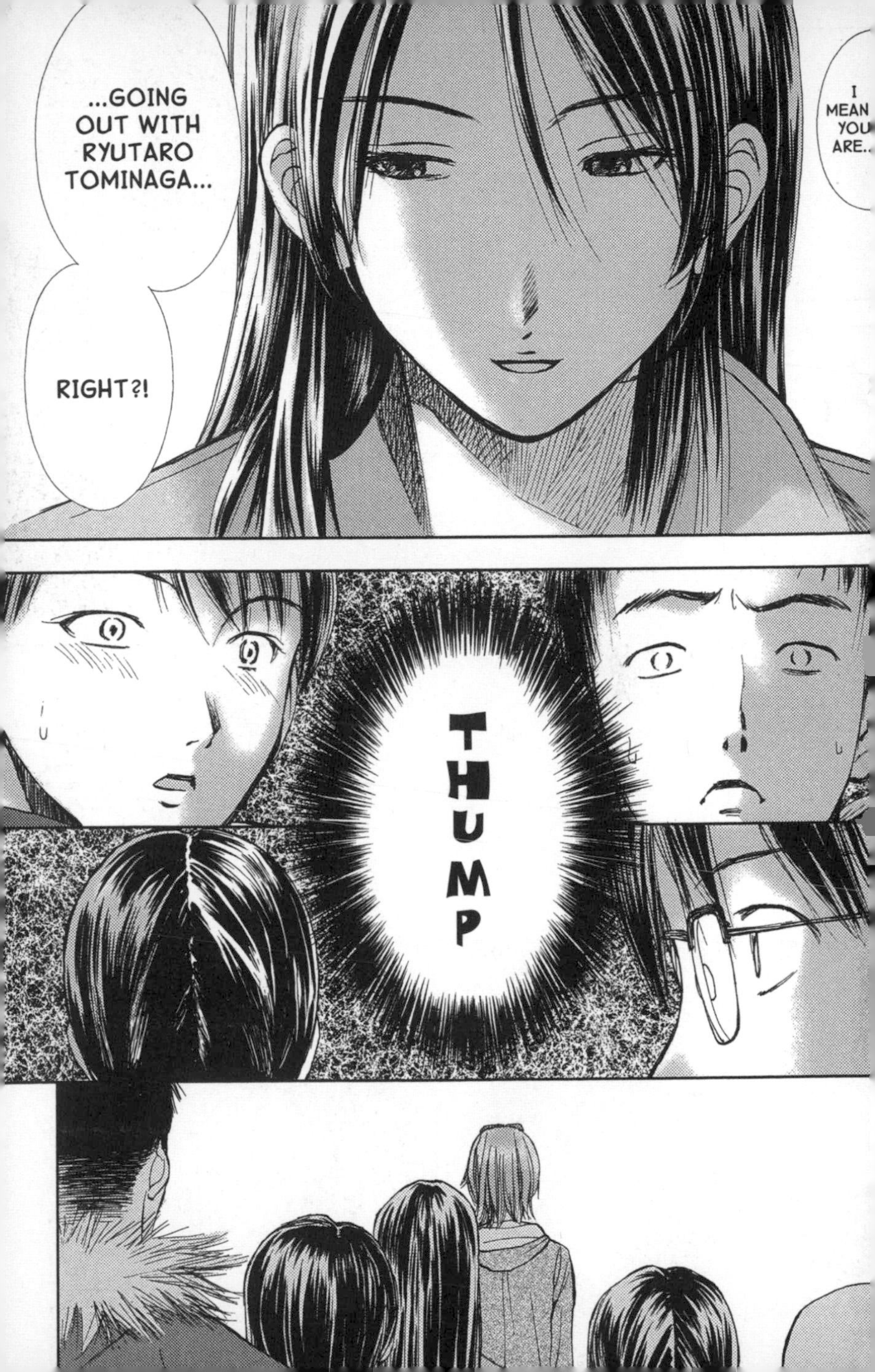
I MEAN YOU ARE..
...GOING OUT WITH RYUTARO TOMINAGA...
RIGHT?!
THUMP

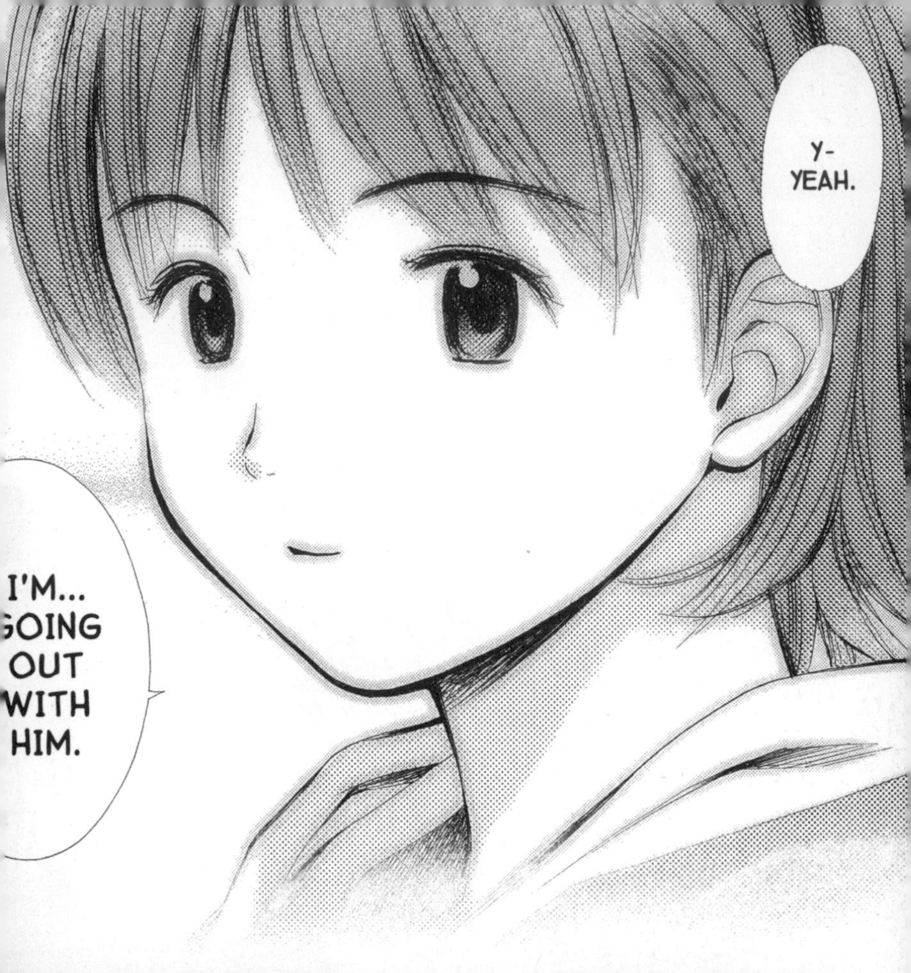
Y-YEAH.
I'M... GOING OUT WITH HIM.
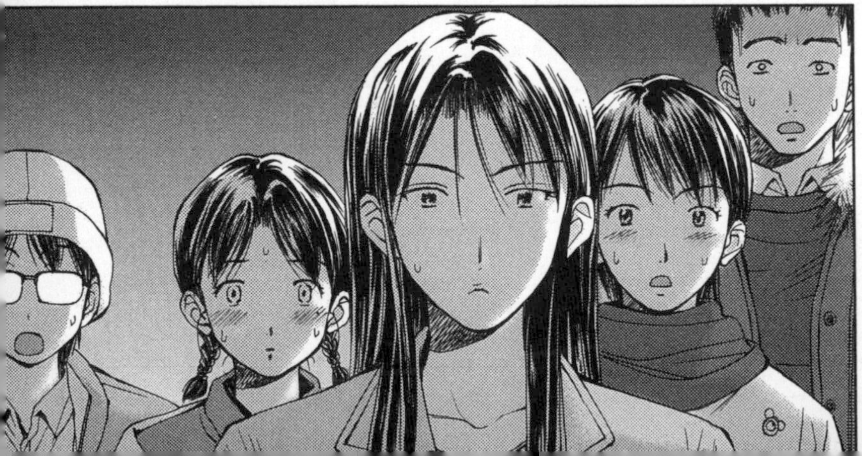

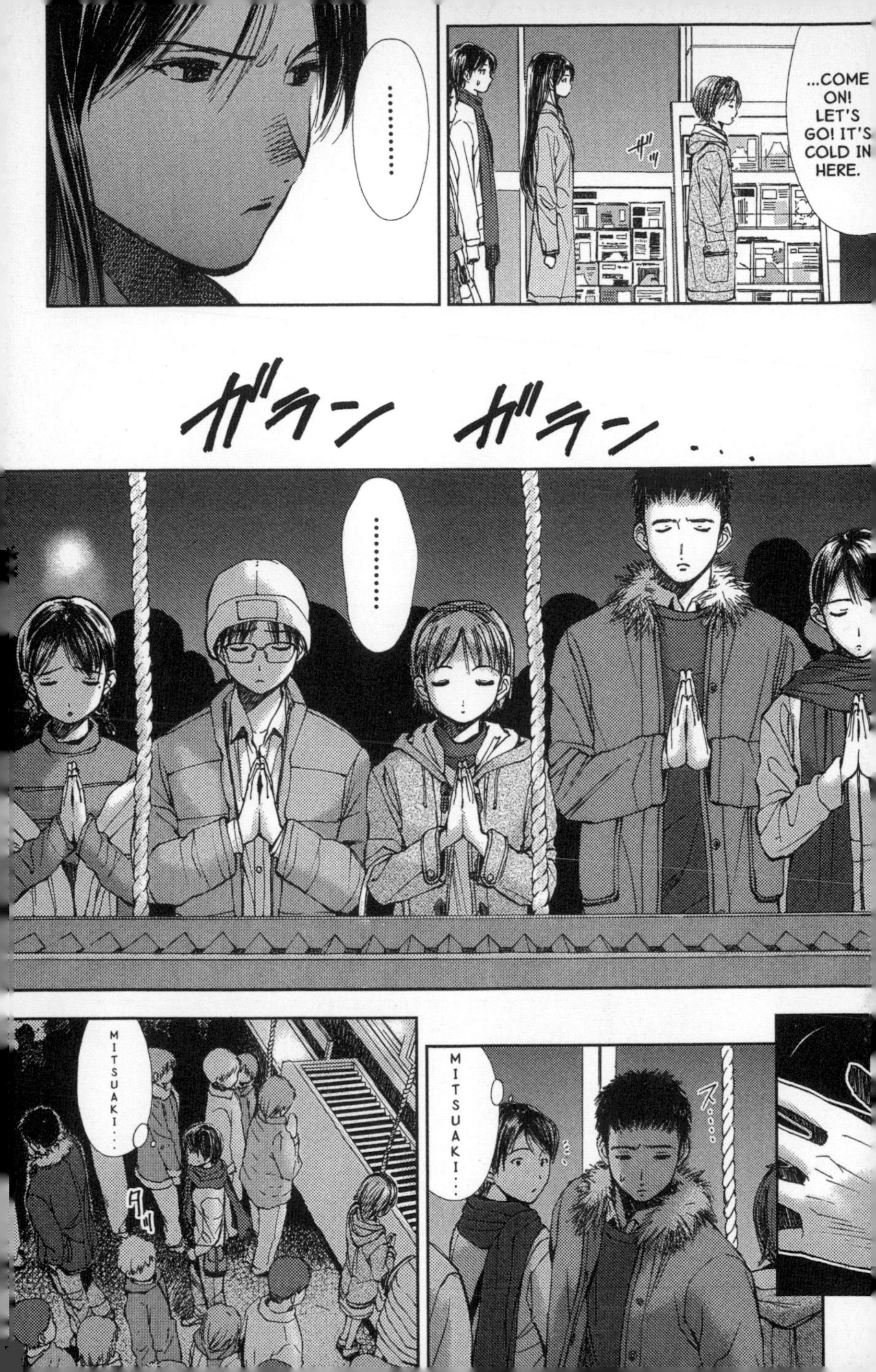
...COME ON! LET'S GO! IT'S COLD IN HERE.
ザッ
....
ガラン ガラン...
....
MITSUAKI...
MITSUAKI...

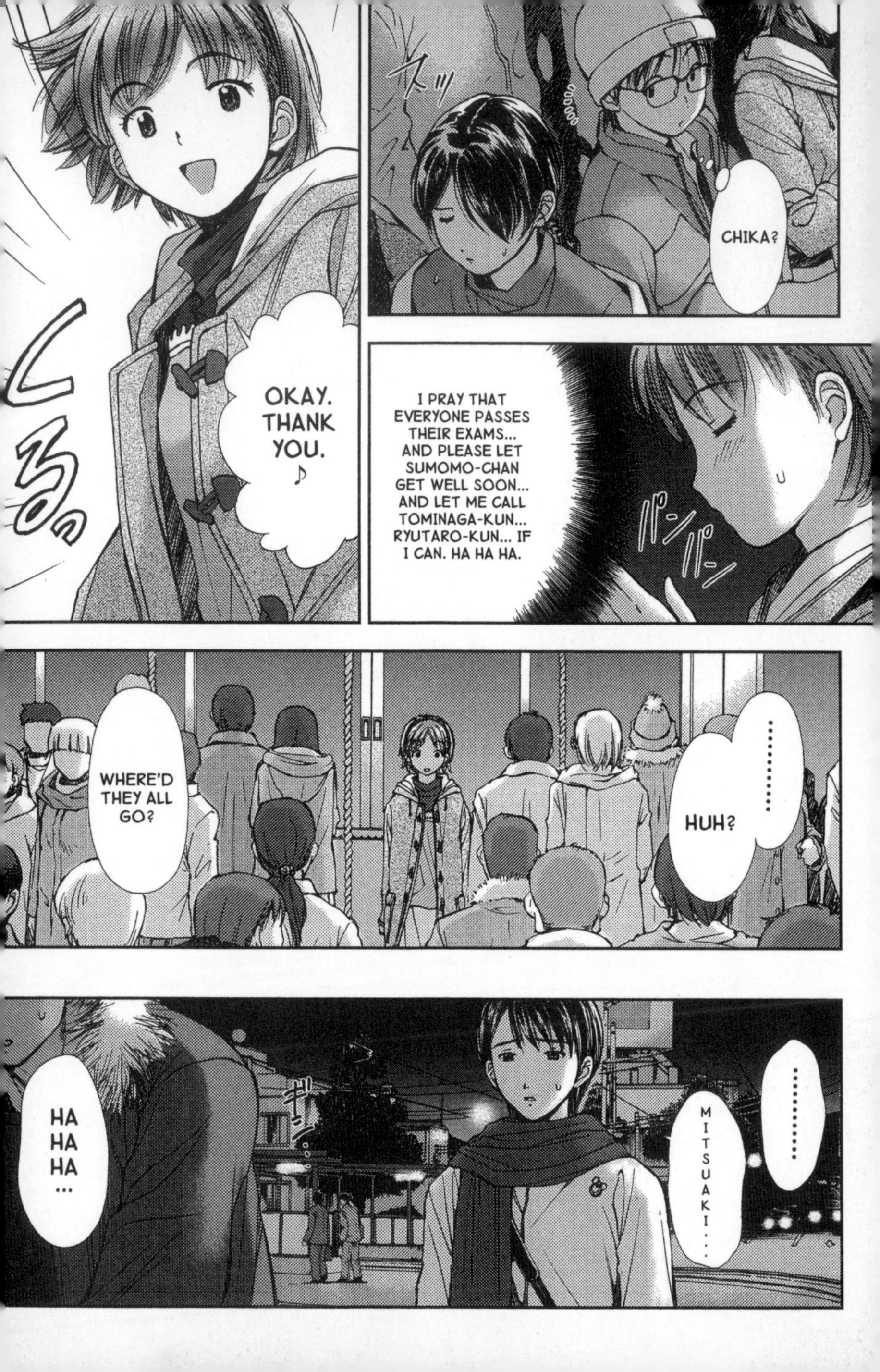
CHIKA?
I PRAY THAT EVERYONE PASSES THEIR EXAMS... AND PLEASE LET SUMOMO-CHAN GET WELL SOON... AND LET ME CALL TOMINAGA-KUN... RYUTARO-KUN... IF I CAN. HA HA HA.
OKAY. THANK YOU. ♪
....
HUH?
WHERE'D THEY ALL GO?
....
MITSUAKI...
HA HA HA...

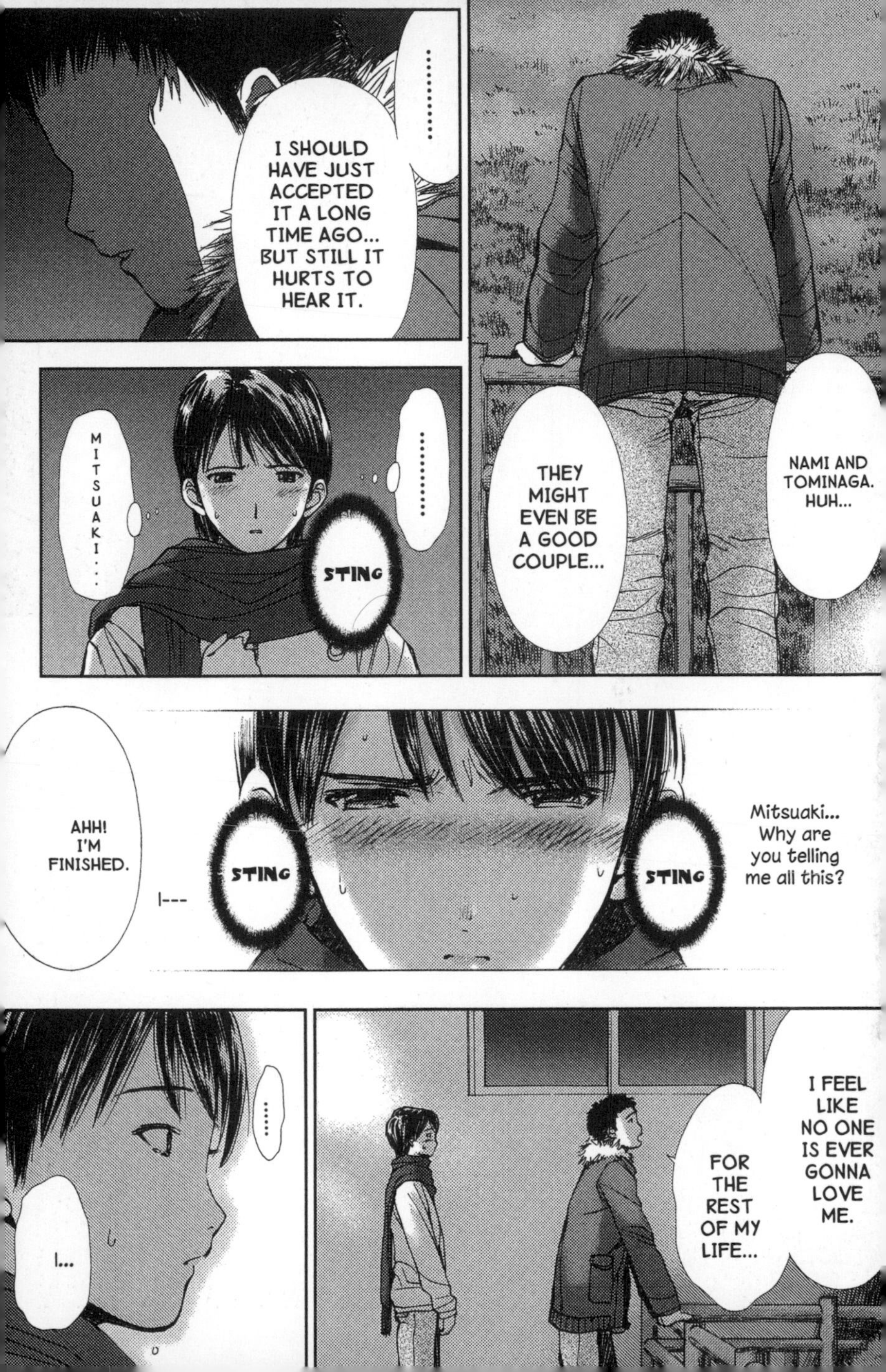
NAMI AND TOMINAGA. HUH...
THEY MIGHT EVEN BE A GOOD COUPLE...
....
I SHOULD HAVE JUST ACCEPTED IT A LONG TIME AGO... BUT STILL IT HURTS TO HEAR IT.
....
STING
MITSUAKI...
Mitsuaki... Why are you telling me all this?
STING
STING
I---
AHH! I'M FINISHED.
I FEEL LIKE NO ONE IS EVER GONNA LOVE ME.
FOR THE REST OF MY LIFE...
......
I...

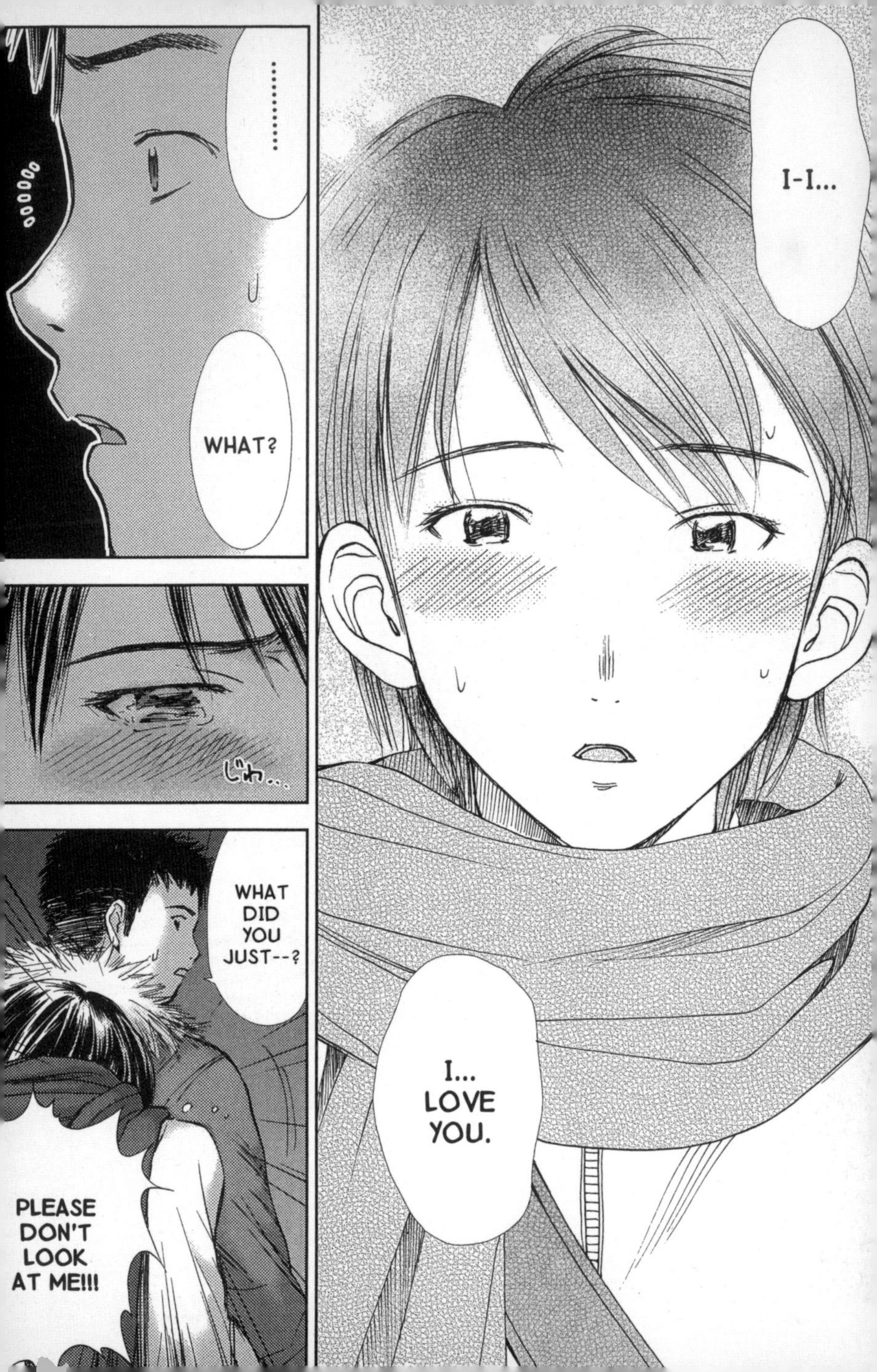
I-I...
I... LOVE YOU.
......
WHAT?
じわ..
WHAT DID YOU JUST--?
PLEASE DON'T LOOK AT ME!!!

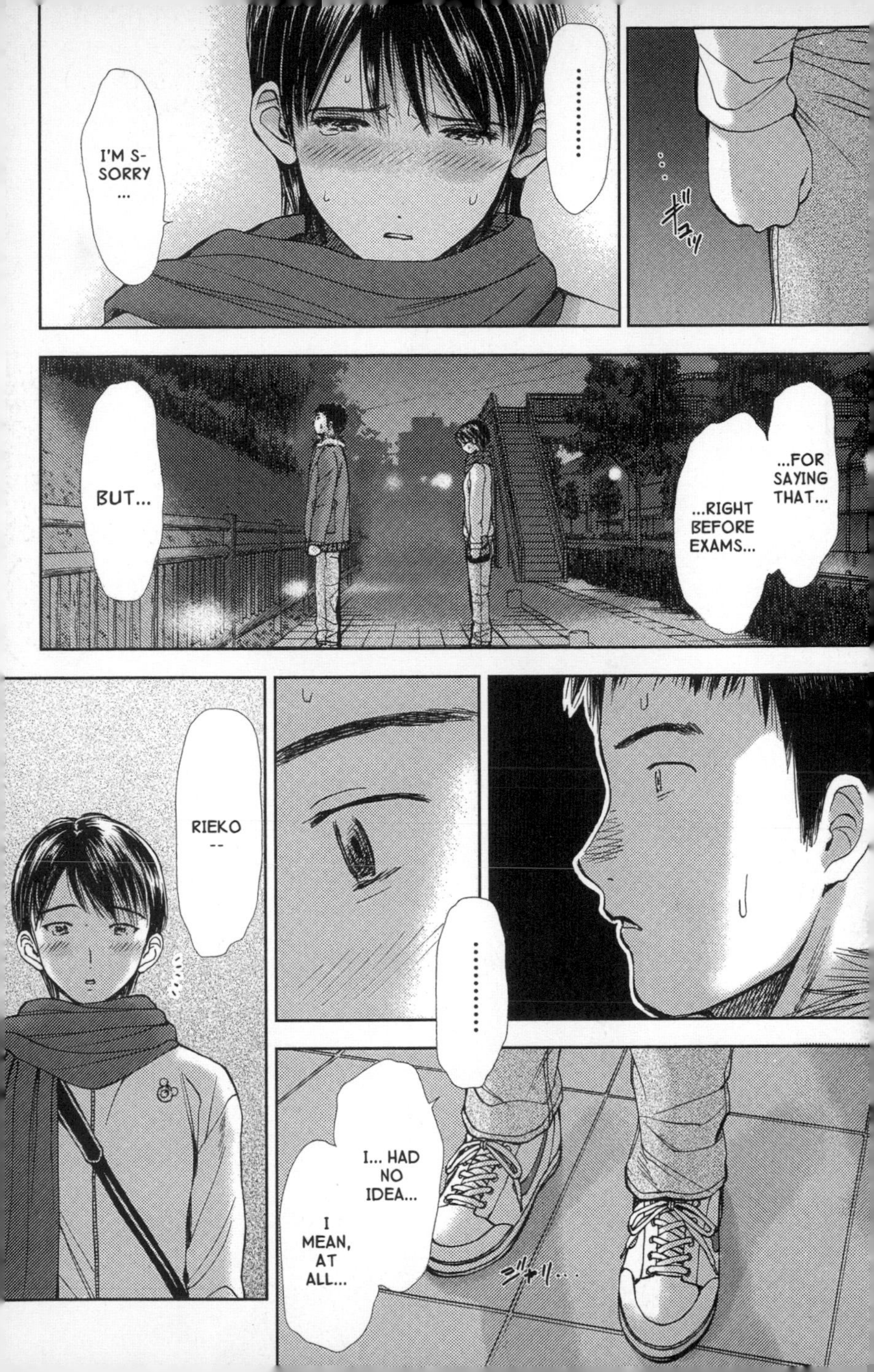
ギュッ
......
I'M S-SORRY ...
...FOR SAYING THAT...
...RIGHT BEFORE EXAMS...
BUT...
......
I... HAD NO IDEA...
I MEAN, AT ALL...
ジャリ...
RIEKO --

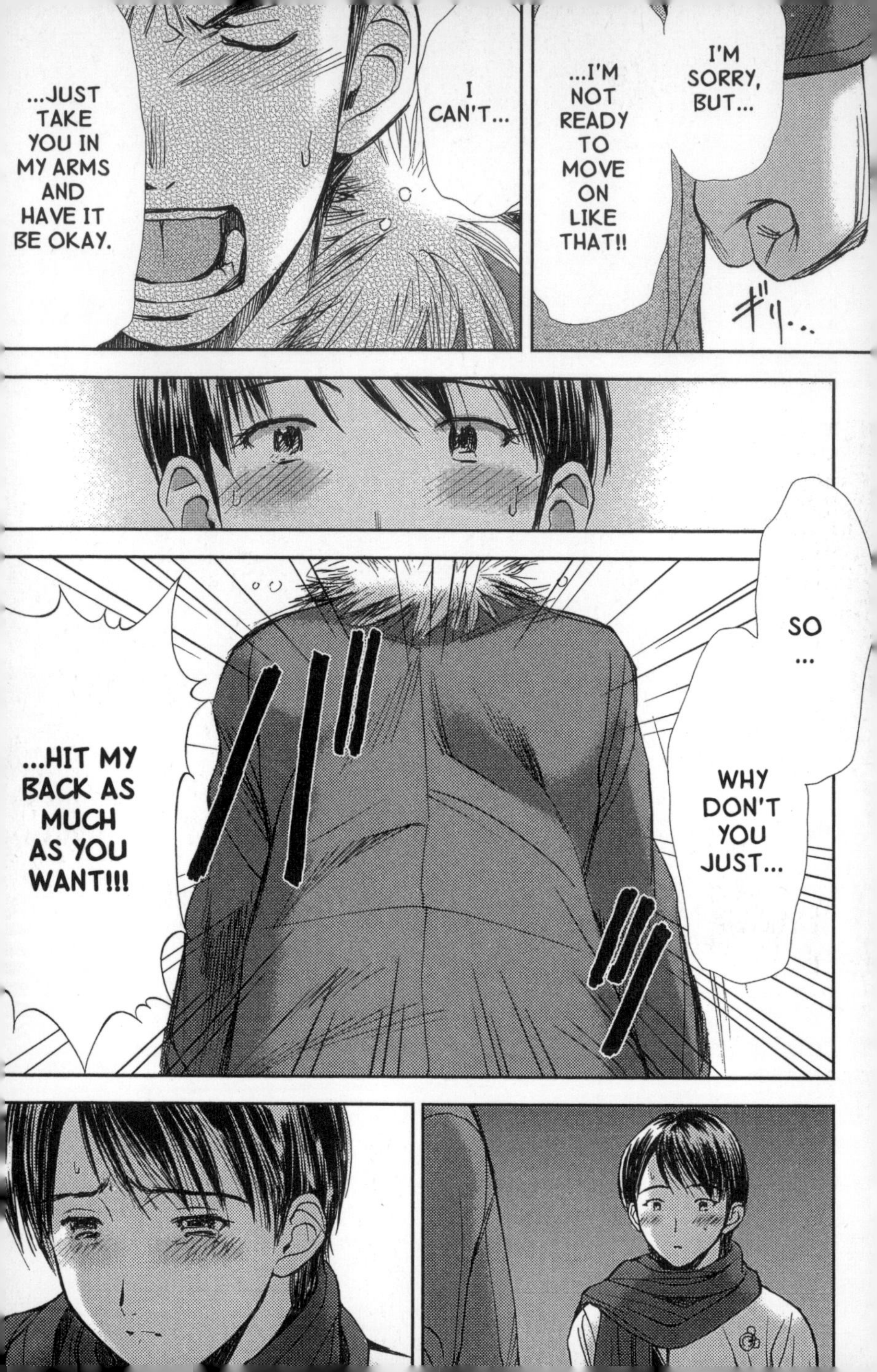
I'M SORRY, BUT...
...I'M NOT READY TO MOVE ON LIKE THAT!!
ギリ...
I CAN'T...
...JUST TAKE YOU IN MY ARMS AND HAVE IT BE OKAY.
SO ...
WHY DON'T YOU JUST...
...HIT MY BACK AS MUCH AS YOU WANT!!!

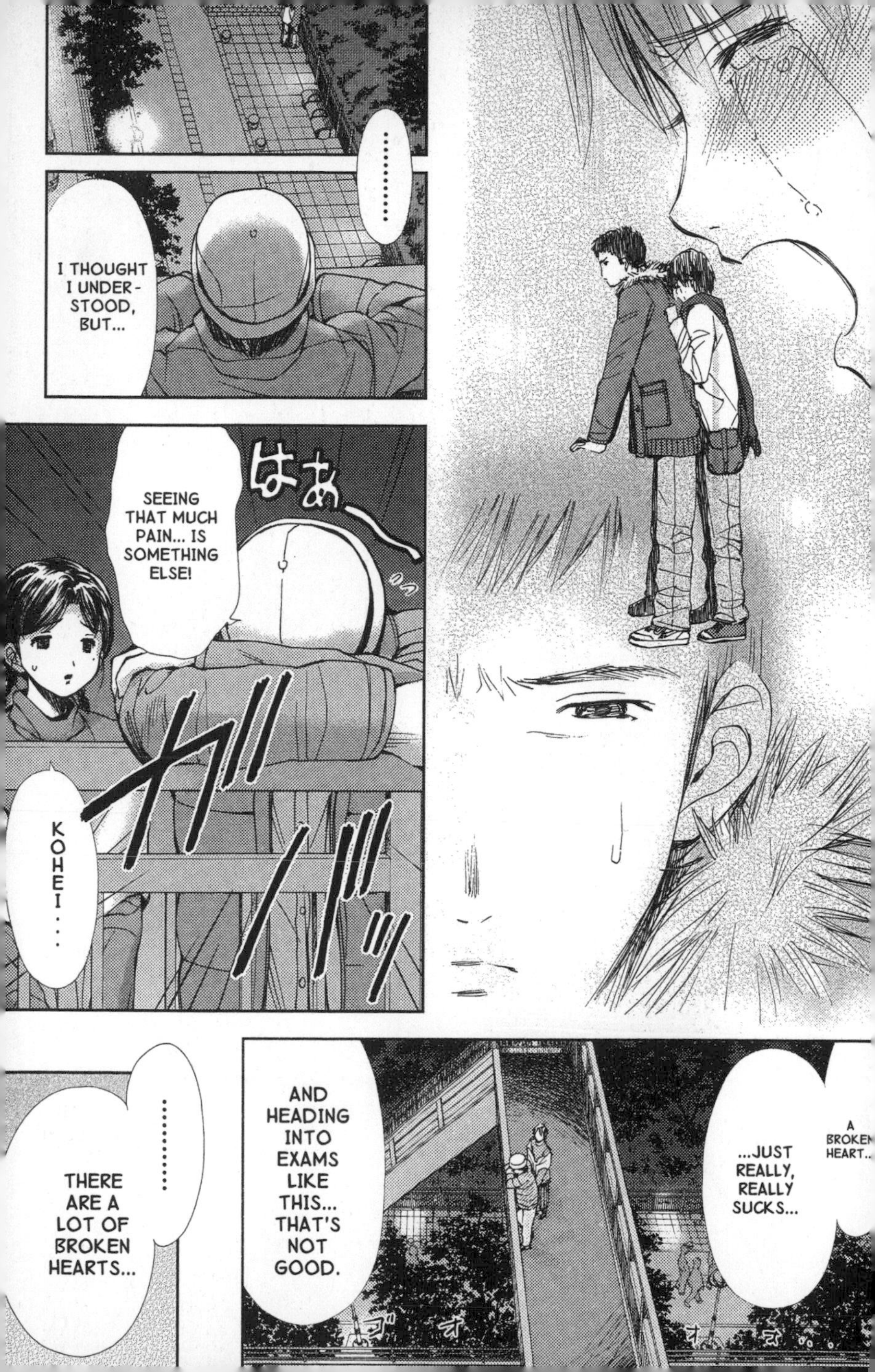
……
I THOUGHT I UNDERSTOOD, BUT...
はぁ~
SEEING THAT MUCH PAIN... IS SOMETHING ELSE!
ガバッ
KOHEI...
A BROKEN HEART...
...JUST REALLY, REALLY SUCKS...
AND HEADING INTO EXAMS LIKE THIS... THAT'S NOT GOOD.
……
THERE ARE A LOT OF BROKEN HEARTS...

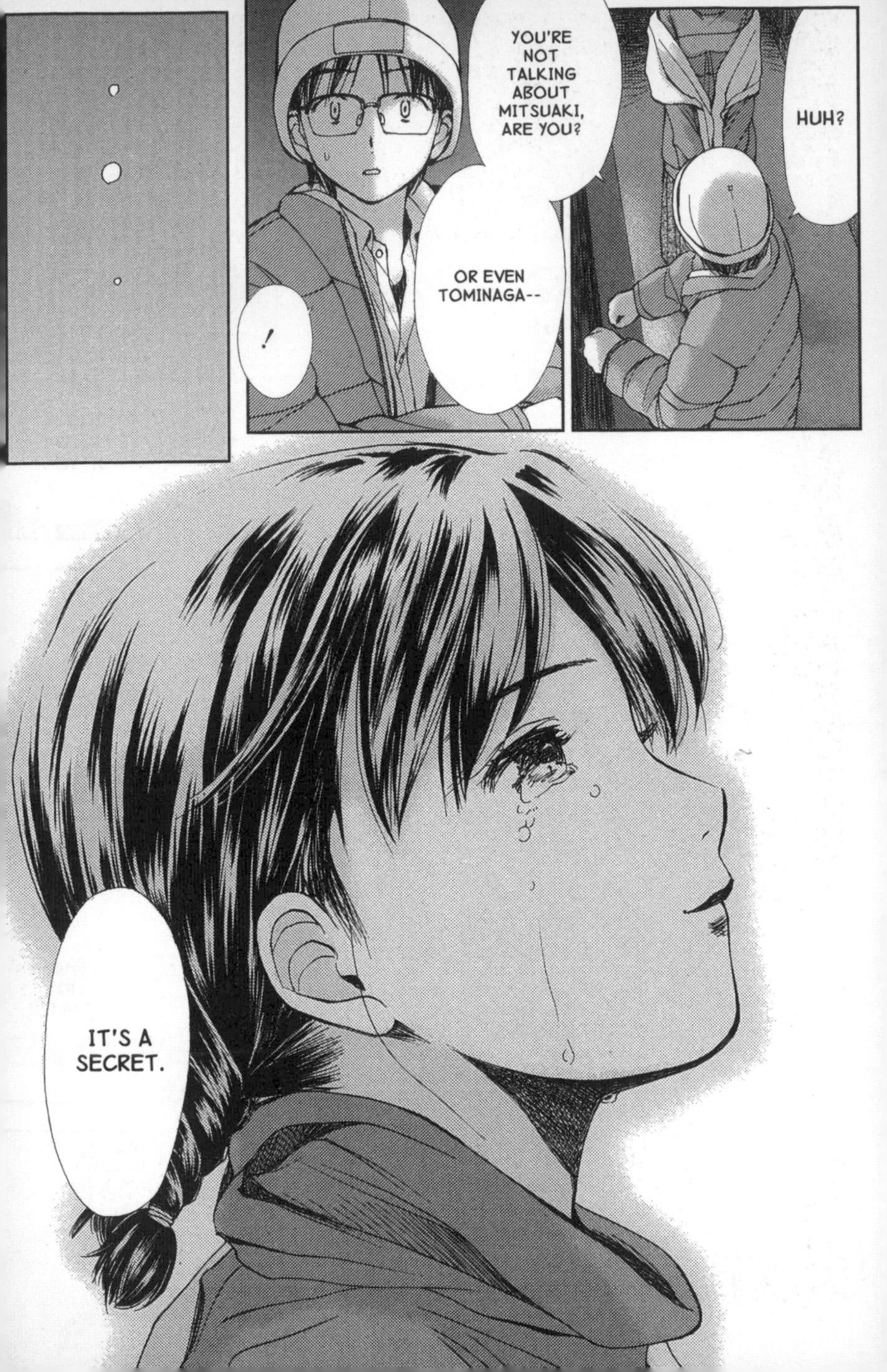
HUH?
YOU'RE NOT TALKING ABOUT MITSUAKI, ARE YOU?
OR EVEN TOMINAGA--
!
IT'S A SECRET.

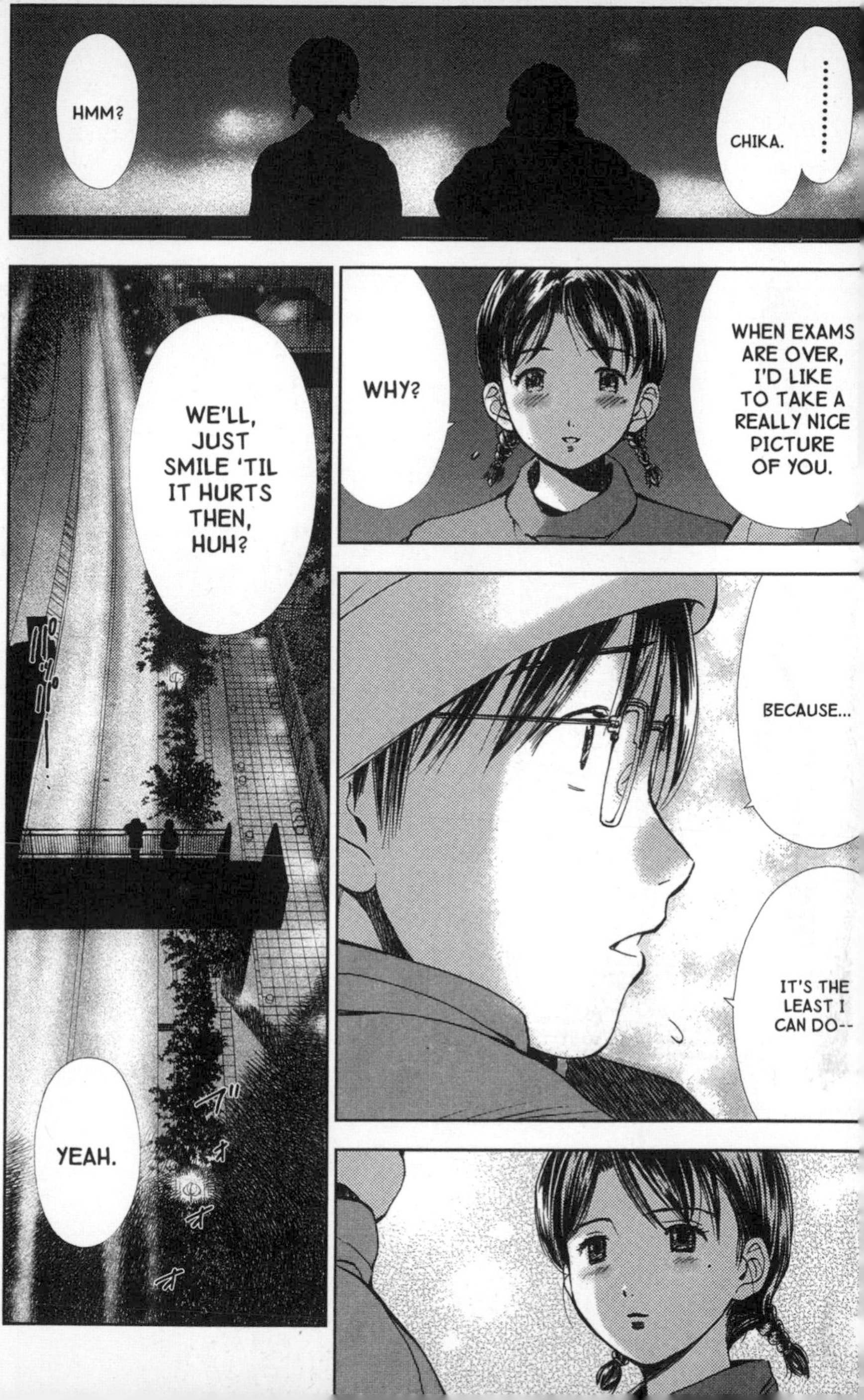

......
CHIKA.
HMM?
WHEN EXAMS ARE OVER, I'D LIKE TO TAKE A REALLY NICE PICTURE OF YOU.
WHY?
BECAUSE...
IT'S THE LEAST I CAN DO--
WE'LL, JUST SMILE 'TIL IT HURTS THEN, HUH?
YEAH.

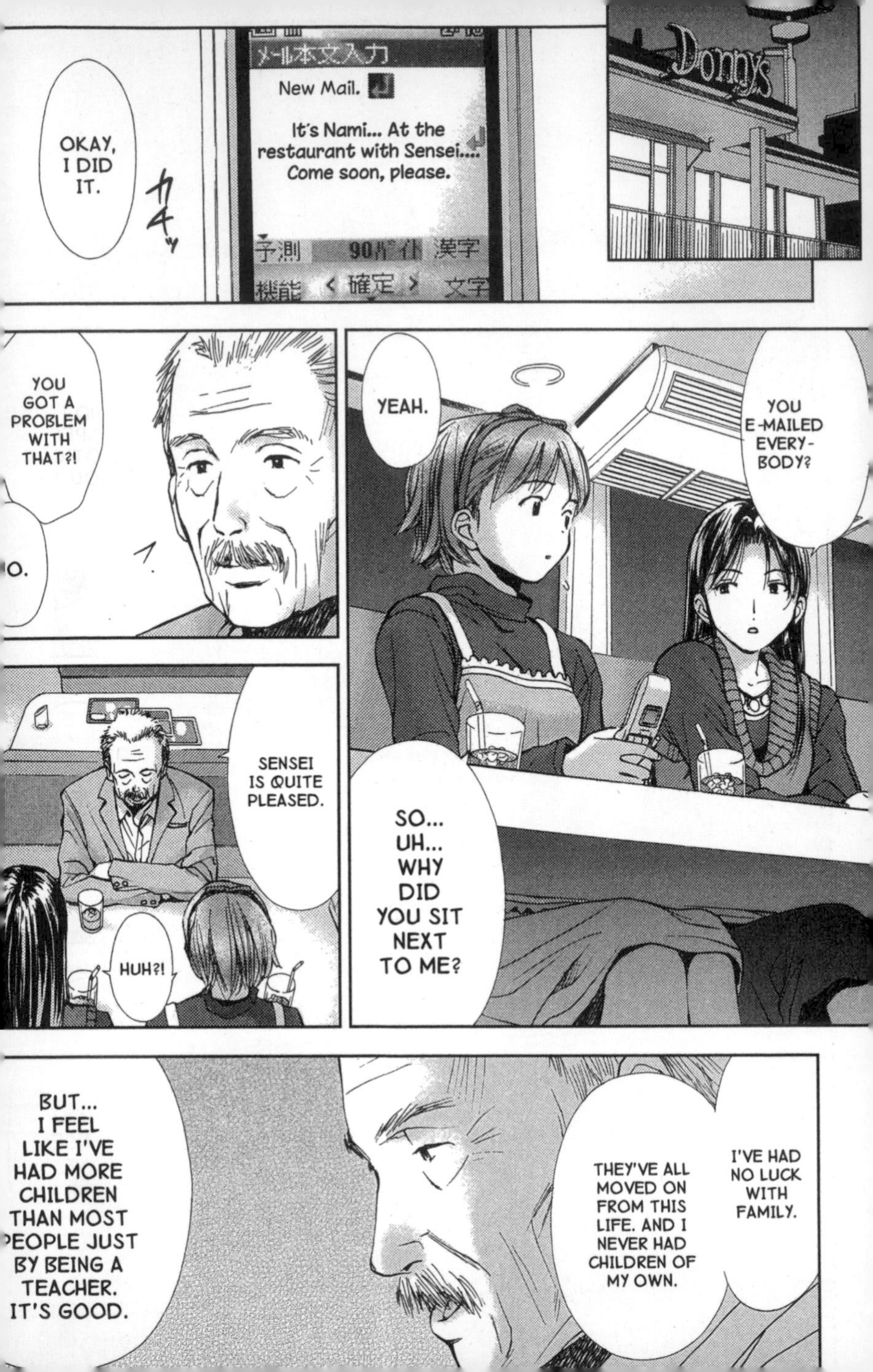
Donny's
メール本文入力
New Mail.
It's Nami... At the restaurant with Sensei.... Come soon, please.
予測 90バイト 漢字
機能 < 確定 > 文字
OKAY, I DID IT.
カチッ
YOU E-MAILED EVERY-BODY?
YEAH.
SO... UH... WHY DID YOU SIT NEXT TO ME?
YOU GOT A PROBLEM WITH THAT?!
O.
SENSEI IS QUITE PLEASED.
HUH?!
I'VE HAD NO LUCK WITH FAMILY.
THEY'VE ALL MOVED ON FROM THIS LIFE. AND I NEVER HAD CHILDREN OF MY OWN.
BUT... I FEEL LIKE I'VE HAD MORE CHILDREN THAN MOST PEOPLE JUST BY BEING A TEACHER. IT'S GOOD.

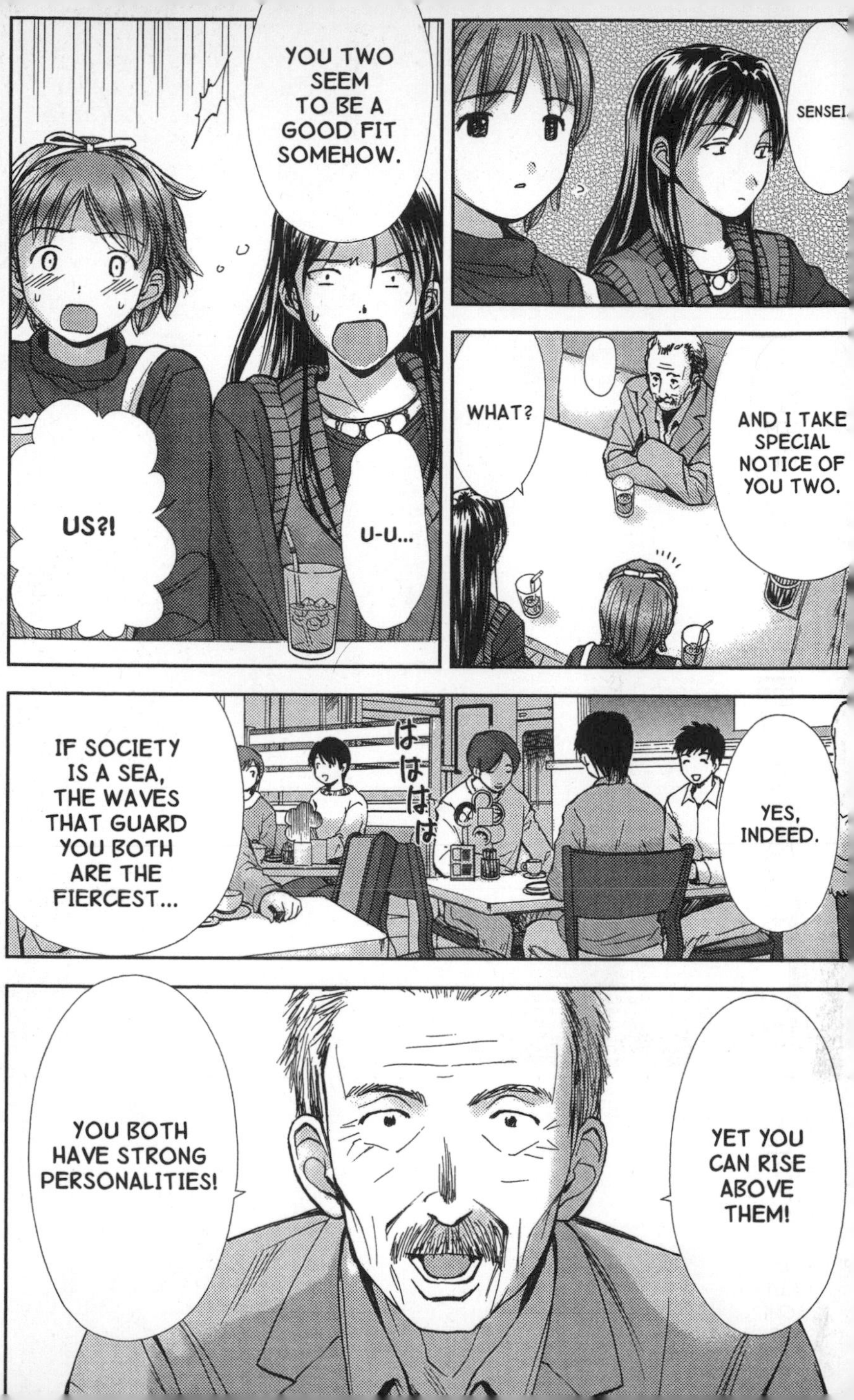
SENSEI.
AND I TAKE SPECIAL NOTICE OF YOU TWO.
WHAT?
YOU TWO SEEM TO BE A GOOD FIT SOMEHOW.
U-U...
US?!
YES, INDEED.
ははは
IF SOCIETY IS A SEA, THE WAVES THAT GUARD YOU BOTH ARE THE FIERCEST...
YET YOU CAN RISE ABOVE THEM!
YOU BOTH HAVE STRONG PERSONALITIES!

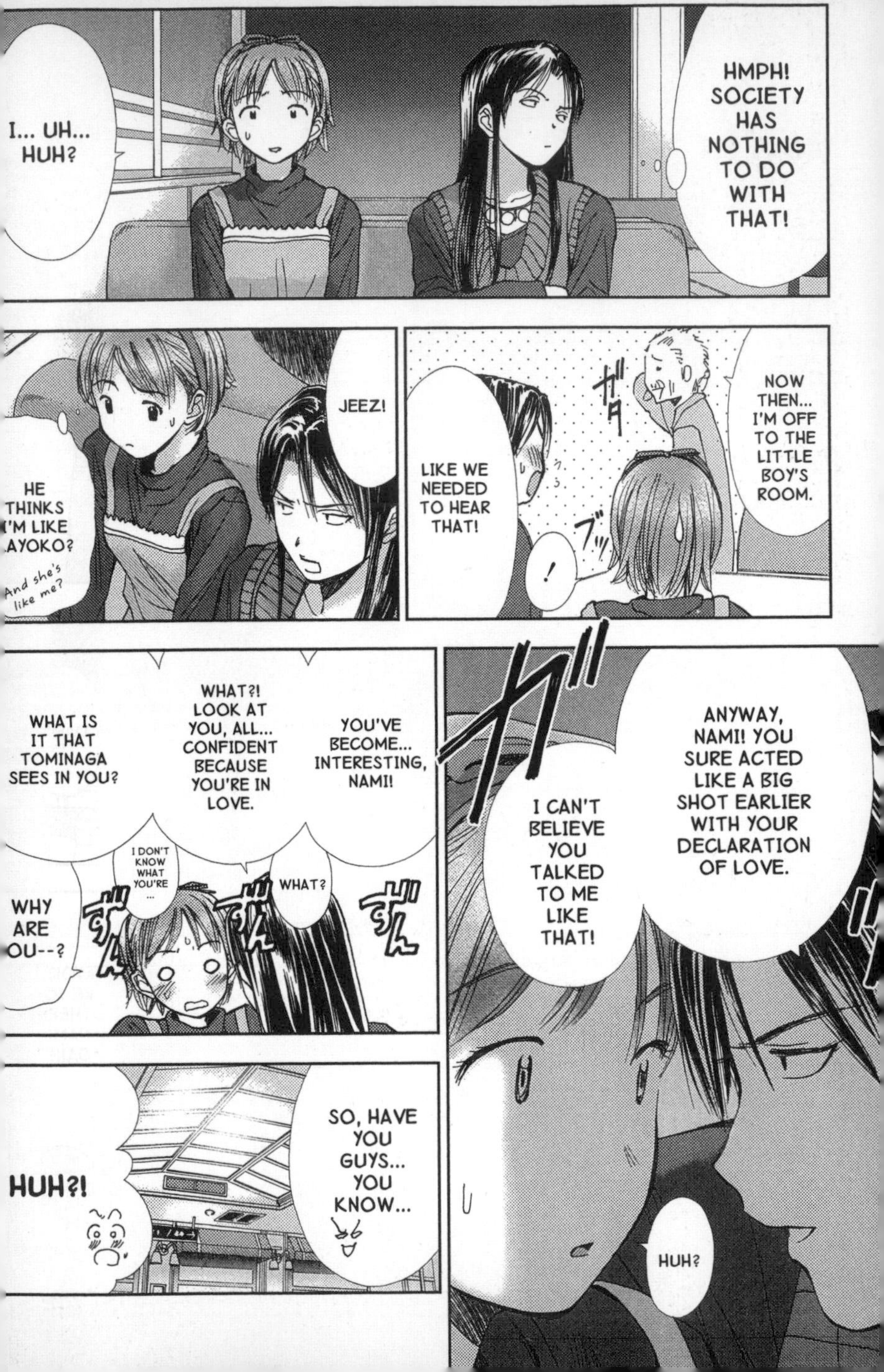

HMPH! SOCIETY HAS NOTHING TO DO WITH THAT!
I... UH... HUH?
NOW THEN... I'M OFF TO THE LITTLE BOY'S ROOM.
ガタ
LIKE WE NEEDED TO HEAR THAT!
ブツ
!
JEEZ!
HE THINKS I'M LIKE AYOKO?
And she's like me?
ガ
ANYWAY, NAMI! YOU SURE ACTED LIKE A BIG SHOT EARLIER WITH YOUR DECLARATION OF LOVE.
I CAN'T BELIEVE YOU TALKED TO ME LIKE THAT!
HUH?
YOU'VE BECOME... INTERESTING, NAMI!
WHAT?! LOOK AT YOU, ALL... CONFIDENT BECAUSE YOU'RE IN LOVE.
WHAT IS IT THAT TOMINAGA SEES IN YOU?
ずん
WHAT?
ずん
I DON'T KNOW WHAT YOU'RE ...
ずん
WHY ARE OU--?
SO, HAVE YOU GUYS... YOU KNOW...
HUH?!

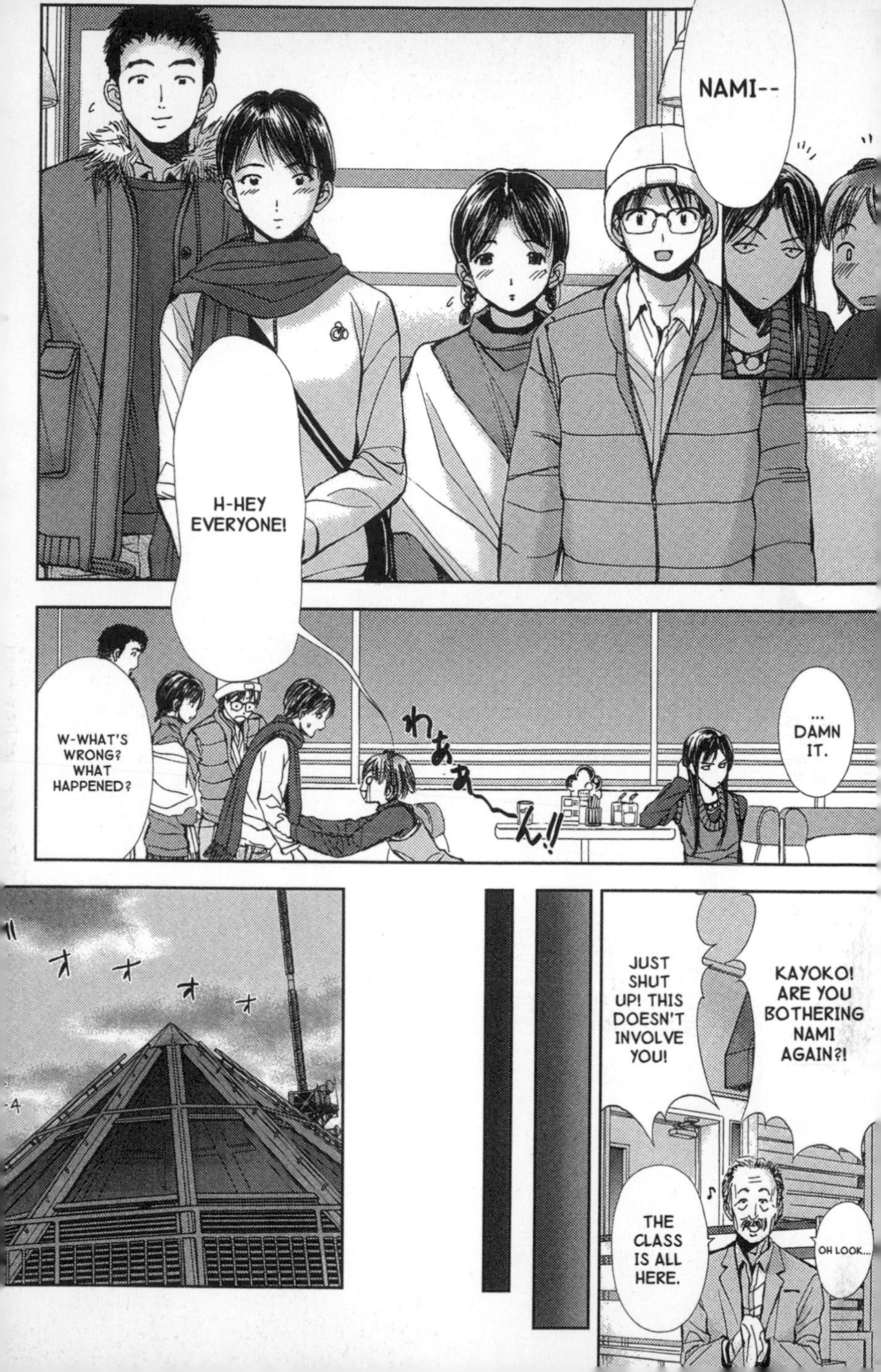
NAMI--
H-HEY EVERYONE!
... DAMN IT.
わあぁん!!
W-WHAT'S WRONG? WHAT HAPPENED?
KAYOKO! ARE YOU BOTHERING NAMI AGAIN?!
JUST SHUT UP! THIS DOESN'T INVOLVE YOU!
OH LOOK...
THE CLASS IS ALL HERE.
オオオオ

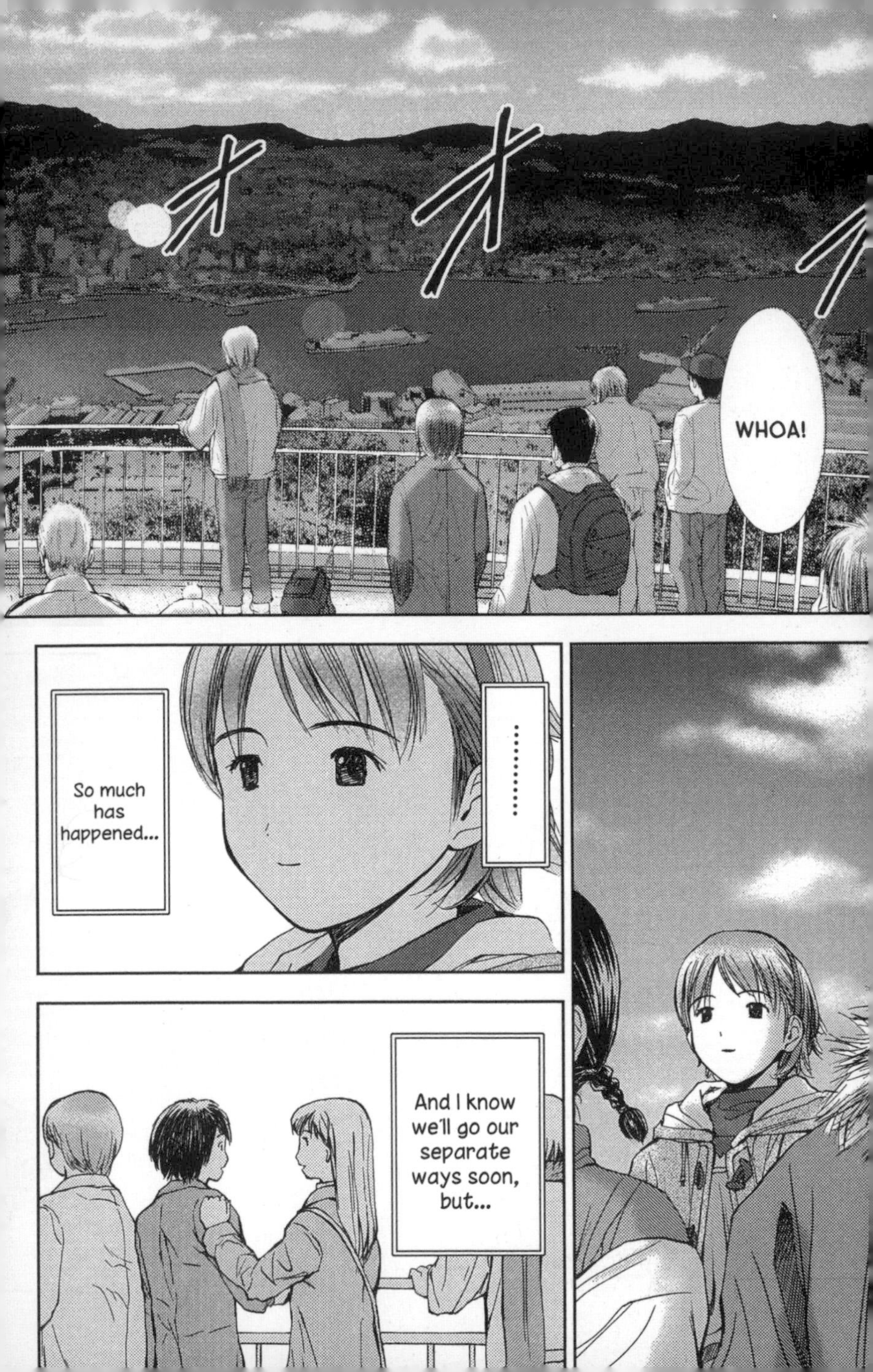
WHOA!
......
So much has happened...
And I know we'll go our separate ways soon, but...

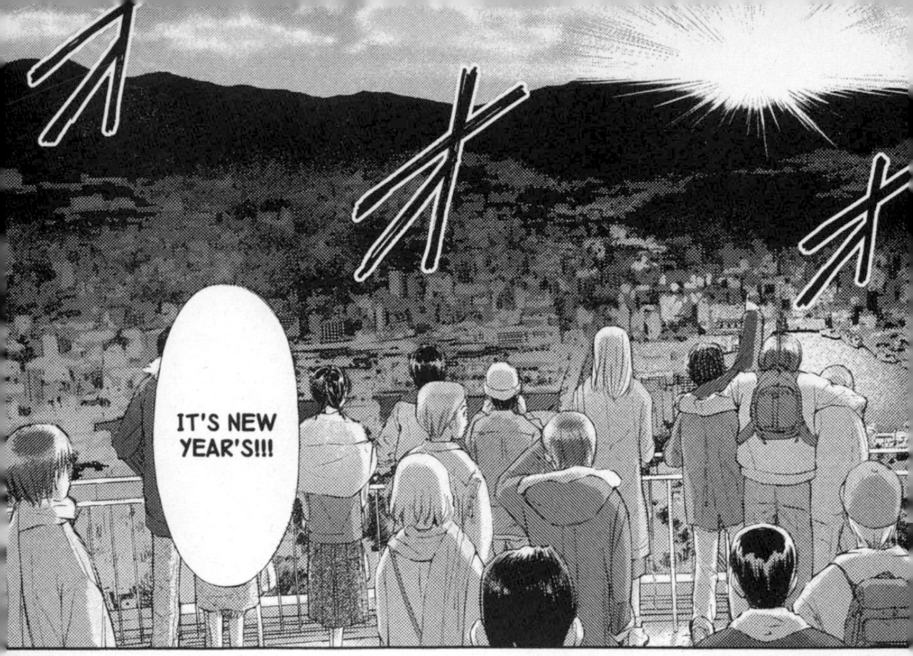
IT'S NEW YEAR'S!!!

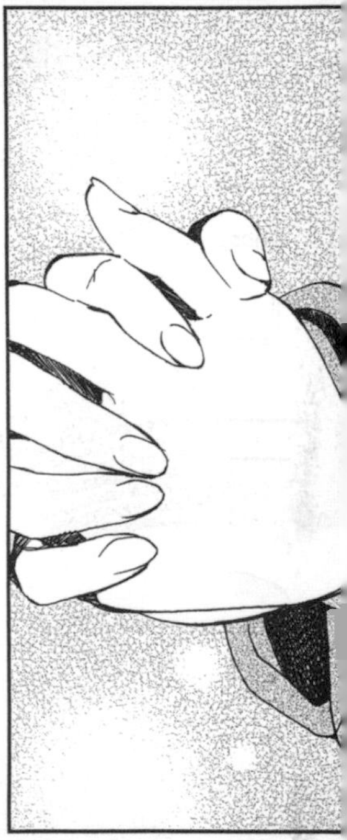

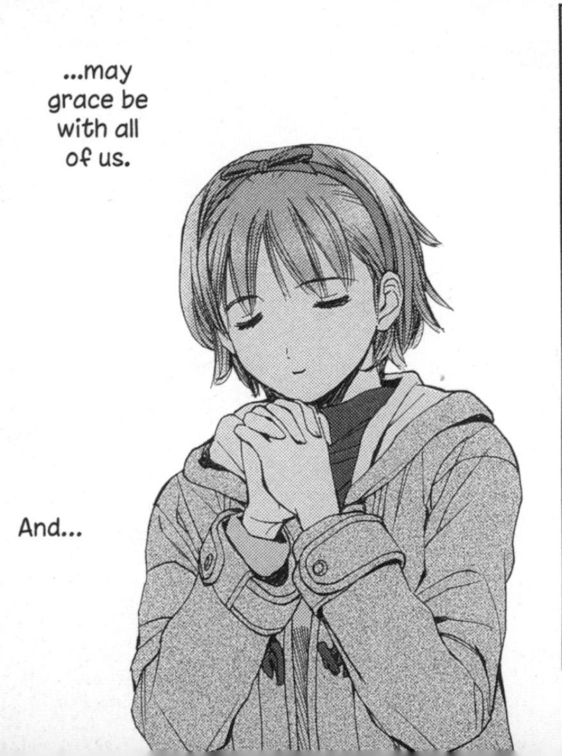
...may grace be with all of us.
And...

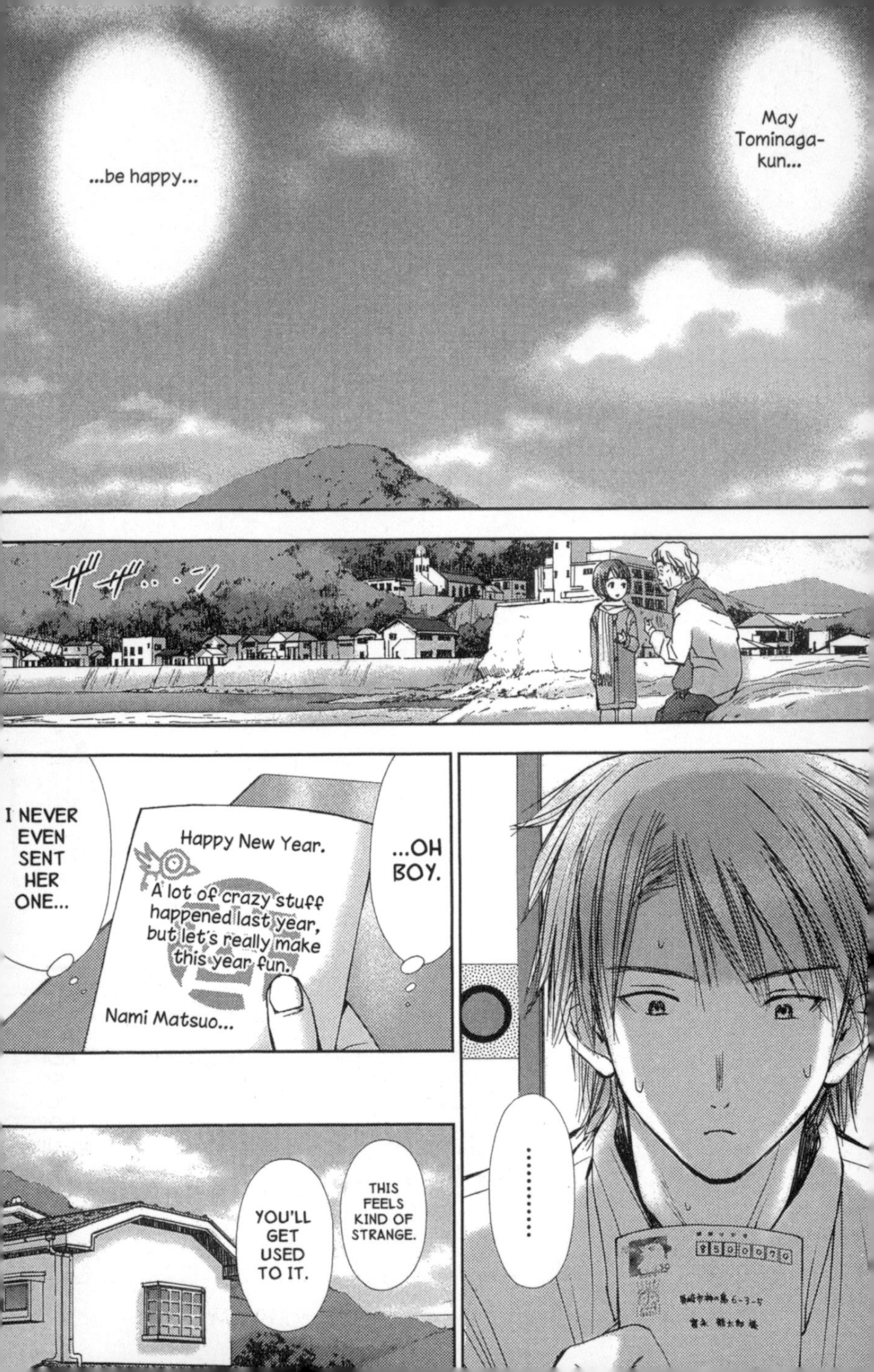
May Tominaga-kun...
...be happy...
....
...OH BOY.
Happy New Year.
A lot of crazy stuff happened last year, but let's really make this year fun.
Nami Matsuo...
I NEVER EVEN SENT HER ONE...
THIS FEELS KIND OF STRANGE.
YOU'LL GET USED TO IT.

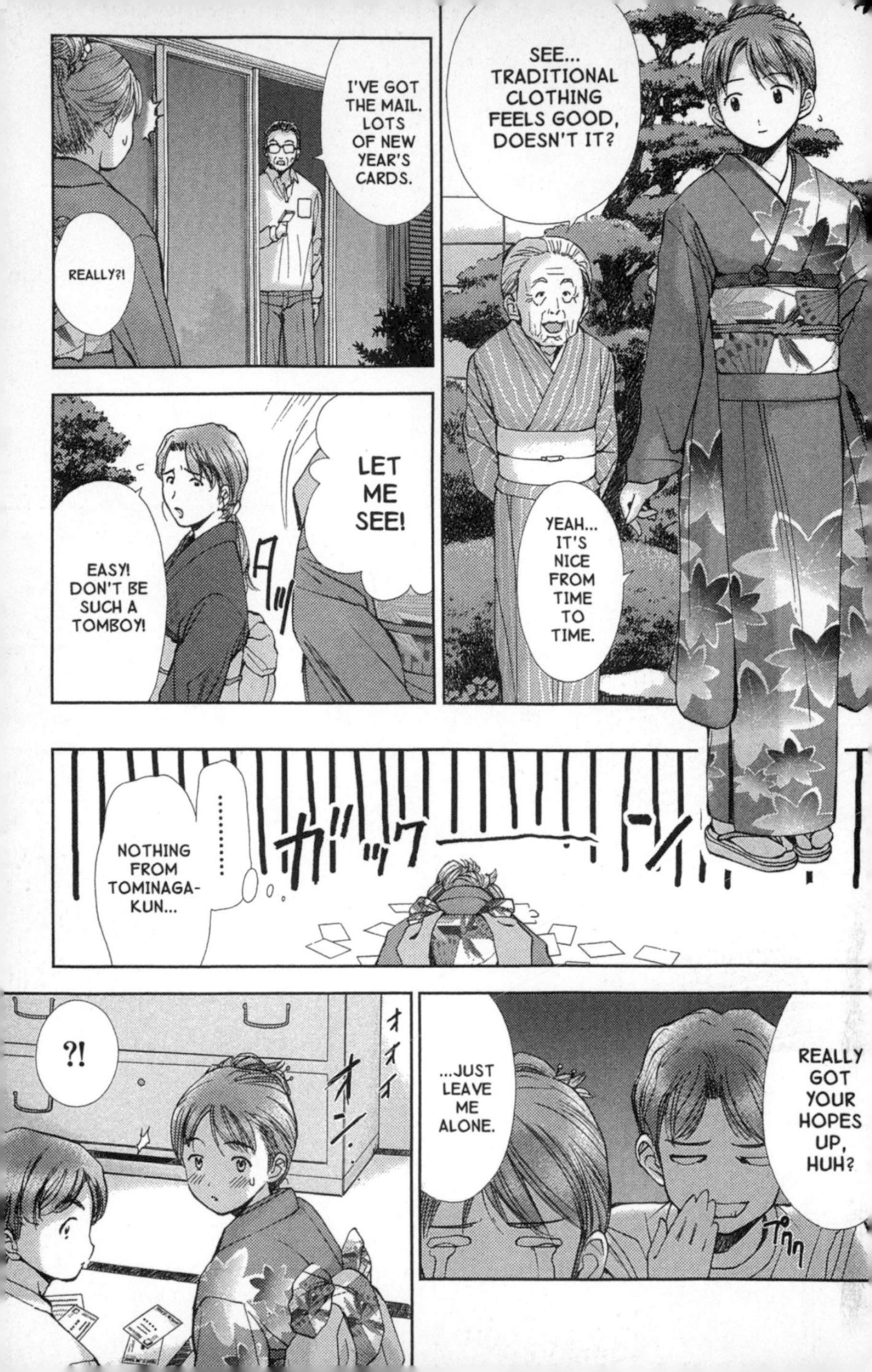
SEE... TRADITIONAL CLOTHING FEELS GOOD, DOESN'T IT?
YEAH... IT'S NICE FROM TIME TO TIME.
I'VE GOT THE MAIL. LOTS OF NEW YEAR'S CARDS.
REALLY?!
LET ME SEE!
EASY! DON'T BE SUCH A TOMBOY!
......
NOTHING FROM TOMINAGA-KUN...
REALLY GOT YOUR HOPES UP, HUH?
...JUST LEAVE ME ALONE.
?!

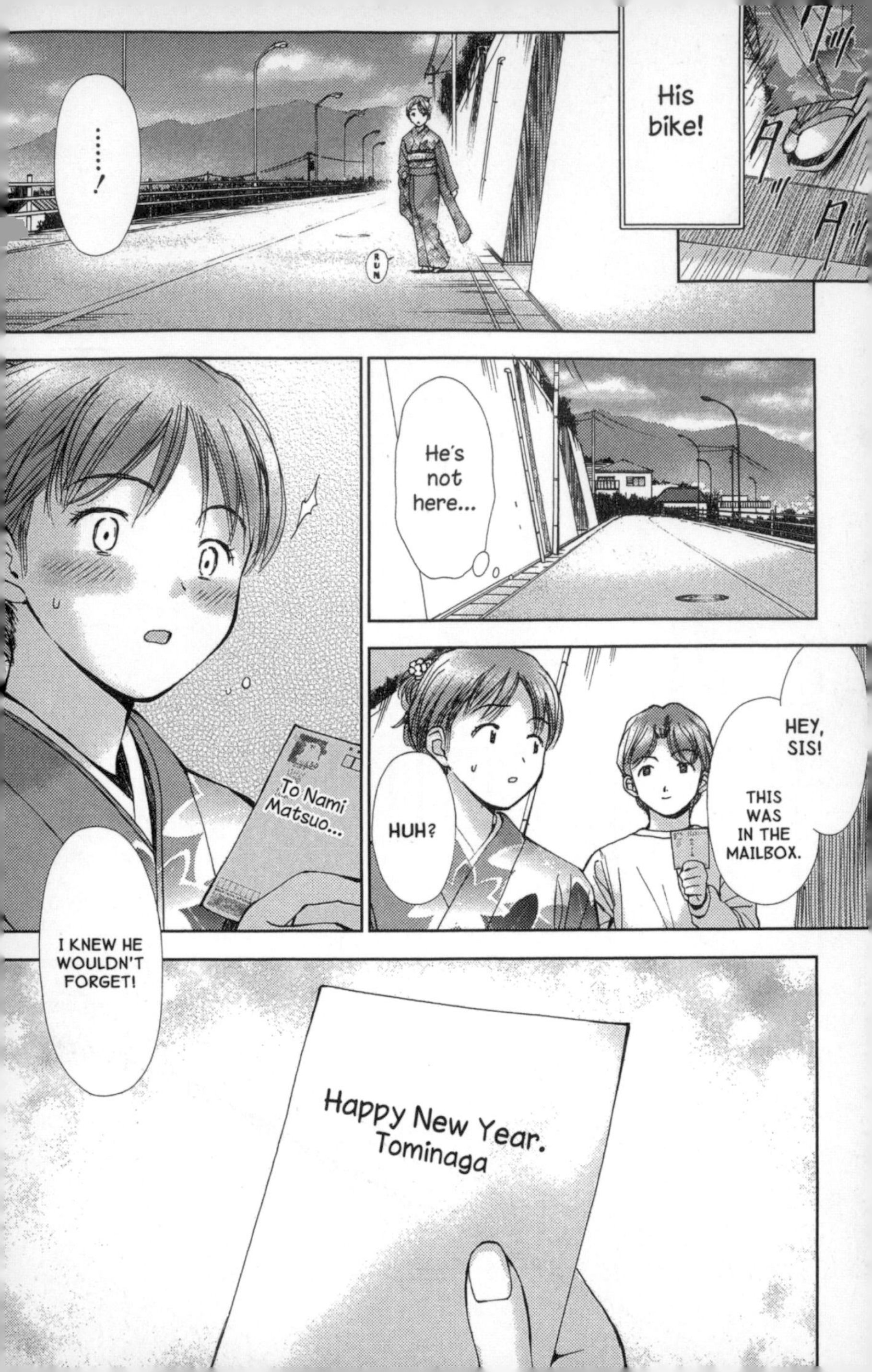

His bike!
RUN
......!
He's not here...
HEY, SIS!
THIS WAS IN THE MAILBOX.
HUH?
To Nami Matsuo...
I KNEW HE WOULDN'T FORGET!
Happy New Year. Tominaga

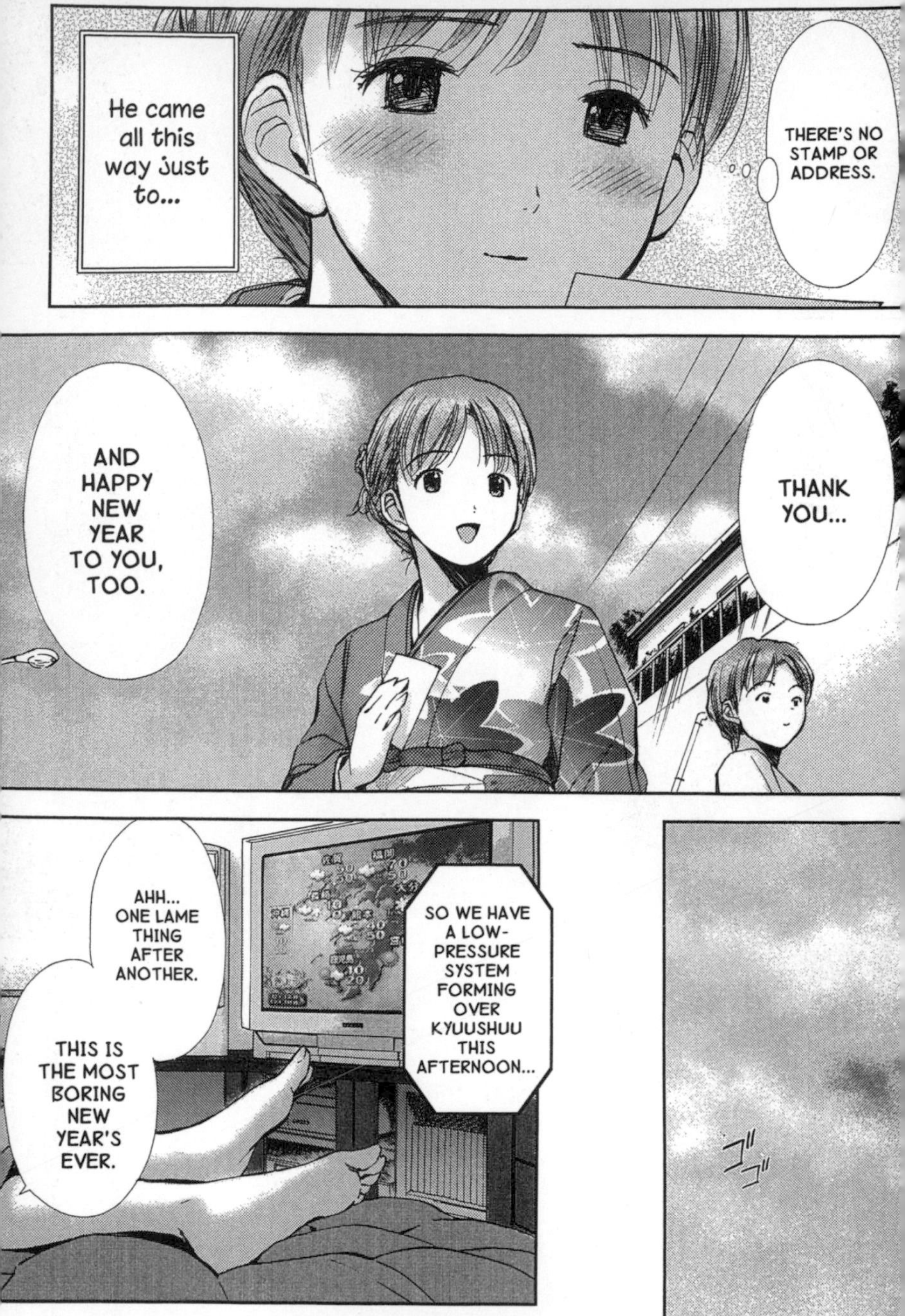
THERE'S NO STAMP OR ADDRESS.
He came all this way just to...
THANK YOU...
AND HAPPY NEW YEAR TO YOU, TOO.
ゴゴ
SO WE HAVE A LOW-PRESSURE SYSTEM FORMING OVER KYUUSHUU THIS AFTERNOON...
AHH... ONE LAME THING AFTER ANOTHER.
THIS IS THE MOST BORING NEW YEAR'S EVER.

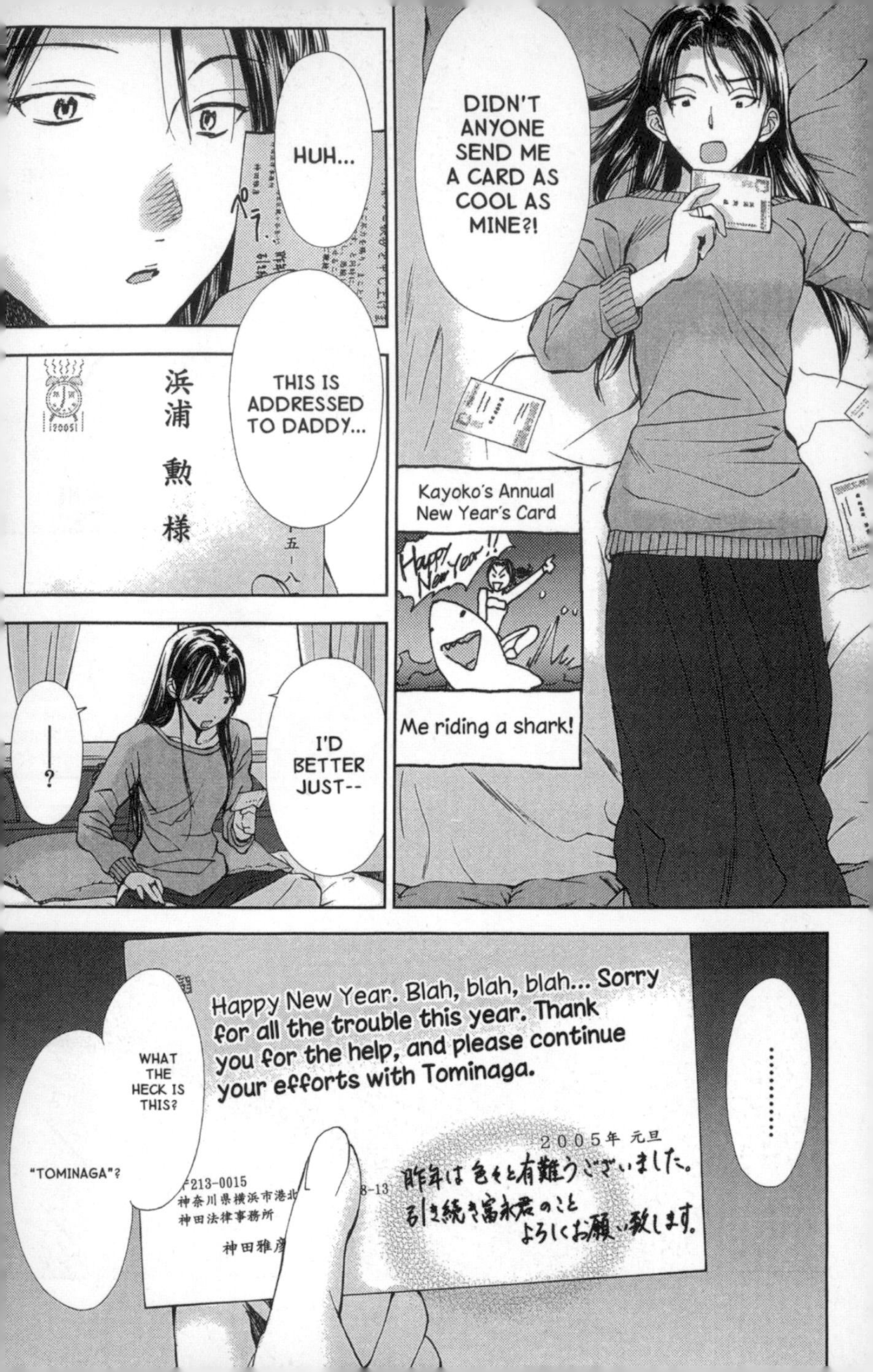

DIDN'T ANYONE SEND ME A CARD AS COOL AS MINE?!
Kayoko's Annual New Year's Card
Happy New Year!!
Me riding a shark!
HUH...
THIS IS ADDRESSED TO DADDY...
浜浦 勲 様
2005
I'D BETTER JUST--
―?
....
Happy New Year. Blah, blah, blah... Sorry for all the trouble this year. Thank you for the help, and please continue your efforts with Tominaga.
2005年 元旦
昨年は色々と有難うございました。
引き続き富永君のこと
よろしくお願い致します。
〒213-0015
神奈川県横浜市港北
8-13
神田法律事務所
神田雅彦
WHAT THE HECK IS THIS?
"TOMINAGA"?

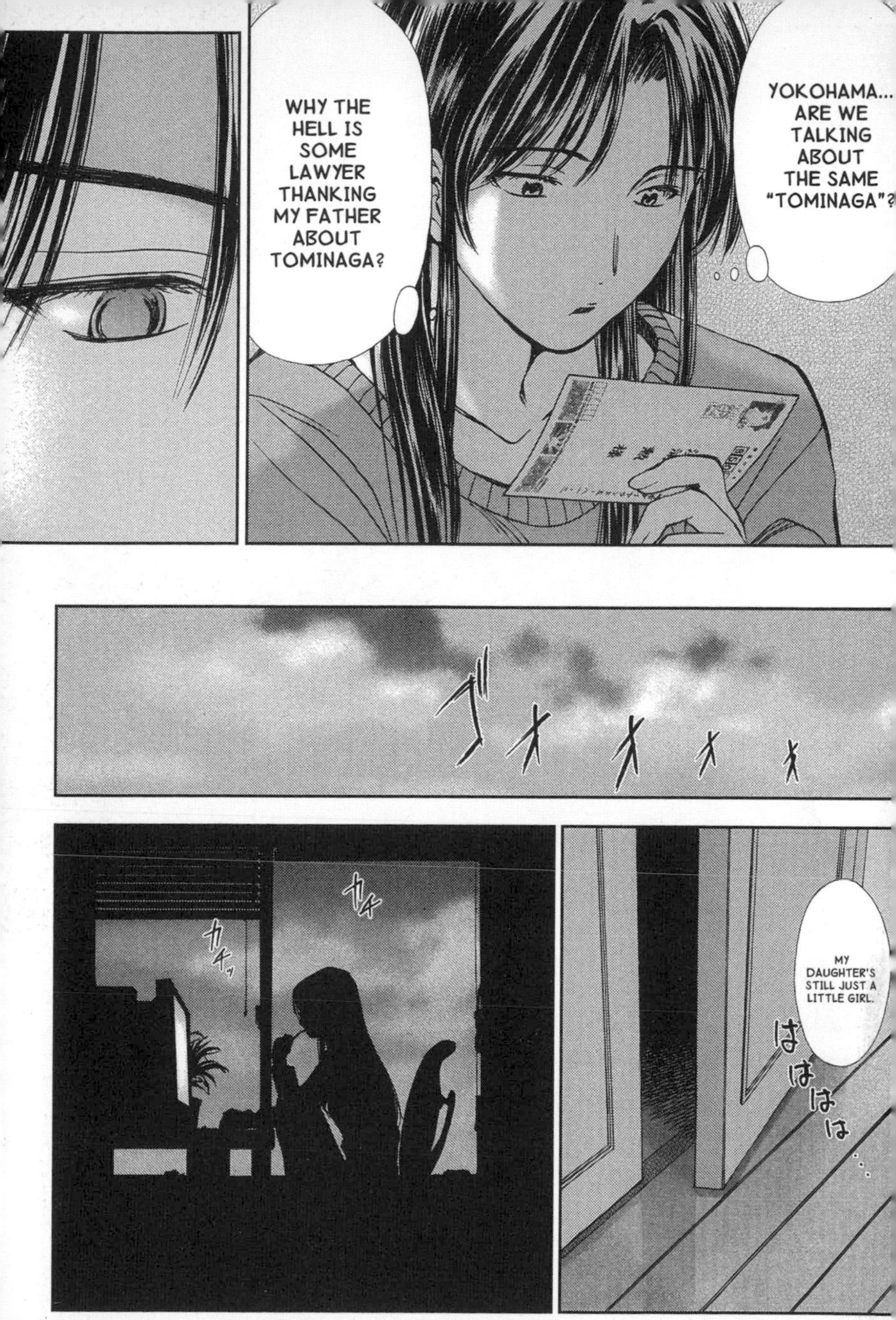
YOKOHAMA... ARE WE TALKING ABOUT THE SAME "TOMINAGA"?
WHY THE HELL IS SOME LAWYER THANKING MY FATHER ABOUT TOMINAGA?
MY DAUGHTER'S STILL JUST A LITTLE GIRL.
はははは...
カチ
カチッ

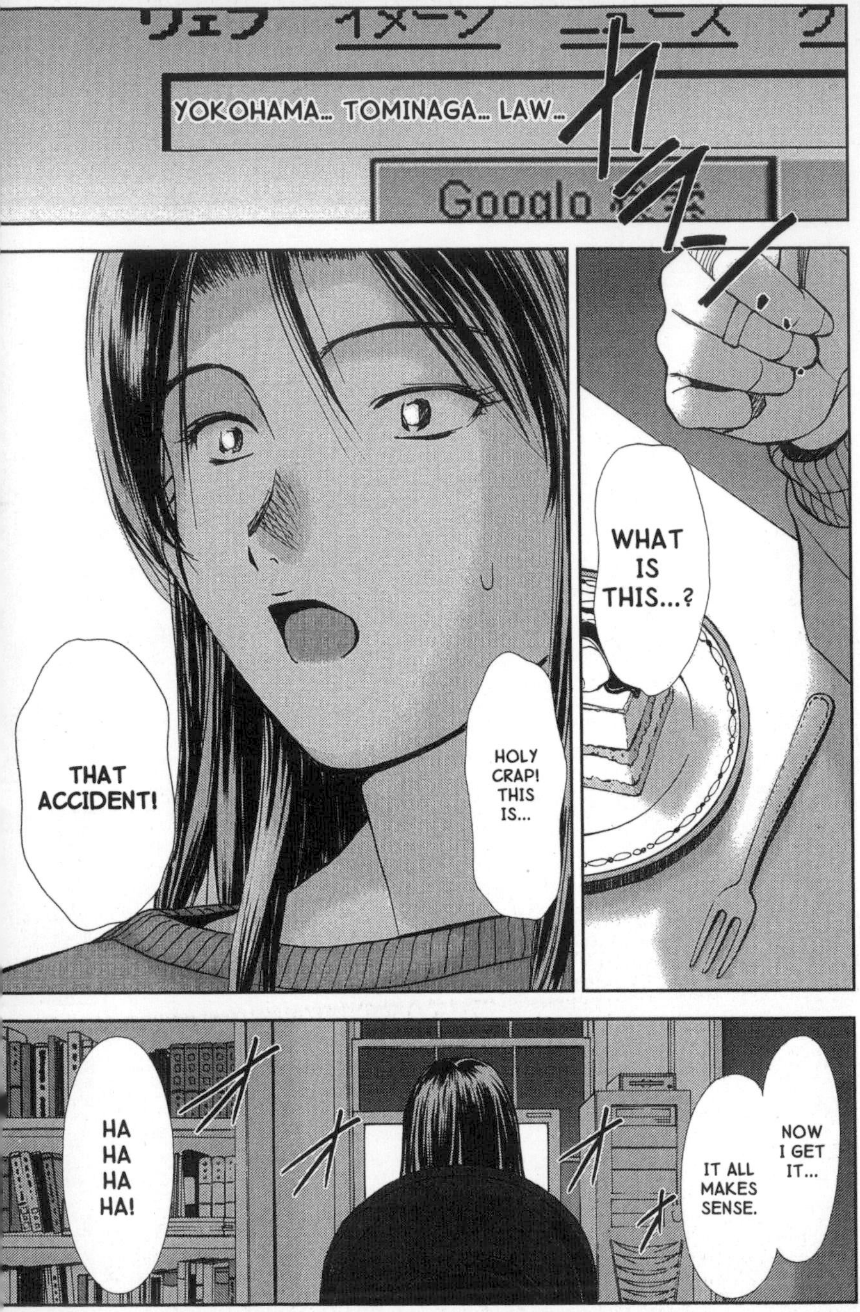
ウェブ イメージ ニュース
YOKOHAMA... TOMINAGA... LAW...
Googlo
WHAT IS THIS...?
HOLY CRAP! THIS IS...
THAT ACCIDENT!
NOW I GET IT...
IT ALL MAKES SENSE.
HA HA HA HA!

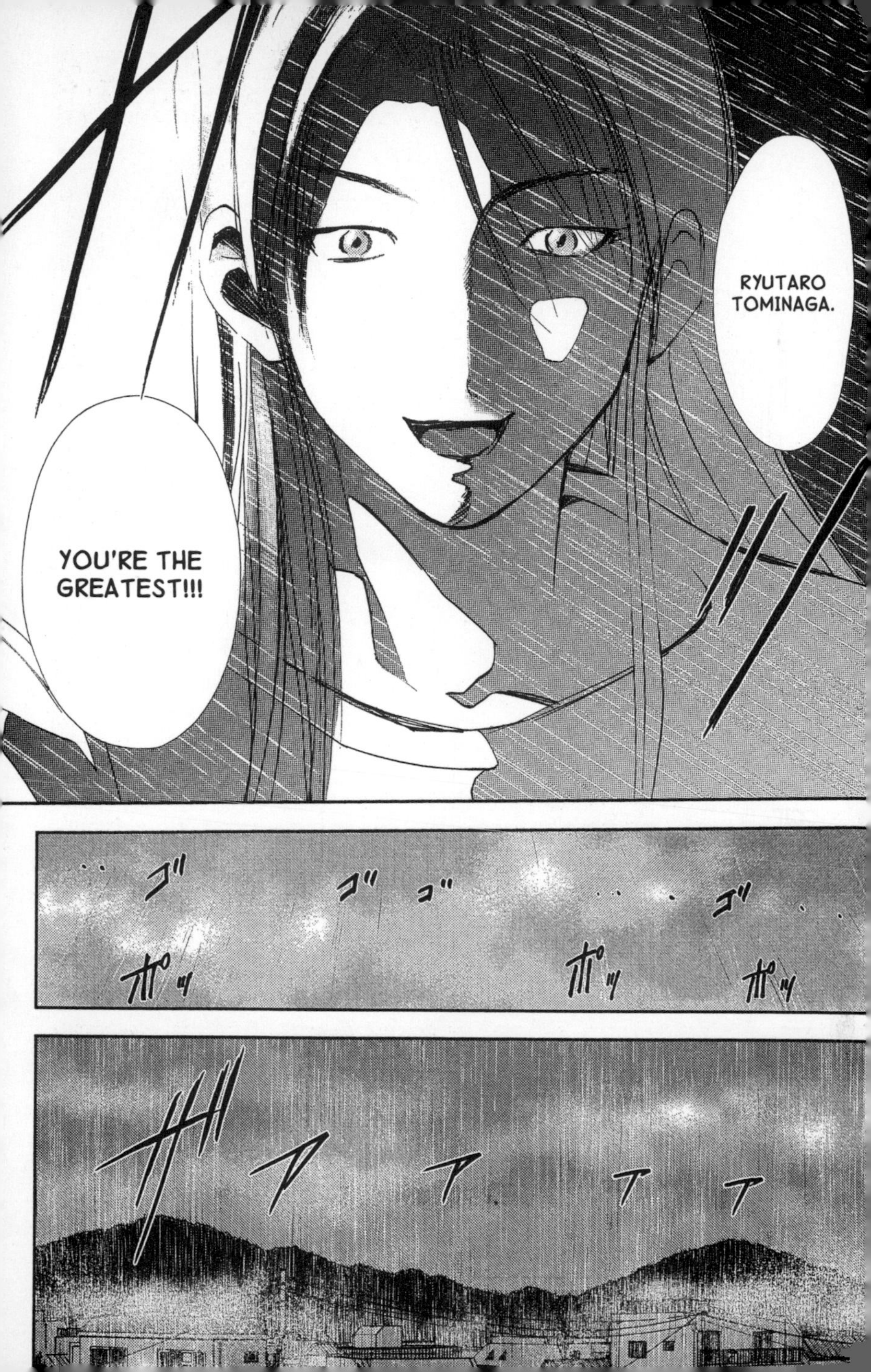
RYUTARO TOMINAGA.
YOU'RE THE GREATEST!!!
ゴ
ゴゴ
ゴ
ポッ
ポッ
ポッ
ザアアアア

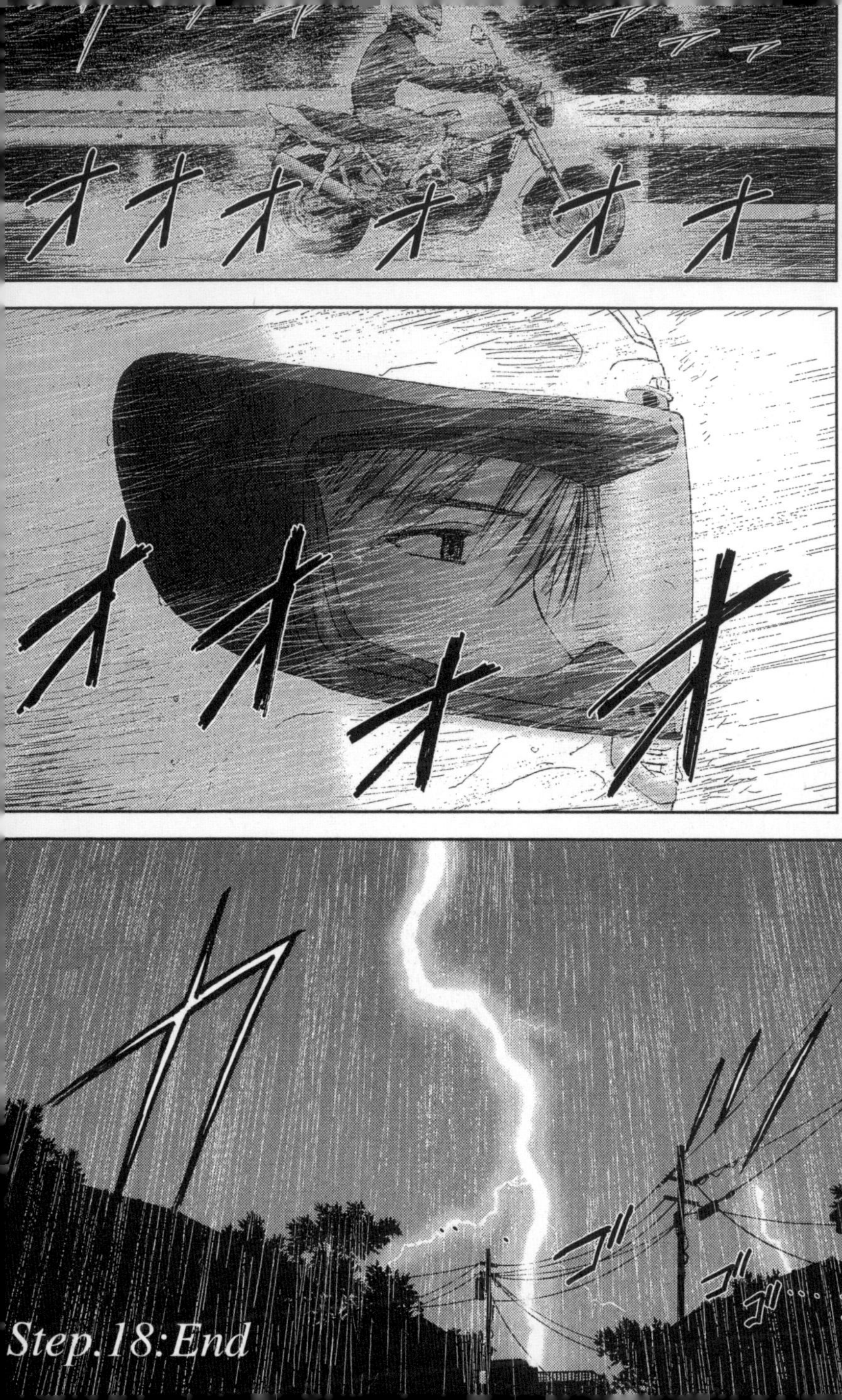
オオオオオオ
オオオオ
カッ
ゴゴゴ…ゴ
Step.18:End

Step 19: The Past Will Always Find You

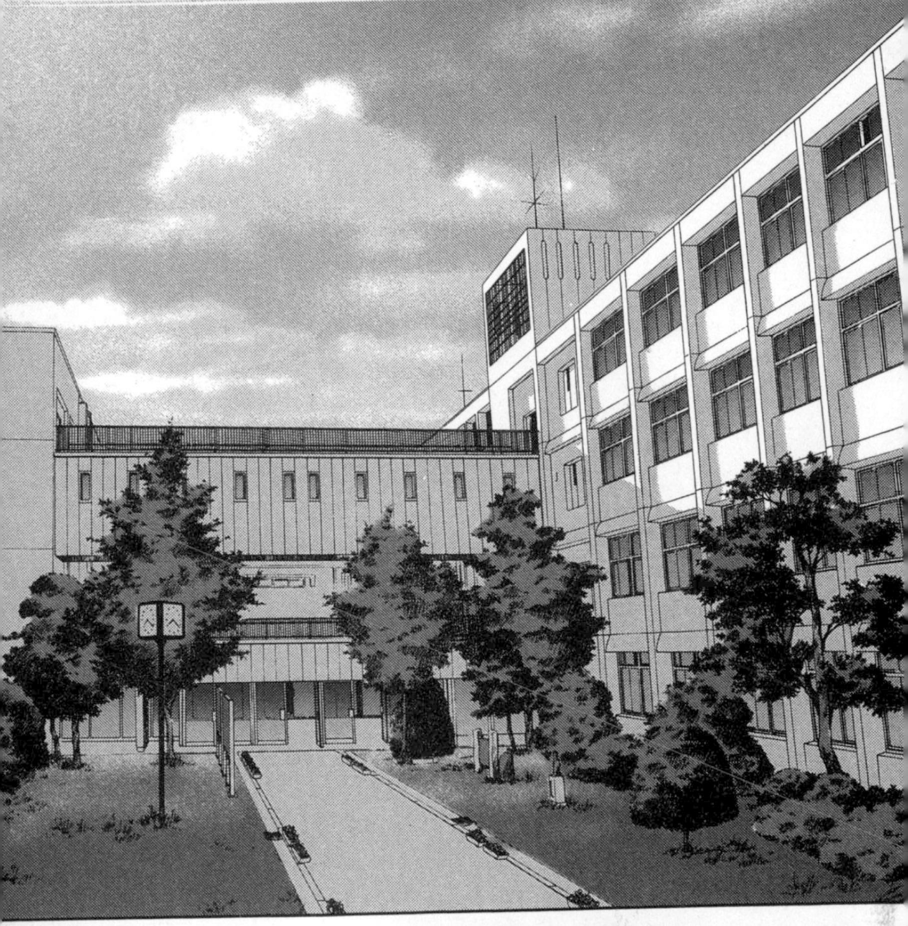

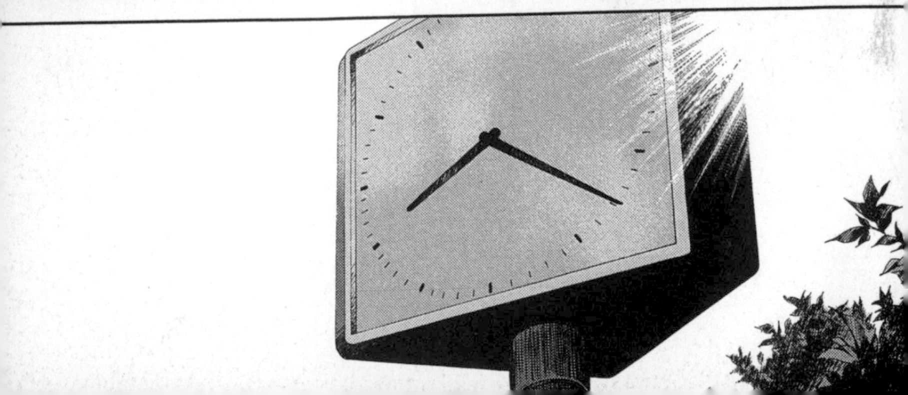

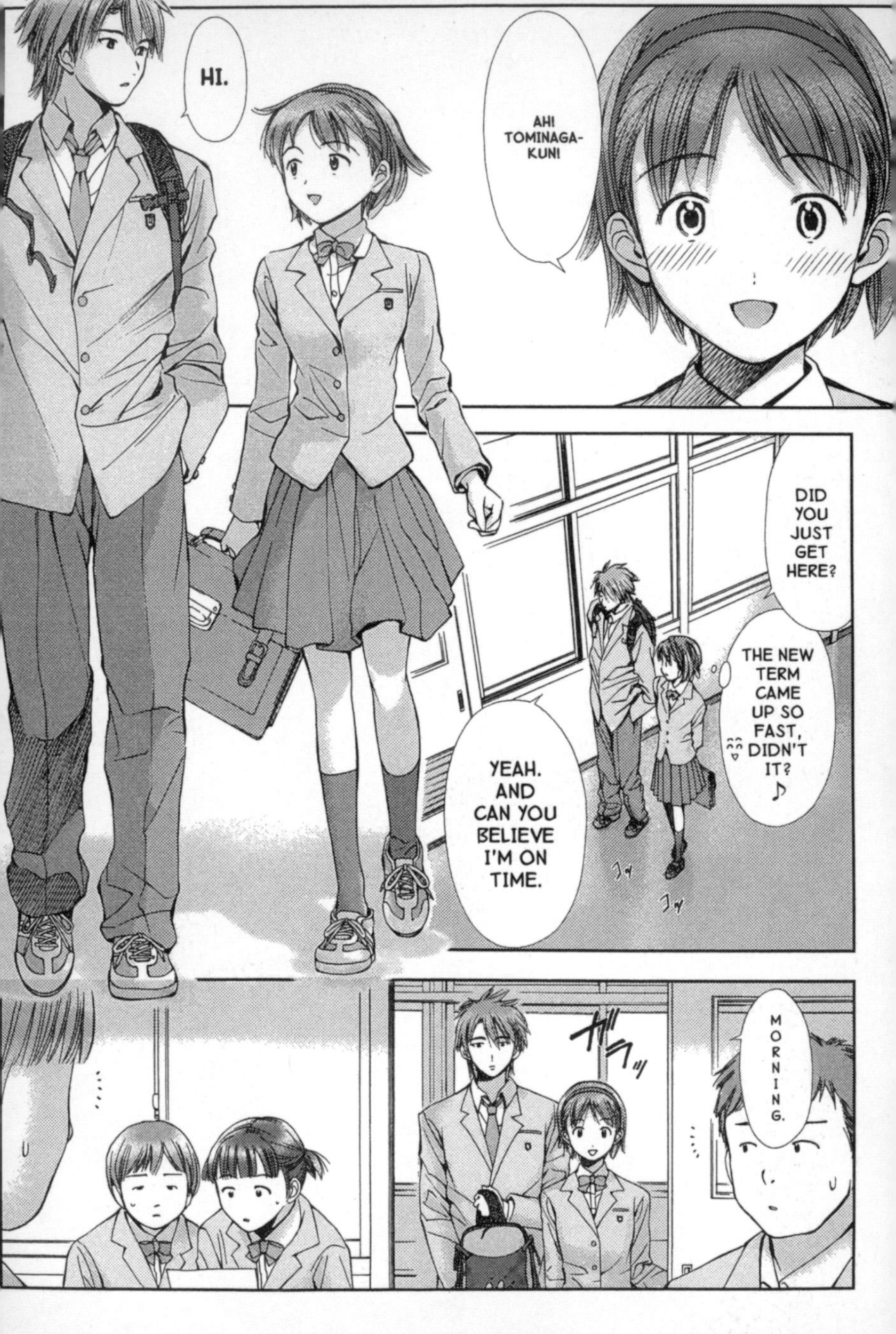
AH! TOMINAGA-KUN!
HI.
DID YOU JUST GET HERE?
THE NEW TERM CAME UP SO FAST, DIDN'T IT? ♪
YEAH. AND CAN YOU BELIEVE I'M ON TIME.
ガラッ
MORNING.

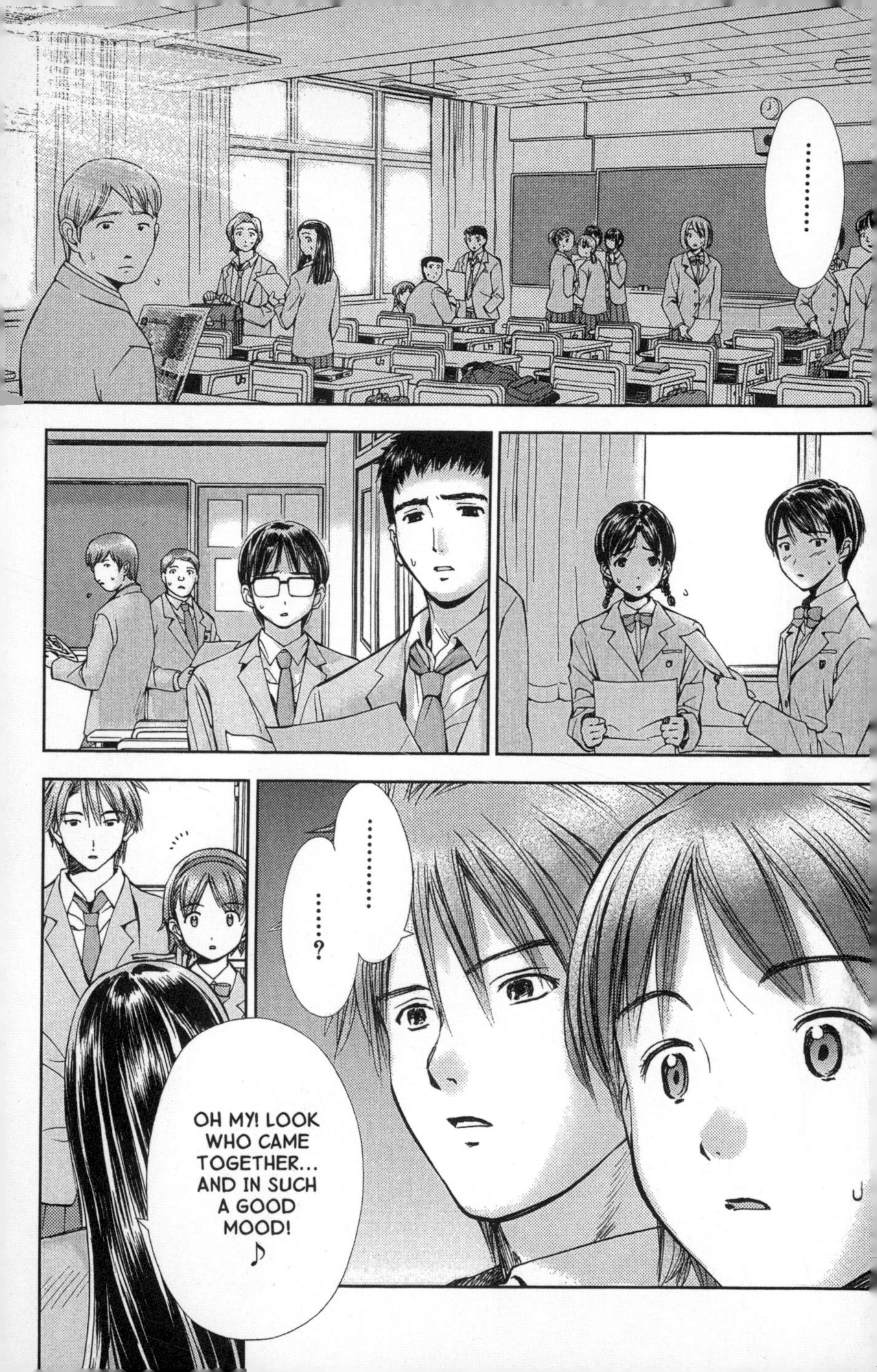
......
......
......?
OH MY! LOOK WHO CAME TOGETHER... AND IN SUCH A GOOD MOOD! ♪

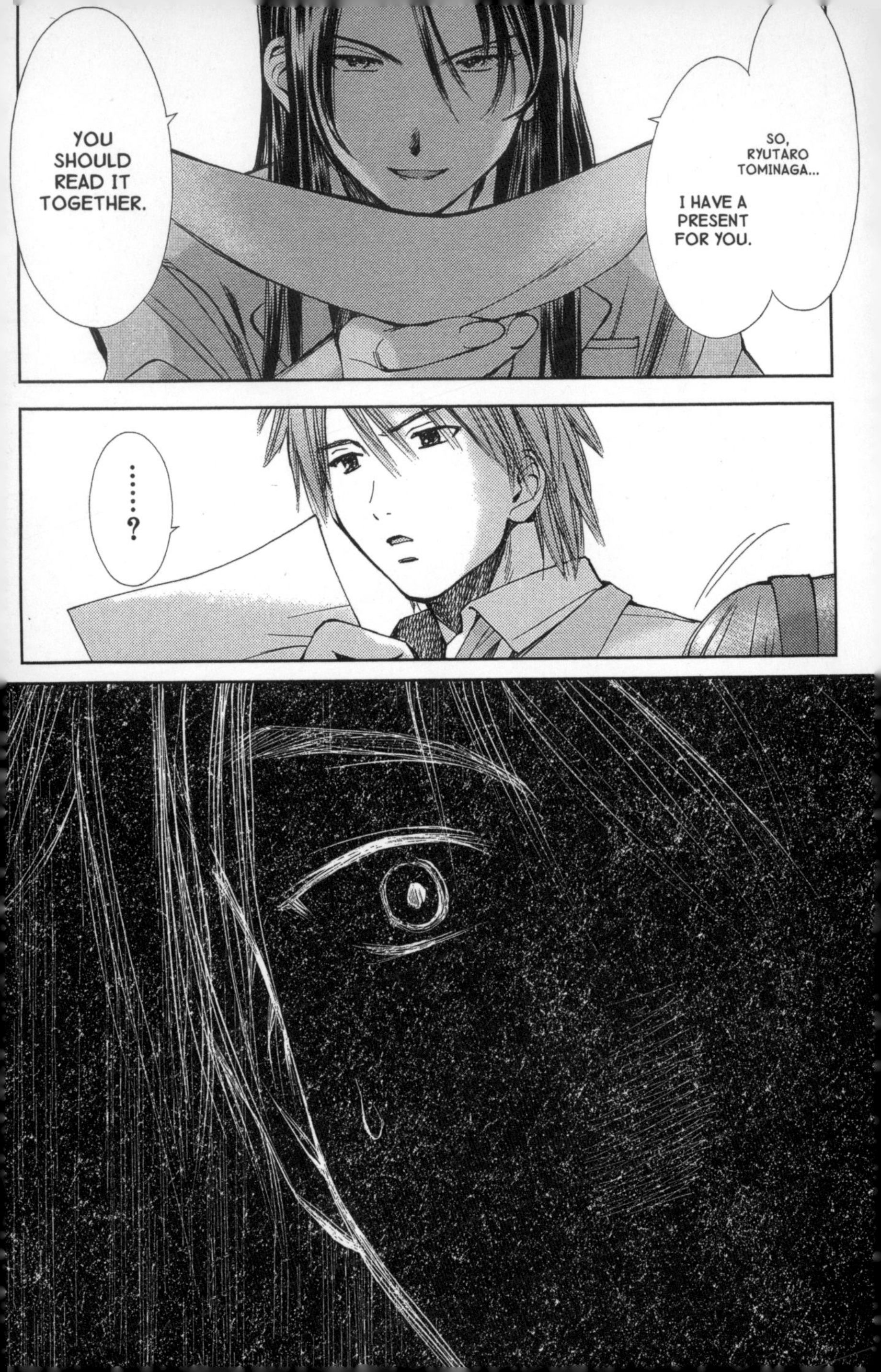
SO, RYUTARO TOMINAGA...
I HAVE A PRESENT FOR YOU.
YOU SHOULD READ IT TOGETHER.
......?

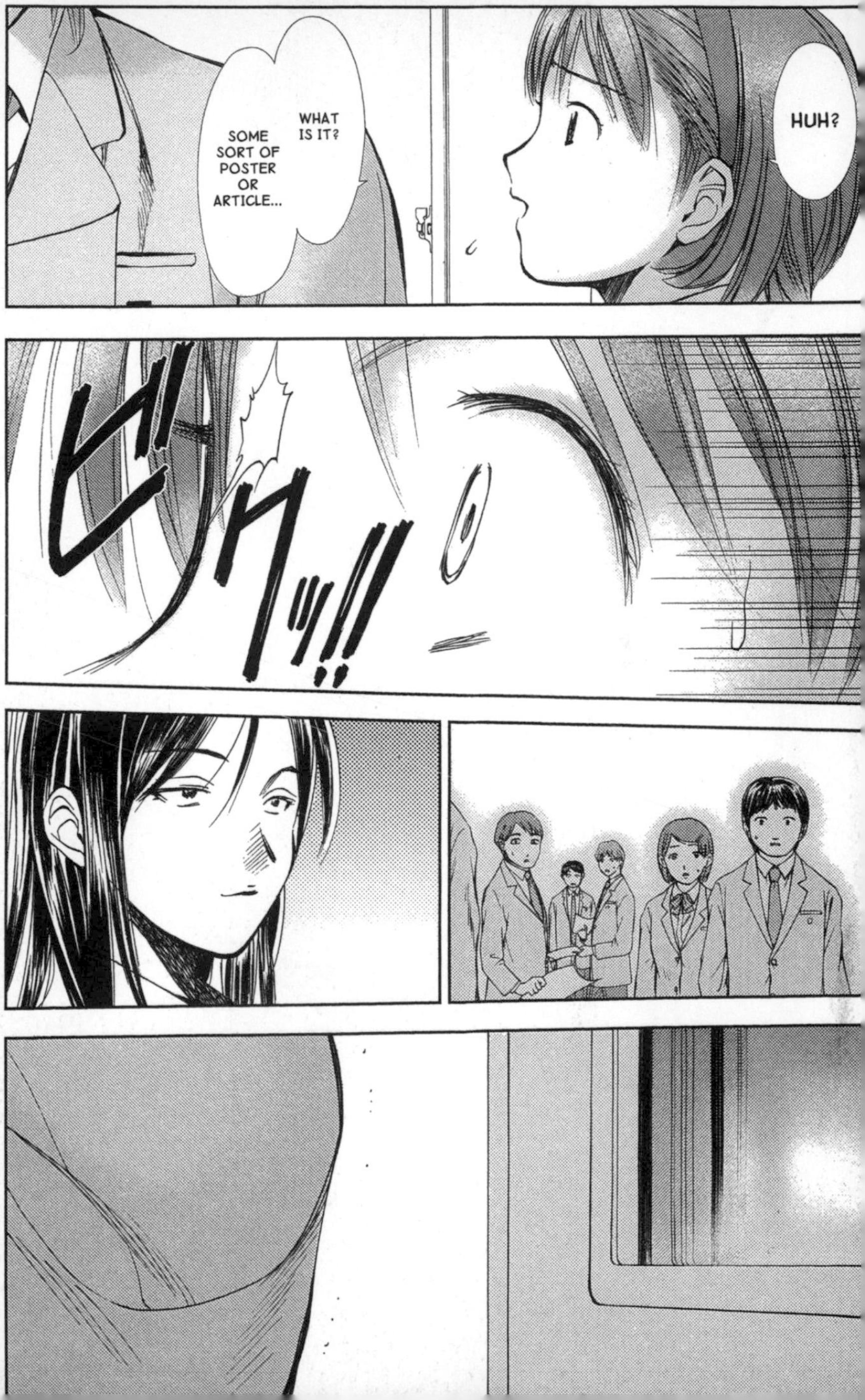
HUH?
WHAT IS IT?
SOME SORT OF POSTER OR ARTICLE...
ビリッ!!

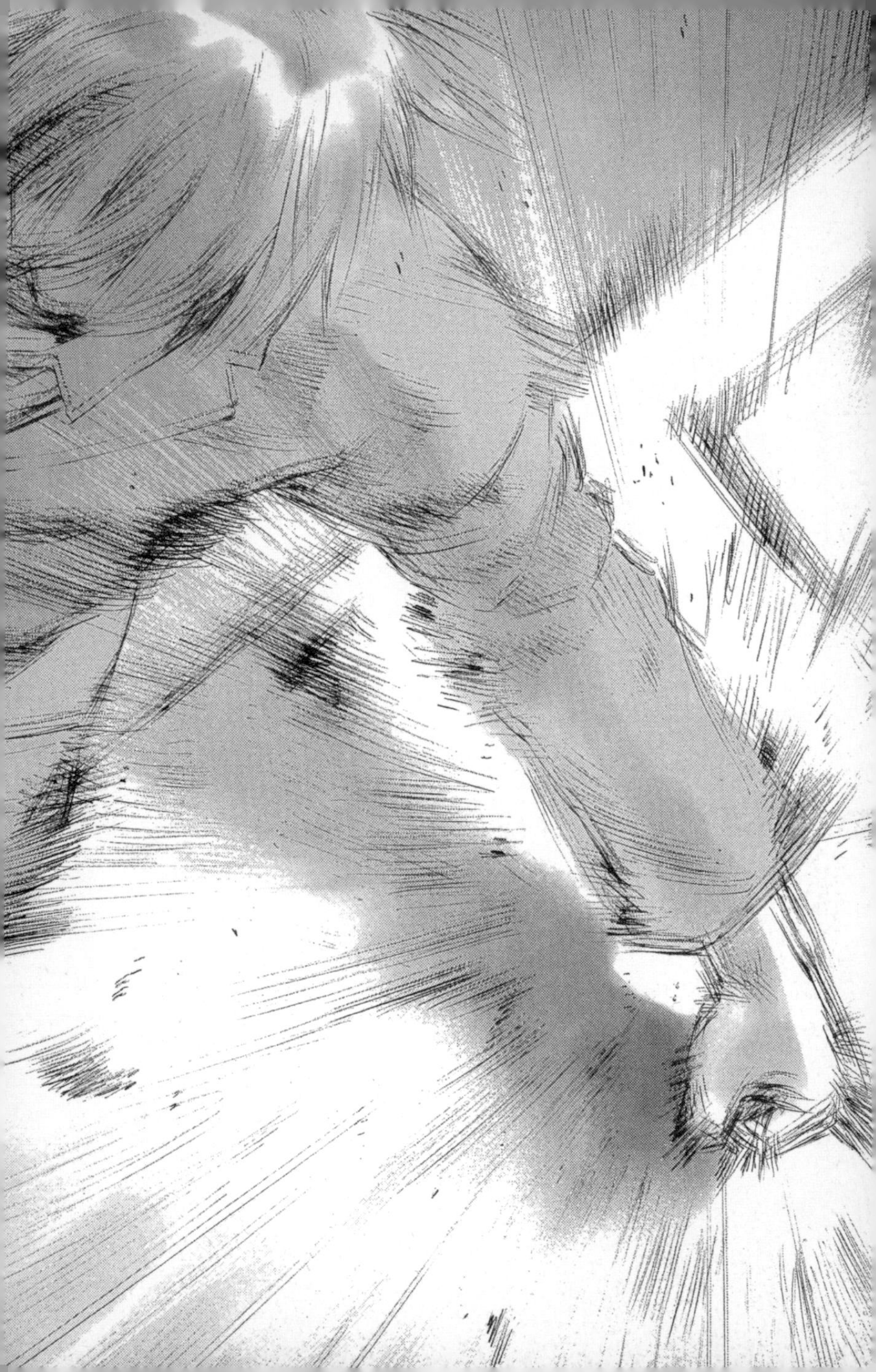

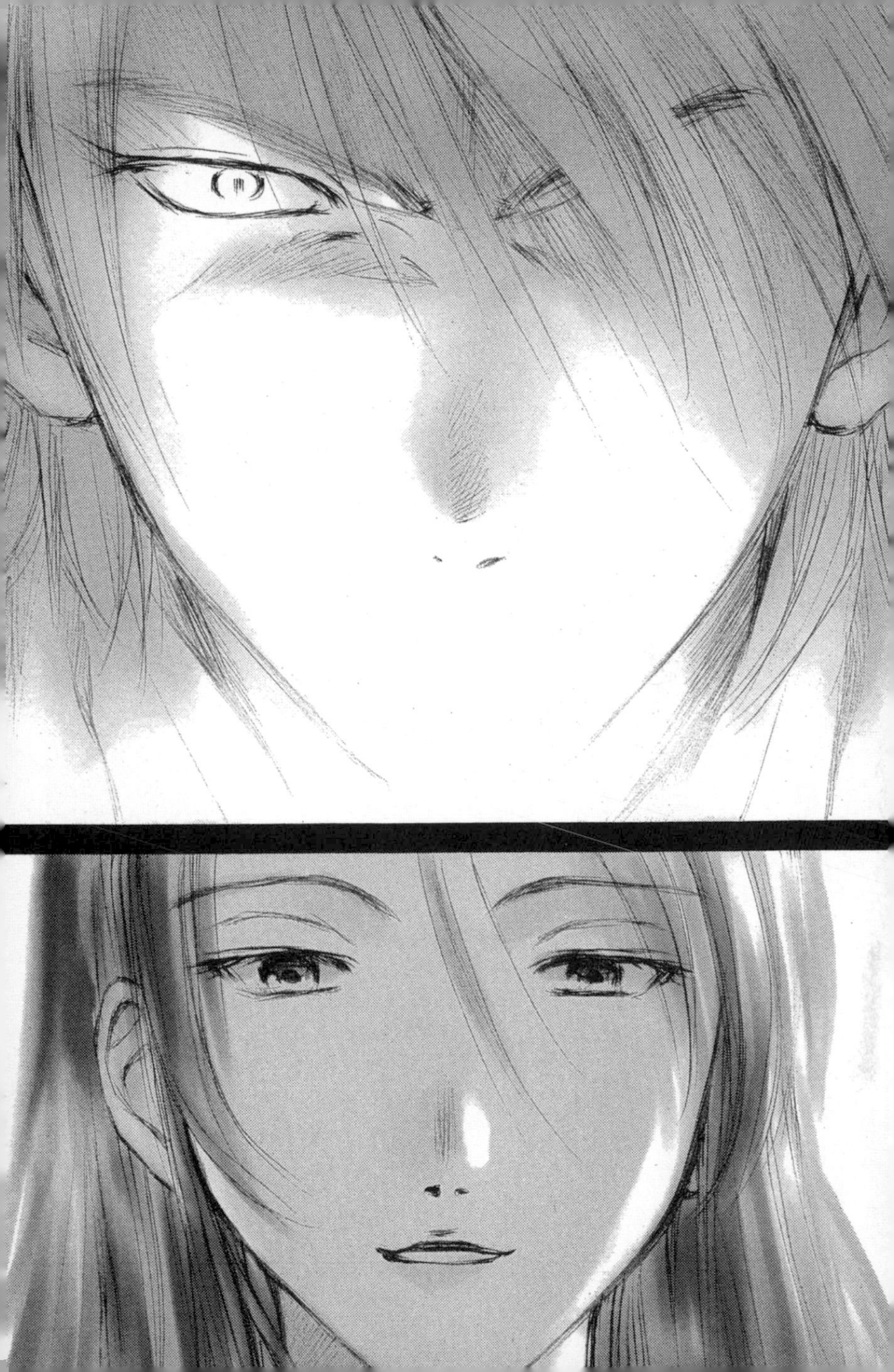

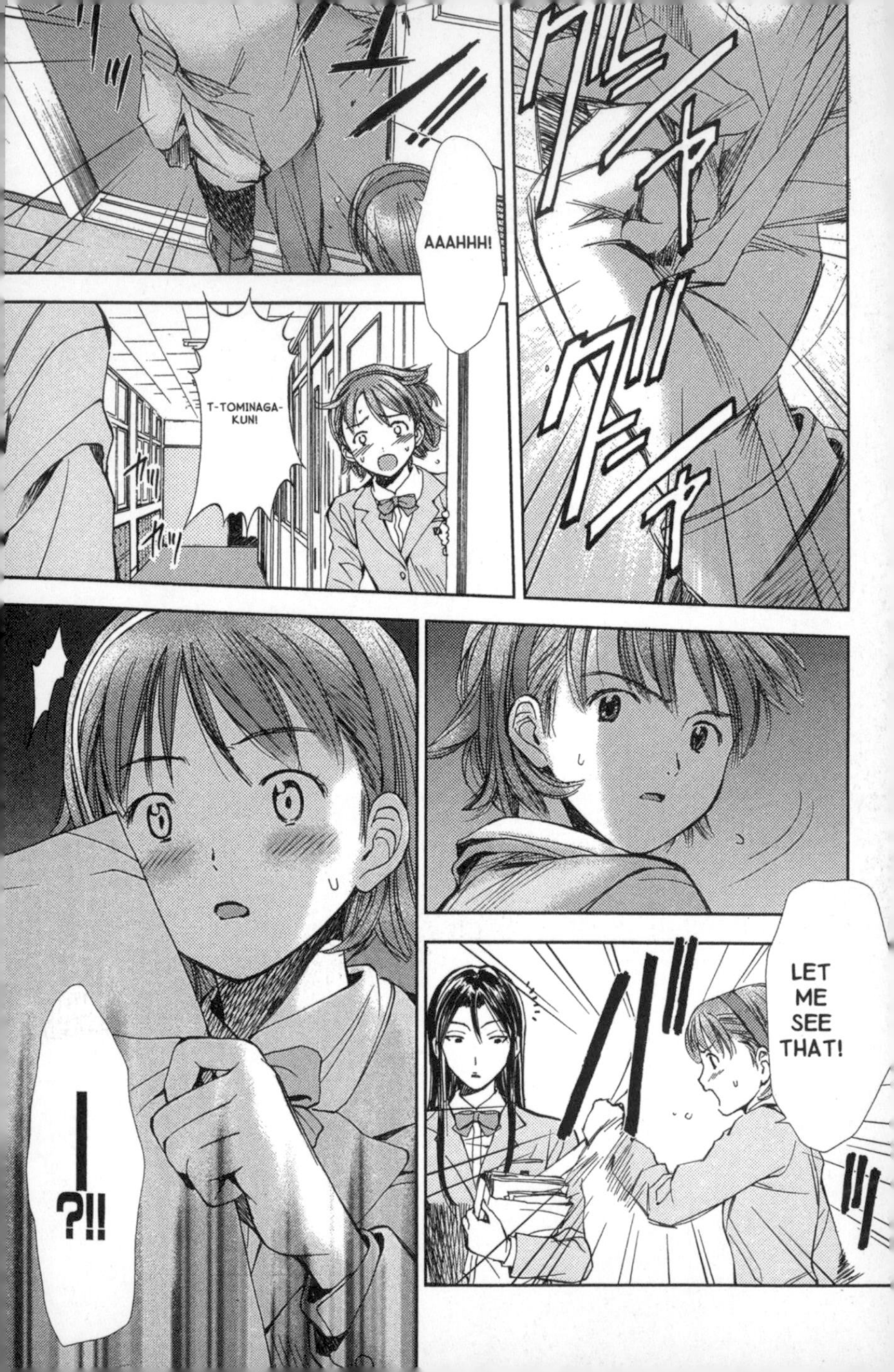
AAAHHH!
T-TOMINAGA-KUN!
LET ME SEE THAT!
?!!

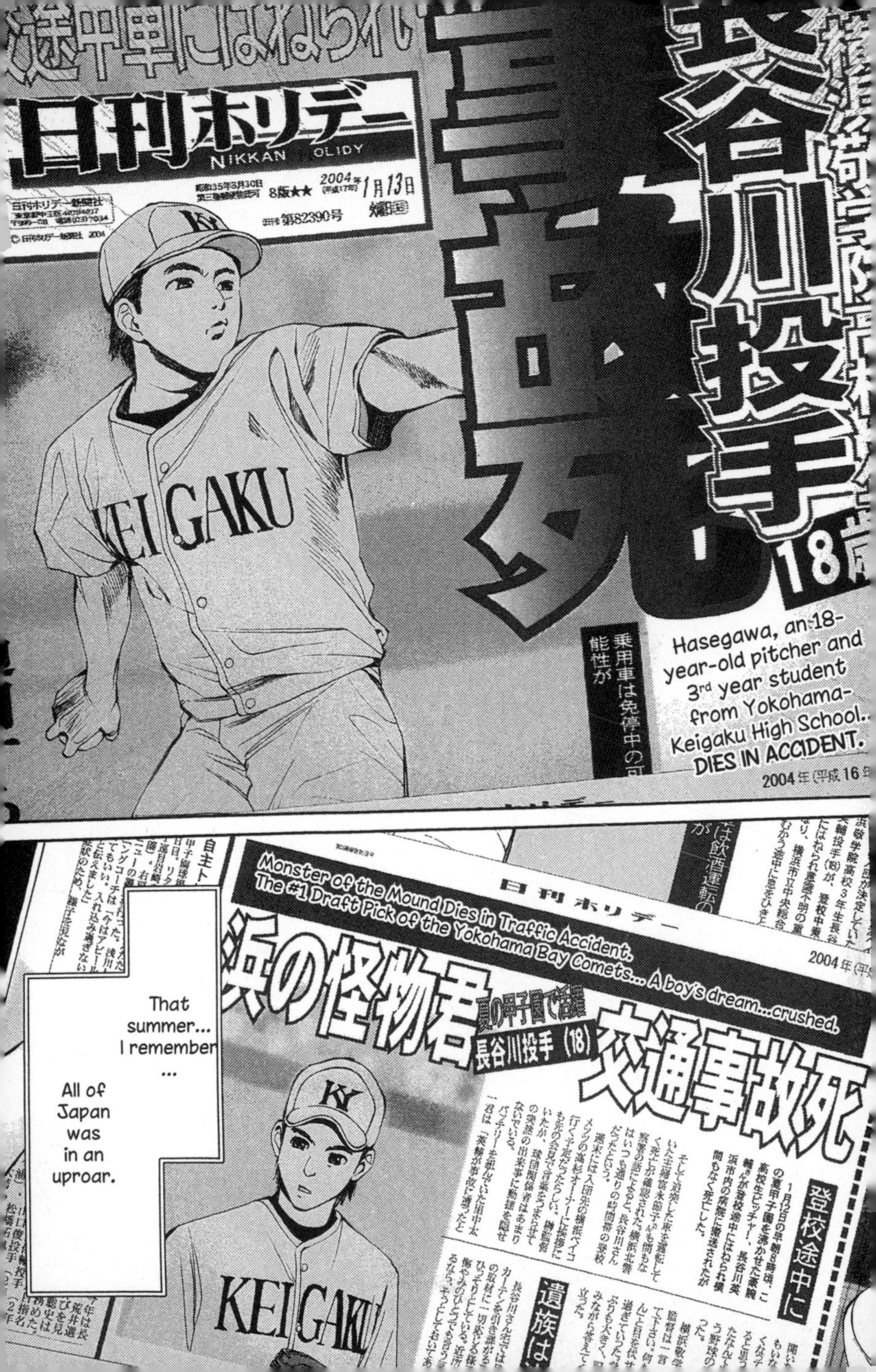
日刊ホリデー
2004年1月13日
長谷川投手
18歳
KEIGAKU
Hasegawa, an 18-year-old pitcher and 3rd year student from Yokohama-Keigaku High School. DIES IN ACCIDENT.
日刊ホリデー
Monster of the Mound Dies in Traffic Accident.
The #1 Draft Pick of the Yokohama Bay Comets... A boy's dream...crushed.
長谷川投手（18）
交通事故死
登校途中に
遺族は
That summer... I remember ...
All of Japan was in an uproar.
KEIGAKU

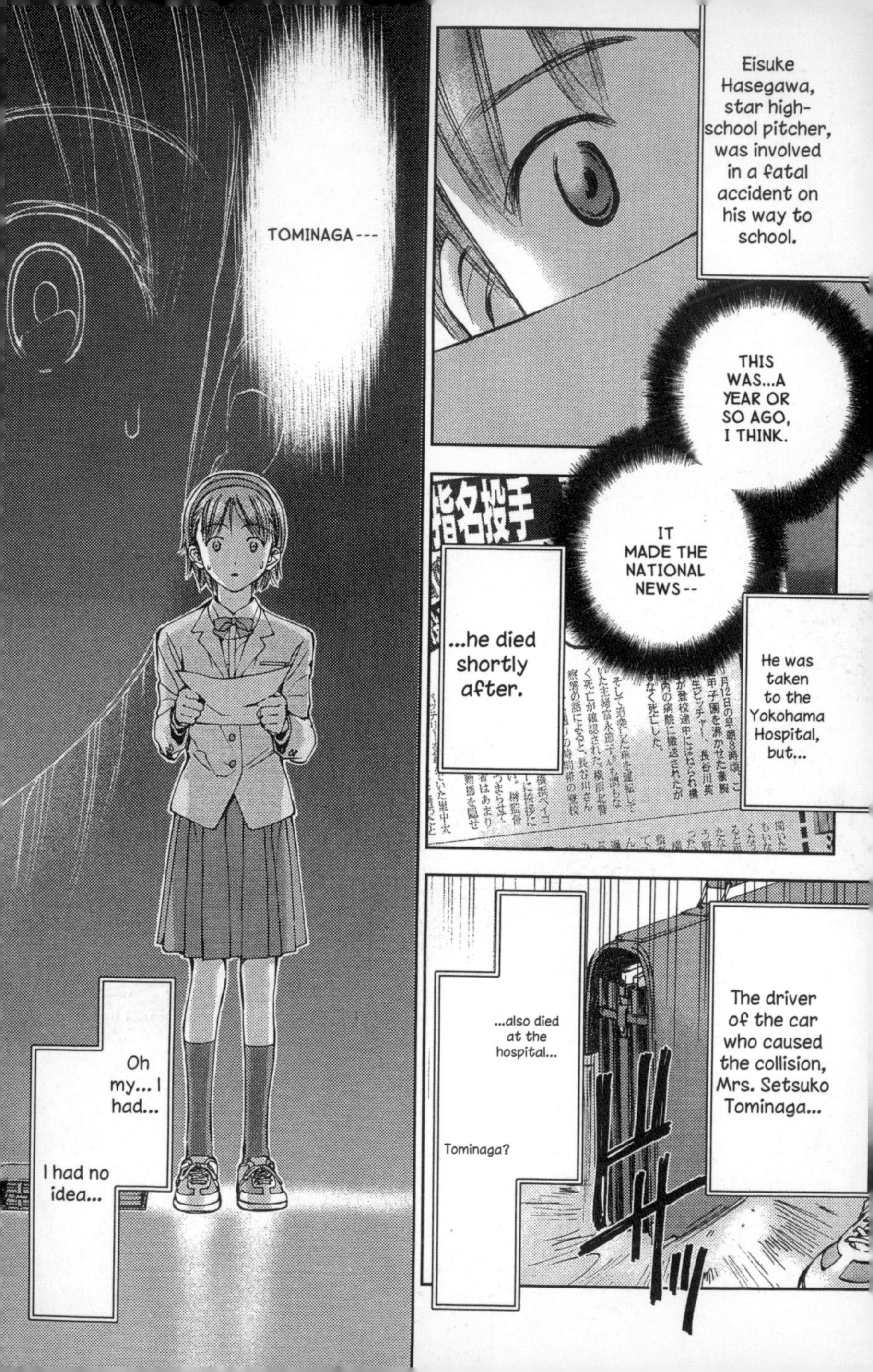
Eisuke Hasegawa, star high-school pitcher, was involved in a fatal accident on his way to school.
THIS WAS...A YEAR OR SO AGO, I THINK.
指名投手
IT MADE THE NATIONAL NEWS--
He was taken to the Yokohama Hospital, but...
...he died shortly after.
The driver of the car who caused the collision, Mrs. Setsuko Tominaga...
...also died at the hospital...
Tominaga?
TOMINAGA---
Oh my... I had...
I had no idea...

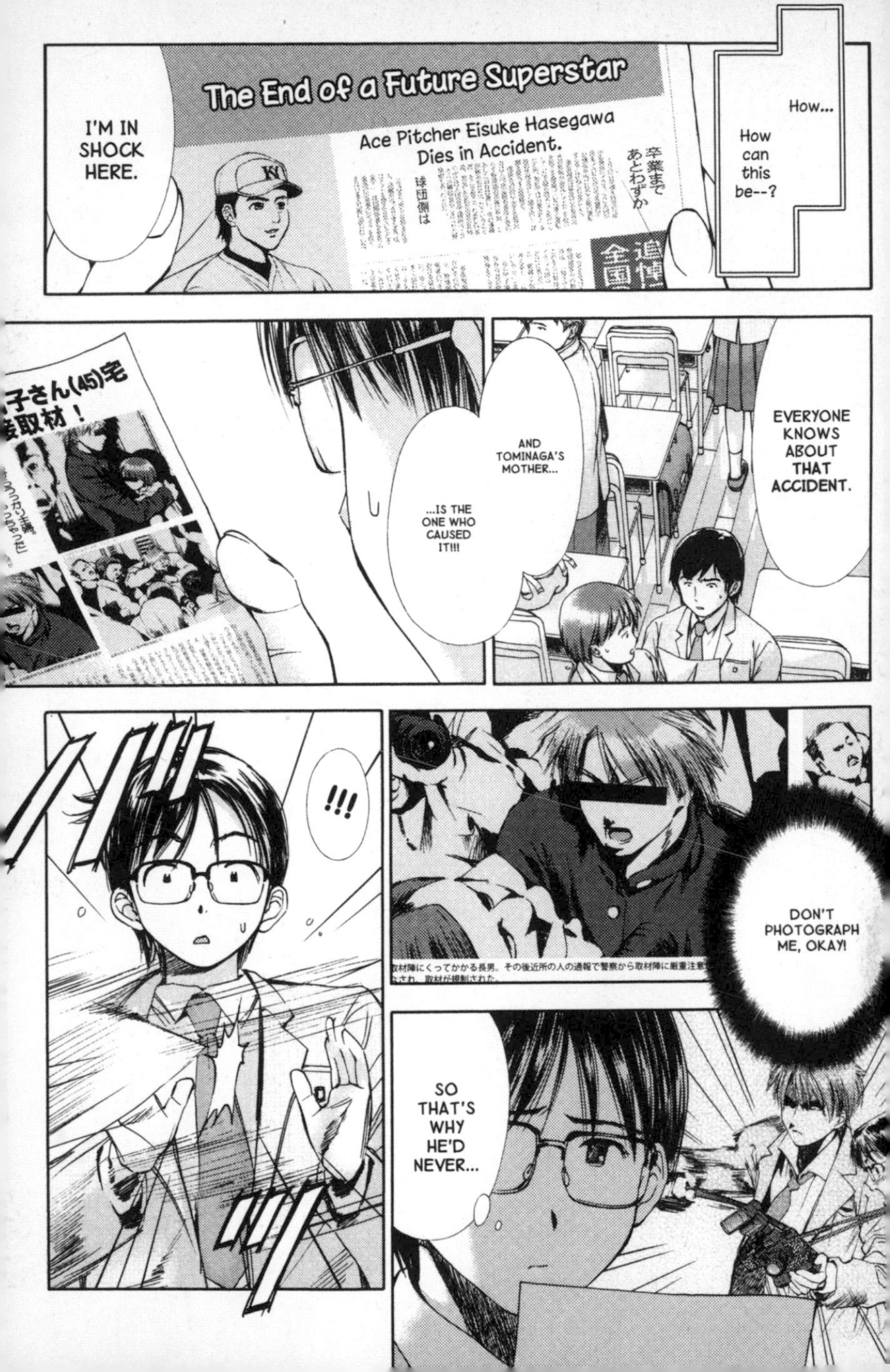
How...
How can this be--?
The End of a Future Superstar
Ace Pitcher Eisuke Hasegawa Dies in Accident.
卒業まであとわずか
球団側は
I'M IN SHOCK HERE.
EVERYONE KNOWS ABOUT THAT ACCIDENT.
子さん(45)宅
接取材！
AND TOMINAGA'S MOTHER...
...IS THE ONE WHO CAUSED IT!!!
DON'T PHOTOGRAPH ME, OKAY!
取材陣にくってかかる長男。その後近所の人の通報で警察から取材陣に厳重注意
され、取材が規制された。
!!!
SO THAT'S WHY HE'D NEVER...

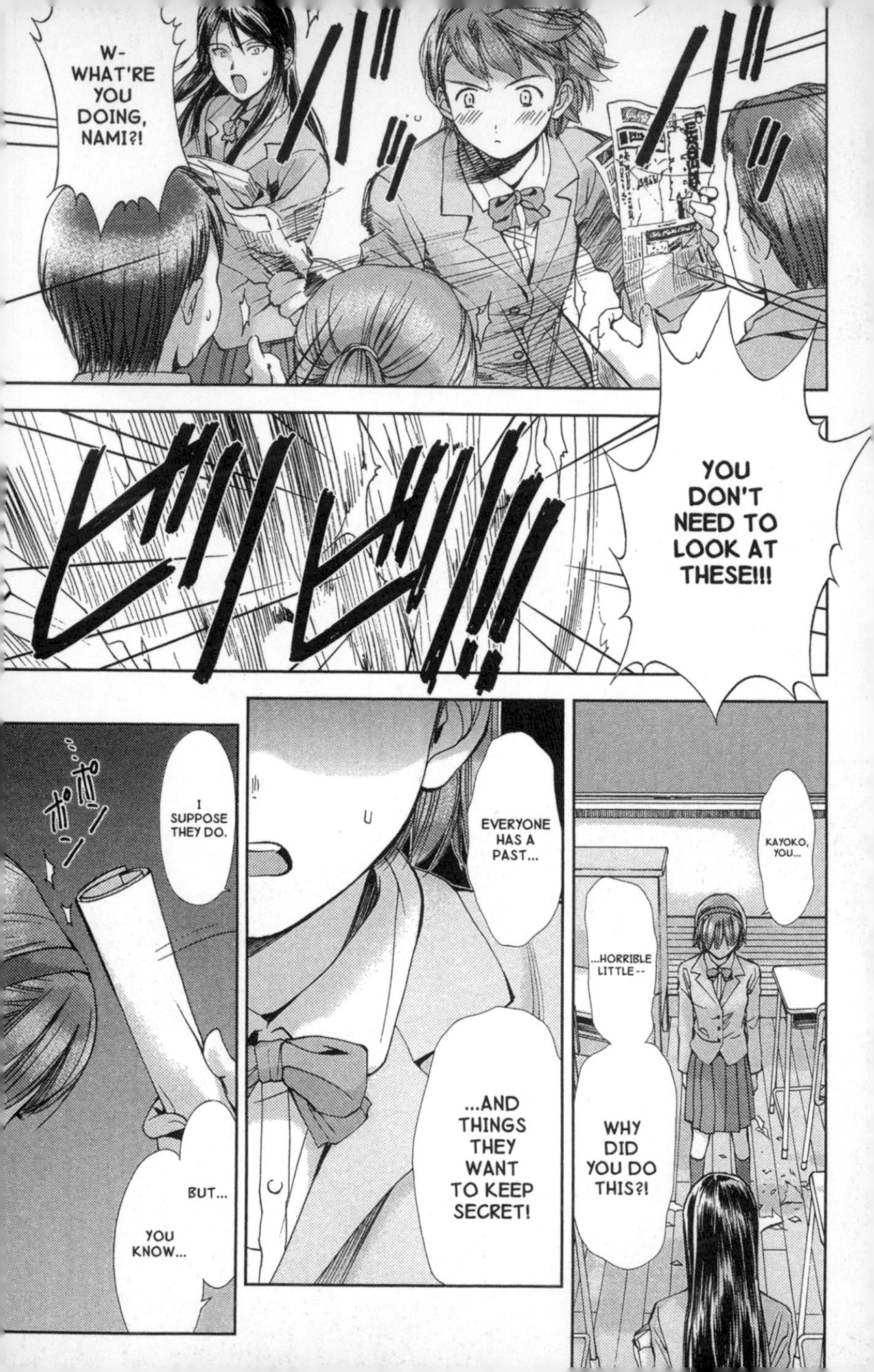
W-WHAT'RE YOU DOING, NAMI?!
YOU DON'T NEED TO LOOK AT THESE!!!
KAYOKO, YOU...
...HORRIBLE LITTLE--
WHY DID YOU DO THIS?!
EVERYONE HAS A PAST...
...AND THINGS THEY WANT TO KEEP SECRET!
I SUPPOSE THEY DO.
BUT...
YOU KNOW...

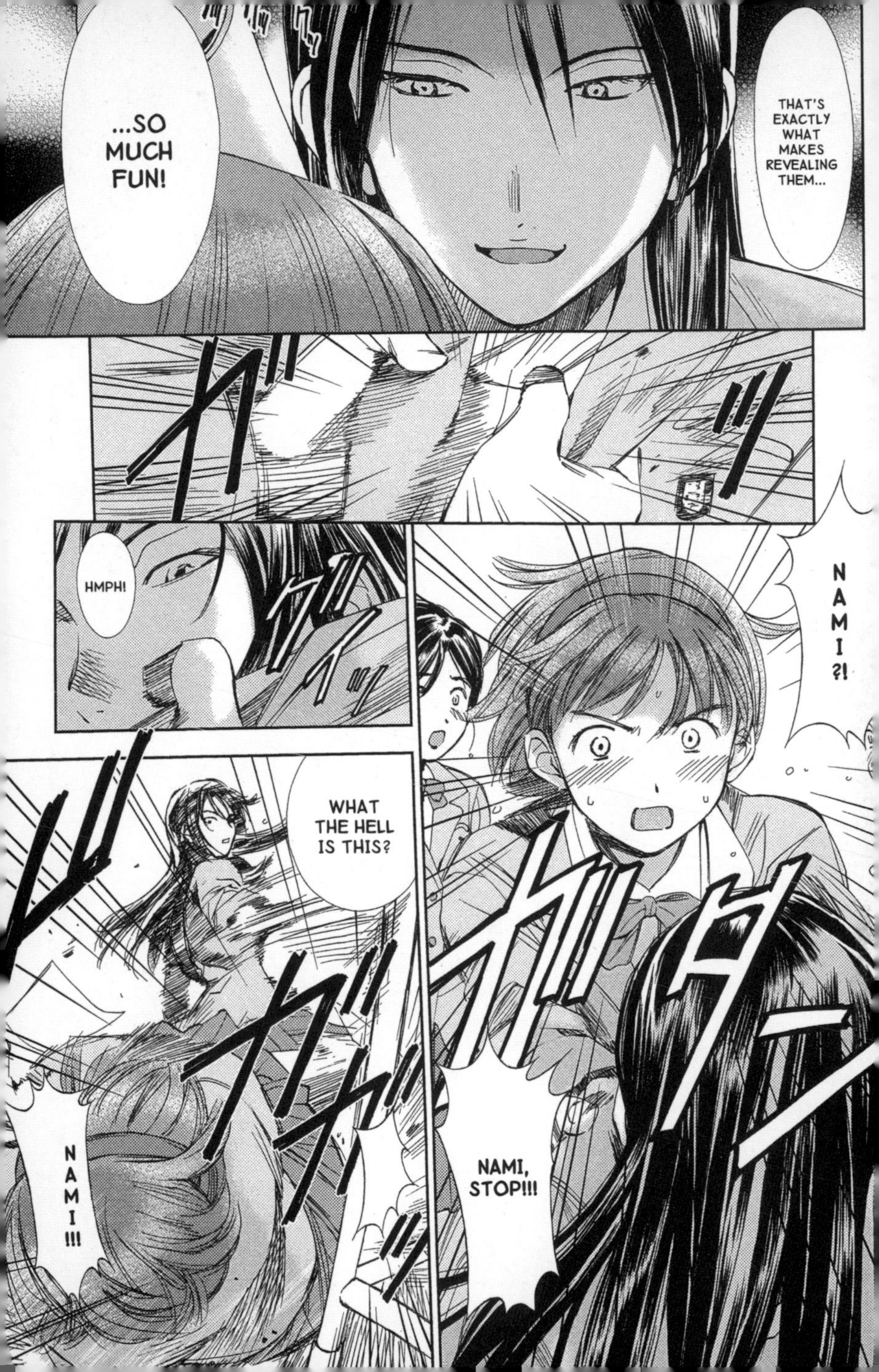
THAT'S EXACTLY WHAT MAKES REVEALING THEM...
...SO MUCH FUN!
NAMI?!
NAMI, STOP!!!
HMPH!
WHAT THE HELL IS THIS?
NAMI!!!

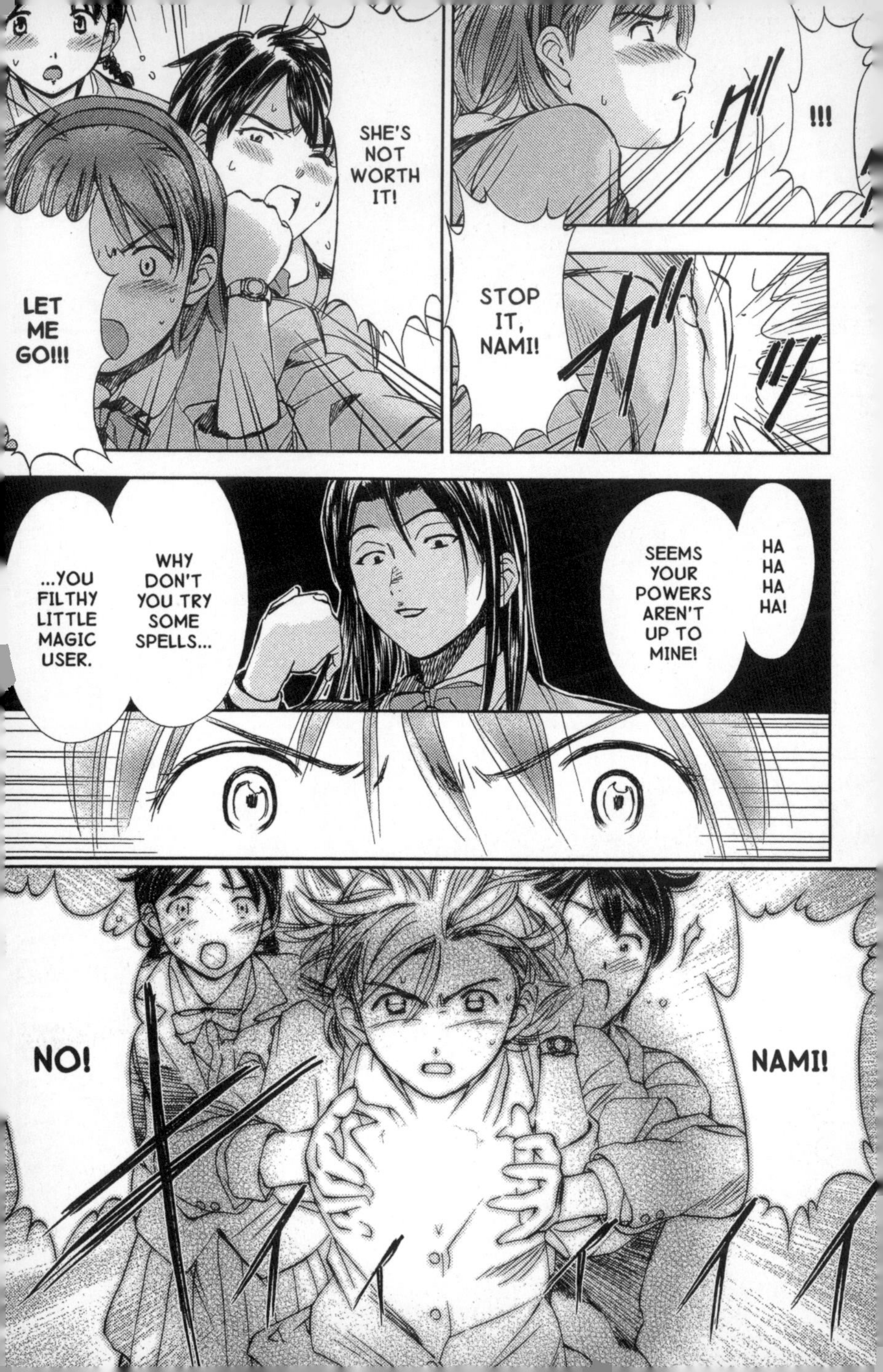
!!!
STOP IT, NAMI!
SHE'S NOT WORTH IT!
LET ME GO!!!
HA HA HA HA!
SEEMS YOUR POWERS AREN'T UP TO MINE!
WHY DON'T YOU TRY SOME SPELLS...
...YOU FILTHY LITTLE MAGIC USER.
NAMI!
NO!

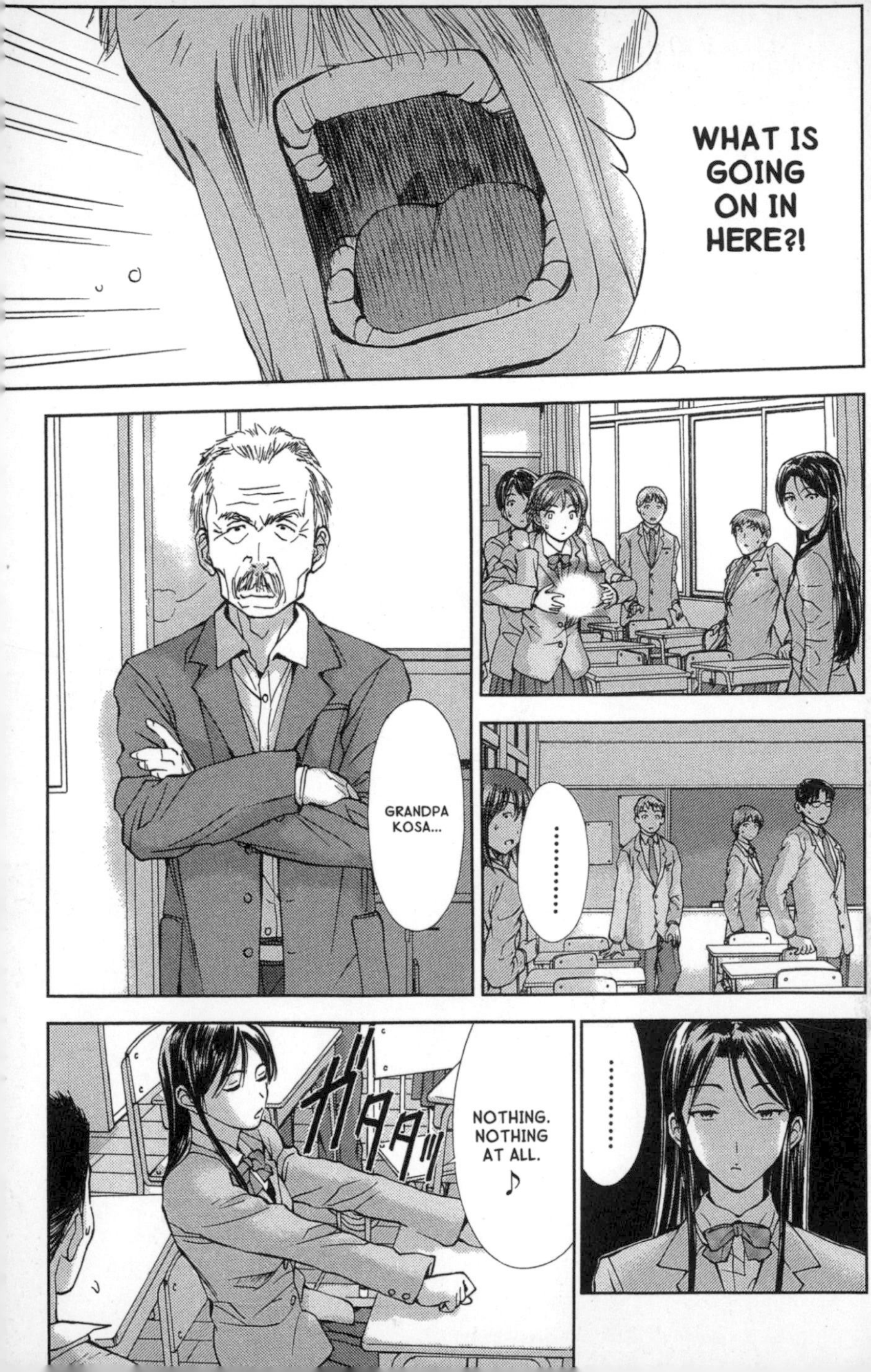
WHAT IS GOING ON IN HERE?!
....
GRANDPA KOSA...
....
ガタタッ
NOTHING. NOTHING AT ALL. ♪

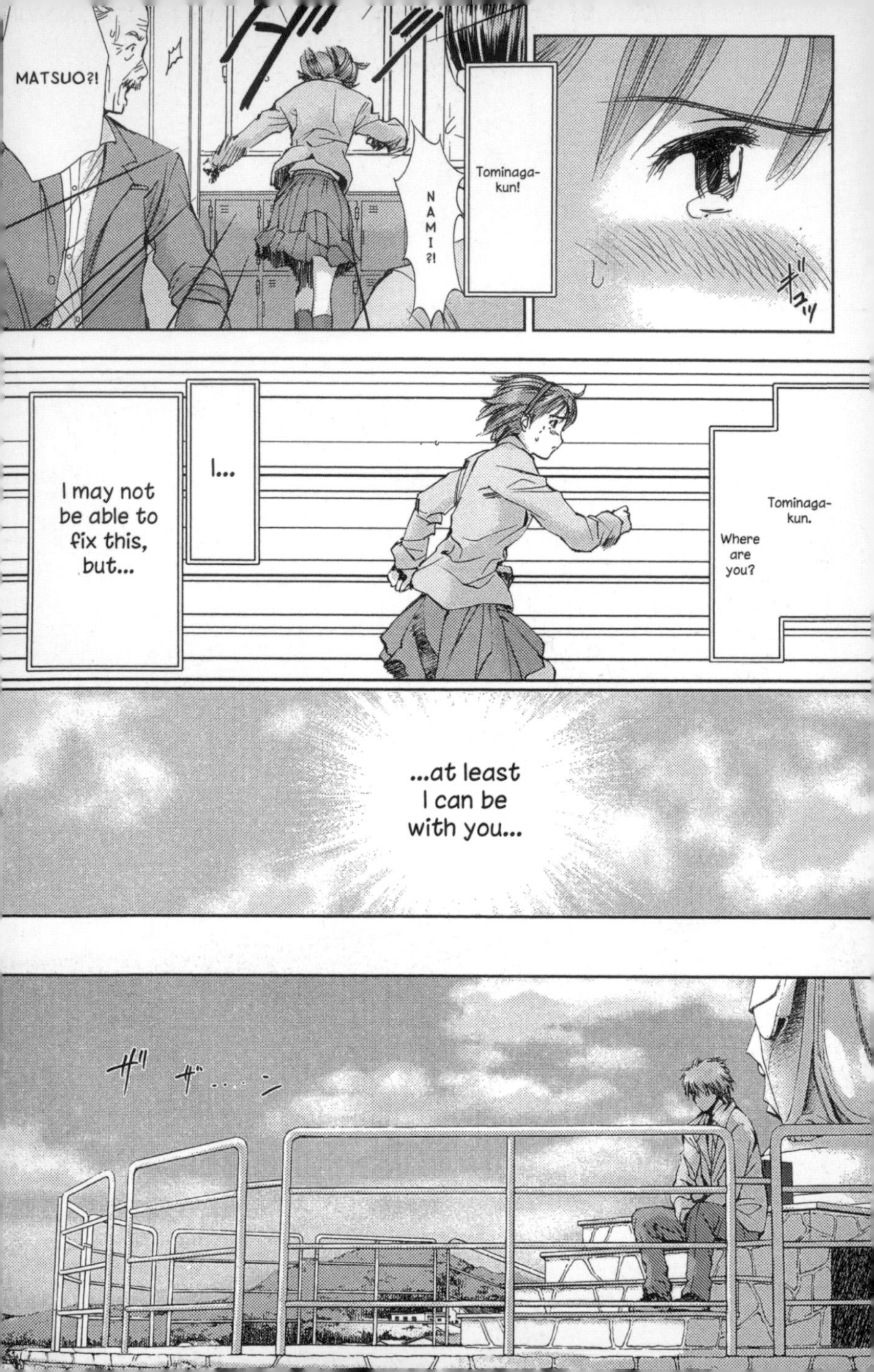
ギクッ
Tominaga-kun!
NAMI?!
MATSUO?!
Tominaga-kun.
Where are you?
I...
I may not be able to fix this, but...
...at least I can be with you...
ザザ…ン

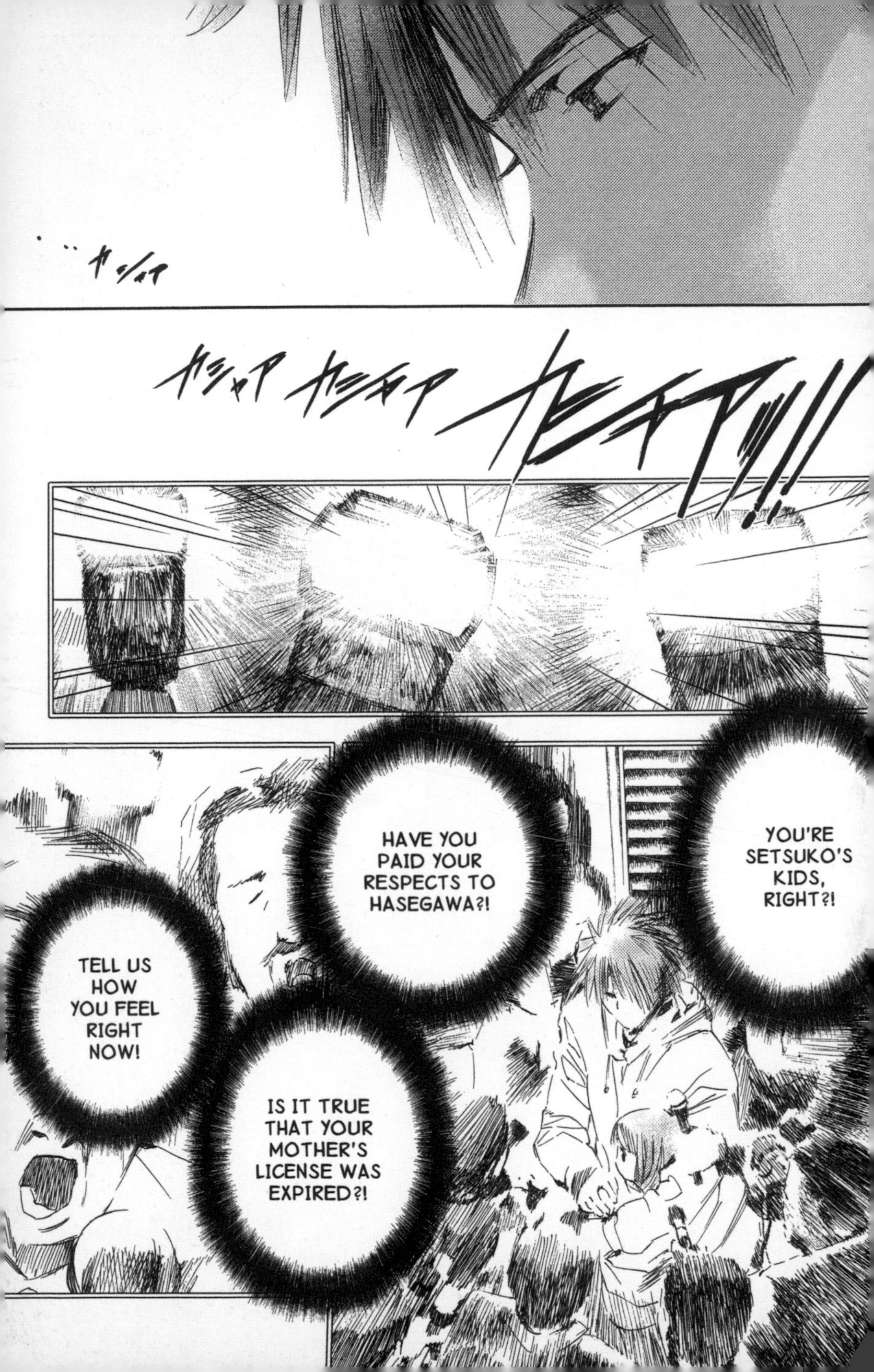
カシャ
カシャア カシャア カシャア!!
YOU'RE SETSUKO'S KIDS, RIGHT?!
HAVE YOU PAID YOUR RESPECTS TO HASEGAWA?!
TELL US HOW YOU FEEL RIGHT NOW!
IS IT TRUE THAT YOUR MOTHER'S LICENSE WAS EXPIRED?!

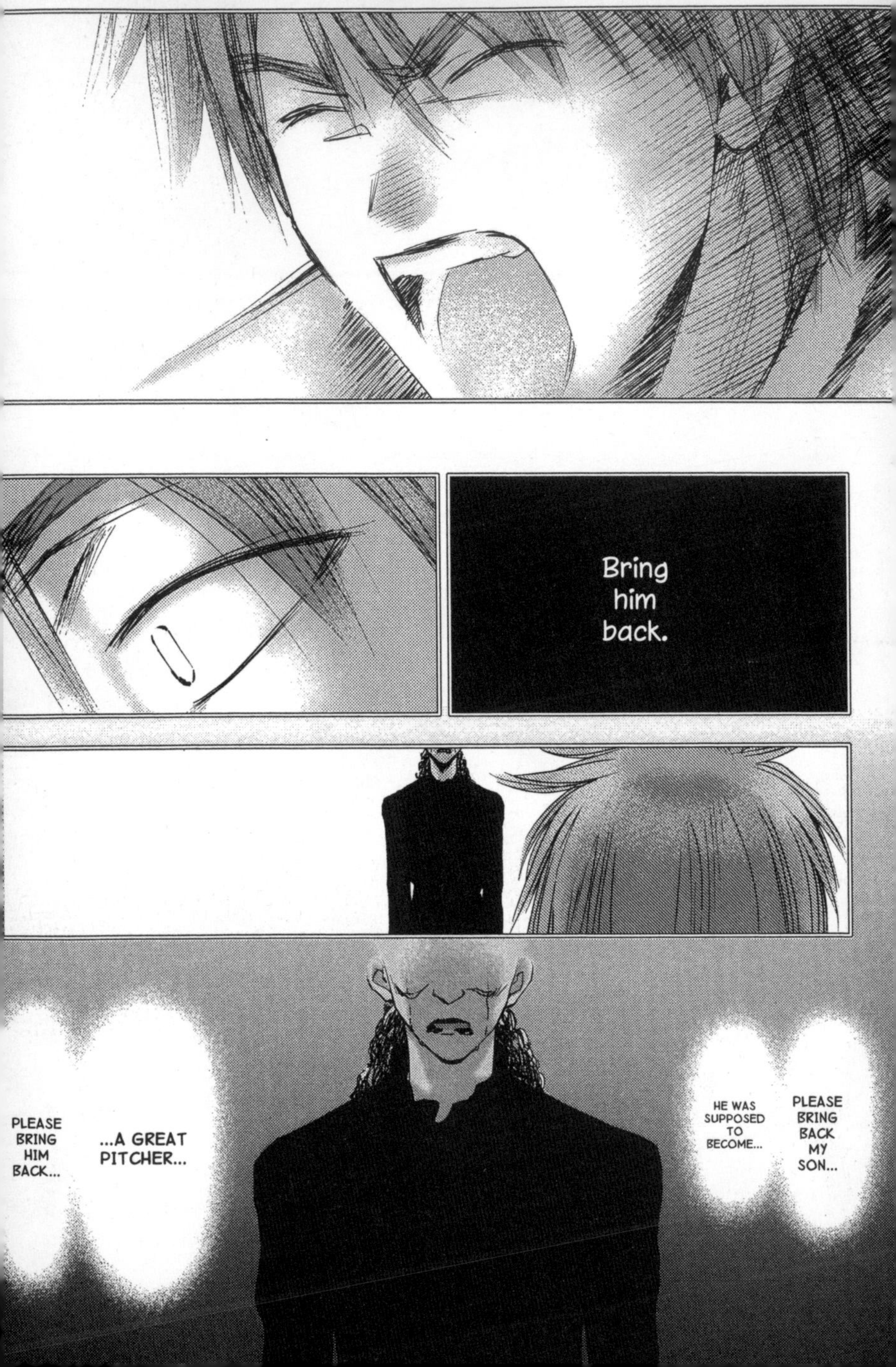
Bring him back.
PLEASE BRING BACK MY SON...
HE WAS SUPPOSED TO BECOME...
...A GREAT PITCHER...
PLEASE BRING HIM BACK...

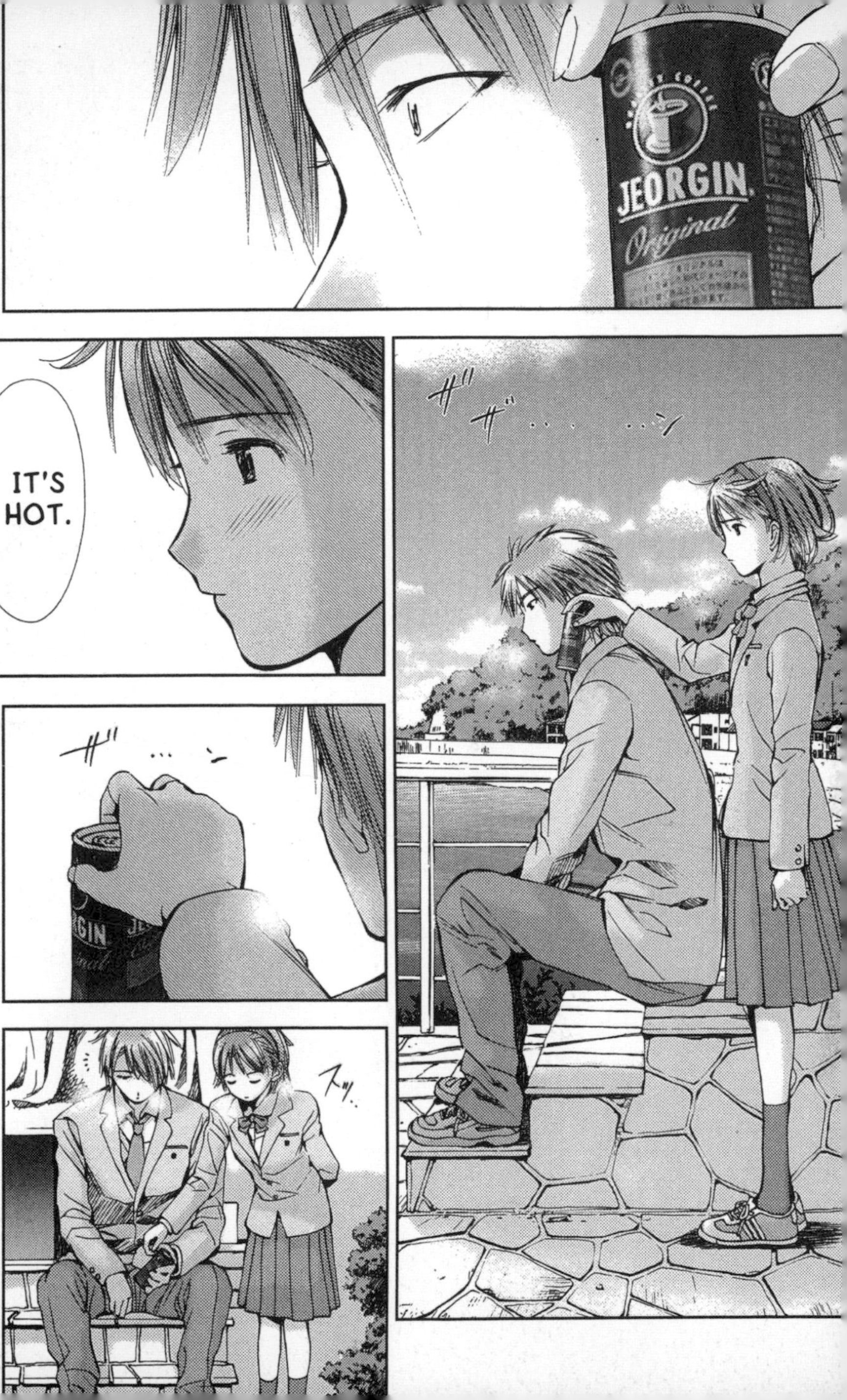
JEORGIN
Original
ザザ・・・・・ン
IT'S HOT.
ザ・・・ン
スッ..

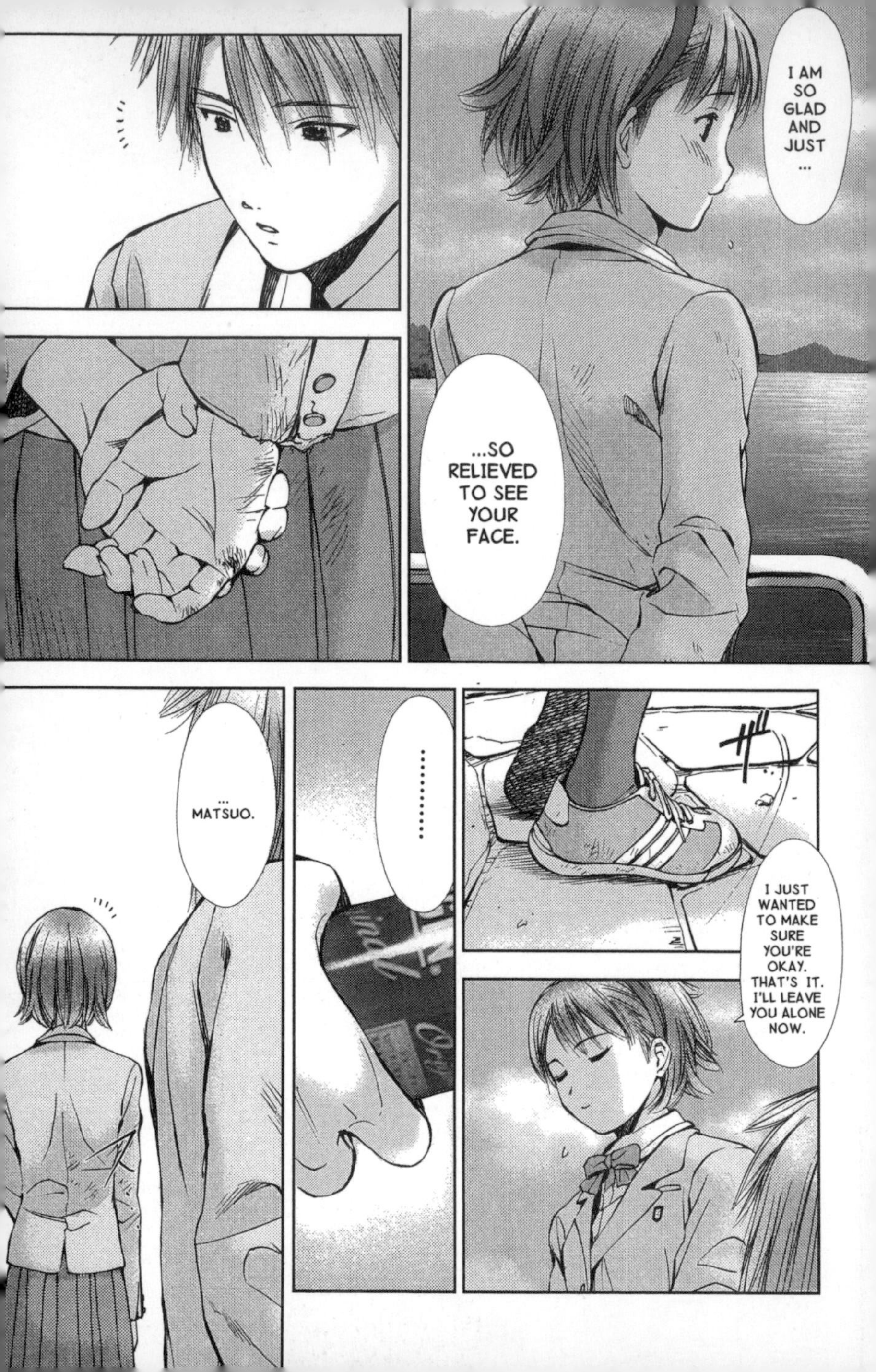
I AM SO GLAD AND JUST ...
...SO RELIEVED TO SEE YOUR FACE.
I JUST WANTED TO MAKE SURE YOU'RE OKAY. THAT'S IT. I'LL LEAVE YOU ALONE NOW.
....
... MATSUO.

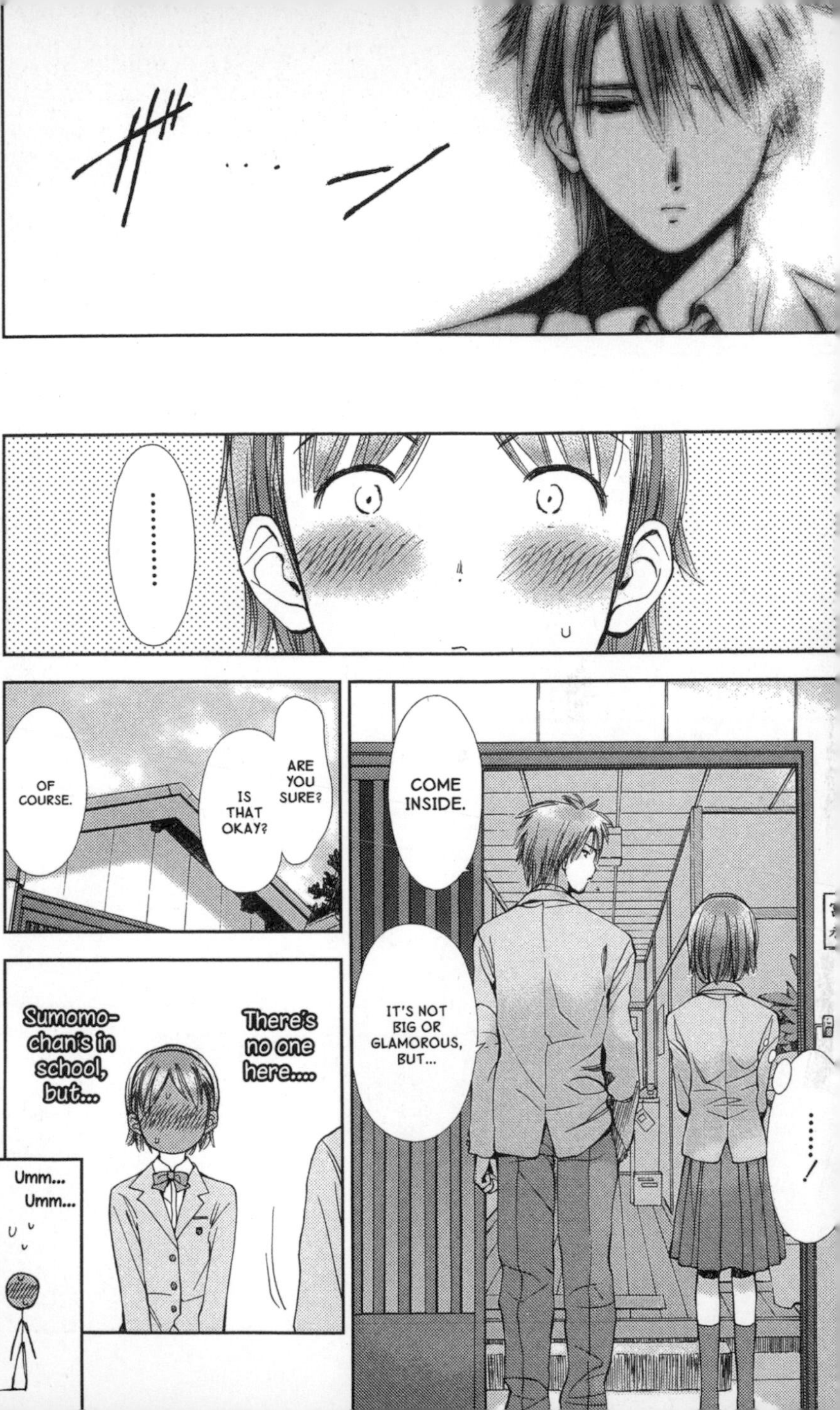
......
COME INSIDE.
IT'S NOT BIG OR GLAMOROUS, BUT...
......!
ARE YOU SURE?
IS THAT OKAY?
OF COURSE.
There's no one here....
Sumomo-chan's in school, but...
Umm... Umm...

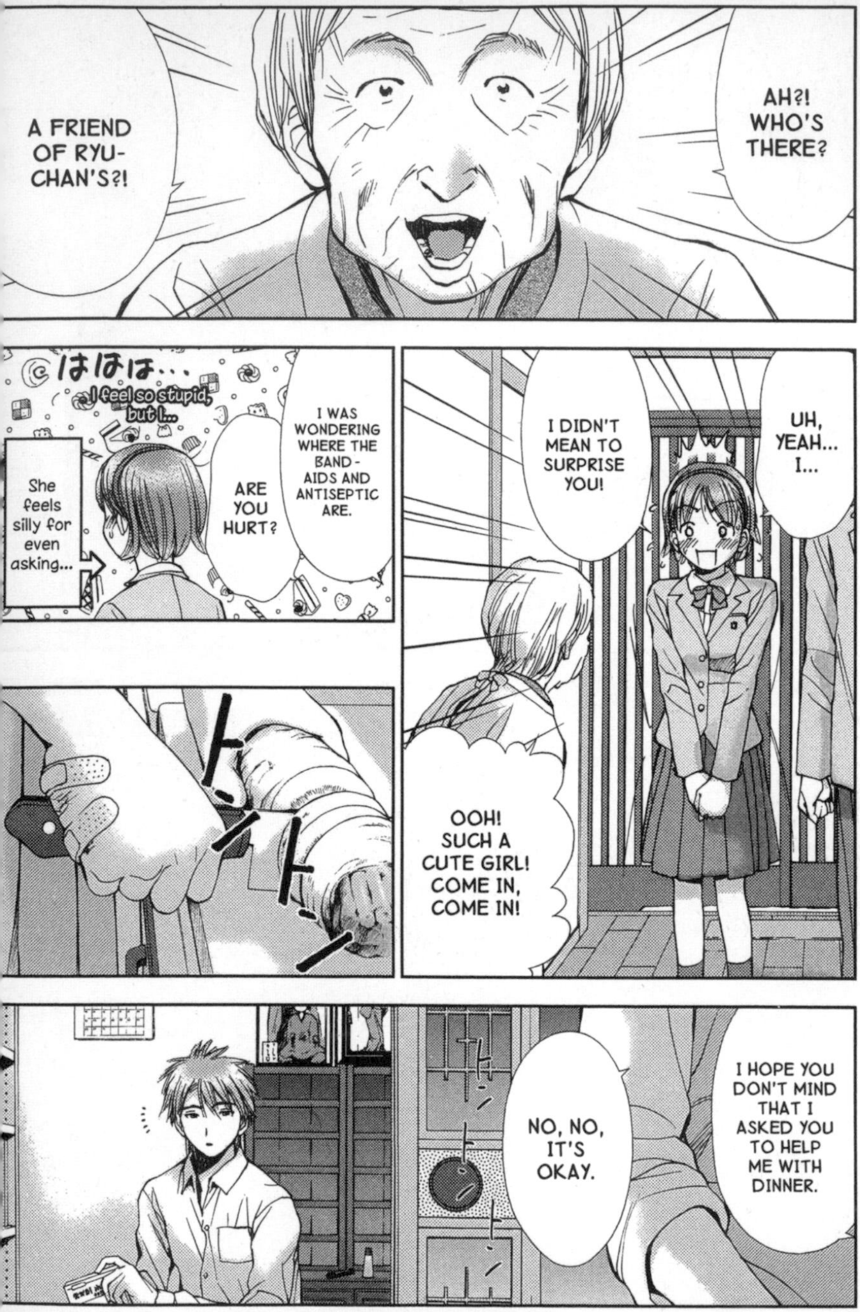
AH?! WHO'S THERE?
A FRIEND OF RYU-CHAN'S?!
UH, YEAH... I...
I DIDN'T MEAN TO SURPRISE YOU!
OOH! SUCH A CUTE GIRL! COME IN, COME IN!
I WAS WONDERING WHERE THE BAND-AIDS AND ANTISEPTIC ARE.
ARE YOU HURT?
ははは…
I feel so stupid, but I...
She feels silly for even asking...
I HOPE YOU DON'T MIND THAT I ASKED YOU TO HELP ME WITH DINNER.
NO, NO, IT'S OKAY.
...

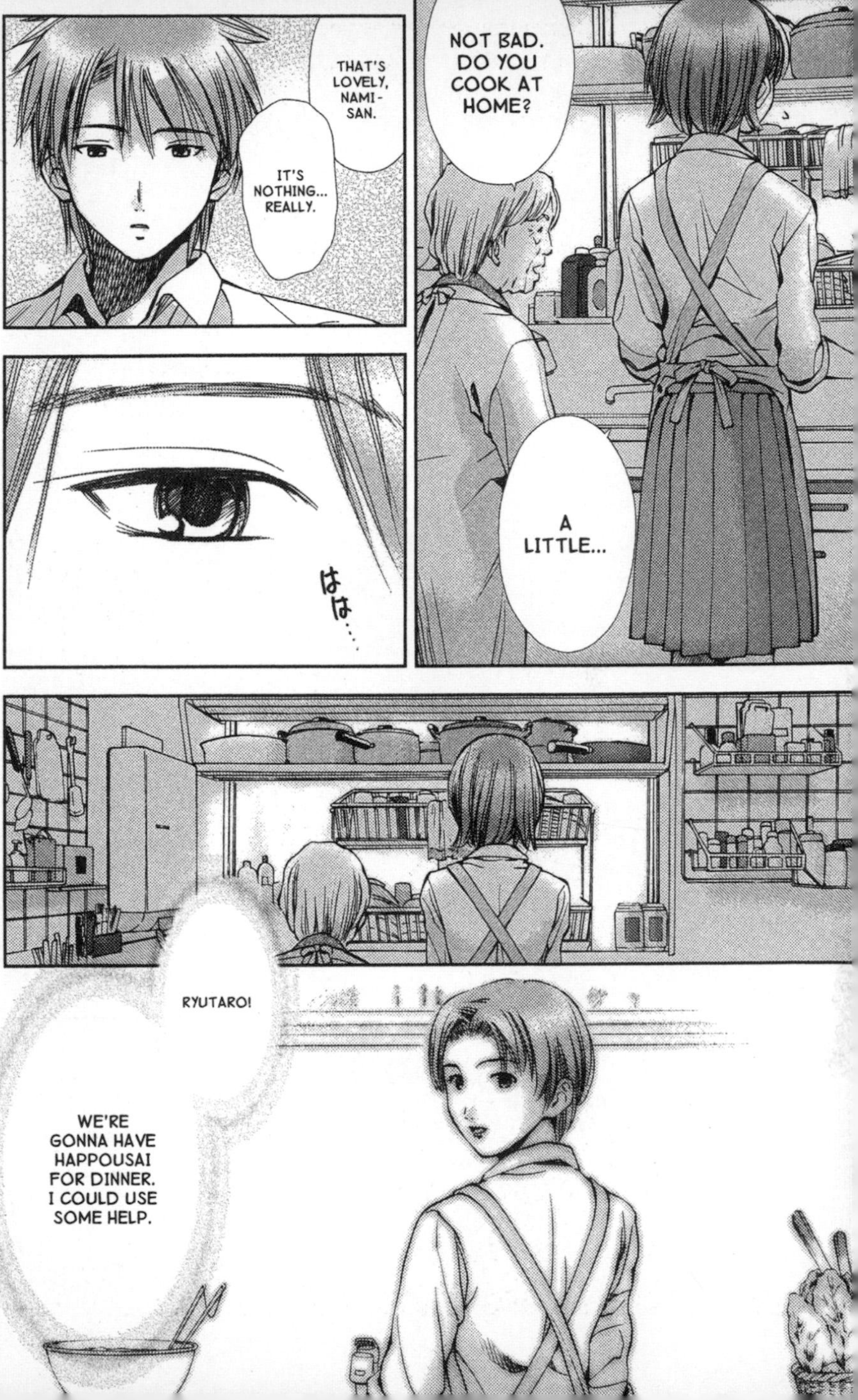
NOT BAD. DO YOU COOK AT HOME?
A LITTLE...
THAT'S LOVELY, NAMI-SAN.
IT'S NOTHING... REALLY.
はは…
RYUTARO!
WE'RE GONNA HAVE HAPPOUSAI FOR DINNER. I COULD USE SOME HELP.

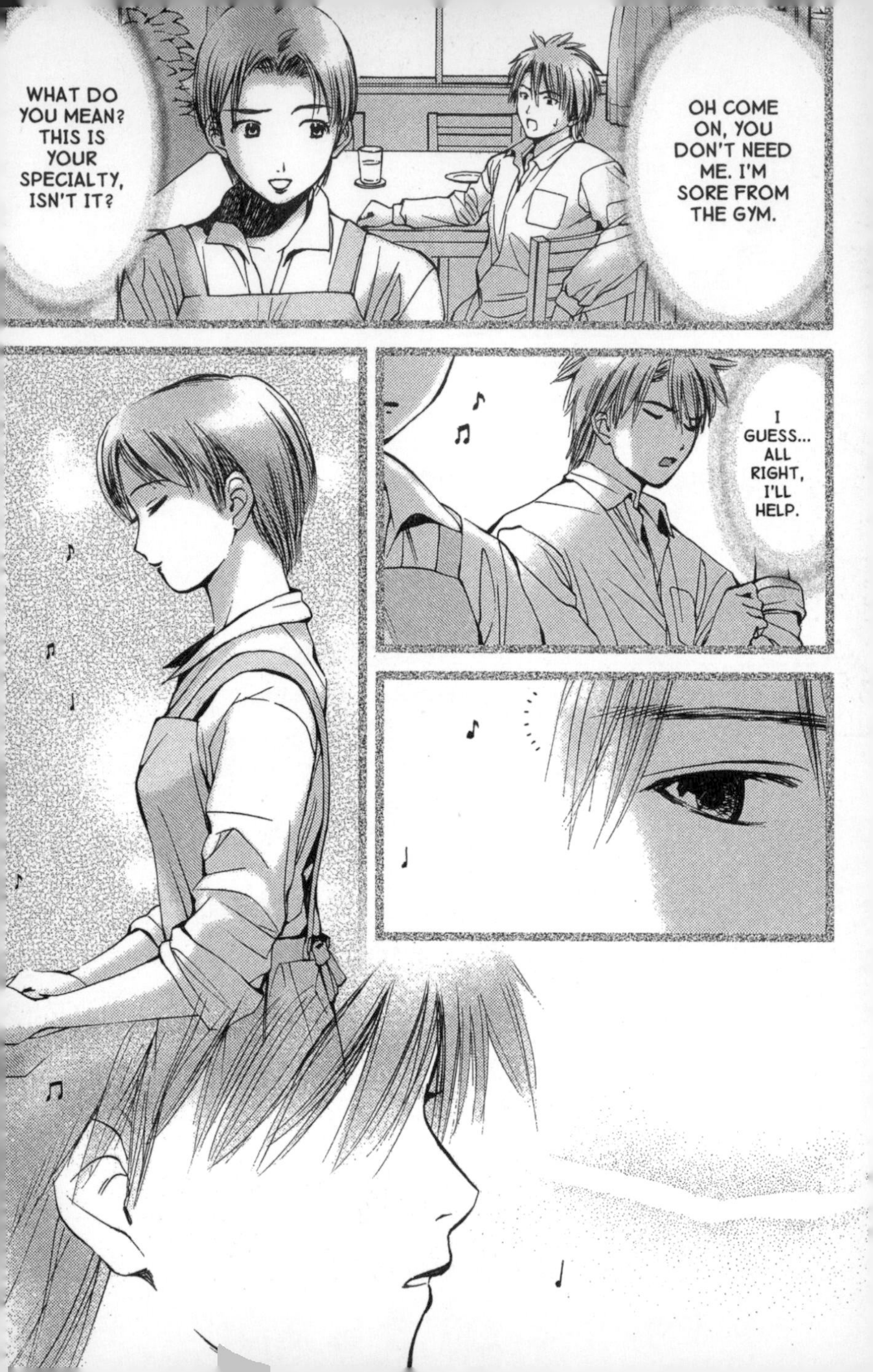
OH COME ON, YOU DON'T NEED ME. I'M SORE FROM THE GYM.
WHAT DO YOU MEAN? THIS IS YOUR SPECIALTY, ISN'T IT?
I GUESS... ALL RIGHT, I'LL HELP.

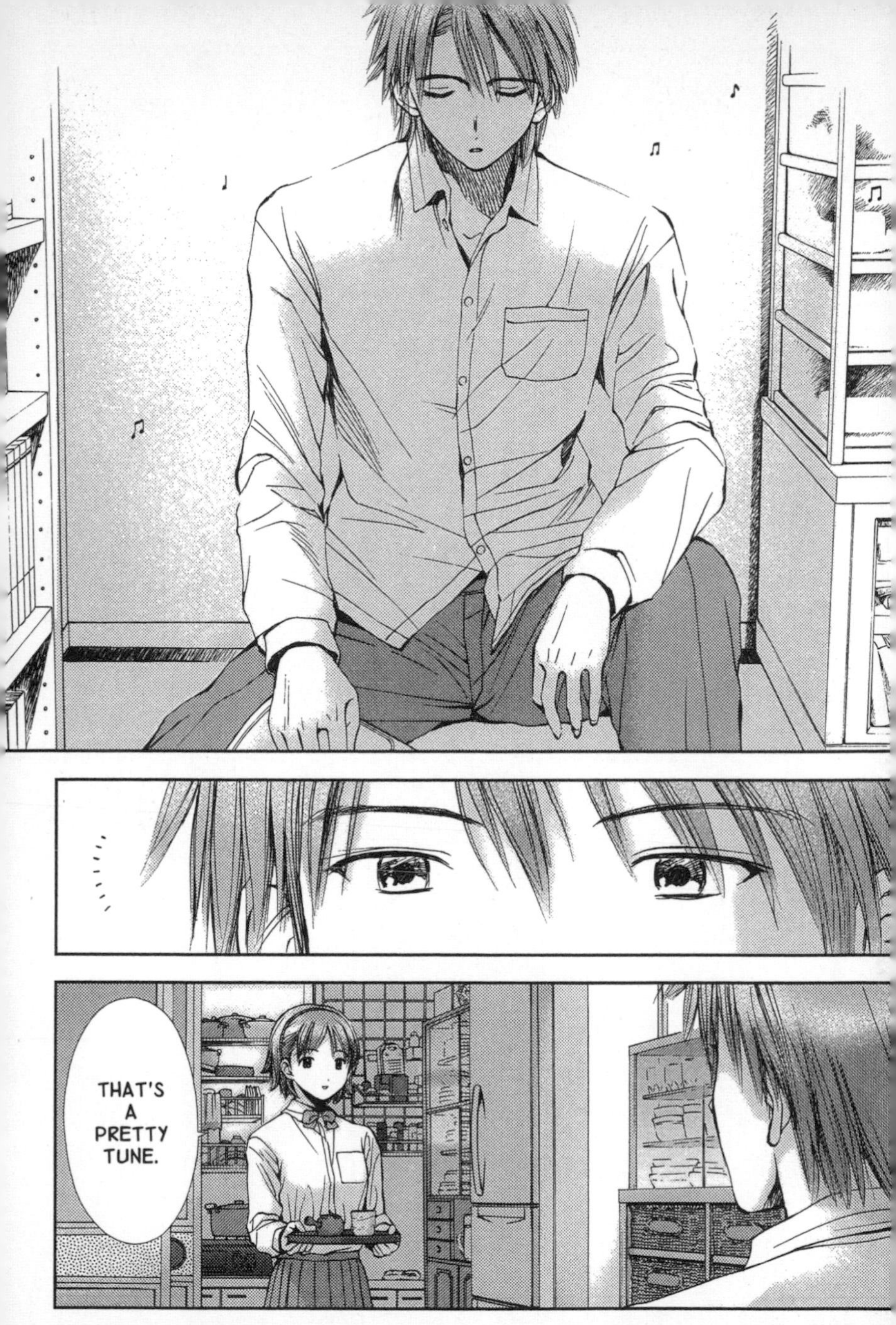
THAT'S A PRETTY TUNE.

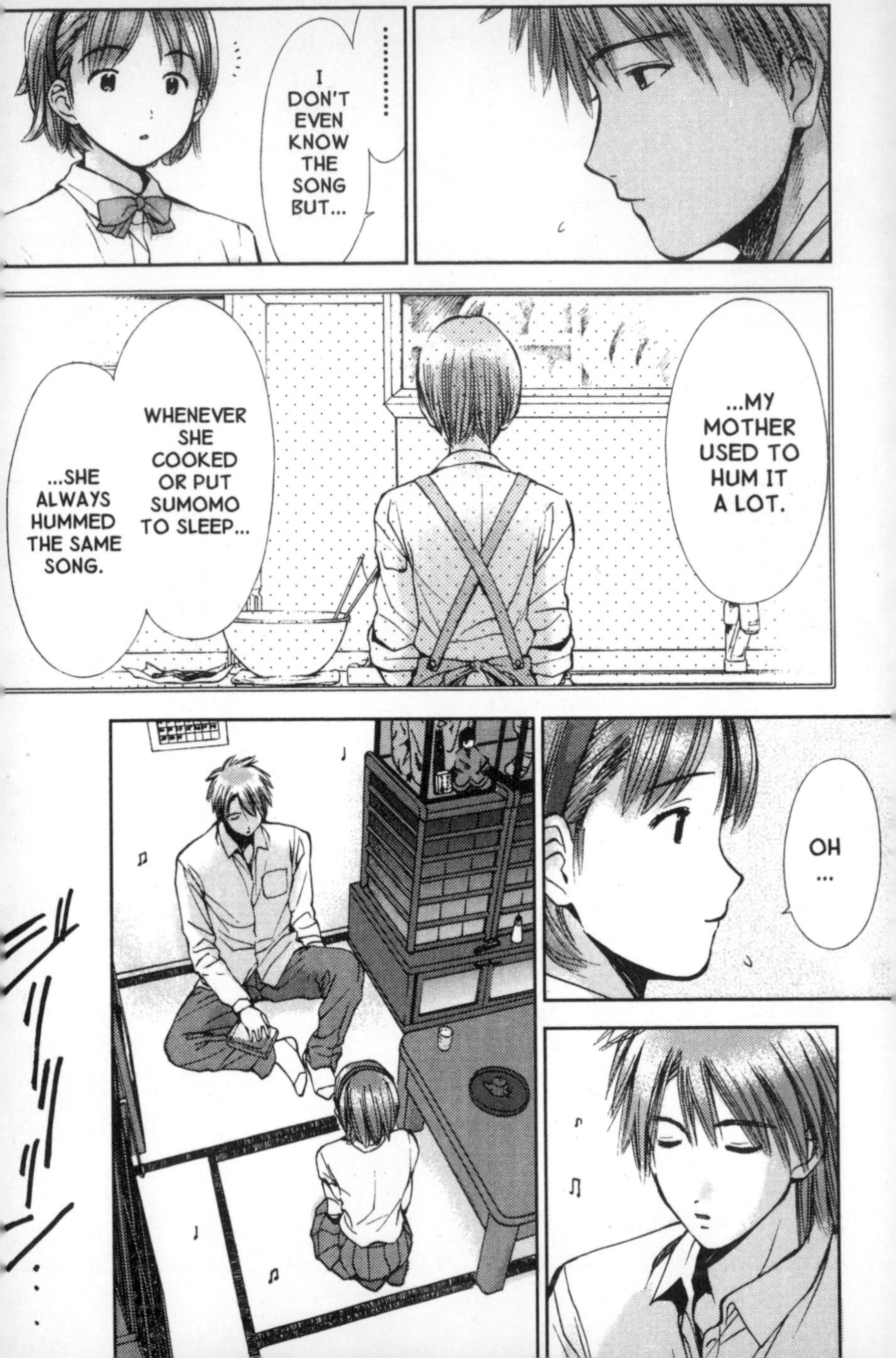
......
I DON'T EVEN KNOW THE SONG BUT...
...MY MOTHER USED TO HUM IT A LOT.
WHENEVER SHE COOKED OR PUT SUMOMO TO SLEEP...
...SHE ALWAYS HUMMED THE SAME SONG.
OH ...

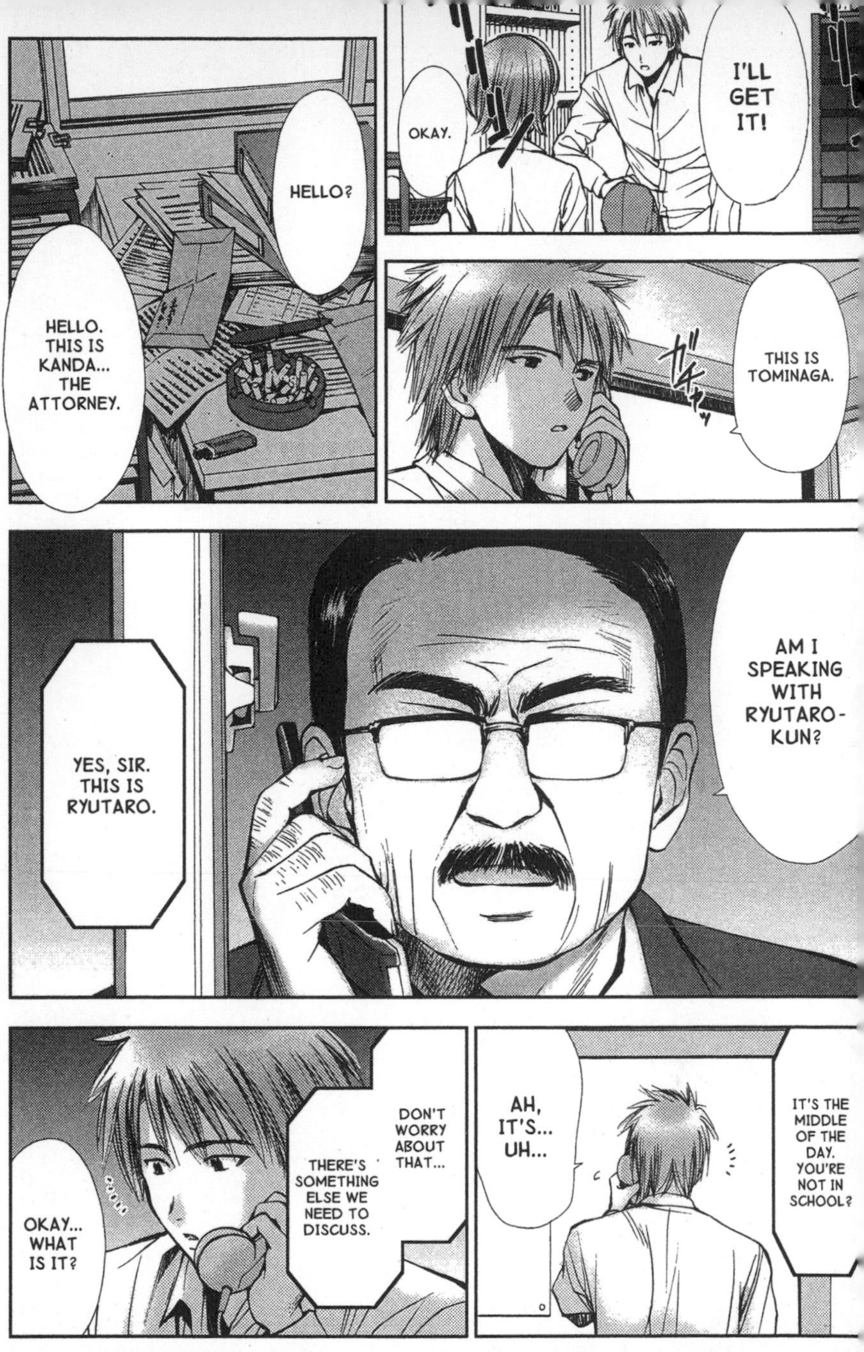
I'LL GET IT!
OKAY.
THIS IS TOMINAGA.
HELLO?
HELLO. THIS IS KANDA... THE ATTORNEY.
AM I SPEAKING WITH RYUTARO-KUN?
YES, SIR. THIS IS RYUTARO.
IT'S THE MIDDLE OF THE DAY. YOU'RE NOT IN SCHOOL?
AH, IT'S... UH...
DON'T WORRY ABOUT THAT...
THERE'S SOMETHING ELSE WE NEED TO DISCUSS.
OKAY... WHAT IS IT?

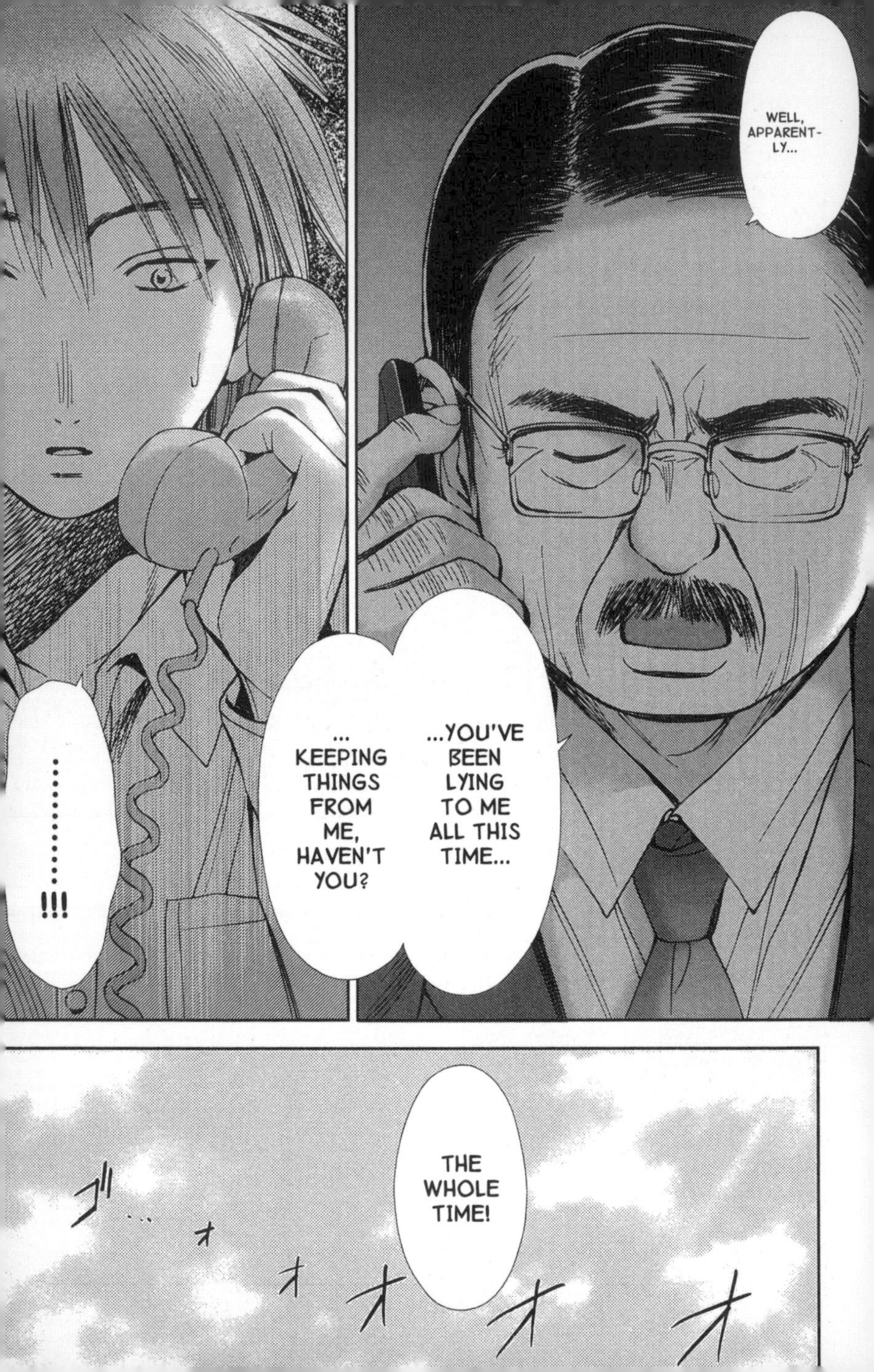
WELL, APPARENT-LY...
...YOU'VE BEEN LYING TO ME ALL THIS TIME...
...KEEPING THINGS FROM ME, HAVEN'T YOU?
.........!!!
THE WHOLE TIME!
ゴ...オオオオオ

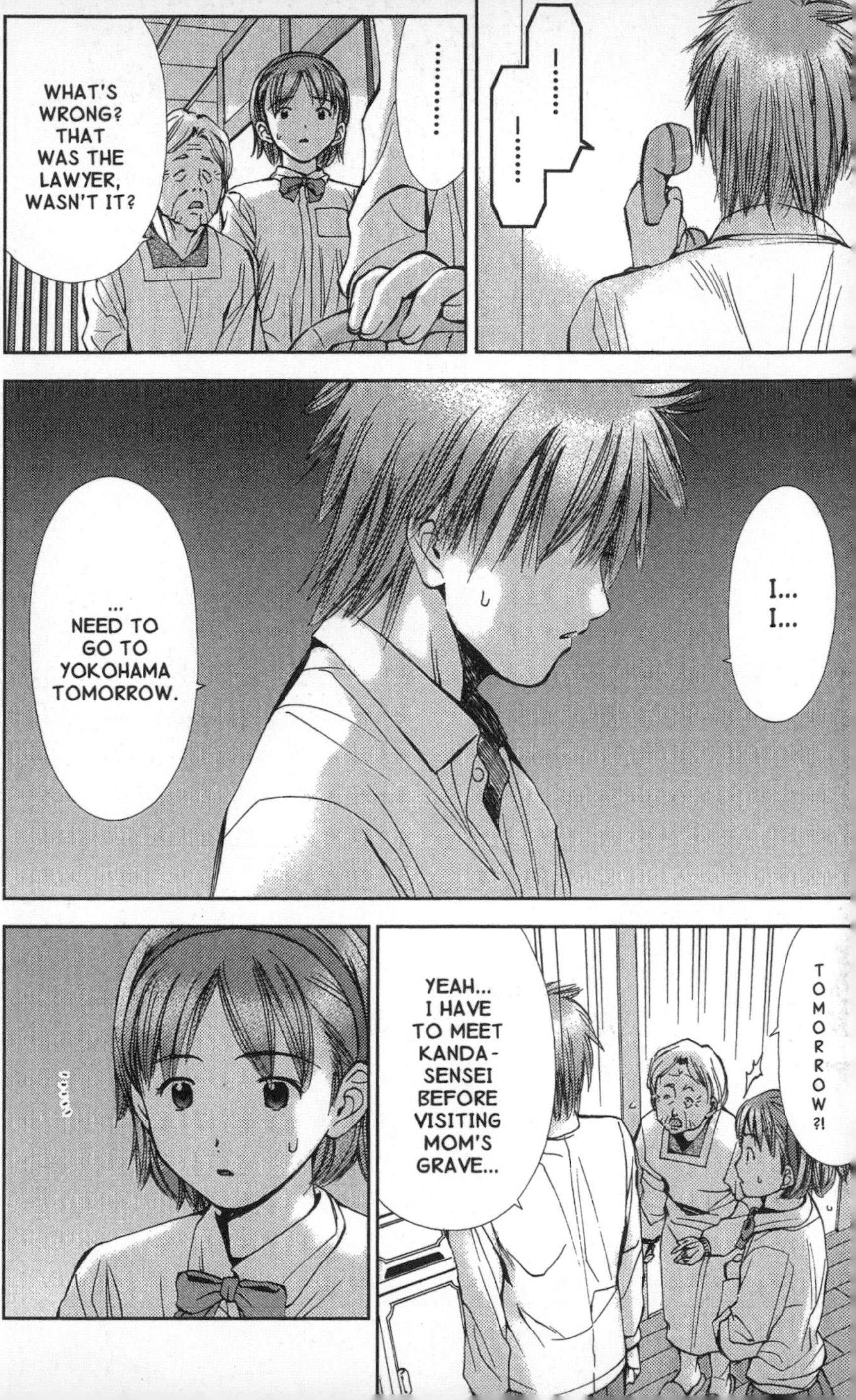
I...... I......
....
WHAT'S WRONG? THAT WAS THE LAWYER, WASN'T IT?
I... I...
... NEED TO GO TO YOKOHAMA TOMORROW.
TOMORROW?!
YEAH... I HAVE TO MEET KANDA-SENSEI BEFORE VISITING MOM'S GRAVE...

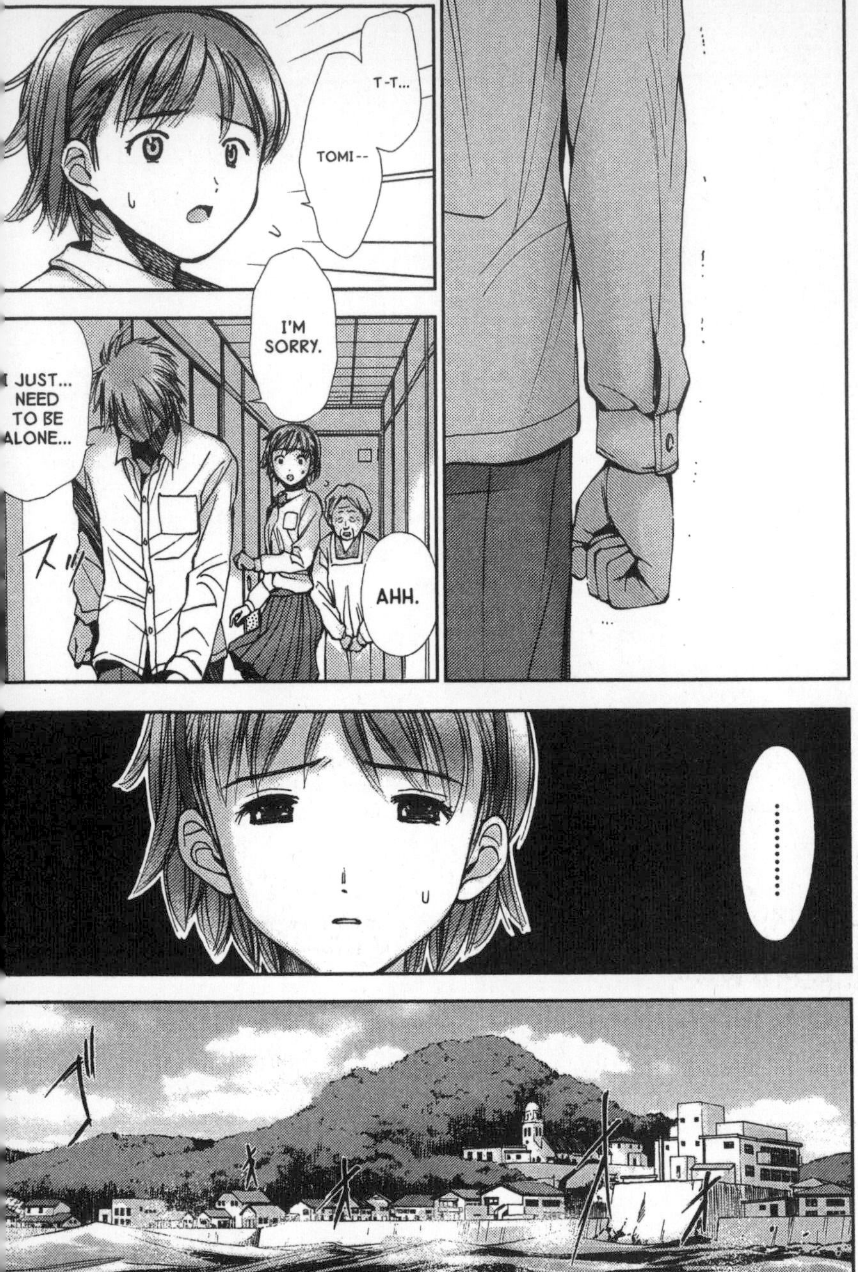
...
T-T...
TOMI--
I'M SORRY.
I JUST... NEED TO BE ALONE...
AHH.
......

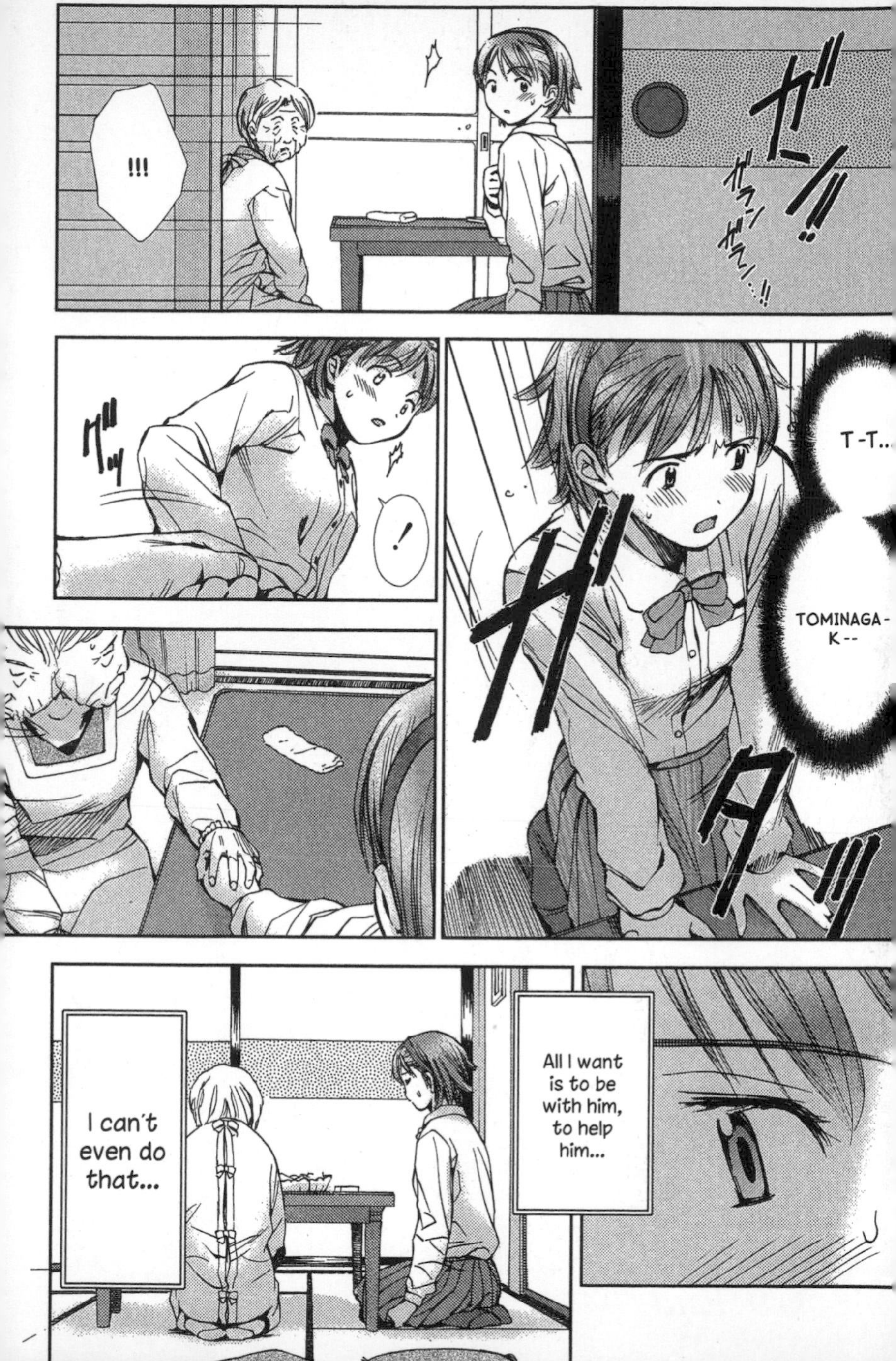
!!!
T-T...
TOMINAGA-K--
!
All I want is to be with him, to help him...
I can't even do that...

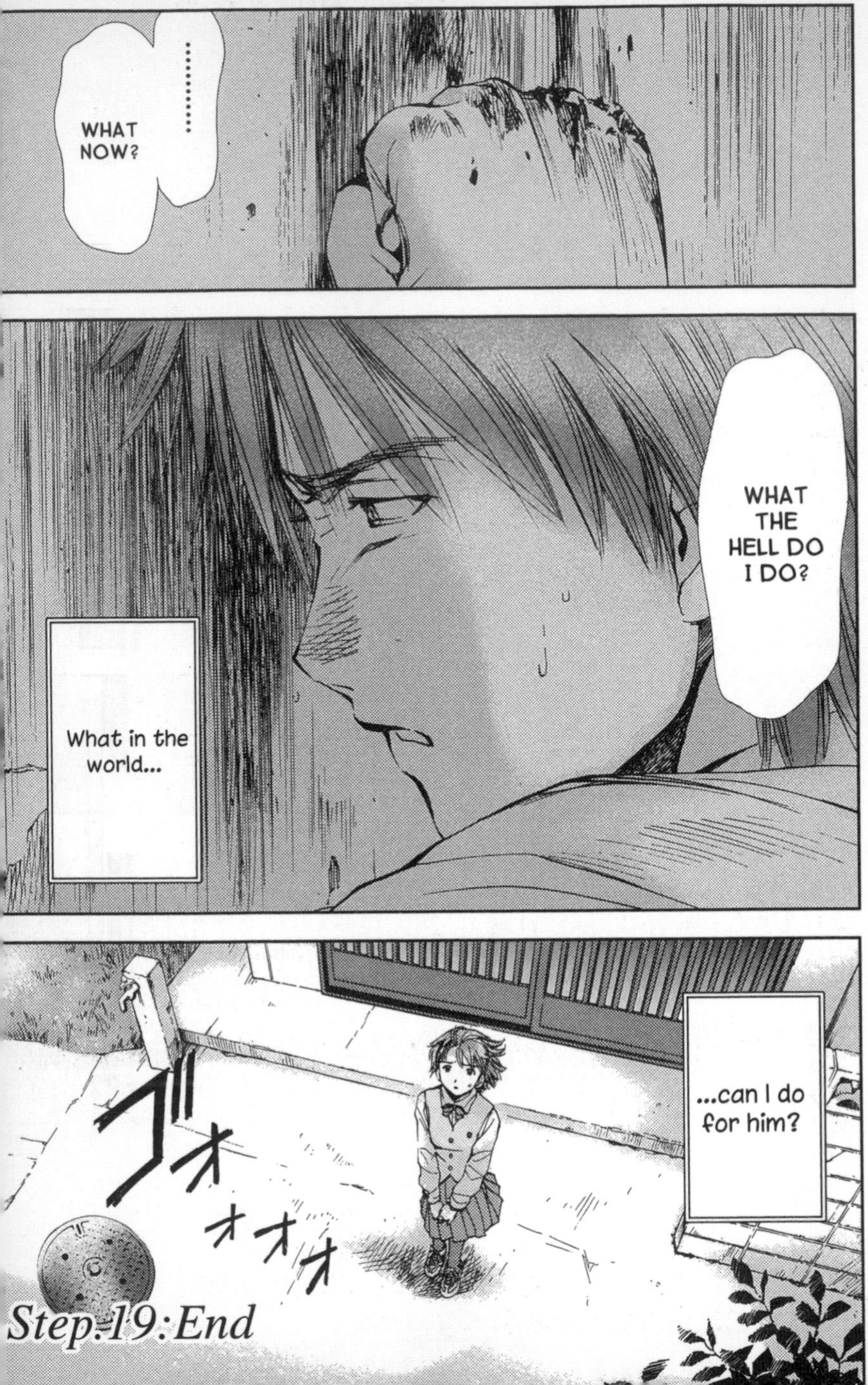
......
WHAT NOW?
WHAT THE HELL DO I DO?
What in the world...
...can I do for him?
ゴオオオオ
Step.19:End

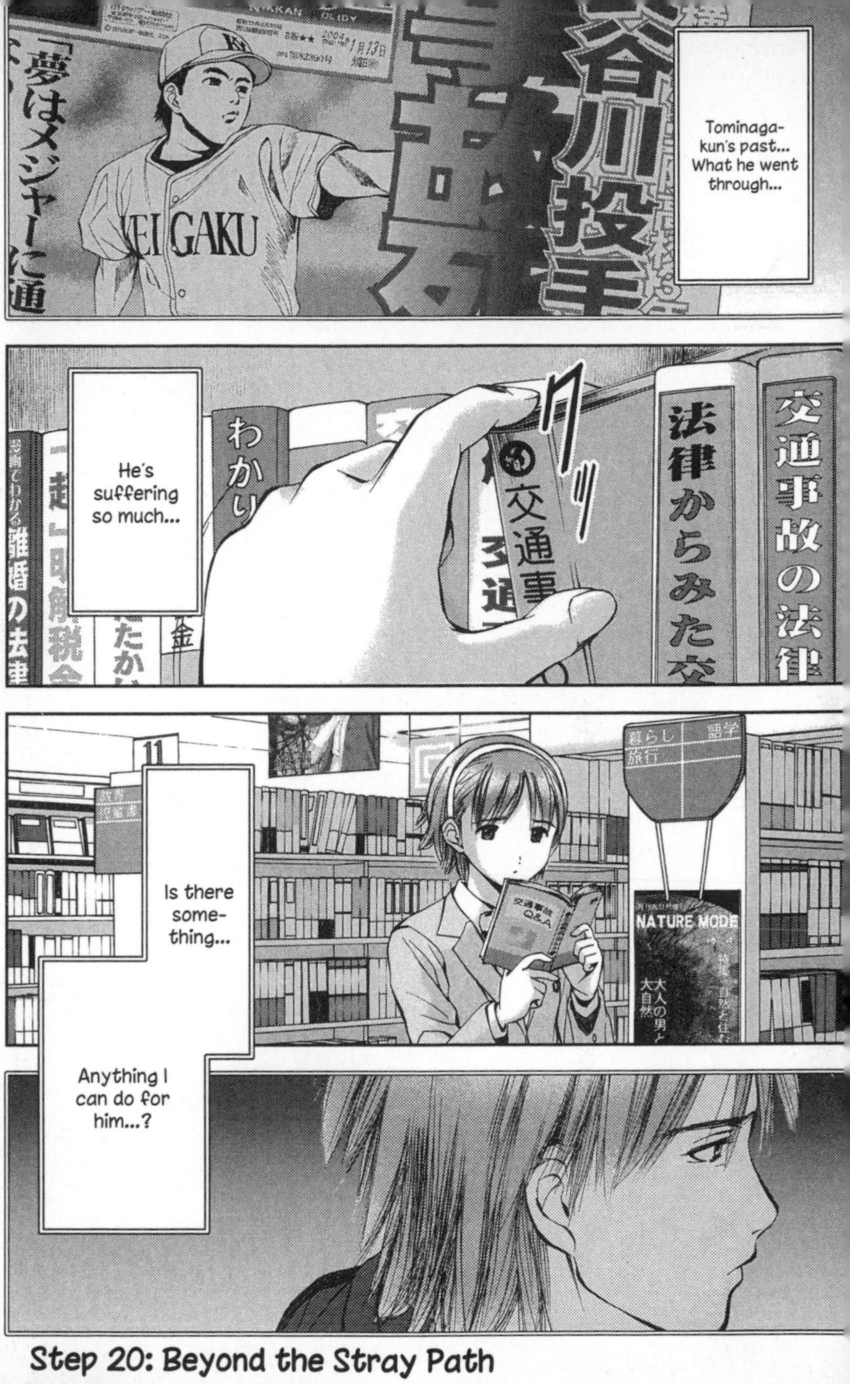
Tominaga-kun's past... What he went through...
「夢はメジャーに通
He's suffering so much...
交通事故の法律
法律からみた交
交通事
わかり
Is there some-thing...
Anything I can do for him...?
暮らし
語学
旅行
交通事故Q&A
NATURE MODE

Step 20: Beyond the Stray Path

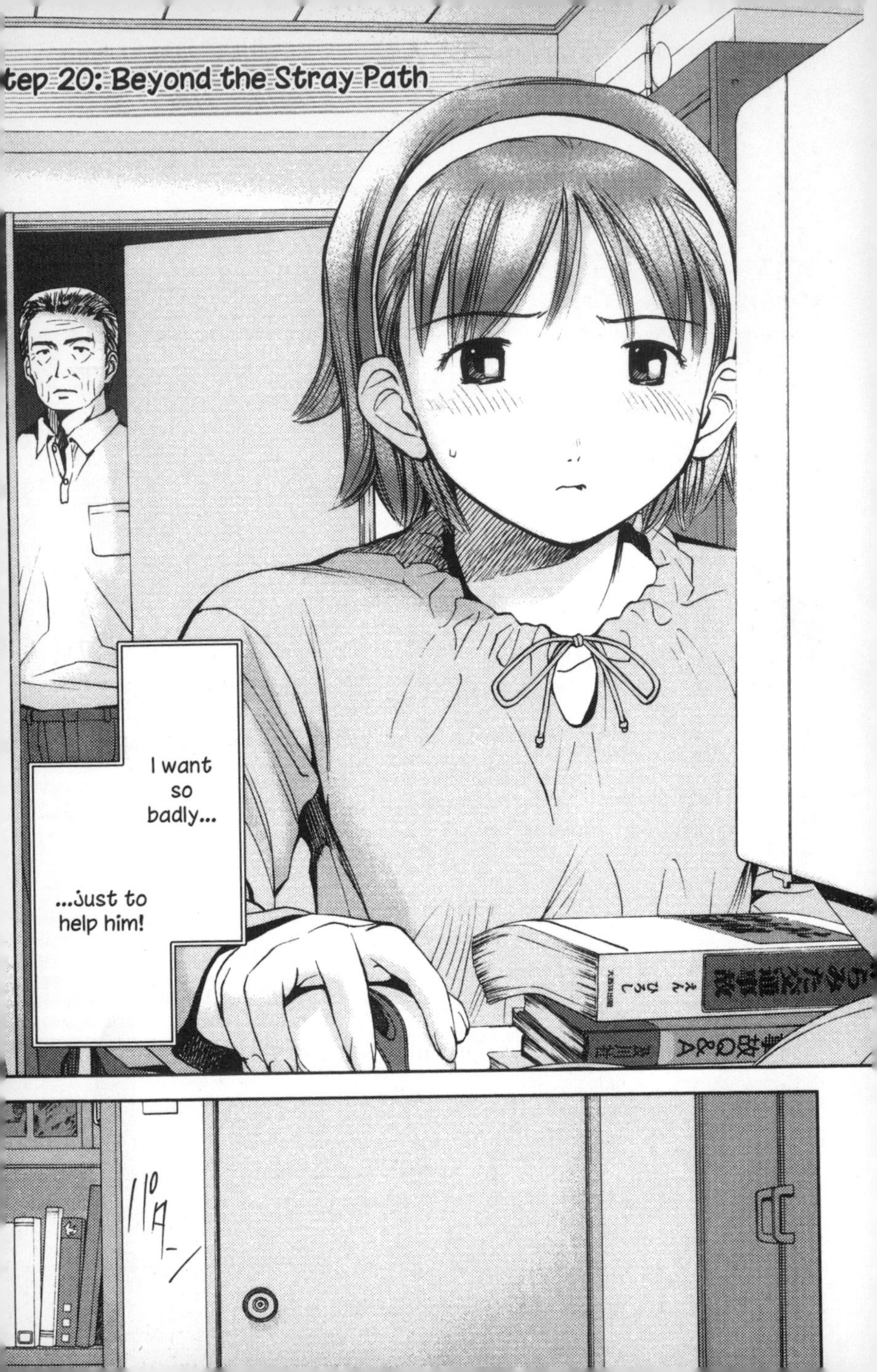
tep 20: Beyond the Stray Path
I want so badly...
...just to help him!
パタ

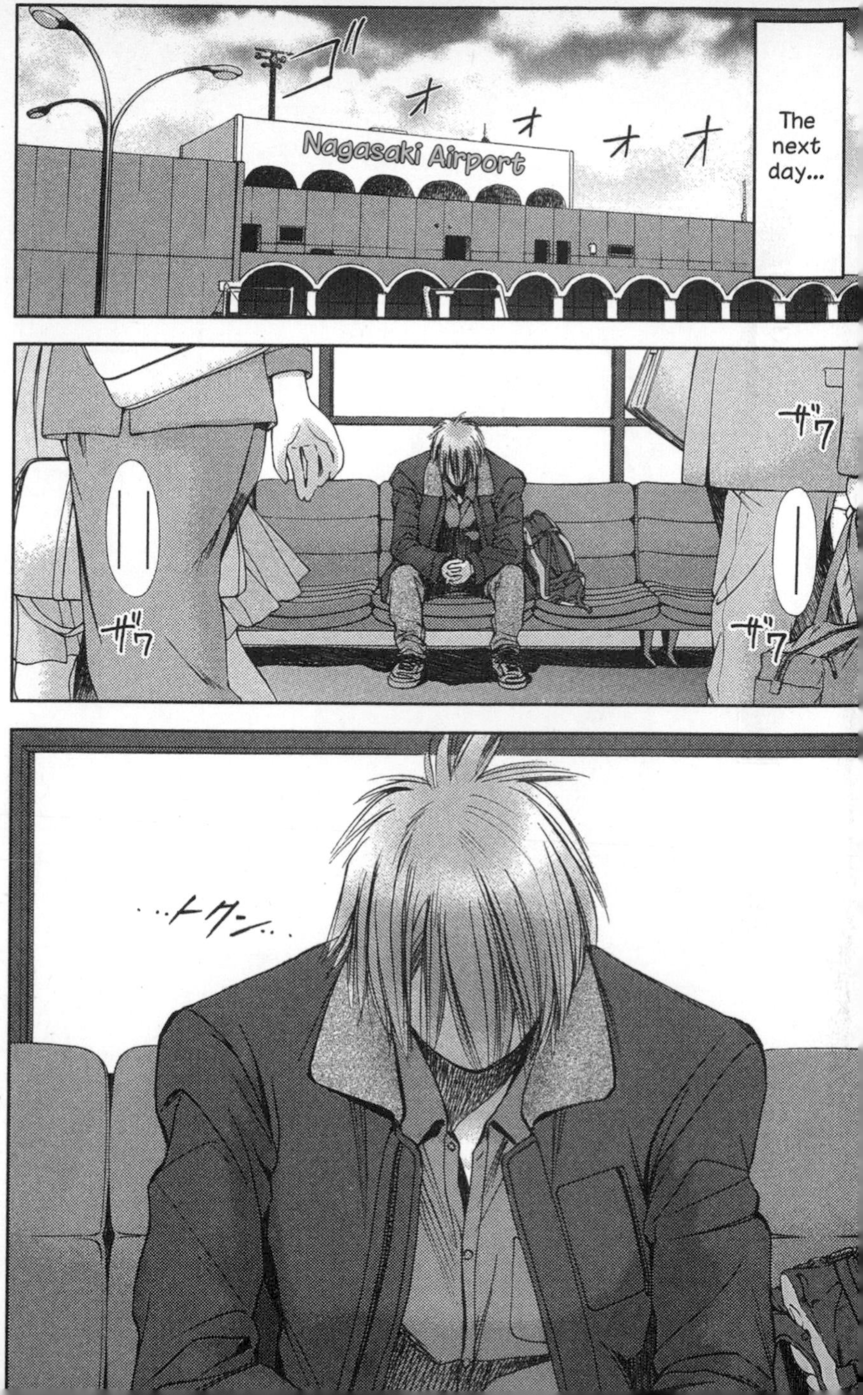
The next day...
ゴオオオオ
Nagasaki Airport
ザワ
ザワ
ザワ
…トクン…

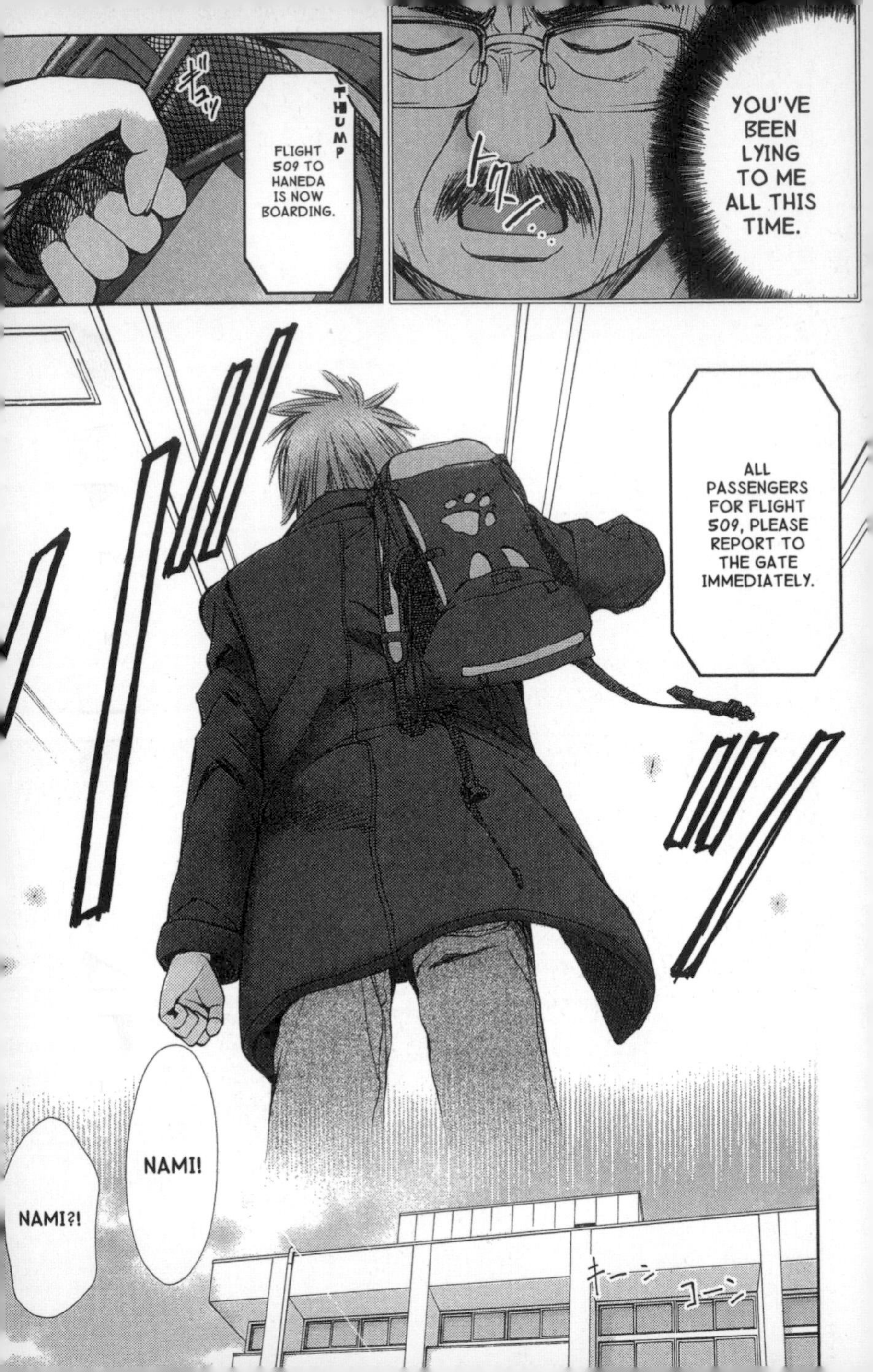
YOU'VE BEEN LYING TO ME ALL THIS TIME.
THUMP
FLIGHT 509 TO HANEDA IS NOW BOARDING.
ALL PASSENGERS FOR FLIGHT 509, PLEASE REPORT TO THE GATE IMMEDIATELY.
NAMI!
NAMI?!

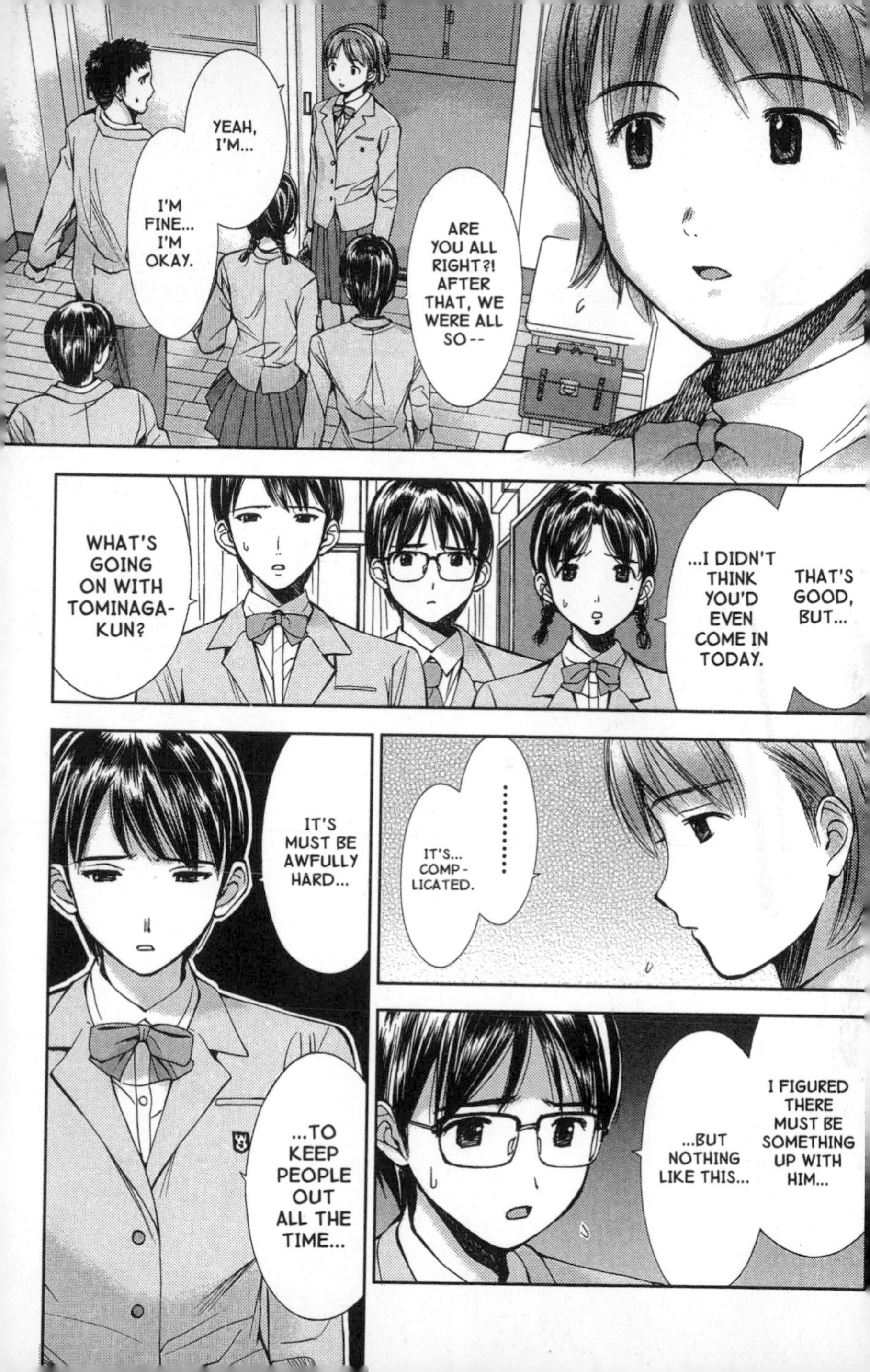
ARE YOU ALL RIGHT?! AFTER THAT, WE WERE ALL SO--
YEAH, I'M...
I'M FINE... I'M OKAY.
THAT'S GOOD, BUT...
...I DIDN'T THINK YOU'D EVEN COME IN TODAY.
WHAT'S GOING ON WITH TOMINAGA-KUN?
....
IT'S... COMP-LICATED.
I FIGURED THERE MUST BE SOMETHING UP WITH HIM...
...BUT NOTHING LIKE THIS...
IT'S MUST BE AWFULLY HARD...
...TO KEEP PEOPLE OUT ALL THE TIME...

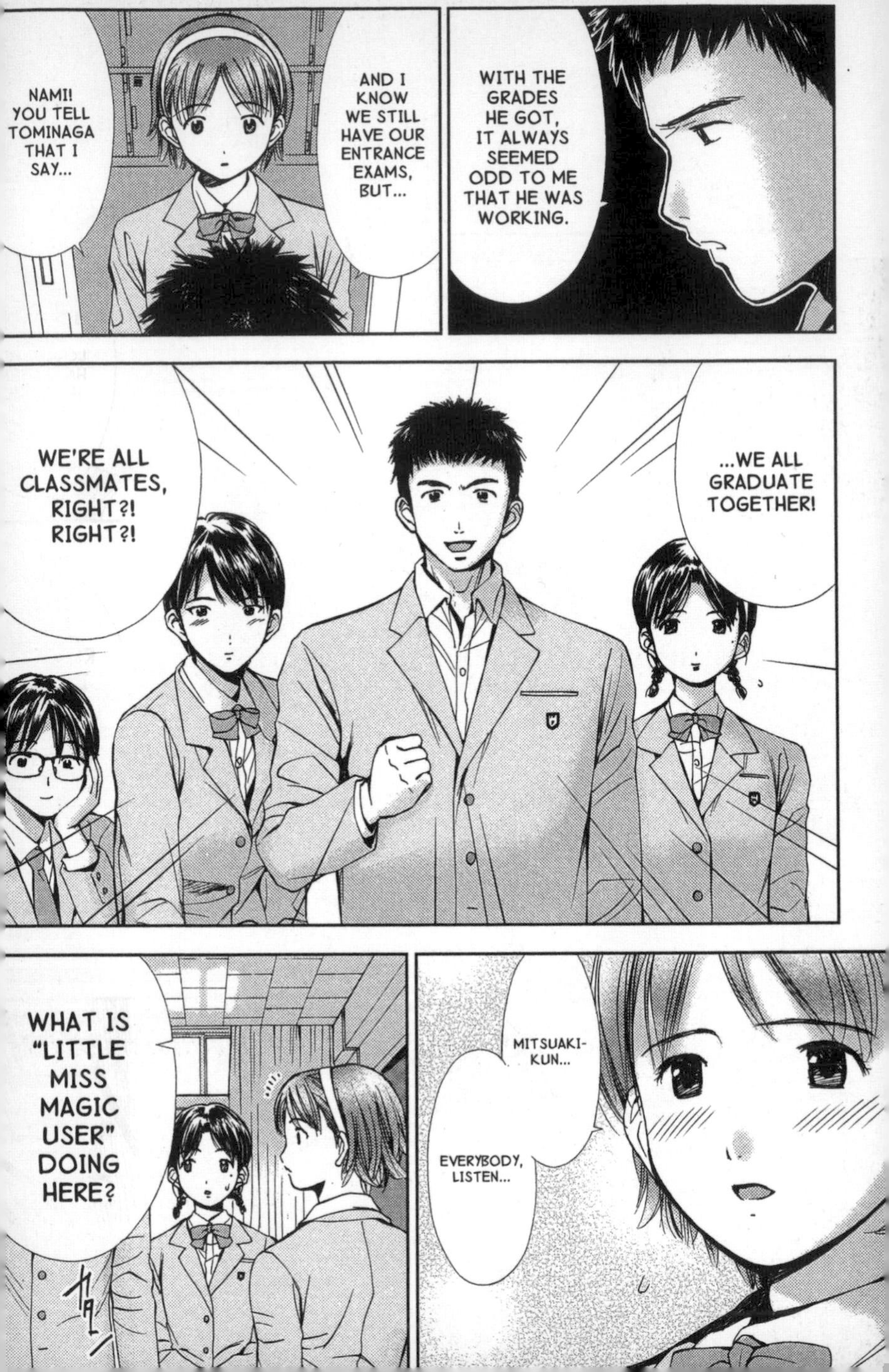
WITH THE GRADES HE GOT, IT ALWAYS SEEMED ODD TO ME THAT HE WAS WORKING.
AND I KNOW WE STILL HAVE OUR ENTRANCE EXAMS, BUT...
NAMI! YOU TELL TOMINAGA THAT I SAY...
...WE ALL GRADUATE TOGETHER!
WE'RE ALL CLASSMATES, RIGHT?! RIGHT?!
MITSUAKI-KUN...
EVERYBODY, LISTEN...
WHAT IS "LITTLE MISS MAGIC USER" DOING HERE?

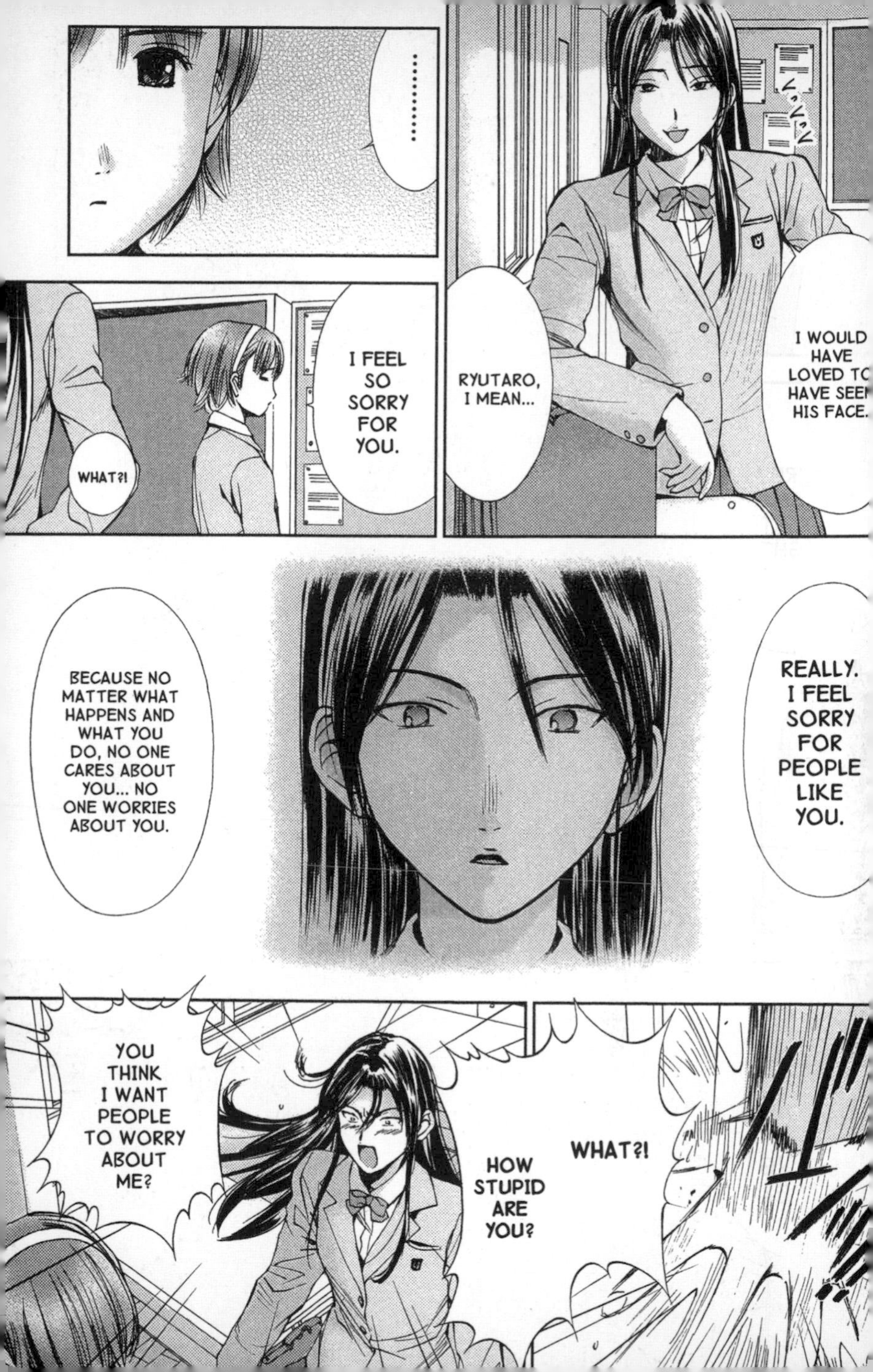
I WOULD HAVE LOVED TO HAVE SEEN HIS FACE.
RYUTARO, I MEAN...
......
I FEEL SO SORRY FOR YOU.
WHAT?!
REALLY. I FEEL SORRY FOR PEOPLE LIKE YOU.
BECAUSE NO MATTER WHAT HAPPENS AND WHAT YOU DO, NO ONE CARES ABOUT YOU... NO ONE WORRIES ABOUT YOU.
WHAT?!
HOW STUPID ARE YOU?
YOU THINK I WANT PEOPLE TO WORRY ABOUT ME?

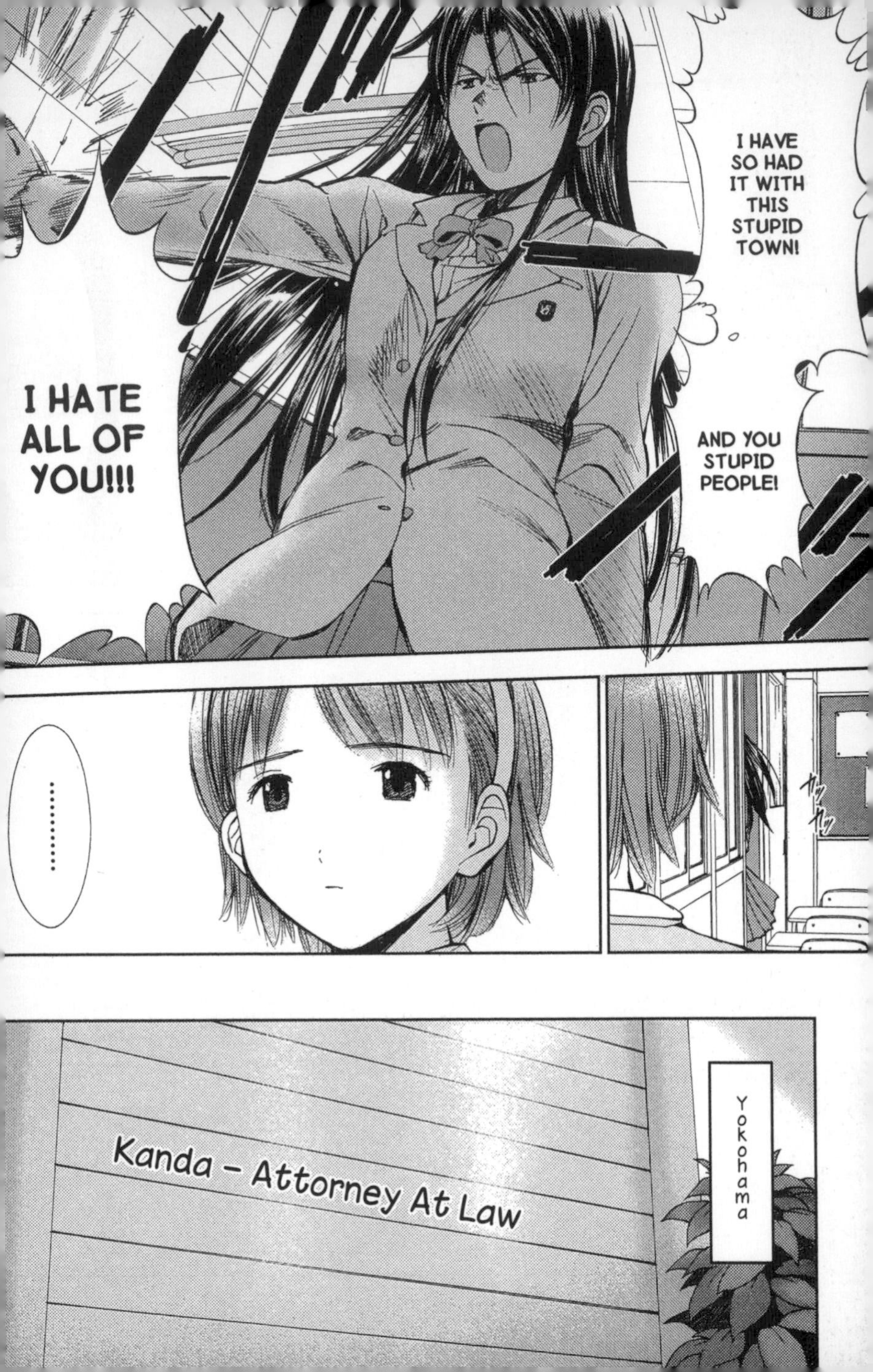
I HAVE SO HAD IT WITH THIS STUPID TOWN!
AND YOU STUPID PEOPLE!
I HATE ALL OF YOU!!!
....
Yokohama
Kanda – Attorney At Law

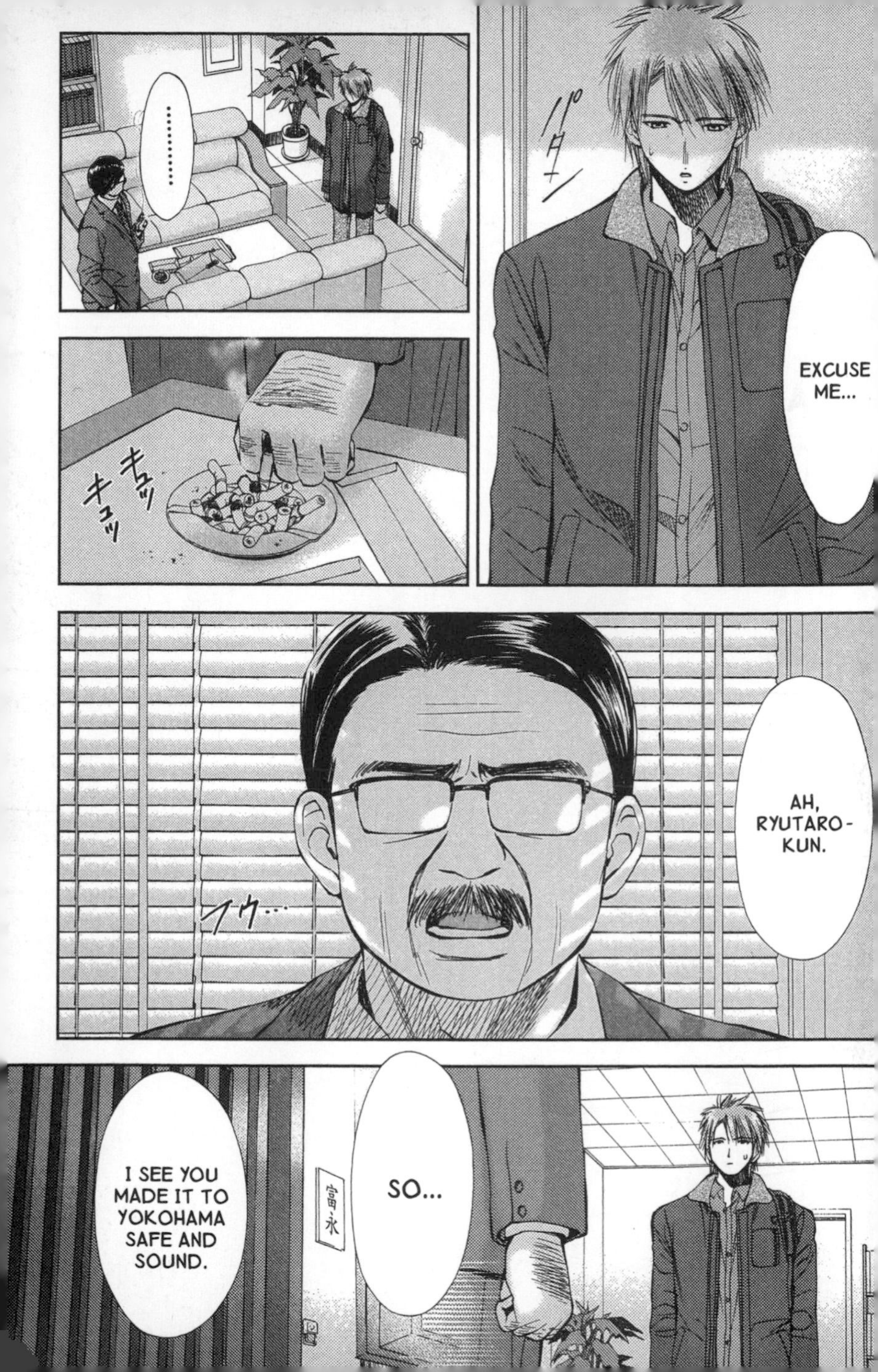
パタン
EXCUSE ME...
......
キュッ
キュッ
AH, RYUTARO-KUN.
フウ…
SO...
富永
I SEE YOU MADE IT TO YOKOHAMA SAFE AND SOUND.

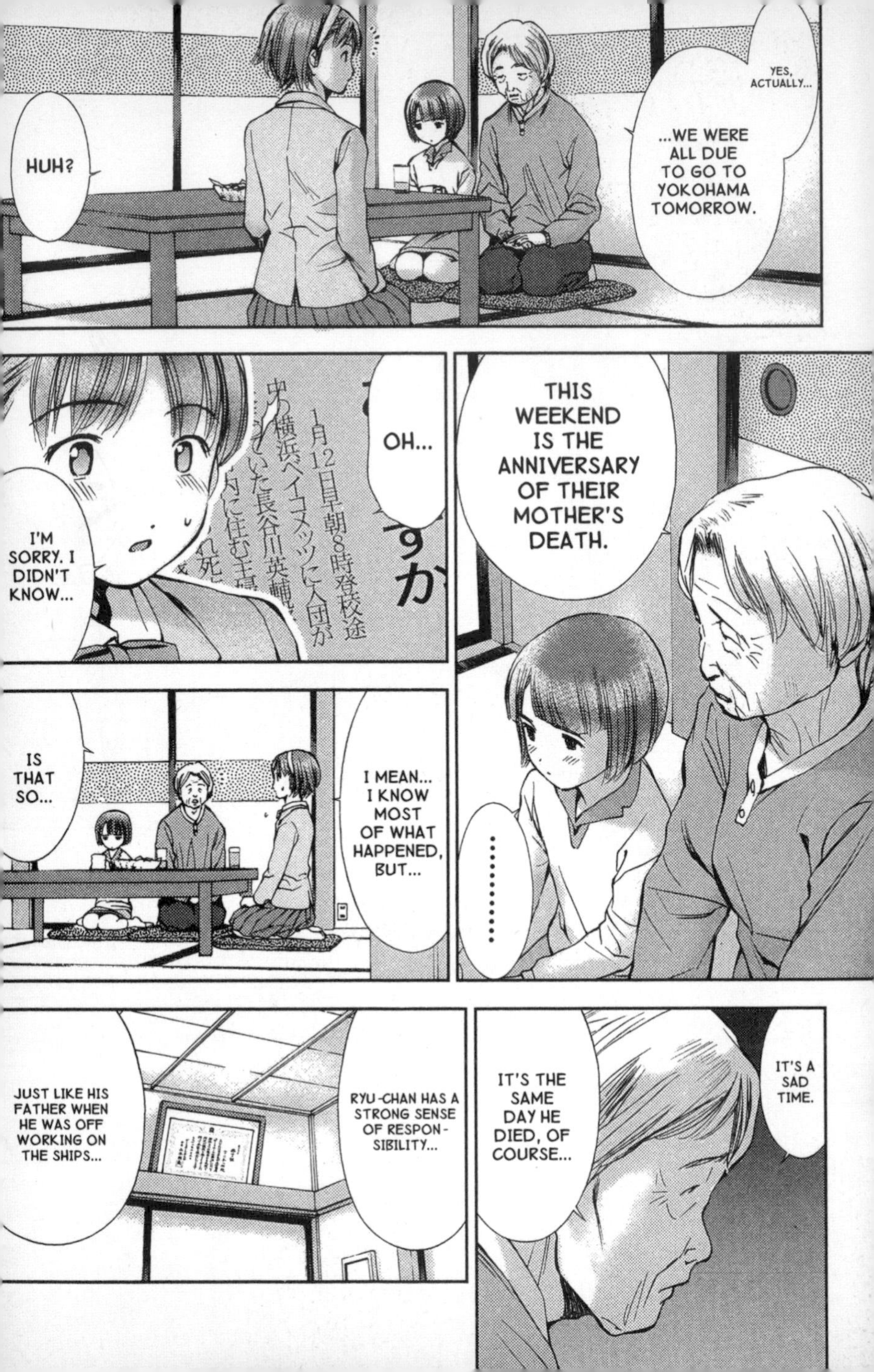
YES, ACTUALLY...
...WE WERE ALL DUE TO GO TO YOKOHAMA TOMORROW.
HUH?
THIS WEEKEND IS THE ANNIVERSARY OF THEIR MOTHER'S DEATH.
......
OH...
I'M SORRY. I DIDN'T KNOW...
1月12日早朝8時登校途
I MEAN... I KNOW MOST OF WHAT HAPPENED, BUT...
IS THAT SO...
IT'S A SAD TIME.
IT'S THE SAME DAY HE DIED, OF COURSE...
RYU-CHAN HAS A STRONG SENSE OF RESPON-SIBILITY...
JUST LIKE HIS FATHER WHEN HE WAS OFF WORKING ON THE SHIPS...

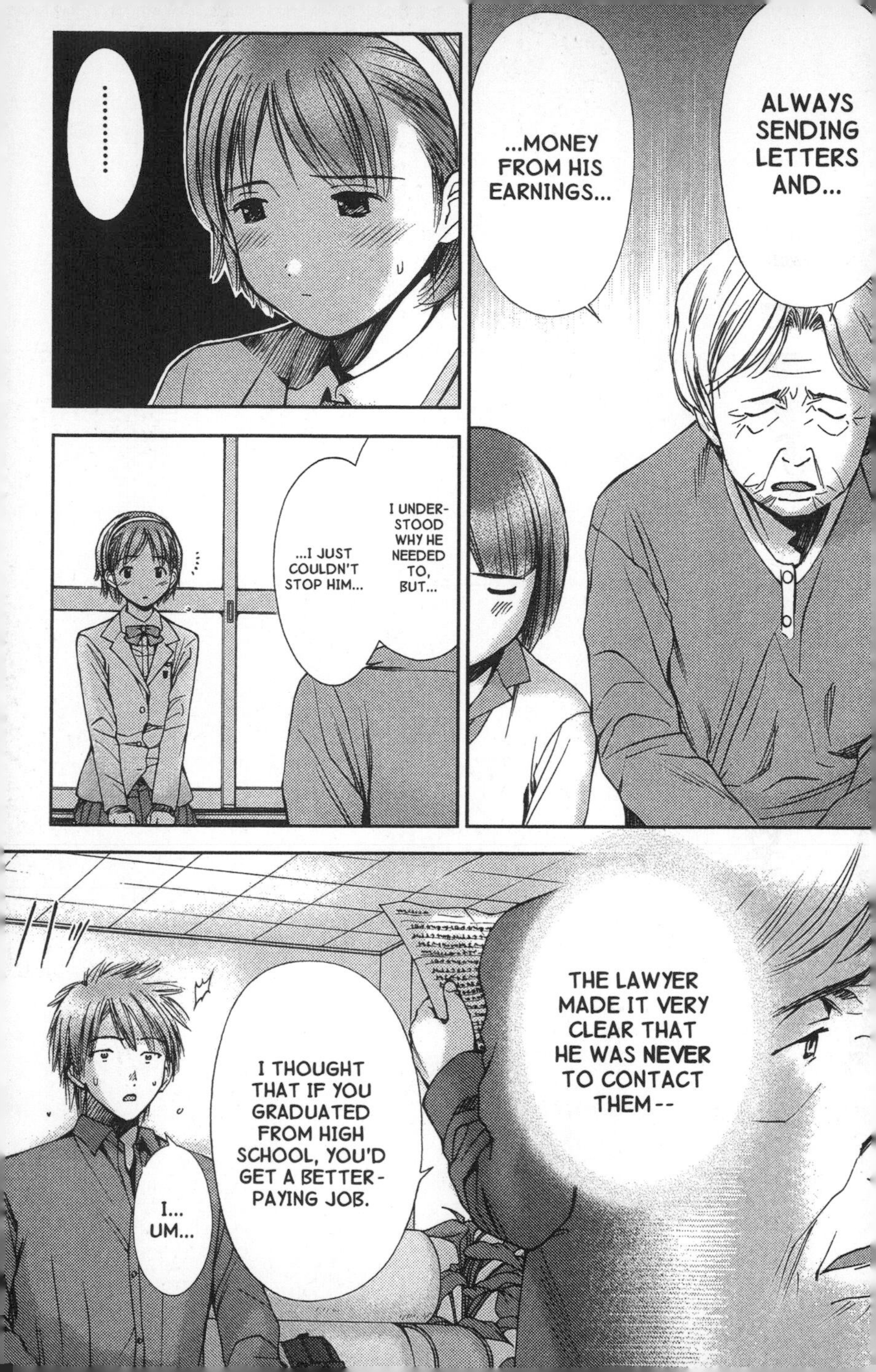
ALWAYS SENDING LETTERS AND...
...MONEY FROM HIS EARNINGS...
......
I UNDER-STOOD WHY HE NEEDED TO, BUT...
...I JUST COULDN'T STOP HIM...
THE LAWYER MADE IT VERY CLEAR THAT HE WAS NEVER TO CONTACT THEM--
I THOUGHT THAT IF YOU GRADUATED FROM HIGH SCHOOL, YOU'D GET A BETTER-PAYING JOB.
I... UM...

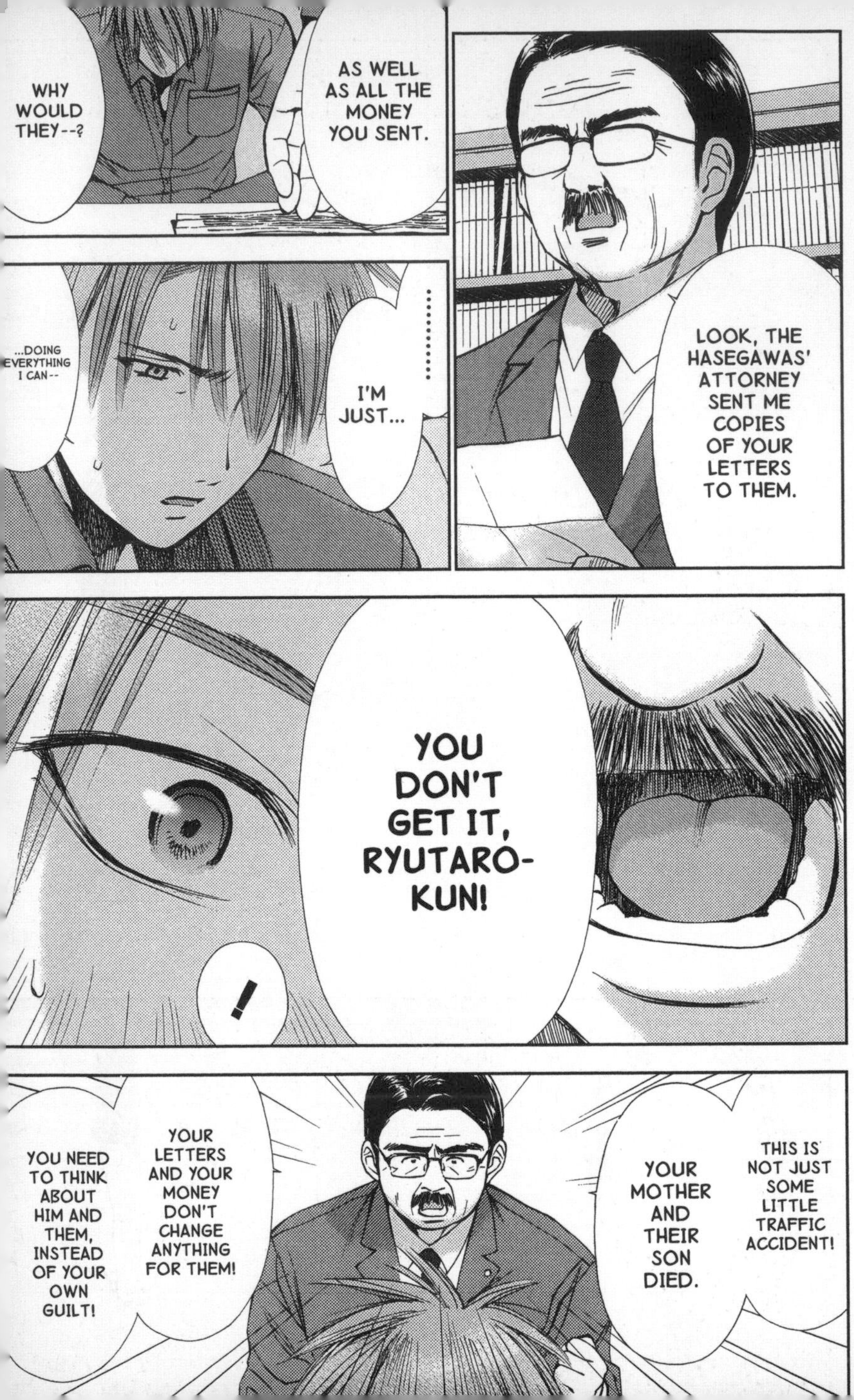
LOOK, THE HASEGAWAS' ATTORNEY SENT ME COPIES OF YOUR LETTERS TO THEM.
AS WELL AS ALL THE MONEY YOU SENT.
WHY WOULD THEY--?
....
I'M JUST...
...DOING EVERYTHING I CAN--
YOU DON'T GET IT, RYUTARO-KUN!
!
THIS IS NOT JUST SOME LITTLE TRAFFIC ACCIDENT!
YOUR MOTHER AND THEIR SON DIED.
YOUR LETTERS AND YOUR MONEY DON'T CHANGE ANYTHING FOR THEM!
YOU NEED TO THINK ABOUT HIM AND THEM, INSTEAD OF YOUR OWN GUILT!

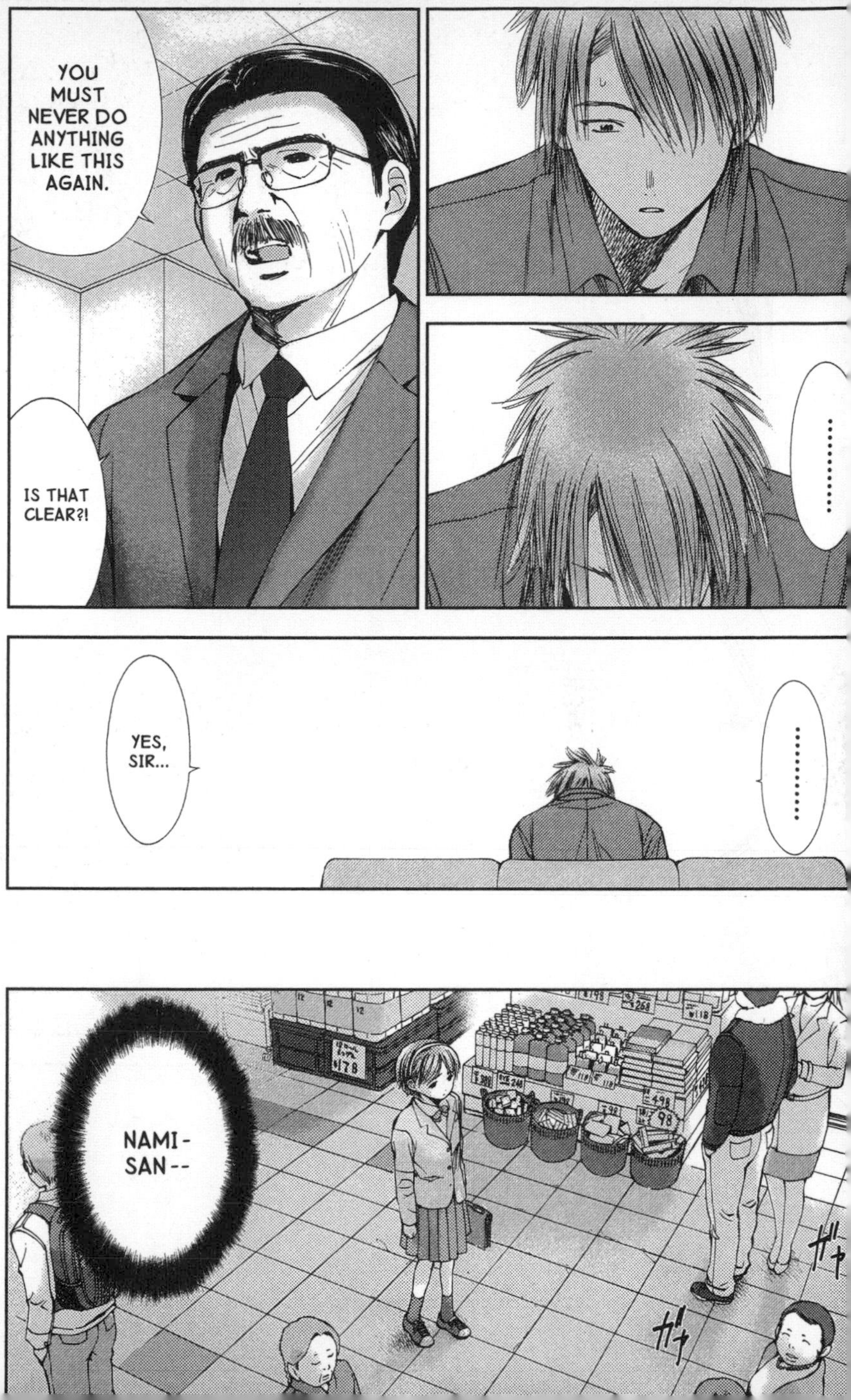
....
YOU MUST NEVER DO ANYTHING LIKE THIS AGAIN.
IS THAT CLEAR?!
....
YES, SIR...
ガヤ
ガヤ
NAMI-SAN--

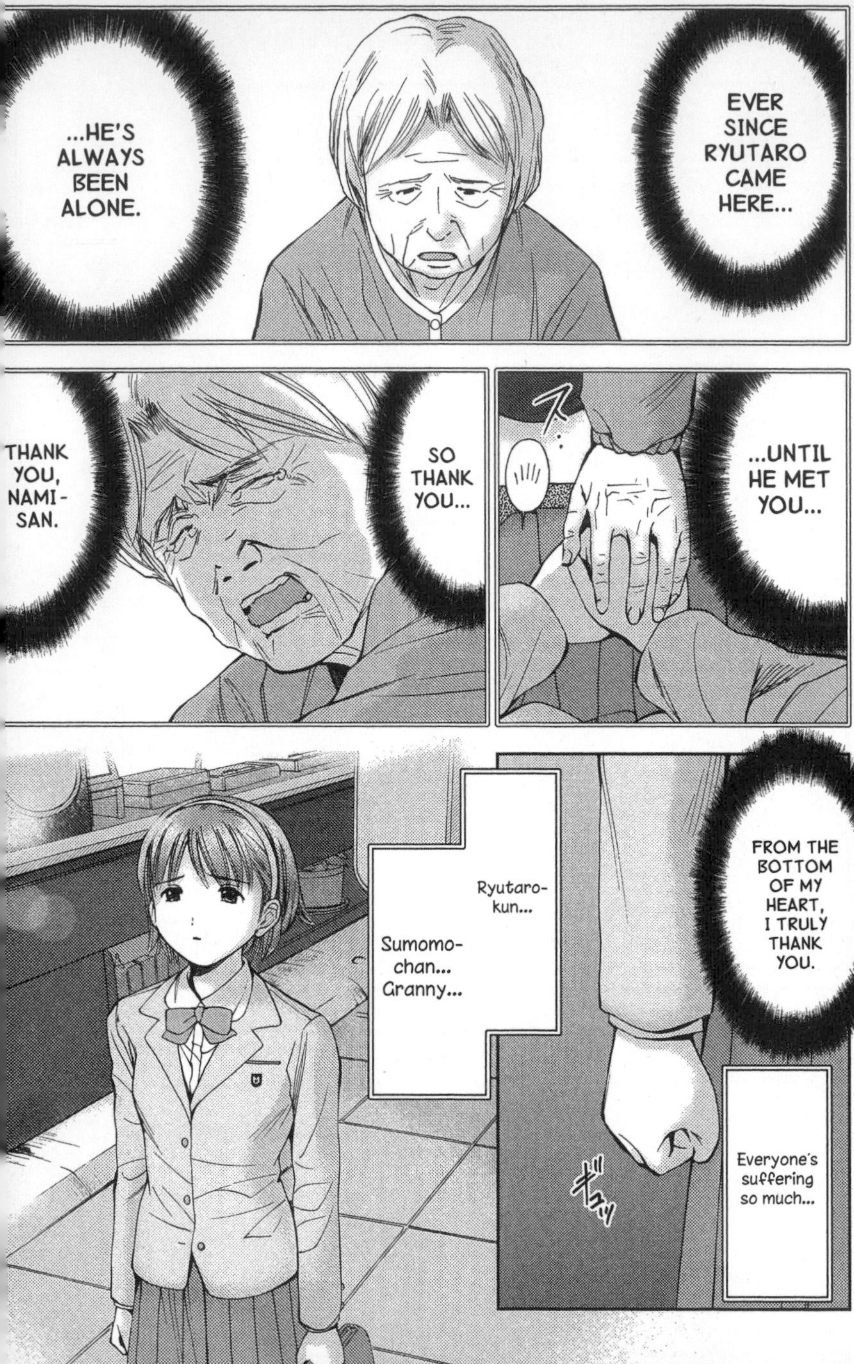
EVER SINCE RYUTARO CAME HERE...
...HE'S ALWAYS BEEN ALONE.
ス
...UNTIL HE MET YOU...
SO THANK YOU...
THANK YOU, NAMI-SAN.
FROM THE BOTTOM OF MY HEART, I TRULY THANK YOU.
ギュッ
Everyone's suffering so much...
Ryutaro-kun...
Sumomo-chan... Granny...

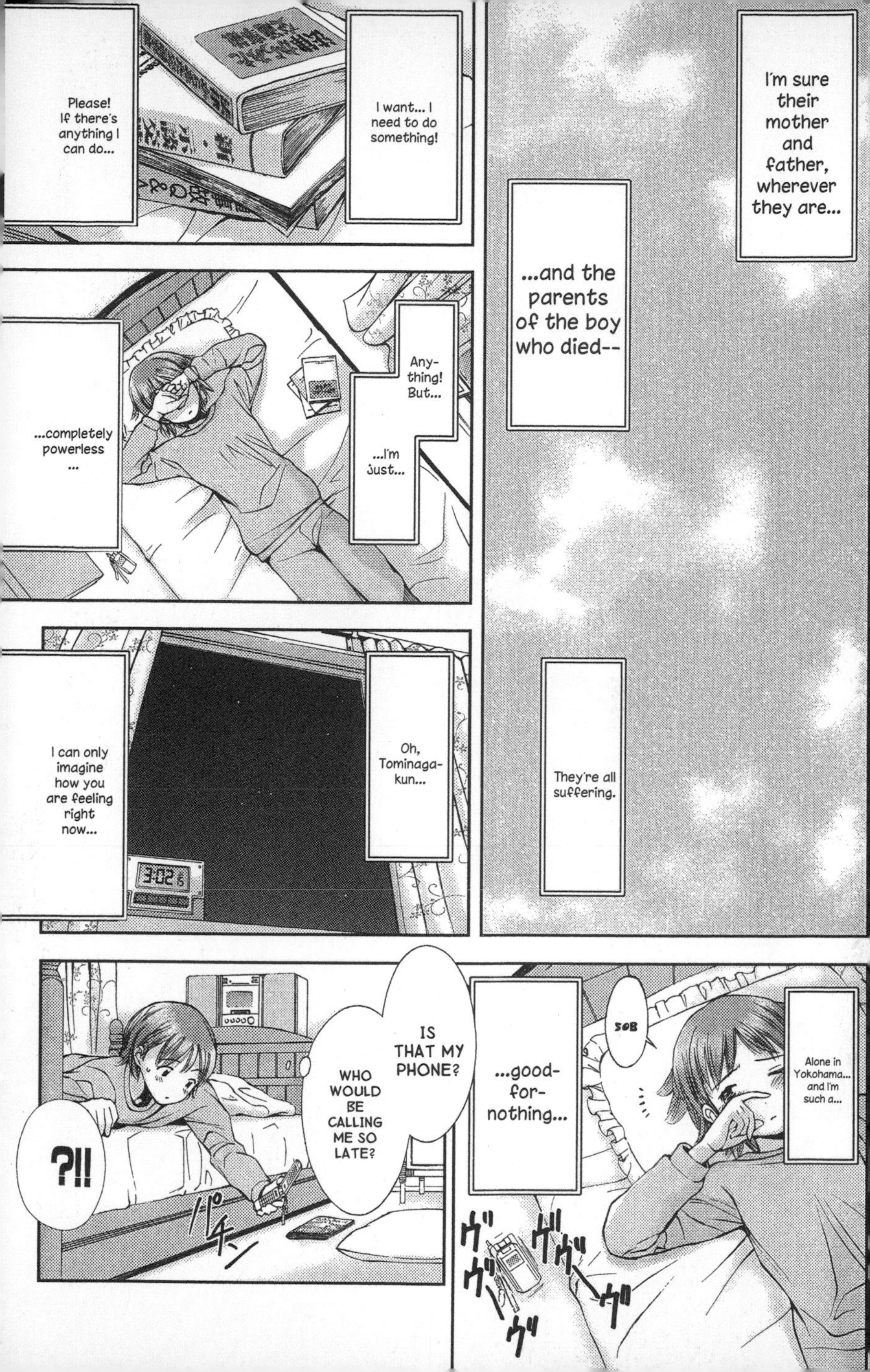
I'm sure their mother and father, wherever they are...
...and the parents of the boy who died--
They're all suffering.
I want... I need to do something!
Please! If there's anything I can do...
Any-thing! But...
...I'm just...
...completely powerless...
Oh, Tominaga-kun...
I can only imagine how you are feeling right now...
Alone in Yokohama... and I'm such a...
SOB
...good-for-nothing...
IS THAT MY PHONE?
WHO WOULD BE CALLING ME SO LATE?
?!!

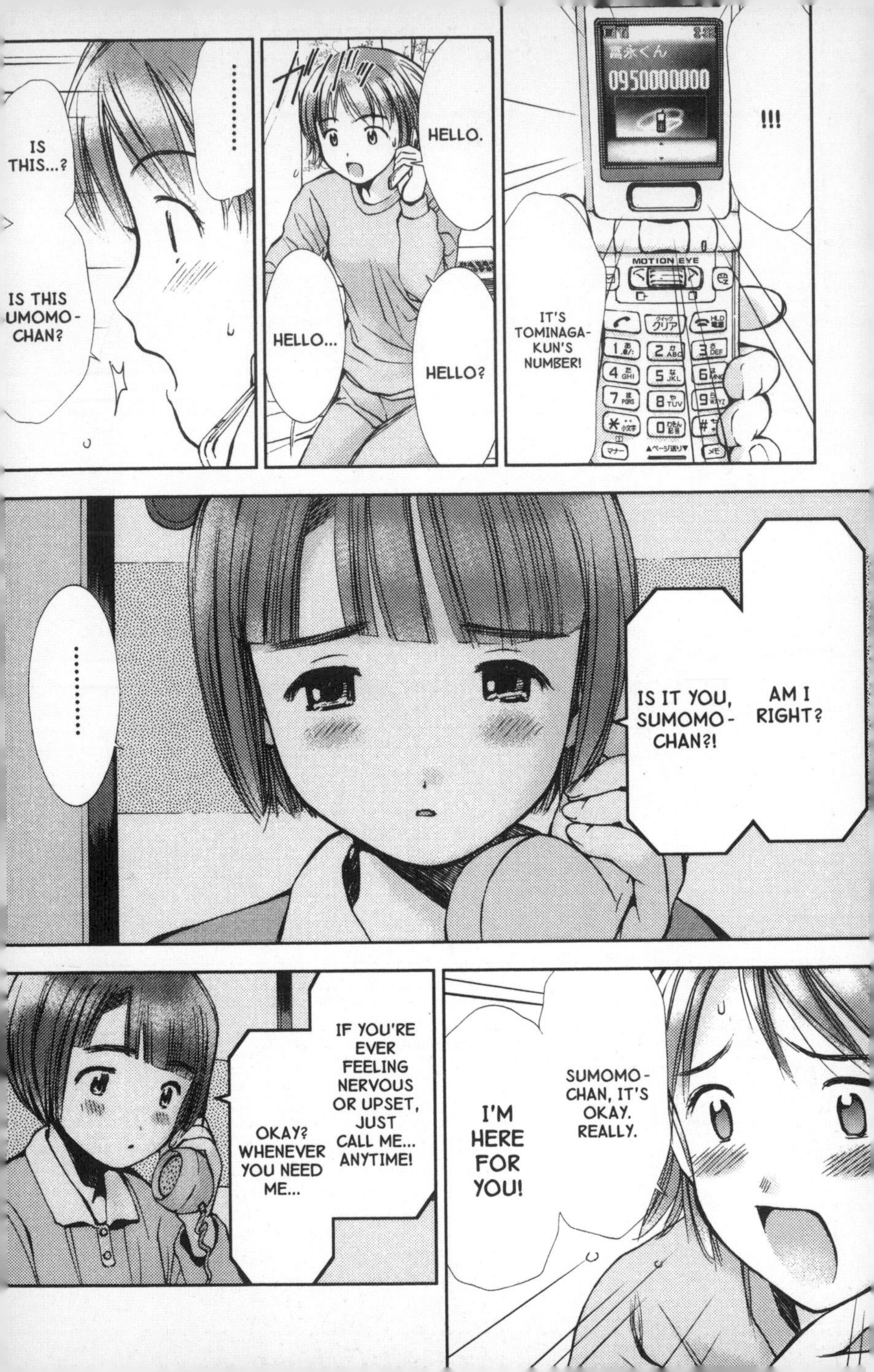
0950000000
MOTION EYE
!!!
IT'S TOMINAGA-KUN'S NUMBER!
HELLO.
HELLO?
HELLO...
......
IS THIS...?
IS THIS UMOMO-CHAN?
AM I RIGHT?
IS IT YOU, SUMOMO-CHAN?!
......
SUMOMO-CHAN, IT'S OKAY. REALLY.
I'M HERE FOR YOU!
IF YOU'RE EVER FEELING NERVOUS OR UPSET, JUST CALL ME... ANYTIME!
OKAY? WHENEVER YOU NEED ME...

......
コン
コン
CLICK
—......
—......
......
ピンポーン
The next day...

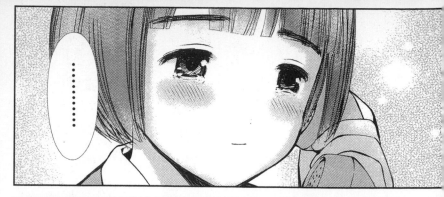

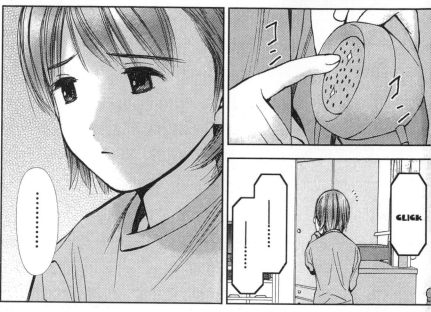

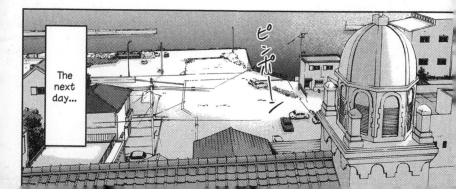

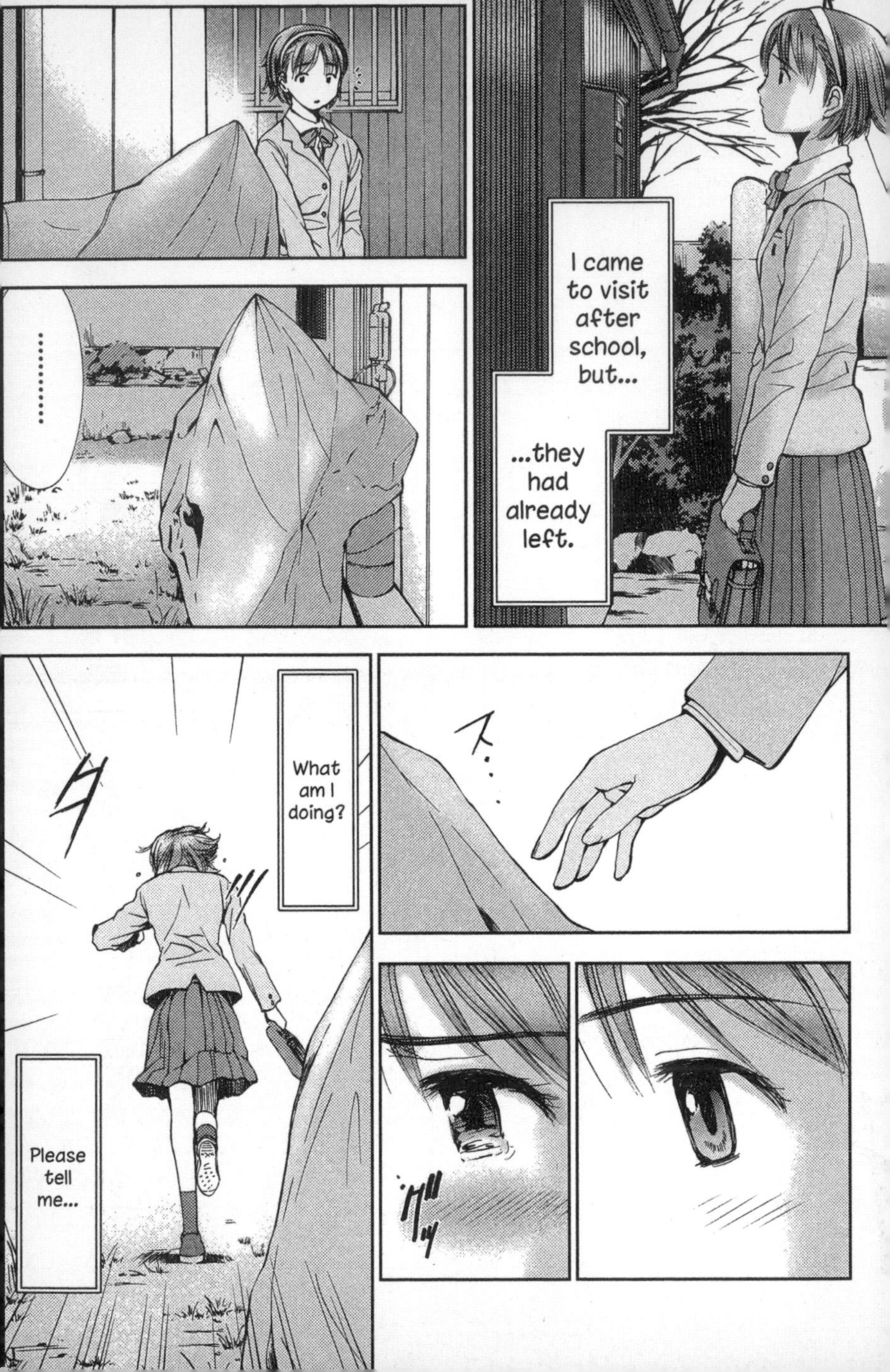
I came to visit after school, but...
...they had already left.
......
What am I doing?
Please tell me...

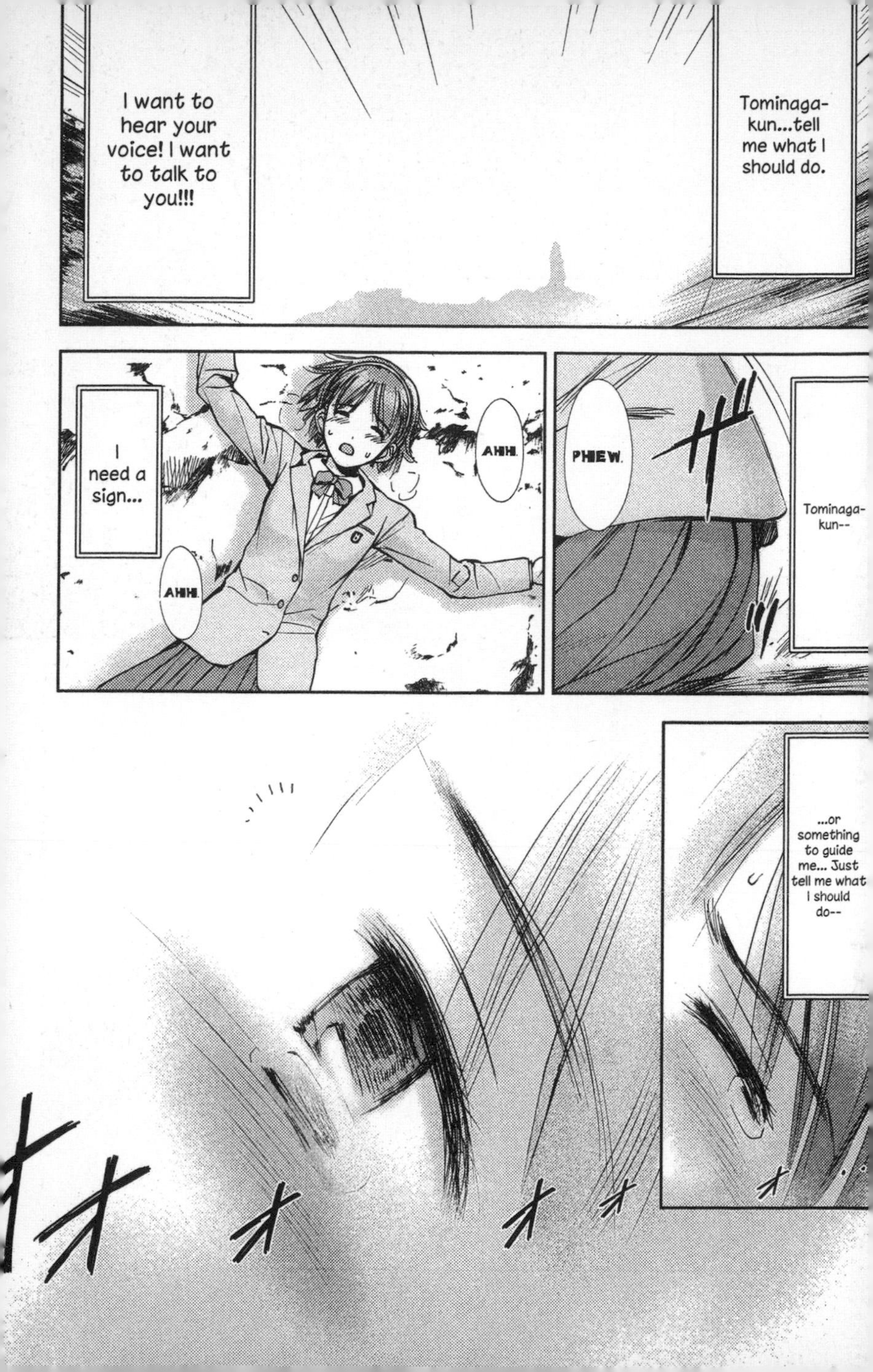
Tominaga-kun...tell me what I should do.
I want to hear your voice! I want to talk to you!!!
Tominaga-kun--
PHEW.
AHH.
I need a sign...
AHH.
...or something to guide me... Just tell me what I should do--

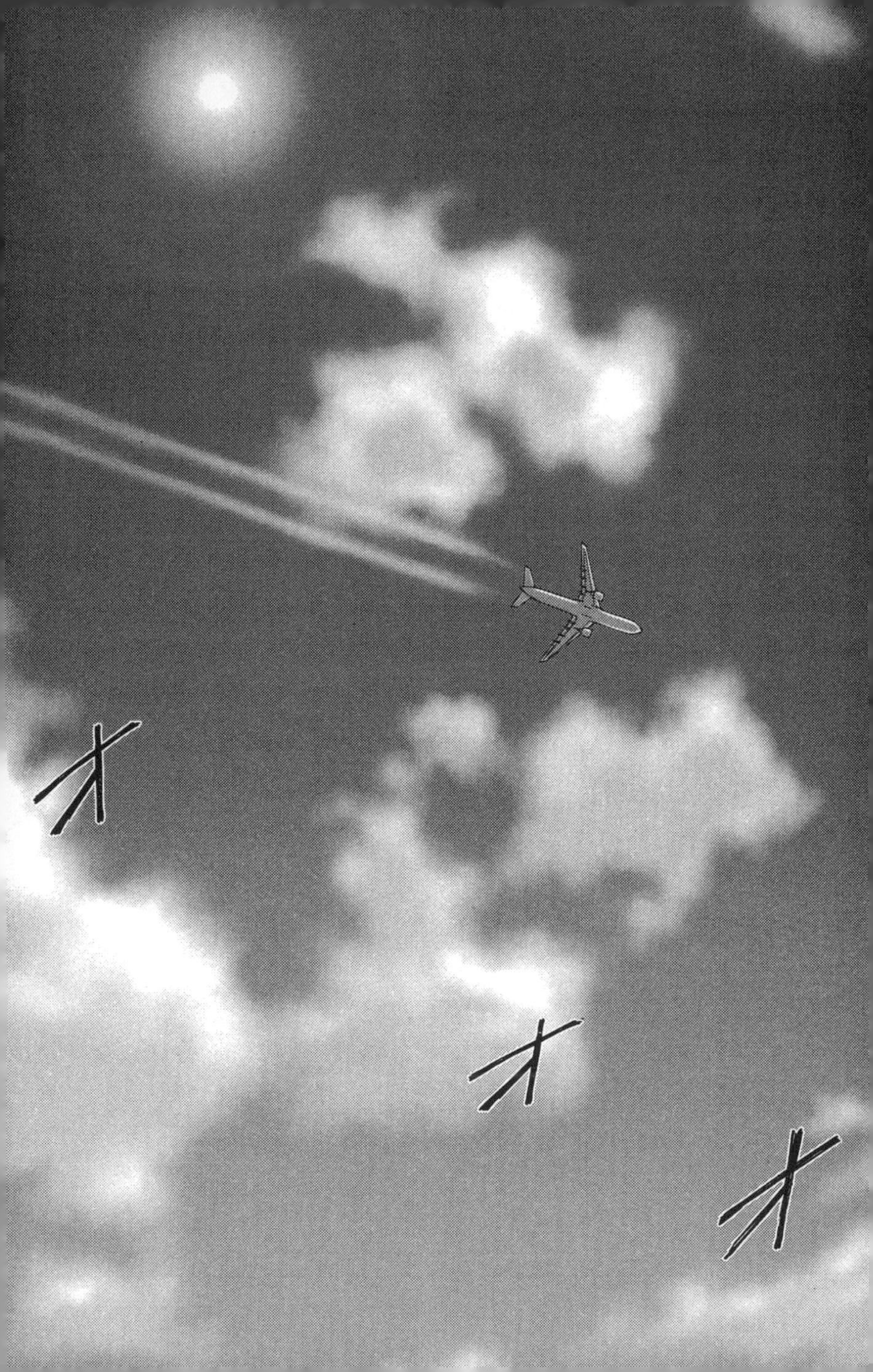
オ
オ
オ

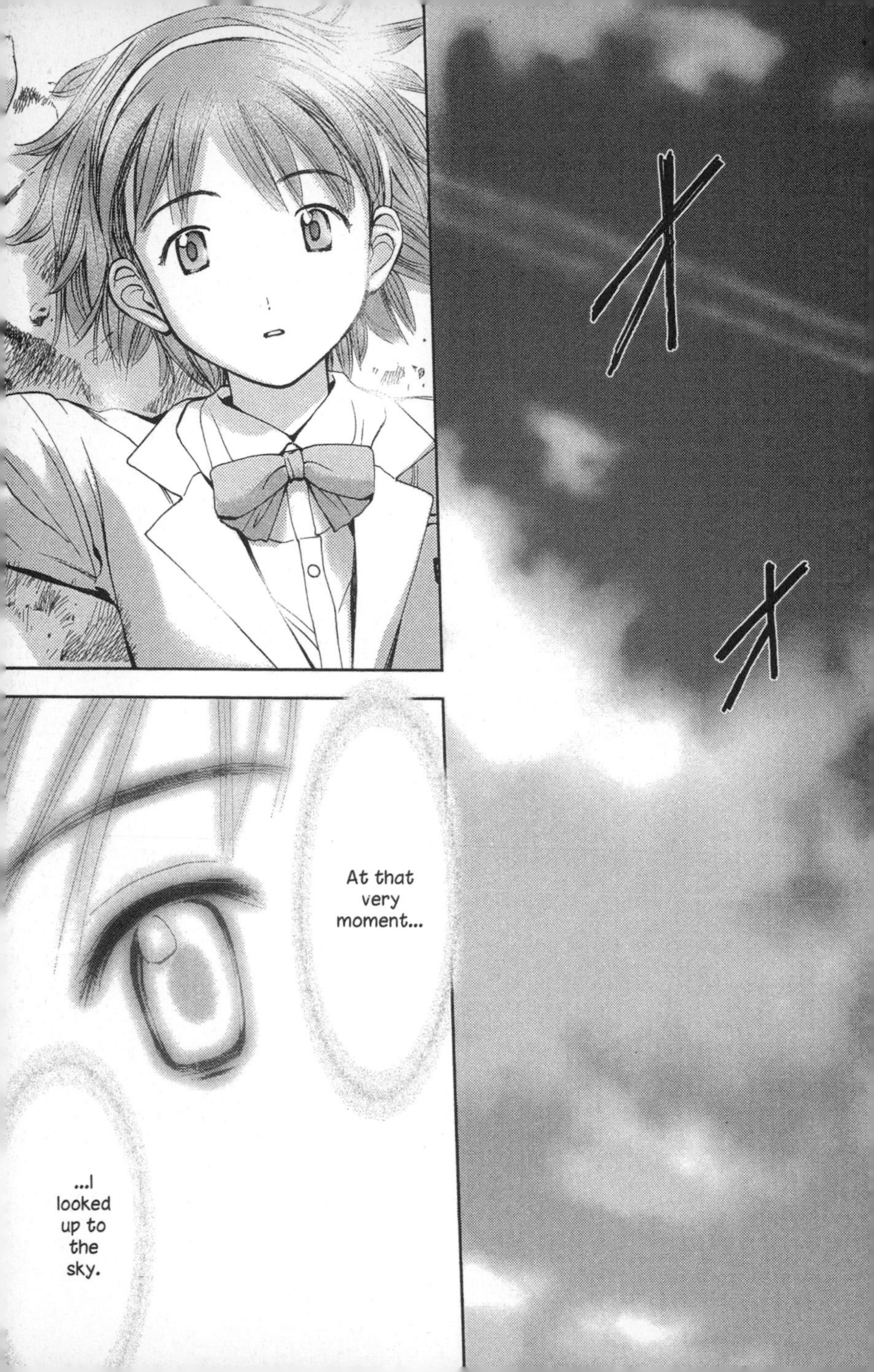
At that very moment...
...I looked up to the sky.

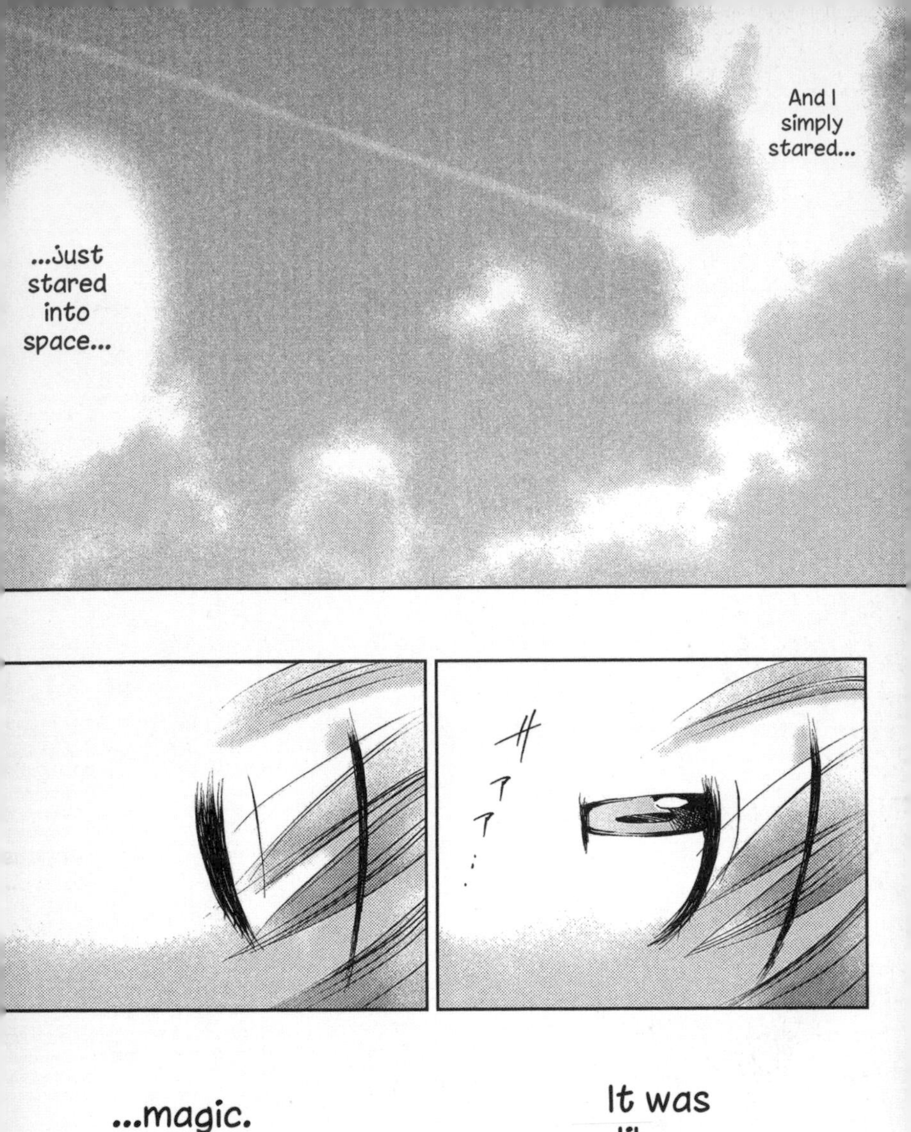
And I simply stared...
...just stared into space...
サァァ・・
It was like...
...magic.

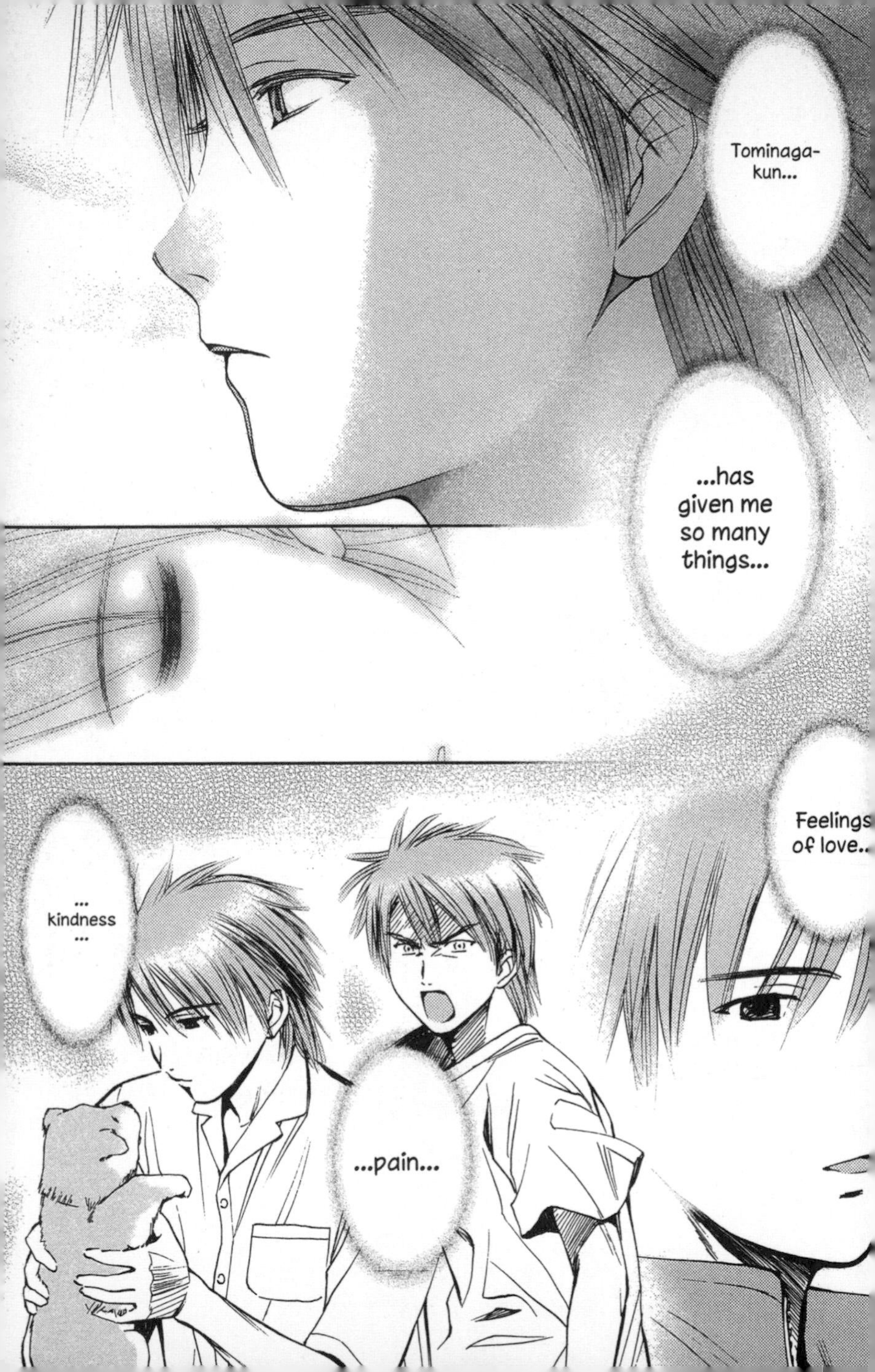
Tominaga-kun...
...has given me so many things...
Feelings of love..
...pain...
...
kindness
...

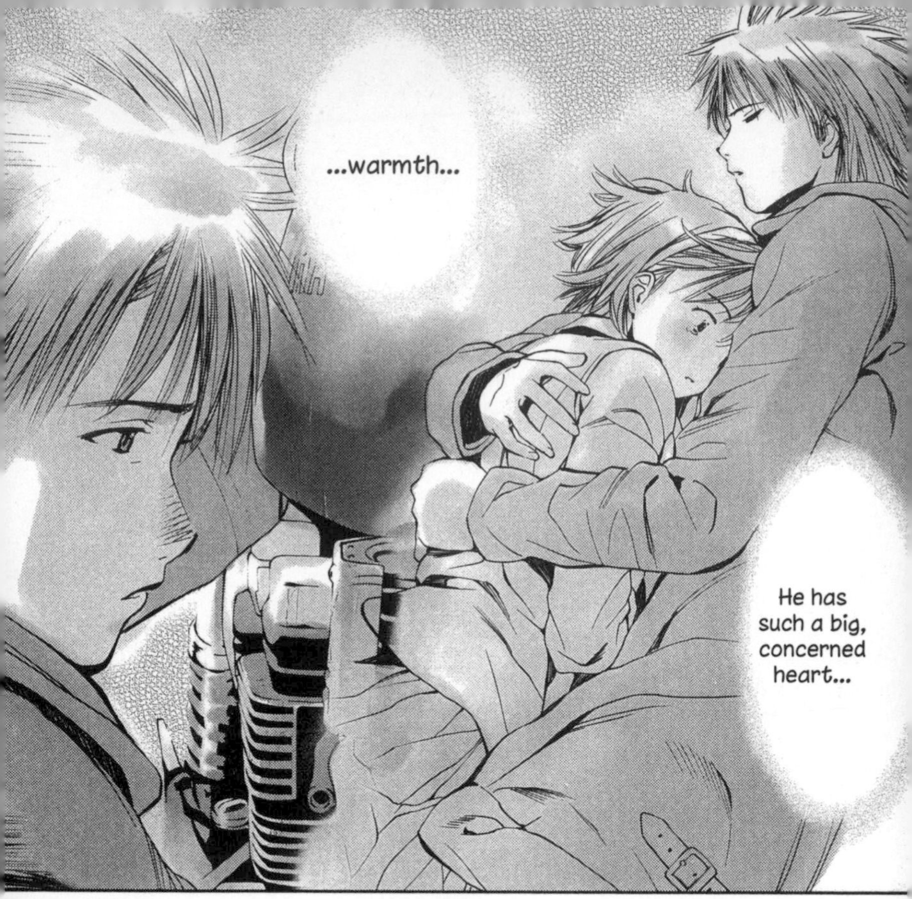
...warmth...
He has such a big, concerned heart...

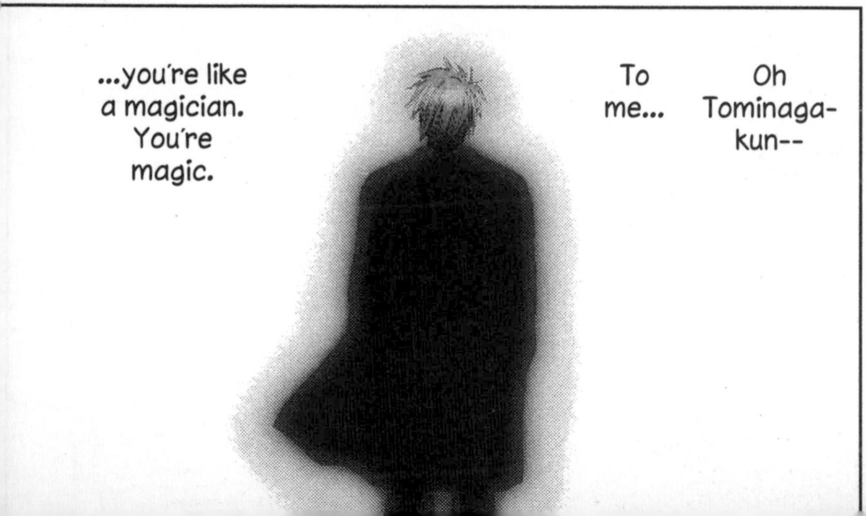
Oh Tominaga-kun--
To me...
...you're like a magician. You're magic.

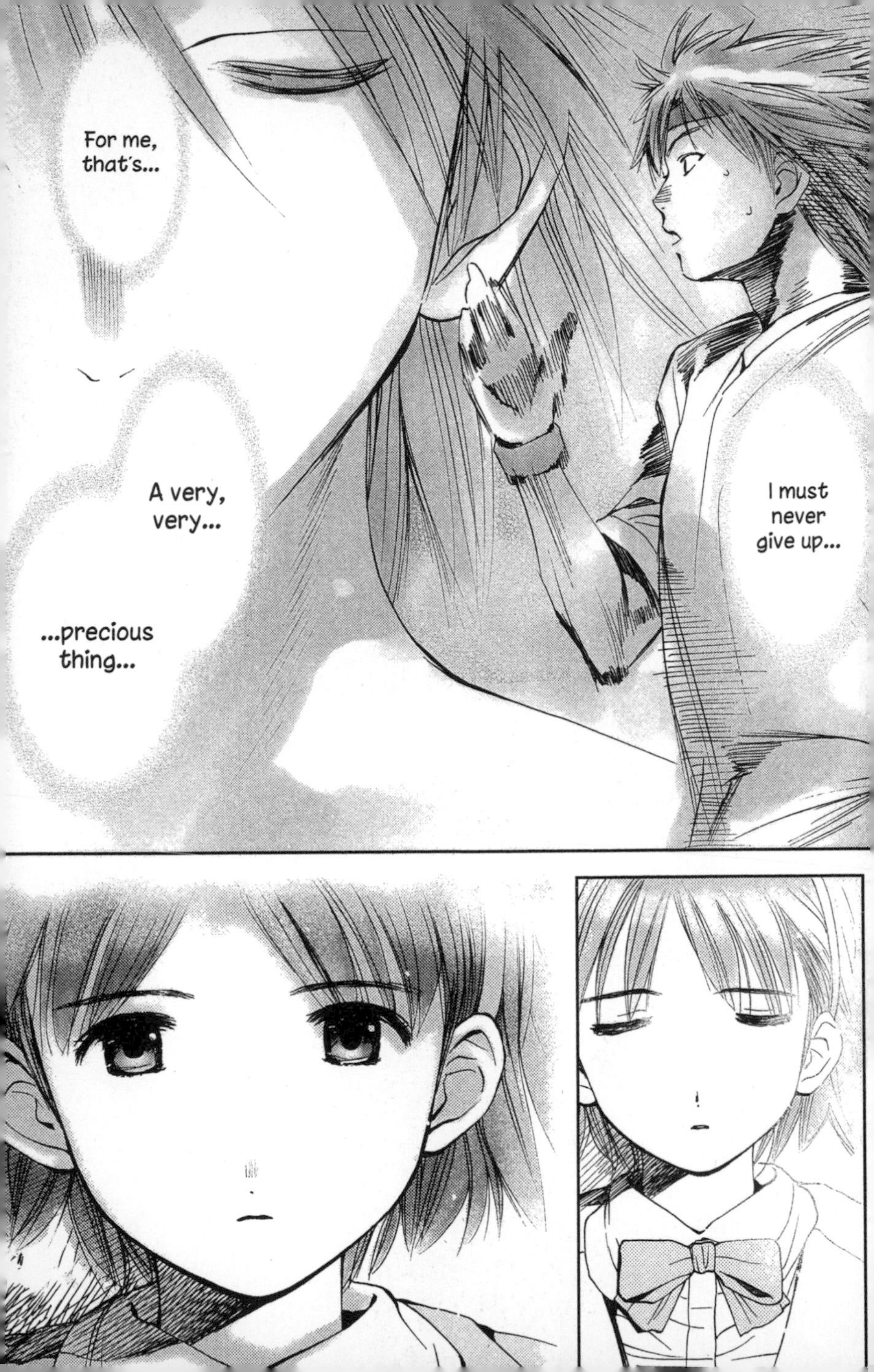
I must never give up...
For me, that's...
A very, very...
...precious thing...

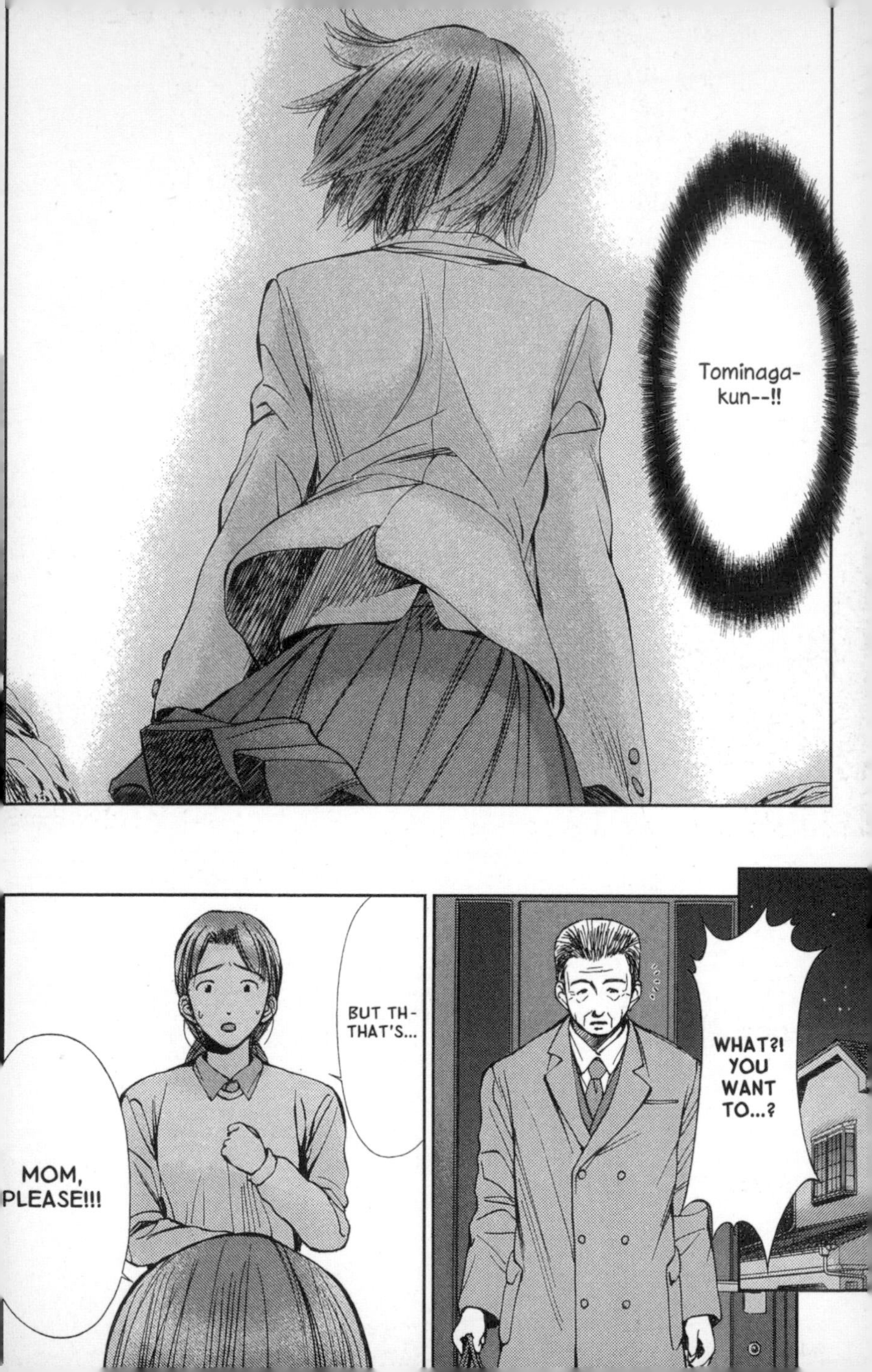
Tominaga-
kun--!!
WHAT?! YOU WANT TO...?
BUT TH-THAT'S...
MOM, PLEASE!!!

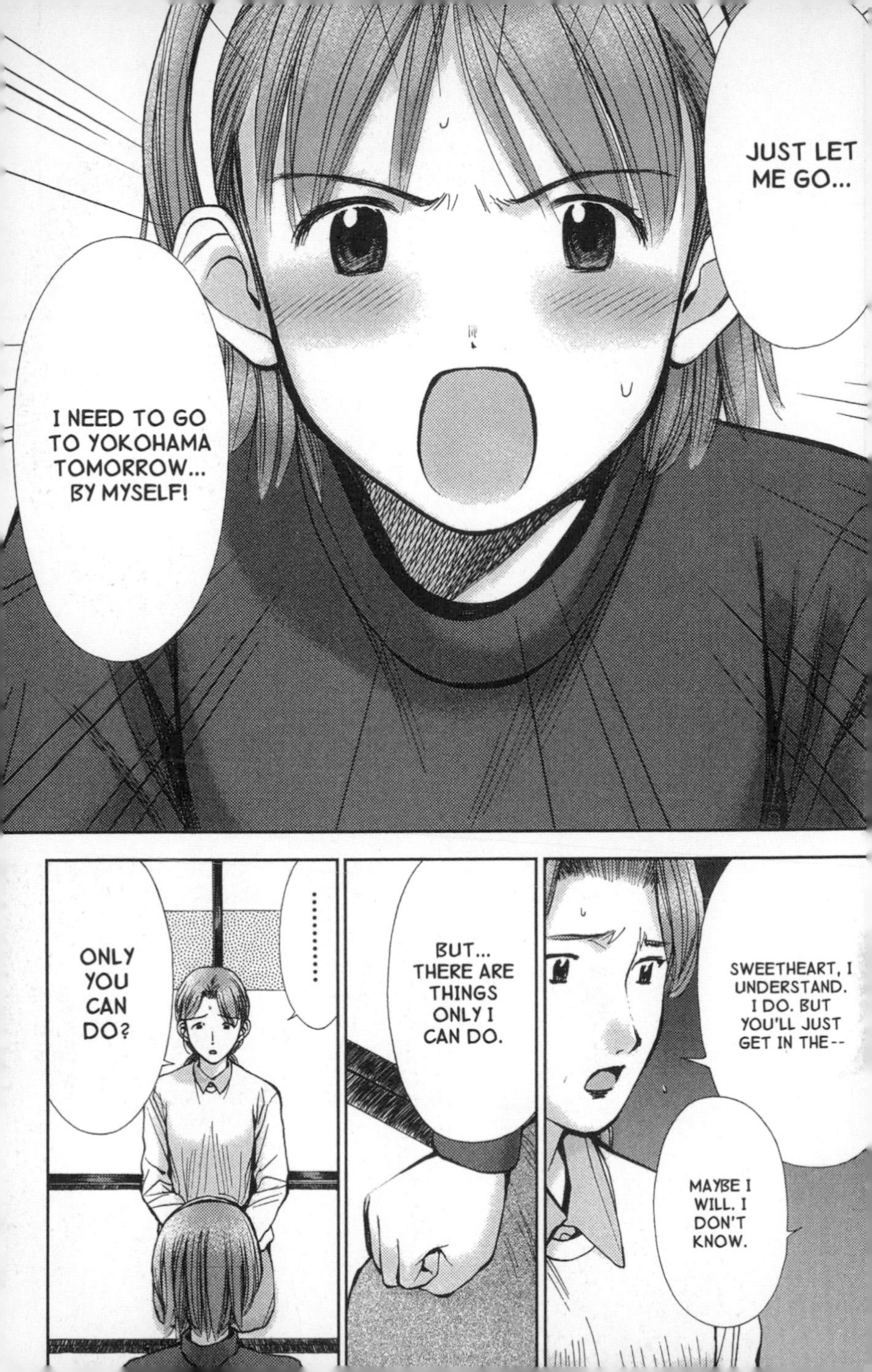
JUST LET ME GO...
I NEED TO GO TO YOKOHAMA TOMORROW... BY MYSELF!
SWEETHEART, I UNDERSTAND. I DO. BUT YOU'LL JUST GET IN THE--
MAYBE I WILL. I DON'T KNOW.
BUT... THERE ARE THINGS ONLY I CAN DO.
....
ONLY YOU CAN DO?

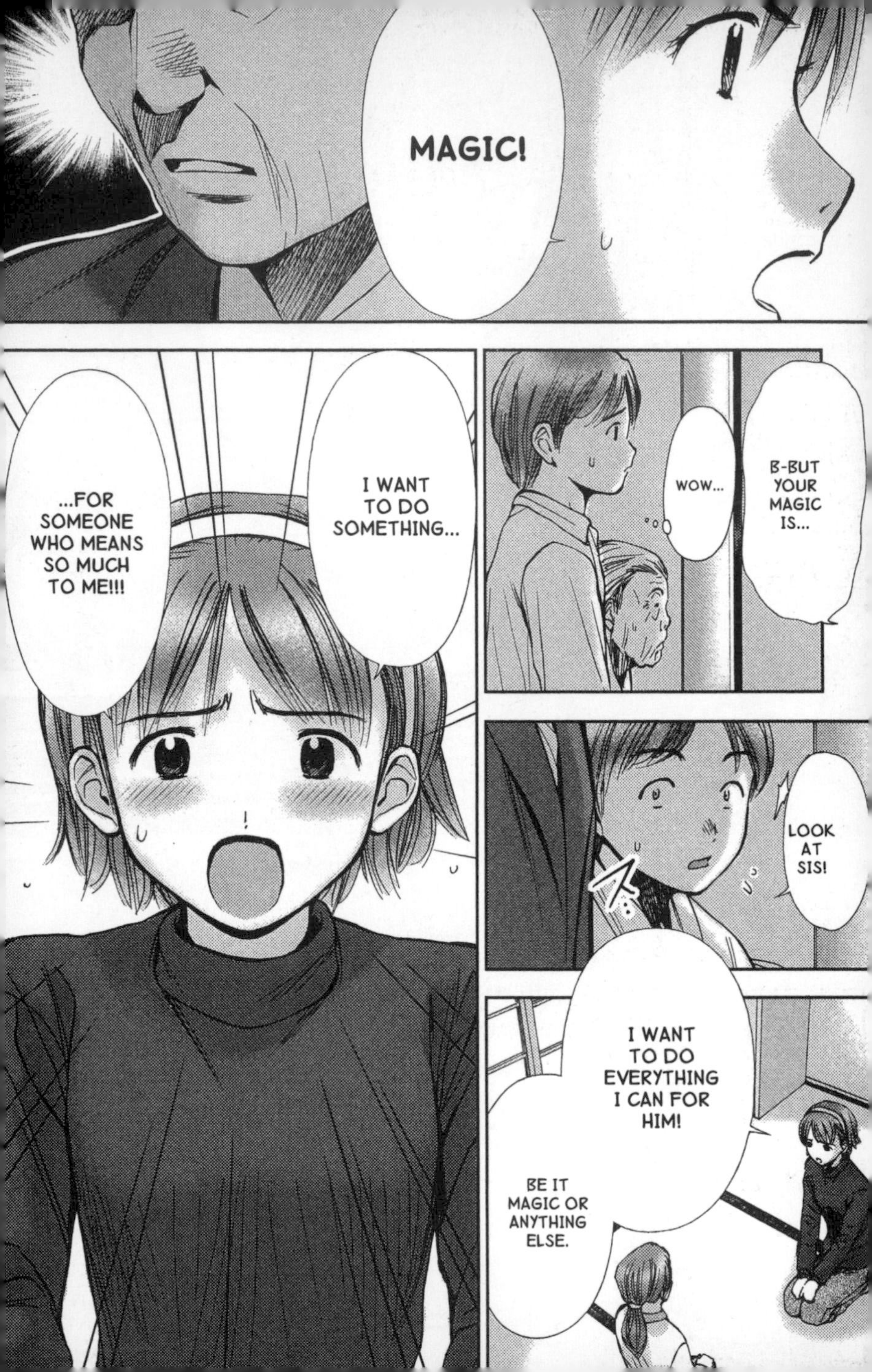
MAGIC!
B-BUT YOUR MAGIC IS...
WOW...
LOOK AT SIS!
I WANT TO DO EVERYTHING I CAN FOR HIM!
BE IT MAGIC OR ANYTHING ELSE.
I WANT TO DO SOMETHING...
...FOR SOMEONE WHO MEANS SO MUCH TO ME!!!

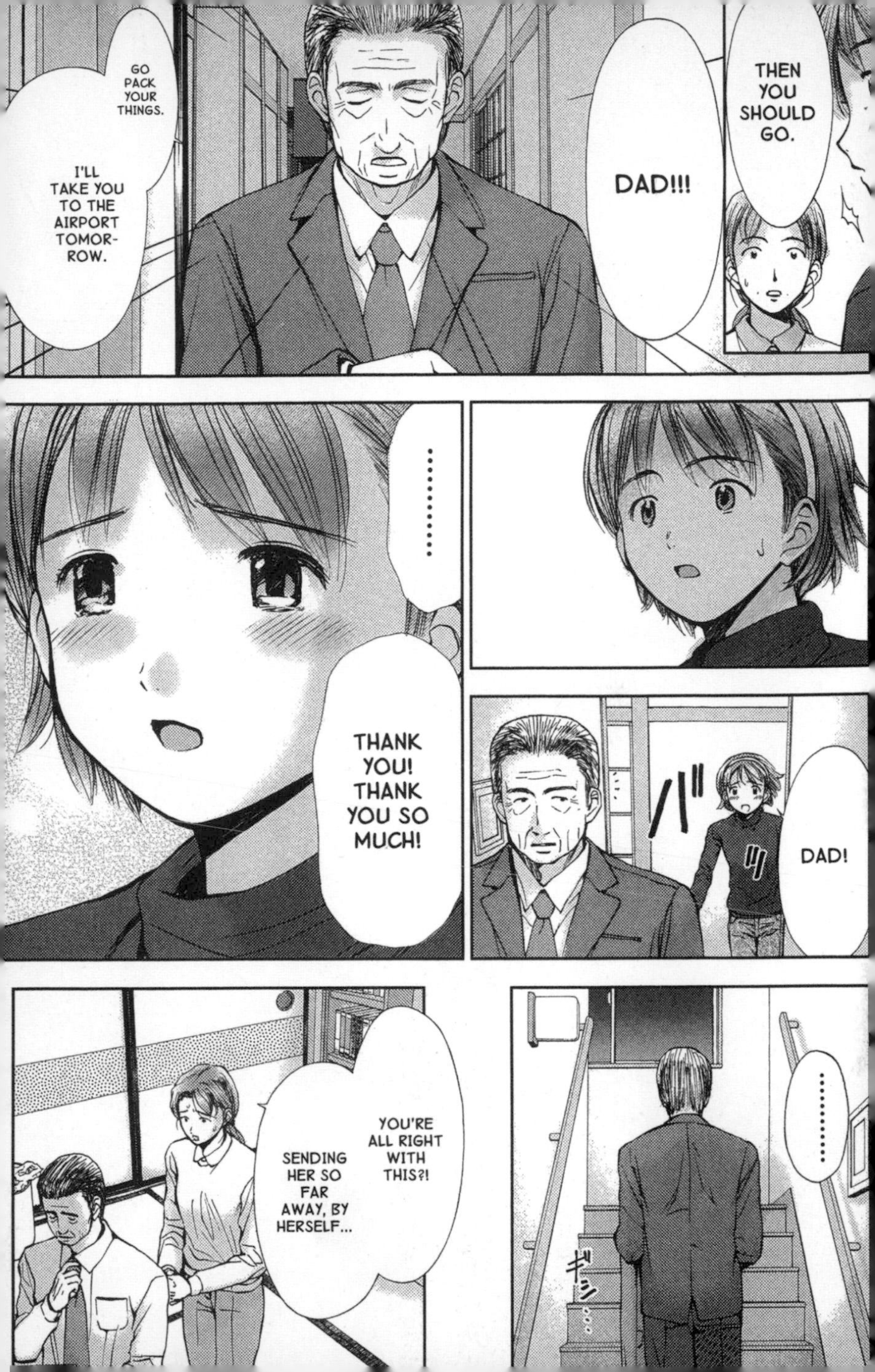
THEN YOU SHOULD GO.
DAD!!!
GO PACK YOUR THINGS.
I'LL TAKE YOU TO THE AIRPORT TOMORROW.
バ
DAD!
......
THANK YOU! THANK YOU SO MUCH!
....
ギシ...
YOU'RE ALL RIGHT WITH THIS?!
SENDING HER SO FAR AWAY, BY HERSELF...

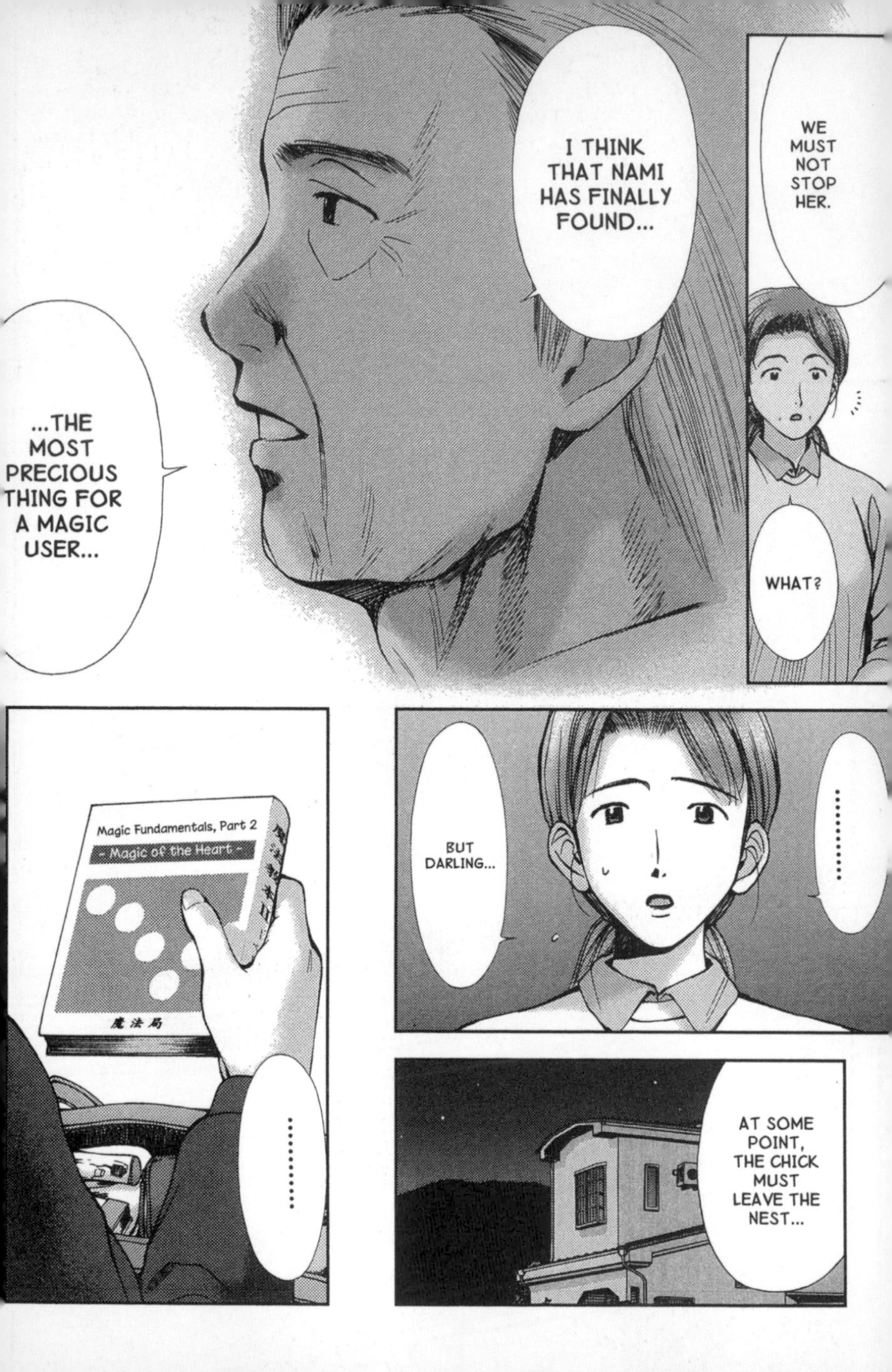
WE MUST NOT STOP HER.
WHAT?
I THINK THAT NAMI HAS FINALLY FOUND...
...THE MOST PRECIOUS THING FOR A MAGIC USER...
......
BUT DARLING...
AT SOME POINT, THE CHICK MUST LEAVE THE NEST...
Magic Fundamentals, Part 2
- Magic of the Heart -
魔法局
....

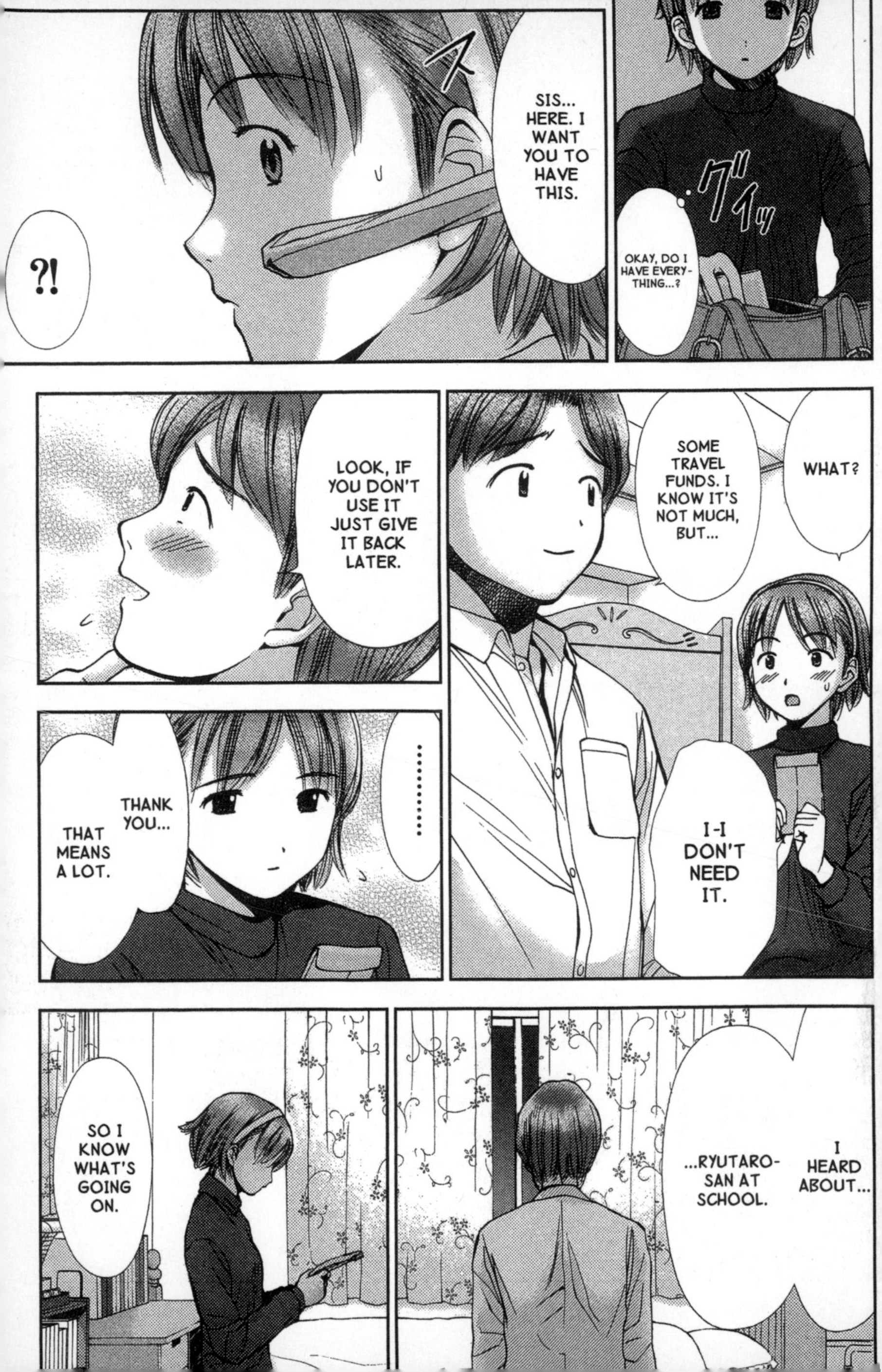
グイッ
OKAY, DO I HAVE EVERYTHING...?
ス
SIS... HERE. I WANT YOU TO HAVE THIS.
?!
WHAT?
SOME TRAVEL FUNDS. I KNOW IT'S NOT MUCH, BUT...
I-I DON'T NEED IT.
LOOK, IF YOU DON'T USE IT JUST GIVE IT BACK LATER.
......
THANK YOU...
THAT MEANS A LOT.
I HEARD ABOUT...
...RYUTARO-SAN AT SCHOOL.
SO I KNOW WHAT'S GOING ON.

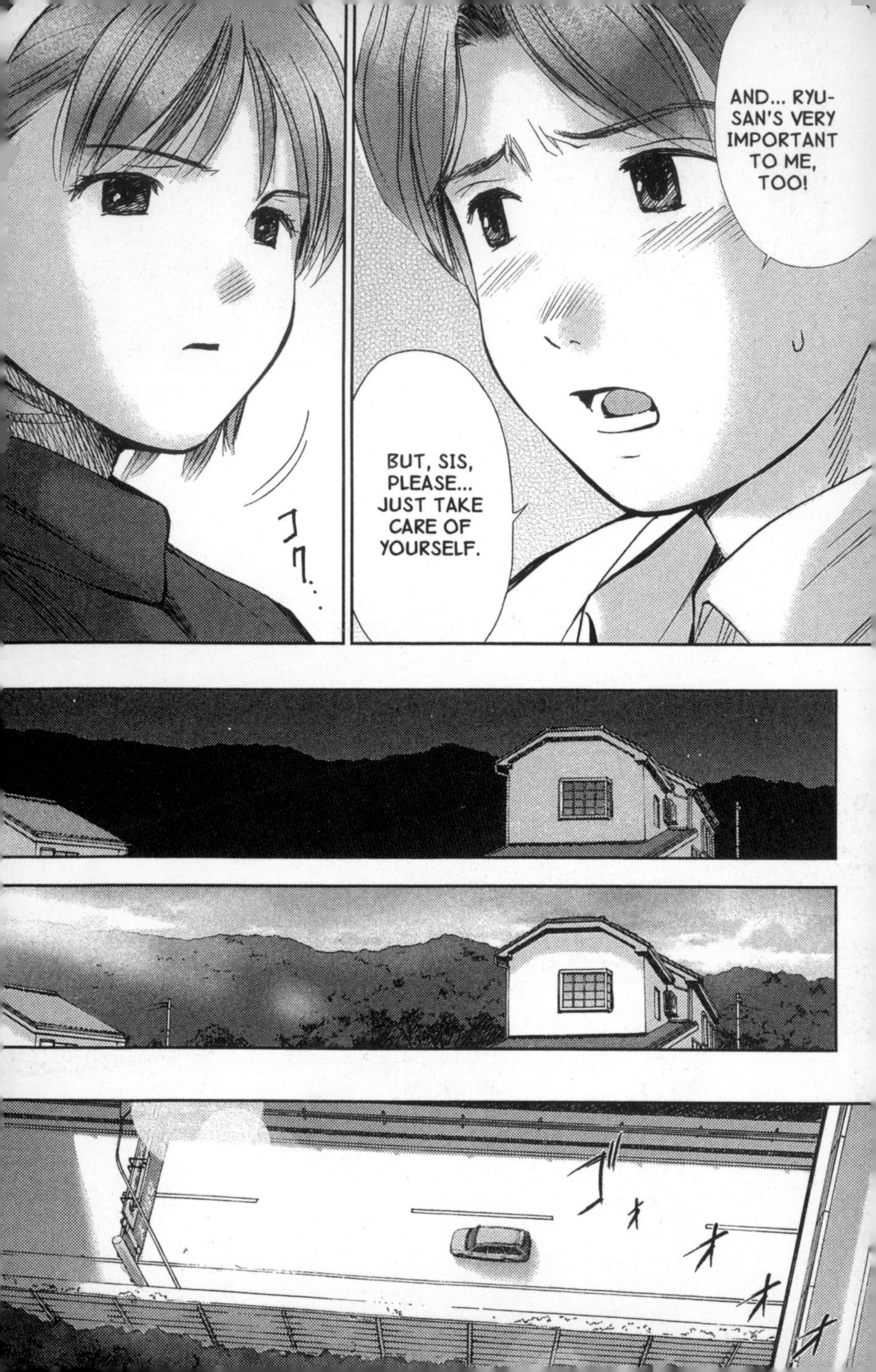
AND... RYU-SAN'S VERY IMPORTANT TO ME, TOO!
BUT, SIS, PLEASE... JUST TAKE CARE OF YOURSELF.

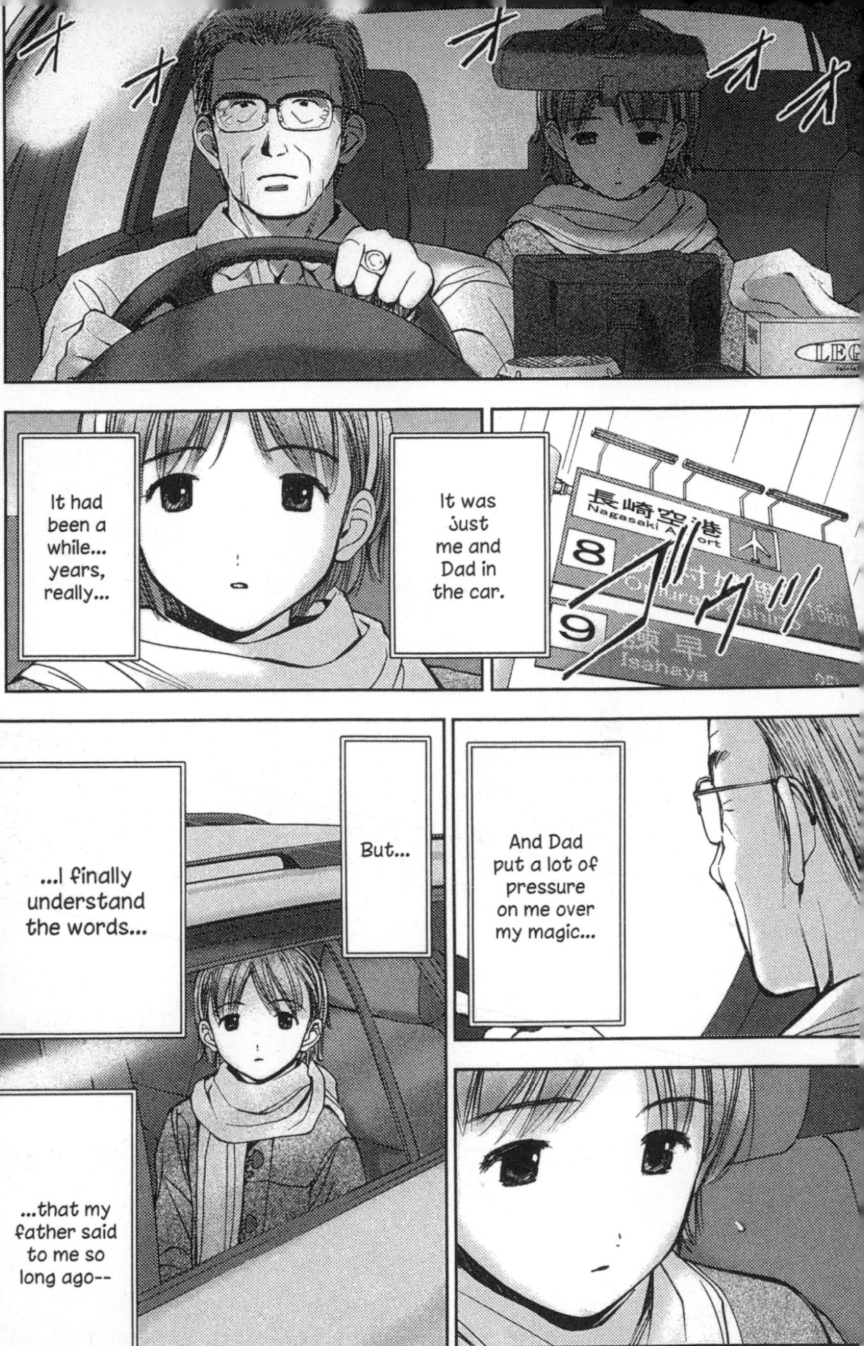
長崎空港
8
9
It was just me and Dad in the car.
It had been a while... years, really...
And Dad put a lot of pressure on me over my magic...
But...
...I finally understand the words...
...that my father said to me so long ago--

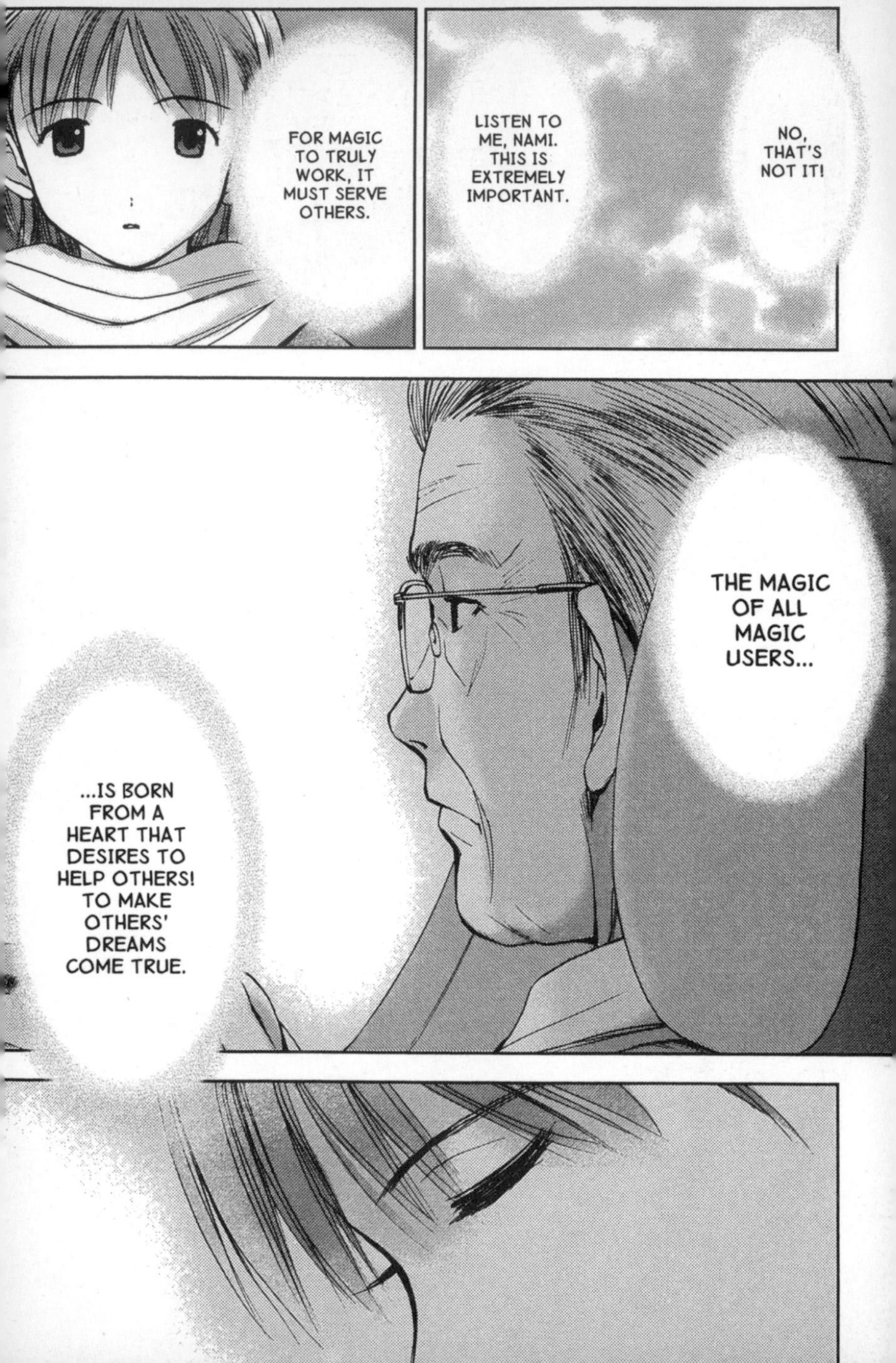
NO, THAT'S NOT IT!
LISTEN TO ME, NAMI. THIS IS EXTREMELY IMPORTANT.
FOR MAGIC TO TRULY WORK, IT MUST SERVE OTHERS.
THE MAGIC OF ALL MAGIC USERS...
...IS BORN FROM A HEART THAT DESIRES TO HELP OTHERS! TO MAKE OTHERS' DREAMS COME TRUE.

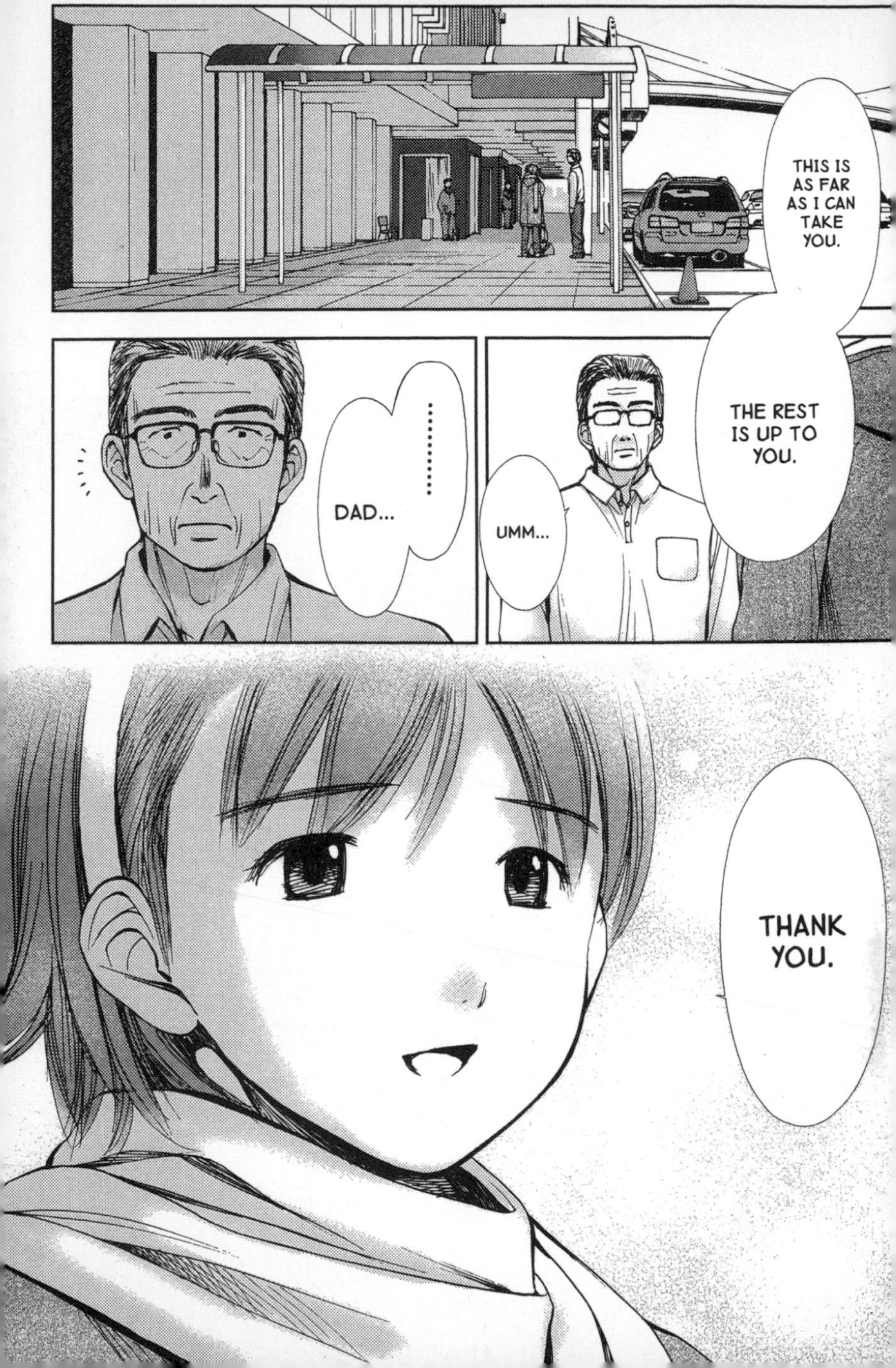
THIS IS AS FAR AS I CAN TAKE YOU.
THE REST IS UP TO YOU.
UMM...
....
DAD...
THANK YOU.

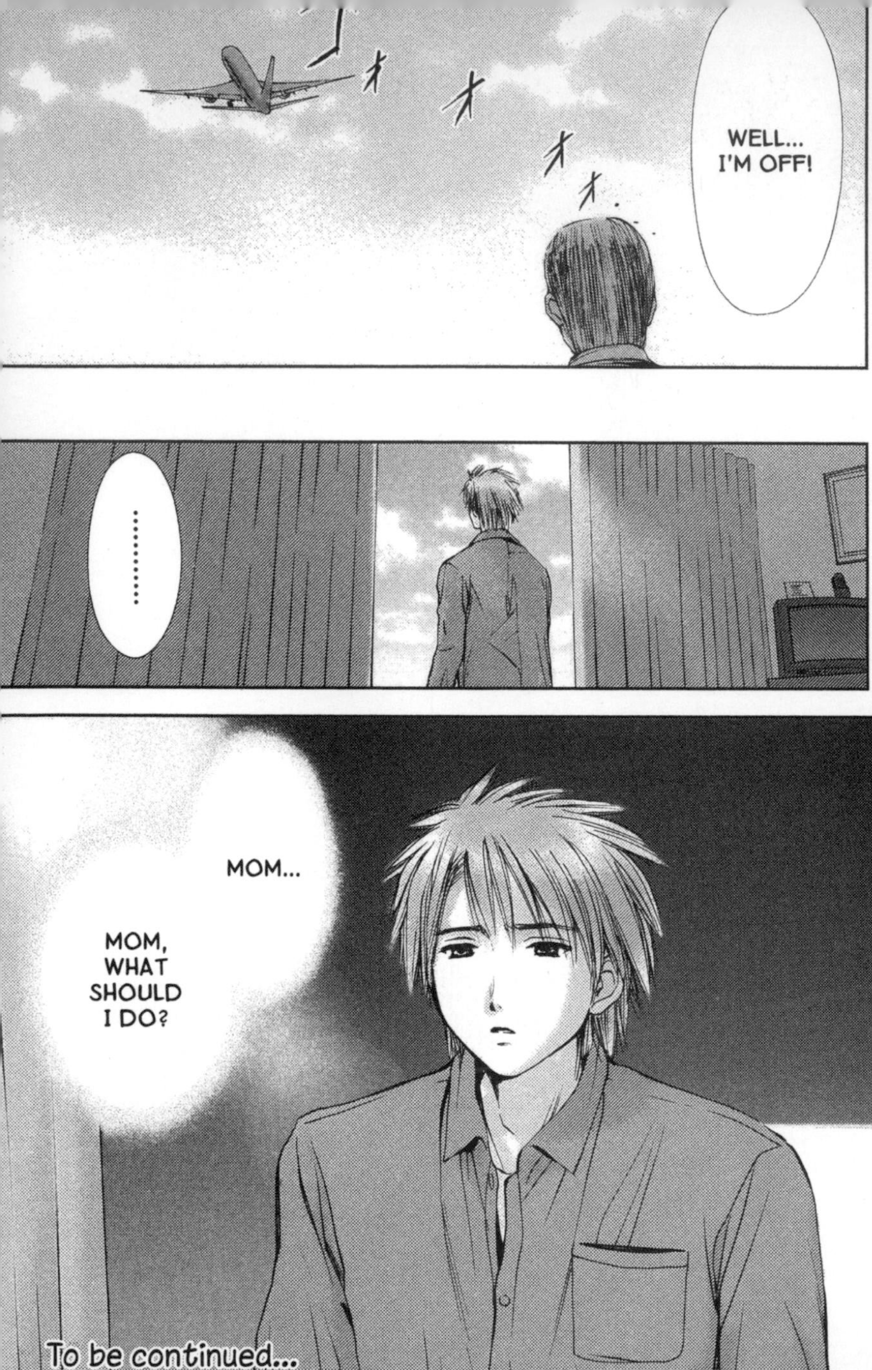
WELL... I'M OFF!
....
MOM...
MOM, WHAT SHOULD I DO?
To be continued...

SOMEDAY'S DREAMERS SPELLBOUND™

Research Assistance

Nagasaki Tourism & Photography Support Center
Nagasaki Senior High
Ooshima Shipyard LLC
Kusano Landscaping LLC
"The Nagasaki" Editors
Natsuko Kogawa

Dialect Advisor

Jun Matsushita

Manga Assistants

Junji Ikeda
Manami Satou
You Kanagaki
Hatsumi Yasunaga

Special Thanks

Izumi Kazuto
Masashi Oyokawa

In the next volume of

SOMEDAY's DREAMERS
SPELLBOUND
™

Upon reaching Yokohama, Nami
overcomes bewilderment and follows
the few leads she has, gaining the
aid of Ryutaro's old friend Masaki.
In her quest, Nami uncovers more
dark secrets from Ryutaro's past...
Will she still be spellbound?

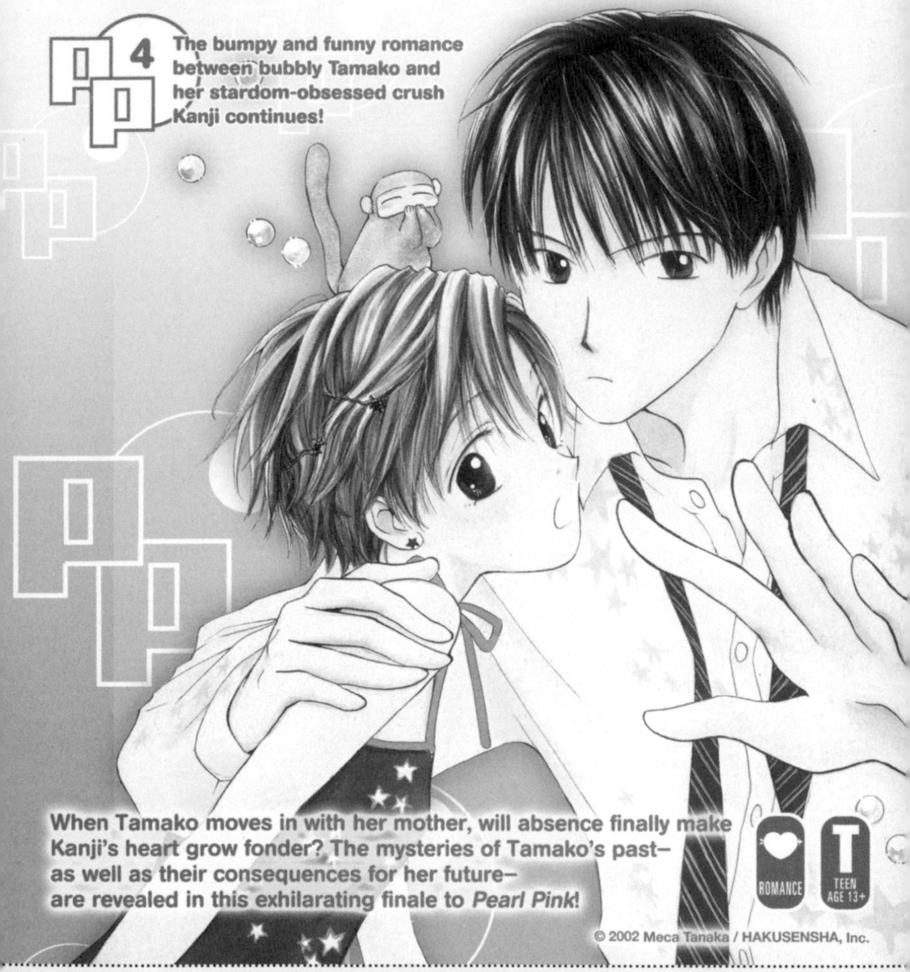

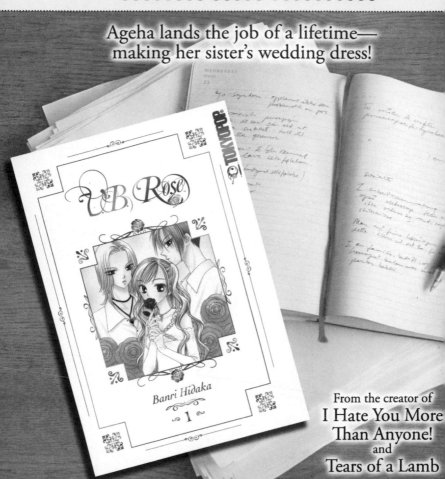

STOP!

This is the back of the book.
You wouldn't want to spoil a great ending!

his book is printed "manga-style," in the authentic Japanese right-to-left ormat. Since none of the artwork has been flipped or altered, readers et to experience the story just as the creator intended. You've been sking for it, so TOKYOPOP® delivered: authentic, hot-off-the-press, nd far more fun!

DIRECTIONS

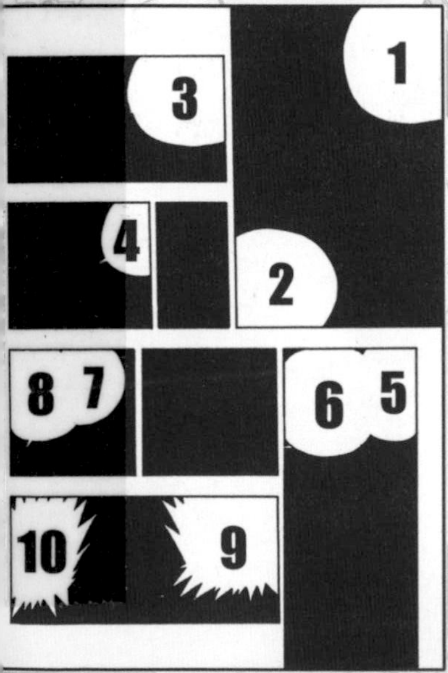
1
2
3
4
5
6
7
8
9
10

If this is your first time reading manga-style, here's a quick guide to help you understand how it works.

It's easy... just start in the top right panel and follow the numbers. Have fun, and look for more 100% authentic manga from TOKYOPOP®!

漫画革命
THE MANGA REVOLUTION · LEADING